Latin American Masses and Minorities:
Their Images and Realities

Volume II

SALALM Secretariat
Memorial Library
University of Wisconsin--Madison

LATIN AMERICAN MASSES AND MINORITIES: THEIR IMAGES AND REALITIES

Volume II

Papers of the Thirtieth Annual Meeting of the
SEMINAR ON THE ACQUISITION OF
LATIN AMERICAN LIBRARY MATERIALS

Princeton University
Princeton, New Jersey
June 19 - 23, 1985

Dan C. Hazen
Editor

SALALM Secretariat
Memorial Library, University of Wisconsin--Madison

ISBN 0-917617-15-0

CONTENTS

Volume 2

Part Four. Research Libraries and the Structure of Latin Americanist Research

Part Five.   The Tools of Understanding: Bibliographies,
Research Guides, and Finding Aids for Latin
American Masses and Minorities

Outline of Contents in Volume I

Latin American Masses and Minorities:
Their Images and Realities

Volume II

Part Four

Research Libraries and the Structure of
Latin Americanist Research

INTRODUCTION

Our focus now shifts from the metaphysics of academic inquiry, the tension between image and reality, and the problematics of diverse sorts of research materials, to the role of libraries and library collections in the study of Latin American masses and minorities. Our concerns are two. In the first place, and despite the flawed collections and resources mentioned so often by students and scholars, there have been and continue to be strong, specialized, and informed efforts to collect materials representative of the moments and the groups addressed in our conference. We thus consider how a number of specialized library collections have developed: the conditions necessary for creating such collections; their nature; and, albeit only implicitly, how we can continue to form them.

Our second concern centers on a different and more troubling aspect of the interplay between research libraries and Latin Americanist scholarship. Here we address our sometimes deliberate, sometimes inadvertent, but always inescapable role as gatekeepers. As we shall see, libraries do control much of the type and the flow of research materials available to students and scholars.

This control takes several forms. One manifestation involves bibliographic access to items already held. Another manifestation centers on the library profession's intensifying efforts to modernize. Too often these efforts would treat all materials, all disciplines, and all collections according to a model devised for fields characterized by technologically innovative forms and formats. Cooperation, to touch on another aspect, is the current panacea for limited acquisitions budgets. Yet cooperation has its limits, both within institutions and on a larger scale. We are likewise limited in our efforts, whether individual or collective, to acquire the nontraditional materials identified throughout this conference. The nature of all these limitations, as they affect both librarians and scholars, must be understood if we are to divine responses and devise solutions.

D.C.H.

I. Specialized Library Collections and the Study
of Latin American Masses and Minorities

33. PRESERVACION DE LA CULTURA CUBANA EN LA BIBLIOTECA DE LA UNIVERSIDAD DE MIAMI

Lesbia Orta Varona

La Biblioteca de la Universidad de Miami recibió y acogió en su seno a los bibliotecarios cubanos que empezaron a llegar a esta nueva comunidad de exiliados, desde la década de los setenta. Su director, Archie L. McNeal, comprendió y apoyó moral y financieramente el esfuerzo de adquirir material para servir a estos nuevos usuarios. Todo esto se efectuó a pesar de que la Universidad es privada y sólo tiende a servir las necesidades de la comunidad universitaria. Esta visión de futuro sigue siendo parte fundamental de la política del nuevo director, Frank Rodgers, quien también brinda su apoyo a nuestros esfuerzos de hacer de nuestra colección cubana, una de las más completas de la nación.

El desarrollo de esta colección no sólo abarca material publicado en Cuba o sobre Cuba antes de la revolución, sino que amplía este ámbito a lo que Cuba produce actualmente y todo aquello que ha surgido fuera de Cuba desde 1959 hasta el presente.

Para la mejor comprensión de esta política, es necesario un recuento histórico del desarrollo de las distintas etapas del exilio cubano.

Primera etapa: Antecedentes, 1959; estampida política y desorientación. Los cubanos de este período tenían como primeros objetivos trabajar y subsistir. Su estado psicológico giraba en torno a la convicción de una vuelta a la isla dentro de corto tiempo. Surge el mito de las 90 millas.

Pasados unos años, la realidad comenzó a perfilarse. Desde 1961, con la situación posterior a la Bahía de Cochinos, el cubano comenzó a trabajar en una nueva sociedad sin por ello olvidar la tierra que dejaba atrás. Este fue el momento en que surgió el interés por mantener vivas nuestras tradiciones y nuestras costumbres. Surge así lo que yo llamo "La Etapa de la Añoranza," y la era del gregarismo cubano. Había que mantenerse juntos bajo todas las presiones apremiantes, y mostrar a la nueva hospitalidad--sin espíritu sectarista--que el cubano tenía cultura y que ansiaba trasmitirla a los demás. La factoría comenzaba su molienda, hombres y mujeres trabajaban con miras al respeto de una vida mejor. Los profesionales miraban hacia su profesión, como meta a seguir. Los intelectuales comenzaron a escribir--entre el paréntesis del pan y la dureza por ganarlo--con esfuerzos incalculables.

El cubano y lo cubano comenzaron a perfilarse no sólo en Miami sino en otros lugares de acogida. Surgieron el refugio y la relocalización. El camino había comenzado y las raíces apuntaban al futuro. Tomada esta decisión, diez años más tarde--década de los setenta--nace el problema de la confrontación cultural cubano-americana. Los jóvenes descendientes de los primeros exiliados rechazan su cultura original. Durante esta etapa los jóvenes trataron de integrarse en cuerpo y alma a la nueva cultura, descartando hasta su propio idioma. En la década de los ochenta resurge el interés hacia sus orígenes, y comienza la etapa de la curiosidad y la investigación: un viaje hacia la semilla.

La juventud actual participa y posee instrumentos de investigación e información tendientes a la búsqueda de su identidad. Aquellos niños de ayer, hoy adultos, no sólo se sienten orgullosos de sus raíces, sino que inculcan a sus hijos el amor y la valoración hacia su cultura y procedencia.

Esta preservación cultural no hubiera sido posible sin el esfuerzo de individuos e instituciones que surgieron y trabajaron infatigablemente hacia la creación de nuevas fuentes de información, que han servido de base para el desarrollo de una colección especial, que sirve hoy no sólo a la comunidad cubana, sino a investigadores en todo el mundo, y que documenta el proceso político, social, económico y cultural de la comunidad cubana en el exilio.

A continuación mencionaré algunas de las instituciones que hicieron posible esta realidad que hoy confrontamos:

Asociación Fraternal Latinoamericana. Fue pionera de las actividades culturales cubanas en Miami, bajo la dirección del poeta Mauricio Fernández. Reunió los pocos poetas, escritores y artistas en la primera Exposición de Arte, Poesía y Cultura del exilio. Aunque creada como institución de salud, apoyó el arte y la cultura cubana.

Cruzada Educativa Cubana. Fundada por el Dr. Vicente Cauce, la Dra. Mercedes García Tudurí y la Dra. María Gómez Carbonell. Creó el Día de la Cultura Cubana y el premio Juan J. Remos, que se otorga a cubanos destacados en todas las ramas de la cultura, incluyendo los valores jóvenes. Creadora también del premio José de la Luz y Caballero para los maestros cubanos más destacados. Creó la "Escuelita Cubana", orientada hacia la juventud para interesar y perpetuar las raíces de su cultura.

Cuban Women's Club. Fundado por Ana Rosa Núñez, Rosita Abella, Julieta O'Farrill, Rosa Gómez y muchas otras mujeres deseosas de continuar la labor del Lyceum Lawn Tennis Club de Cuba.

Asociación de Municipios Cubanos en el Exilio. Creada para mantener la cohesión política, social y cultural de la colonia cubana en Miami. La mayoría de los municipios preservan su herencia a través de sus publicaciones periódicas, sus reuniones, y romerías que se celebran en la Ermita de la Caridad del Cobre, de acuerdo a la fecha del patrón de cada municipio.

Museo Cubano de Arte y Cultura. Fundado por Mignon Medrano, Martha de Castro, Rosita Abella, Ana Rosa Núñez y otros en 1973. Inicialmente era un museo sin paredes, activo en distintos locales de la ciudad. Al fin, en la década de los 80 cuenta con su propio local, cedido por la ciudad de Miami, aportando a la ciudad valiosos actos culturales y exposiciones artísticas retrospectivas y actuales de artistas cubanos.

Cuban American National Foundation. Radicada en Washington, realiza una gran labor en pro de la propagación de la situación actual política y social de los cubanos, tanto dentro como fuera de la Isla. Sus publicaciones, investigaciones, seminarios y conferencias son de una alta calidad.

Cámara de Comercio Latina. Fundada en la década de los setenta para agrupar hombres de negocios e instituciones bancarias, comerciales, etc. Ha publicado un sinnúmero de documentos sobre economía, negocios y estadísticas.

Bancos. Bajo este nombre se agrupan una serie de bancos que auxilian a la propagación de la cultura cubana, tanto por su participación en actos culturales, políticos, sociales y económicos, como por su aporte económico a tales fines.

La producción teatral también ha aportado desde los principios del exilio su grano de arena a la preservación de nuestra cultura. Entre los más destacados se encuentran:

Añorada Cuba. Dirigida por el padre Chabebe, agrupó a los artistas de todos los géneros. Fue la primera muestra de actividad teatral.

Teatro Las Máscaras. Dirigido por Salvador Ugarte y Alfonso Cremata. Esta compañía presentó obras clásicas y comedias, alcanzando grandes éxitos hasta nuestros días.

Gran Teatro Lírico Grateli. Dirigido por Martha Pérez, Pili de la Rosa y Demetrio Pérez, presenta tanto artistas nacionales como internacionales.

Fórum. Bajo la dirección de René Alejandro, de donde surgieron muchos valores actuales.

Sociedad Artística, Cultural de las Américas. Bajo la dirección de Manuel Ochoa con proyección a la música cubana, zarzuelas y teatro.

Repertorio Español. Surge en Miami, y ya con éxitos obtenidos en New York. Presenta obras de autores cubanos como Santa Camila de La Habana Vieja y El Super, llevada después al cine con gran acogida.

Teatro "La Danza". Presentó teatro clásico, cubano, latinoamericano y experimental.

Teatro Bellas Artes. Presenta obras clásicas, españolas, cubanas, latinoamericanas y recitales musicales y poéticos, así como teatro guiñol.

Teatro Avante. Fundado por Mario Ernesto Sánchez, Alina Interián y Teresa María Rojas. Una obra de recordación fue Aire Frío de Virgilio Piñera, dramaturgo distinguido cubano.

Teatro Prometeo. Miami Dade New World Campus. Fundadora: Teresa María Rojas, dedicada a enseñar a valores jóvenes, haciendo mutis como actriz por varios años.

Koubek Center. Division of Continuing Education de la Universidad de Miami. Sirve a los actos teatrales, recitales, conferencias, etc., de la comunidad hispano-parlante. Actualmente, en su programa "Audiciones," pone gran énfasis en la cultura cubana.

Se ha hecho hincapié en la importancia de la producción teatral, ya que nuestra colección de afiches, programas, fotos y críticas, nutrió una exposición de teatro hispanoamericano en los Estados Unidos, que se está llevando a cabo en estos momentos en las ciudades más importantes de este país, donde existen grandes núcleos de hispano-parlantes.

Como consecuencia de estas instituciones y de sus actividades, así como del constante celo de los bibliotecarios cubanos de nuestra biblioteca en adquirir la producción intelectual de todo lo que se ha publicado y se publica, surgieron orientaciones e informaciones bibliográficas que han servido de base al investigador en distintas areas de interés. Podemos poner como ejemplos los siguientes volúmenes:

La obra de Seymour Menton, La Narrativa de la Revolución Cubana, que fue uno de los primeros en recoger el aporte literario del exilio cubano.

Las obras de Richard R. Fagen, Cuba: The Political Content of Adult Education y Cubans in Exile, fueron unos de los primeros esfuerzos hacia el estudio de nuestro exilio.

La bibliografía de Thomas D. Boswell, Cuba and the Cubans, así como infinidad de artículos que ha publicado sobre el tema.

La nueva bibliografía de Lyn MacCorkle, Cubans in the United States; A Bibliography for Research in the Social and Behavioral Sciences, 1960-1983, que se publicó recientemente.

Hugh Thomas con sus investigaciones históricas como Cuba: The Pursuit of Freedom, publicada en 1971, y The Revolution on Balance en 1983.

Juan Clark, que se dedica a la investigación social y económica de las distintas etapas del exilio cubano, y tiene publicados varios libros y artículos, entre ellos Cubans in the U.S. y Refugees & Escapees: The Cuban Exodus.

Irving L. Horowitz, investigador sociológico y político que ha escrito varios libros sobre Cuba como Cuba and the U.S.: A Reappraisal y The Cuban Lobby.

Carlos Alberto Montaner, autor y periodista cuya columna sindicada aparece en los mejores rotativos del mundo, y cuyos libros como Secret Report on the Cuban Revolution han sido publicados en varios idiomas.

Carlos Ripoll ha escrito varios libros sobre historia y literatura cubana como La Generación del 23 en Cuba y Writers & Intellectuals in Today's Cuba. Sus artículos se han publicado en el New York Times, Partisan Review, etc. Ha escrito extensivamente sobre la obra y vida de José Martí.

Otro gran aporte para los investigadores es la colección de periódicos publicados por cubanos exiliados. Actualmente la Biblioteca de la Universidad de Miami cuenta con una colección que sobrepasa los 300 títulos. Muchos de estos periódicos son de variable frecuencia, debido a las condiciones económicas impuestas por el medio; otros se han mantenido desde los inicios del exilio y aún se siguen publicando. Iguales condiciones caracterizan a las revistas. No obstante, el material que ofrecen es de suma importancia en el conocimiento de la vida y de la orientación que, en distintos momentos, sigue el exiliado.

Es importante enfatizar la labor efectuada por nuestra biblioteca que, siendo de una institución privada, ha mantenido abiertas sus puertas a investigadores, tanto extranjeros como locales, interesados en la búsqueda de información útil para el estudio de la comunidad cubana del exilio. En la actualidad está brindando estos mismos servicios a la comunidad nicaragüense.

Hemos podido comprobar por cartas personales y reconocimientos en prólogos de obras y disertaciones ya publicadas, que en este campo, nuestra colección es una de las más importantes en la nación.

34. NOTES ON THE ACQUISITION AND ORGANIZATION OF GOVERNMENT DOCUMENTS AT THE PUERTO RICAN COLLECTION OF THE UNIVERSITY OF PUERTO RICO'S RIO PIEDRAS CAMPUS LIBRARY SYSTEM

Carmen Mí Costa de Ramos

Introduction

As the title suggests, this short paper aims to present some of the special characteristics and problems pertaining to the government documents collection at the Puerto Rican Collection. I do not probe into the documents of the Spanish Administration of Puerto Rico (1493-1898), nor those of the early and middle years of the American Administration (1898-1952), because they are mostly the province of the Historical Archives of Puerto Rico. Government documents from 1952 on provide the focus for this paper.

In 1950, President Truman signed Public Law 600 of the 81st Congress. This law, adopted in the nature of a compact, enlarged Puerto Rico's powers and autonomy over its internal matters and authorized it to write its own constitution. In 1952, in a special referendum, a constitution for Puerto Rico was approved and a new status, "Estado Libre Asociado," translated into English as "Commonwealth," was established.* The government structure defined in this constitution remains in force; it is the documents issued by the units within this structure that concern us here. (See Appendix A.)

Acquisition

The Puerto Rican Collection was designated as a depository library for all public documents by Law number 5 of December 8, 1955, later amended on June 4, 1979. Article 15 states that: "Las oficinas gubernamentales remitirán a la Biblioteca General de Puerto Rico y a la Colección Puertorriqueña de la Universidad de Puerto Rico una copia o ejemplar de toda información, boletín, revista o libro que se publique y circule en el gobierno."

However, there is no provision for enforcing this law. We must rely on the cooperation and goodwill of the departments, agencies, public corporations, and their subordinate bureaus, offices, and the like to receive their publications.

The sole person encharged with public documents at the Puerto Rican Collection spends considerable time and effort writing and calling all the government units in an effort to

---

*Juan M. García Pasalacqua, Puerto Rican Constitutional Law (San Juan, PR: Colegio de Abogados de Puerto Rico, 1974).

acquire as many documents as possible. Inclusion on several mailing lists has been helpful. Even then, though, not everything is received.

Several additional factors compound our acquisition problems:

1. The officials responsible for information at all levels of government are usually both ignorant of and little concerned with our depository status.

2. The government itself has relatively little interest in preserving public documents.

3. There is no centralization in the publication and distribution of public documents. Each department has its own printing press, and/or its own methods for distribution.

4. The Anuario Bibliográfico Puertorriqueño, our closest approximation to a national bibliography, has not been published since the issue corresponding to 1973-74. In the absence of other listings to verify titles for selection, we must rely on our requests being met in a comprehensive manner by the agencies we approach.

5. The lack of bibliographic information likewise impedes the acquisition of retrospective material. There is no way to identify back titles unless they represent titles in series, or are mentioned in another publication or bibliography.

Scope and Organization

Notwithstanding these special acquisition problems, we have the Island's most complete current government document collection. These documents for the most part represent the executive, legislative, and judicial branches. The Island is subdivided into seventy-eight municipalities, but these only enjoy limited responsibilities because the Commonwealth government is highly centralized. (See Appendix B.)

The Commonwealth's documents range from periodicals and mimeographed reports and books, to pamphlets, annuals, looseleaf editions, maps, posters, and the like. Until the early '70s, the official documents received full cataloging. These materials appear in our card catalog by author, title, and subject. Except for the documents in nonsuitable formats, they are shelved with the rest of the books.

In more recent years, the documents have gone through two successive organizational schemes. A system based on the U.S. Superintendent of Documents' classification system was employed for several years. It was dropped after six years because of the time it required. (There was, and there remains, a critical shortage of staff.) At the present time, each document is registered only under its issuing agency and the body highest within the administrative hierarchy under which that agency falls. For example: Puerto Rico, Junta de Planificación. Negociado de Análisis Económico y Social. Serie histórica de desempleo en Puerto Rico. Año 1978.

These cards are not filed in the card catalog, but are instead kept in a special sequence. There are obvious drawbacks to this system, including access by only a single descriptive entry, and the need to search an additional file while trying to gather information on documents and other sources. However, because of our personnel limitations, this is the only system that can be used if we want to have the official documents available to our readers as speedily as possible.

The person in charge of processing government documents has been slowly reregistering all documents, save those classified by Dewey, to unify access in accord with the current system.

Bibliographic Control

Some documents were, until 1973-74, listed in the seemingly defunct Anuario Bibliográfico Puertorriqueño. A few documents are usually listed in the Monthly Checklist of State Publications, which is compiled at the Library of Congress.

The Planning Board's Office of Statistics Coordination initiated a new effort at bibliographic control in 1980. The person in charge of the project wrote a letter to all the government's units, urging each to comply with the law by sending its publications to the Puerto Rican Collection. This request had scant results, and follow-ups have not fared any better. The Planning Board's intention was to enter into a cooperative program with the Puerto Rican Collection, whereby we would receive the publications, and then prepare and send bibliographic information to the Board's computer. In return, we would receive copies of their printouts. The ultimate value of these listings would, of course, depend upon the cooperation extended by the agencies.

Beginning in 1982, we sent copies of all our document catalog cards to the Planning Board, as well as quarterly accessions lists. The Planning Board has produced a listing of the documents classified by Dewey, but still has to process the rest of the titles. The project is now on hold, pending a review by the Board's new head. Budgetary constraints mean that this project has little chance of success, since publications and their control have an extremely low priority with respect to anything else.

Access and Pattern of Use

Our document collection is available to both the university community and the general public. The library's extended service hours, and our location on the largest campus of the University of Puerto Rico and in a densely populated area, are assets in that we are easily accessible to a large number of readers.

However, even though the documents represent a significant part of our resources, these materials are underused. They remain unfamiliar to many of our users, who more often turn to books and periodicals. A small percentage of titles accounts for a high proportion of the documents used, which means that a wealth of information is not being tapped. It takes an interested reader, in combination with an alert librarian, to elicit that which is dormant. Documents whose access cards are filed in our card catalog, and statistical works such as those produced by the Planning Board, comprise the most frequently used titles. Legal materials, especially Decisiones de Puerto Rico and Leyes Anotadas de Puerto Rico, are also widely used by law school students.

Concluding Remarks

This brief account has discussed certain aspects of Puerto Rico's official publications: questions of acquisition, organization, bibliographic control, and use. Other topics also merit attention and should be kept in mind. These include the creation of a government information policy that would provide readily available channels for disseminating its communications to the public, a centralized production and distribution system for documents, a higher level of budgetary support, and the expanded availability of computerized databases.

Appendix A

ORGANIZATION CHART OF THE GOVERNMENT

OF THE COMMONWEALTH OF PUERTO RICO

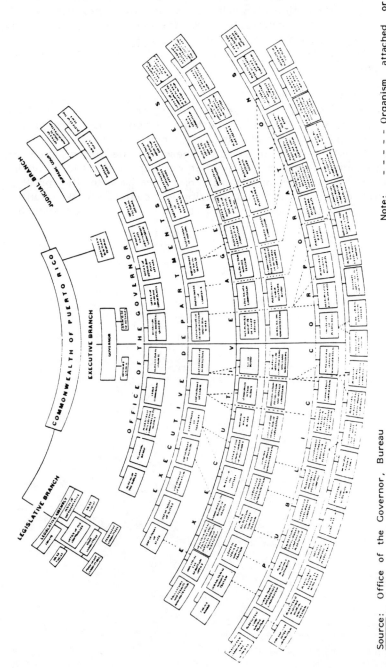

Note: – – – – Organism attached or related administratively by law to a department or agency but autonomous in its operation.

Source: Office of the Governor, Bureau of the Budget

Appendix B

POLITICAL SUBDIVISIONS OF PUERTO RICO

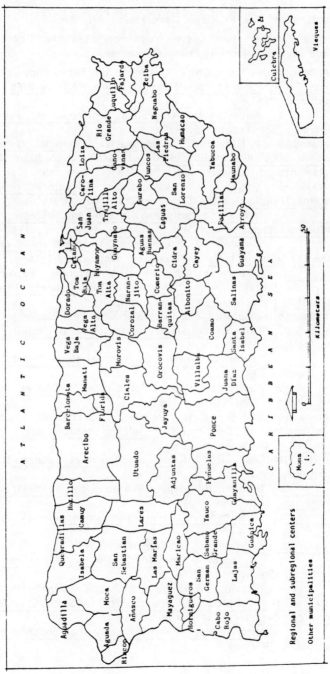

Source: Office of the Governor, Puerto Rico Planning Board

Appendix C

SELECTED LISTS

Publications of Puerto Rican Government Agencies

The date in the open entry corresponds to the first available issue in the Colección Puertorriqueña.)

Departamento de Agricultura. Oficina de Estadísticas Agrícolas. Facts and Figures on Puerto Rico's Agriculture 1960/61. Santurce, 1961--.

_____. Anuario de estadísticas agrícolas de Puerto Rico 1968/69. Santurce, 1961--.

Departamento de Hacienda. Comparative Financial Condition of Commercial Banks in Puerto Rico 1956/57. San Juan, 1957--.

Departamento de Instrucción Pública. Area de Planificación, Información y Desarrollo Educativo. Directorio de escuelas públicas/Public Schools Directory 1979/80. Hato Rey, 1980--.

_____. Informe estadístico: Primer mes escolar, 1981/82/ Statistical Report First School Month. Hato Rey, 1982--.

_____. División de Información. Informe anual estadístico 1955/56/Annual Statistical Report. Hato Rey, 1956--.

_____. Programa Educativo, Vocacional, Técnico y de Altas Destrezas. Annual Accountability Report: Fiscal Year 1980/81. Hato Rey, 1981--.

Departamento de Salud. Administración de Facilidades y Servicios de Salud. Informe anual de estadísticas de salud: 1971/72. Río Piedras, 1972--.

_____. Informe anual de estadísticas vitales: 1930. Río Piedras, 1931--.

_____. Registro Control del Cáncer. Cáncer en Puerto Rico: 1966. Río Piedras, 1967--.

Departamento de Servicios Sociales. Secretaría Auxiliar de Planificación y Desarrollo. Boletín estadístico: año fiscal 1976-77. Santurce, 1977--.

Junta de Planificación. Informe económico al gobernador: 1950. Santurce, 1951--.

_____. Balanza de pagos, Puerto Rico, 1941-42/Balance of Payments. Santurce, 1942--.

_____. Indicadores económico mensuales. Santurce, 1968--.

_____. Boletín social. Santurce, 1981--.

_____. Ingreso y producto, P.R., 1959/Income and Product. Santurce, 1960--.

Junta de Planificación. Area de Planificación Económica y Social. External Trade Statistics, Puerto Rico: 1954/55/Estadísticas de Comercio Exterior. Santurce, 1955--.

_____. Informe de recursos humanos al gobernador: 1970. Santurce, 1971.

Oficina de Presupuesto y Gerencia.   Presupuesto para el año
fiscal 1945/46. San Juan, 1946--.
_____. Guía de funcionarios del Estado Libre Asociado de
Puerto Rico. San Juan, 1959--.
_____. Manual de organización del gobierno de P.R.
San Juan, 1955--. (The most comprehensive publication about
the government and its organization.)
Oficina del Procurador del Ciudadano.   Primer informe anual,
1979/80. San Juan, 1980.

Periodicals Issued by Puerto Rican Government Units

El Aljibe. Autoridad de Acueductos y Alcantarillados.

Anales de investigación histórica. Universidad de Puerto Rico.

Boletín de seguro. Oficina del Superintendente de Seguros.

Cuentagotas. Oficina de Energía.

Diálogos. Universidad de Puerto Rico.

Educación. Departamento de Instrucción Pública.

Enlace. Departamento del Trabajo y Recursos Humanos.

Noticias estadísticas. Junta de Planificación.

Noticiero de la Asociación. Asociación de Empleados del E.L.A.

Nuevos horizontes. Oficina para el Desarrollo Integral del
Impedido.

Personal. Oficina Central de Administración de Personal.

Plerus. Universidad de Puerto Rico.

Presupuesto y Gerencia. Oficina de Presupuesto y Gerencia.

P.R. Business Review. Banco Gubernamental de Fomento.

P.R. Monthly Economic Indicators/Indicadores económicos
mensuales. Banco Gubernamental de Fomento.

Qué pasa in Puerto Rico. Compañía de Turismo.

Revista del Instituto de Cultura Puertorriqueña.   Instituto de
Cultura Puertorriqueña.

Revista del Trabajo. Departamento del Trabajo.

35. HUMAN RIGHTS IN LATIN AMERICA, 1960-1980

Georgette M. Dorn

It was primarily concern over violations of human rights that led the first colonists to populate the area we know today as the United States. Concerns over basic rights also lent much of the impetus to the North American Revolution and the framing of the Constitution. In the twentieth century, human rights issues have contributed to United States involvement in international conflicts, to its efforts to establish organizations such as the League of Nations and the United Nations, and above all to its attempts to promote and encourage the enforcement of a wide spectrum of human rights.[1]

Recognition of the need for the protection of human rights has grown since the early 1960s, in parallel with the proliferation of repressive and/or authoritarian regimes that have contributed to widespread violations. Some Latin American governments also developed ideological justifications to disregard constitutional guarantees and legal protections of rights.[2] At the same time, human rights issues have often become an explicitly stated component of United States foreign policy.

The number of publications concerning human rights in Latin America has increased markedly over the last two decades, while the concept of protected rights has undergone a noticeable redefinition and expansion. Since the middle and late 1960s the literature on human rights, traditionally oriented toward constitutional protections, philosophical writings, and legal procedures, has begun to change. The sharp increase in wholesale violations under repressive regimes has brought human rights to the fore, and the literature has begun to emphasize social and ethical issues, economic and social rights, and questions of equality.

A substantial number of basic publications on human rights were and still are generated by organizations such as the International Court of Justice, the International Commission of Jurists, the United Nations, the Organization of American States, Amnesty International, the U.S. Department of State, and the U.S. Congress (especially during the 1970s). Publications by international and national governmental agencies, and by non-governmental organizations, have been supplemented by a steady flow of materials that are testimonial or polemical, and popular rather than scholarly. Many deal with human rights violations in such major countries as Brazil, Argentina, and Chile. Most of this literature has tended to be of protest and opposition, embodying the expression of those "on the outside." Some publications are produced within countries in which rights are being violated, for example, in Chile; others are published in exile, as with Cuba.

The genesis of a pamphlet collection entitled "Human Rights in Latin America," which has been assembled by the Hispanic Division of the Library of Congress, is the focus of this paper. Under the direction of then-chief Mary Ellis Kahler, the Hispanic Division began in 1977 to systematically set aside items on human rights. The materials thus collected were those that the Library would not normally catalog fully as separate titles. I, for instance, while attending a conference in Rio de Janeiro, was able to gather a number of items on human rights in Brazil published by organizations such as the Ordem dos Advogados do Brasil, the Catholic Church, and ad hoc human rights groups. These initial acquisitions marked the start of this pamphlet collection. The Library's office in Rio became an excellent source for additional materials relating to human rights. Most items were sent on to the general collections of the Library, and only those not selected for cataloging remained in the pamphlet collection.

In the fall of 1977, Patricia Weiss Fagen, chairperson of the Academic Freedom and Human Rights Committee of the Latin American Studies Association (LASA), approached Mary Kahler to suggest that the Hispanic Division cooperate with LASA in compiling a bibliography specifically concerned with human rights in Latin America. The scholarly community felt that there was an extensive body of little-known literature on human rights, written by Latin Americans both in their own countries and in exile. The Hispanic Division and LASA agreed to cooperate in this venture.

Early in 1978, the Executive Council of LASA secured a grant from the Ford Foundation to gather materials and compile a bibliography on human rights in Latin America. The Hispanic Division and LASA agreed that this collection would include discussions of general and specific human rights, and would incorporate works on politics, philosophy, religion, economics, and law. Formats would include books and periodicals, as well as pamphlets. Most of the materials to be acquired during the project would be fully cataloged and added to the Library's collections. Those not selected for cataloging would be added to a fledgling pamphlet grouping.[3] A supplemental grant awarded by the Organization of American States (OAS) helped the project toward its completion in 1981.

Under the terms of the Ford grant, Patricia Fagen traveled to South America and Mexico in 1979. There she met with staff members of human rights organizations and brought back approximately 50 items, mainly pertaining to rights violations in Chile and Brazil. The Hispanic Division sent a circular letter to more than 200 human rights organizations in North America, Latin America, and Europe.[4] About half these centers responded. The new materials were then organized by country or by subject.

When William Carter succeeded Mary Kahler as chief of the Hispanic Division in 1979, the Human Rights Project was well under way. Two persons were engaged in classifying and describing the materials. They also searched the Library's data-bases, catalogs, and book and periodical collections for additional materials for the bibliography. The staffers found a wealth of human-rights related materials in LC's Law Library, especially in legal journals and in publications issued by international organizations.

The Human Rights Pamphlet Collection, 1960-1980, contains approximately 700 items on topics ranging from jurisprudence and official reports to first-hand description of torture and murder. Many of the items were produced by either church organizations or by church-supported programs or centers, Catholic or Protestant, throughout the world. A total of 120 items in the pamphlet collection were published by these church-related agencies, such as the Vicaría de la Solidaridad of the Arzobispado de Santiago and the Academia de Humanismo Cristiano, both in Chile; the American Friends Service Committee, the Inter-Church Committee on Human Rights in Latin America, the National Assembly of Women Religious, the United Presbyterian Church in the U.S., the U.S. Catholic Conference, and others. We placed under the heading "Churches--Latin America" publications dealing with Latin America in general, with theoretical issues, or with more than one country. Church-related publications dealing with a specific country were placed under that country. Thus, the larger portion of publications by the Vicaría de la Solidaridad can be found under "Chile," rather than "Churches."

Newsletters and reports by solidarity groups concerning human rights, some of them short-lived, are of historical interest and often difficult to acquire: these groups usually disband when the repressive regime they opposed changes and human rights violations cease. Cases in point are such solidarity groups as the Committee in Solidarity with the Uruguayan People of Brooklyn, N.Y.; the Committee for the Defense of Human Rights in Argentina of Port Credit Station, Ontario, Canada; and the Nicaraguan Support Fund of London. Thanks to its aggressive search for human rights materials, the Library was able to acquire all the back issues of Paz y Justicia, published in Buenos Aires. This publication was cataloged and added to the general collections.

The pamphlet collection contains 70 items under the heading "General--Latin America." Of special interest are the Notre Dame Symposium on International Human Rights and American Foreign Policy (1977), a pamphlet entitled Why Police States Love the Computer (1977), and publications on the relation between peace, equality, and human rights. There are an additional 17 listings for bibliographies on human rights in Latin America, including materials produced by Amnesty International, the U.S.

Department of State, the Index on Censorship, and the Estudio bibliográfico by the Vicaría de la Solidaridad (1978).

There are 287 titles listed under individual countries, with the largest numbers corresponding to Chile, Brazil, and Haiti. A good deal of the literature has a leftist cast, since many Latin American countries were governed by regimes of the political right during the period under consideration. Those countries with very strict control over publishing tend to be represented by fewer items than those that imposed less control, as seen in the abundance of materials on Chile and Brazil and the relative sparsity for Cuba and Uruguay.[5] The reason for the numerous entries pertaining to Haiti, on the other hand, is that individual issues of the periodical Construction were each counted as a single item.

The materials on Argentina include reports by the Argentine Commission for Human Rights, publications on legal and constitutional matters, and reports on torture, cases of desaparecidos, and repression of trade unions. Many of the Brazilian items were published by the Ordem dos Advogados do Brasil. The entries under Bolivia center on publications dealing with the repression of campesinos and of members of indigenous groups. The materials on Chile include items on arrests, torture, and disappearances. The pamphlets on Colombia were produced in large part by the Asociación Colombiana pro Derechos Humanos, and were published within that country. Cuban entries include publications based on the testimony of former political prisoners and of prisoners who were religious dissidents. The items pertaining to El Salvador relate to disappearances, murder, and torture, as do those on Nicaragua. Most of the latter hail from the Somocista era, although a few recent acquisitions deal with the Sandinista regime, for instance in its treatment of the Miskito Indians. The Guatemalan materials deal with repression of rights, as well as labor union questions. The items on Paraguay largely represent the results of international inquiries. The materials concerning Uruguay are varied and extensive. In fact, the pamphlets on the Southern Cone area form the backbone of the "countries" cluster within the pamphlet collection.

Under the heading "Amnesty International," one finds largely Spanish-language reports, many providing country-by-country surveys on human rights violations. Some items present case reports of torture or murder, while others are the published findings of conferences. The Library keeps only English-language materials by Amnesty in its general collection.

Publications by the Organization of American States' Inter-American Commission on Human Rights form a cluster of 36 items, mostly reports by working committees and the texts of resolutions on human rights. Here one also finds specific and comprehensive surveys on individual countries, such as those for Argentina, Chile, Uruguay, and Cuba. One of the most recent

acquisitions is the 7th edition of The Situation of Human Rights in
Cuba (1983). These documents, often in Spanish, highlight the
international concern to protect human rights and to document
repression, as can be seen from the following titles: Examen
comparado de los proyectos de convención sobre derechos humanos
del Consejo Interamericano de Jurisconsultos (1966); and
Terrorismo con fines políticos e ideológicos como fuente de
violación de los derechos humanos (1970). A separate group of
eight pamphlets produced by the OAS Inter-American Commission
on Women demonstrates the commission's efforts to promote
broader political participation of women. Some of them document
discrimination on the basis of gender. One noteworthy item in
this group is a bibliography, published in 1977, which lists works
on Women in Latin America in the Columbus Memorial Library.

The United Nations documents in this collection tend to
represent theoretical treatments of human rights, and to analyze
the broad issue of protecting them. Several items deal with
interpretations of the Universal Declaration of Human Rights,
while a few contain more specific reports. The Library's general
collections maintain fairly complete holdings of U.N. materials.

Thirty-four pamphlets were issued by the Washington Office
on Latin America (WOLA), an organization sponsored by several
churches in the United States, which monitors repression in the
Americas and also analyzes the impact of human rights concerns
on U.S. foreign policy. The pamphlet collection features several
years of WOLA's newsletter, Update.

Another center of interest to those studying human rights is
Human Rights Internet, a worldwide clearinghouse on rights
violations established in 1976, which moved to Washington, DC in
1977. The center's Human Rights Reporter, published six times a
year, provides systematic information about research, human
rights publications, unpublished reports, and conference proceedings. The center has also published two editions of a Human
Rights Directory: Latin America, Africa, Asia, the latest in 1981,
which will be superseded by the publication of individual directories for each part of the world. The Latin American volume is
scheduled to appear in 1986.

The LC Hispanic Division's Human Rights Pamphlet collection,
of about 700 items, was copied on microfiche in 1984. This select
collection consists only of those materials not cataloged
individually by the Library, in addition to a few duplicates
included for purposes of relevance. Those studying human rights
developments in the 1960-1980 period should begin by consulting
the bibliography that grew out of this joint undertaking of the
Library of Congress and LASA, namely, Human Rights in Latin
America: A Selective Annotated Bibliography, 1964-1980 (1983).
This compilation encompasses 1,827 entries. In addition to the
headings mentioned above in describing the pamphlets, the
bibliography contains additional selections under the following

categories: U.S. Congressional Documents; U.S. Policy Relating to Human Rights in Latin America; Newsletters; and Bibliographies and Directories. An appendix listing organizations dealing with human rights issues enhances this reference tool.

The Hispanic Division, under the direction of Sara Castro-Klarén, continues to acquire materials on human rights. Items not selected for the general collections are retained in the pamphlet collection. Acquisitions during the last five years have included new materials, as well as retrospective items from the 1970s. The new materials tend to contain more information on labor groups; for instance, we now receive a newsletter entitled Informativo CLAT (Central Latinoamericana de Trabajadores). There are also more items on discrimination against women, and other women's issues, as well as materials concerning infringements of indigenous people's rights, for example, in the Amazon region. Exiles from Latin American countries often alert the Hispanic Division staff to the formation of new human rights organizations and to new titles. The materials at hand suggest that materials continue to be produced in Chile. A few, for the most part dealing with the trials of the military, even come from Argentina. Nothing, however, seems to be published on Uruguay. Materials on post-Mariel Cuba and Guatemala form interesting new topics within the collection.

The human rights pamphlet collection, as it continues to develop, offers the researcher a selective subset of this literature of outsiders, a subset that in many libraries tends to "get lost." Many of these materials document worsening human rights conditions, as systematic official violations of civil and political rights become a means of social control. The violation or protection of human rights is more often than not at the heart of intellectual discourse in Latin America. For this reason alone, these ephemeral materials are indispensable. Greater access will contribute to scholarship and to an enhanced general awareness of the violations. This, in turn, may facilitate the creation, maintenance, or restoration of societies in which individual rights are fully respected.

NOTES

1. William E. Carter, "Introduction," Human Rights in Latin America: A Selective Annotated Bibliography, 1964–1980, comp. and ed. by the Hispanic Division (Washington, DC: Library of Congress, 1983), pp. v–vi.

2. Margaret E. Crahan, ed., Human Rights and Basic Needs in the Americas (Washington, DC: Georgetown University Press, 1982), pp. 6–7.

3.   Patricia Weiss Fagen to Mary Ellis Kahler, Nov. 11, 1977.   Library   of   Congress,   Hispanic   Division   archives (hereafter, LC/HD).

4.   Circular letter by Georgette M. Dorn, July 10, 1978. LC/HD.   The letter solicited materials relating to human rights.

5.   Carter, Human Rights, p. v.

36. THE HISTORICAL AND PROGRAMMATIC DIMEN-
SIONS OF MEXICAN AMERICAN RESEARCH
COLLECTIONS AT STANFORD

Roberto G. Trujillo

Collection Development at Stanford

The collection development effort at Stanford University really began with the development of academic programs for and about the Mexican American. Stanford Chicano students established the Chicano Reference Library in 1971. At the same time, the Stanford University Libraries were acquiring most materials published by major and university presses. Neither effort, however, proved adequate for developing a research-level collection. By 1980, with the establishment of the Stanford Center for Chicano Research (SCCR), a major new effort was essential. A formal collection evaluation was conducted of holdings within the Stanford University Libraries in August of 1981.[1] The evaluation identified major areas of collection weaknesses, reviewed existing efforts to develop primary source material collections (i.e., the Mexican American Manuscript Collections at Stanford), and recommended a plan of action to develop a "research level" collection. One recommendation included the elimination of duplication between the University Libraries and the Chicano Reference Library.

In September, 1982, a curatorial office for Mexican American collections was established. The office was to develop the collection of secondary source material (books, serials, microform sets, retrospective and current items, selected audiovisual materials) to a level that was comparable with research collections at other universities. The most notable collection programs were at the University of California's Santa Barbara, Los Angeles, and Berkeley campuses, and at the University of Texas at Austin. The Stanford effort was also to encompass primary source collections, including both manuscripts and archives.

At Stanford, the student-run Chicano Reference Library closed. Parts of that collection which did not duplicate University Library holdings were incorporated within Stanford's social science and humanities research facility, the Cecil H. Green Library. Within a two and a half year period, short-term goals and objectives for the Mexican American collections program were reached. The collections of literature, history, reference, serials, general social sciences, and the humanities were greatly increased. Antiquarian and subject trade specialists provided those materials that Stanford had lacked. The collection grew by approximately 3,000 titles and approximately 650 retrospective serial titles, all acquired in addition to the ongoing acquisition of federal and state government documents, and ERIC microfiche materials. The archival records of the Mexican American Legal Defense and Educational Fund--one of the most important primary source collections on the contemporary social and political history of the Mexican American people--was a capstone to this period of consolidation and expansion. The collections were also augmented by an important videotape series on Mexican American literature, comprising interviews with prominent creative writers and literary critics. Other acquisitions included an extensive nine-hour PBS interview with artist and activist Pedro J. González, microform sets, machine-readable files, and microfilm of retrospective Chicano newspapers.

According to ALA's 1979 criteria for library collections, Stanford's collections were no more than "basic" at the time the Mexican American curatorial office was created. By 1985, the Stanford collections had become some of the most comprehensive in the entire country, and they match the institution's ongoing commitment to an academic program of intensive research and instruction. Stanford's Mexican American manuscript collections are the largest in the country in terms of linear footage, and they include papers from some of the most important social and political movements, and leaders, of the Mexican American community.

During the last decade, Stanford has acquired an out-standing group of manuscript collections pertaining to the Mexican American experience in its historical, legal, educational, political, and social aspects. With approximately 2,000 linear feet of material, Stanford's Mexican American manuscripts constitute the largest special collection currently available on this subject. These holdings, which are comprised of papers of individuals and records of organizations, reflect many differing viewpoints. A few examples are:

- The Mexican American Legal Defense and Educational Fund (MALDEF), a national civil rights advocacy organization with extensive archives.
- El Centro de Acción Social Autónomo (CASA), a Los Angeles-based Marxist-Leninist organization founded in 1968.
- The papers of the late Dr. Ernesto Galarza, prominent educator and former research director of the National Agricultural Workers Union.
- The papers of Bert Corona, long-time labor leader and political activist.
- The papers of Manuel Ruiz, Jr., attorney and former commissioner on the United States Civil Rights Commission.
- The papers of Eduardo Quevedo, former president of the Mexican American Political Association (MAPA).
- The papers of Dr. Edward Valenzuela, founder of IMAGE, a national Spanish-speaking organization concerned with government employees.

The papers of Father Victor P. Saldini, a social activist priest best known as an advocate of the Mexican American community and of the California farm laborers' cause, and a close associate of César Chávez, director of the United Farm Workers Union.

The papers of Anne Draper, who achieved prominence in the 1960s as a California leader of labor, feminist, and peace movements, active with the farm labor organizing of César Chávez and the United Farm Workers.

The papers of Father James L. Vizzard, a university professor, author, and legislative representative for the National Catholic Rural Life Conference (1955-1968) and for the United Farm Workers (1972-1977).

In addition to these collections, which are housed in the Department of Special Collections, the Stanford University Archives (which collects records and publications generated by the University) has amassed primary source materials documenting the history of Stanford's Mexican American community. Included are the following:

The records of the Assistant Provost and Advisor to the President for Chicano Affairs.

The records of the Stanford Center for Chicano Research.

The papers of the late Dr. Alfredo Castaneda, Professor of Education and Stanford's first Mexican American faculty member.

The records of the Chicano Fellows Program, Undergraduate Studies on Chicano Society and Culture.

The records and publications of the local chapter of MECHA, a national Chicano student organization.

To be sure, the Mexican American collections program at Stanford is "program driven": that is, the collection's direction and scope reflect the research and teaching at Stanford University. This response to the academic program is truer for manuscript and University Archives materials than for published secondary source material. The acquisition of secondary source materials is primarily driven by publishing activity, though the great bulk of Chicano published material is "fugitive," and difficult to acquire. The Stanford University Libraries has explicitly assumed responsibility for developing "research level" collections on the Mexican American. Stanford has also assumed explicit primary collection responsibility, within the Research Libraries Group (RLG), for Mexican American literature. Scholars can consequently expect that most, if not all, published material on the Mexican American will be acquired. Only children's literature is not collected.

The Libraries' collections are being developed in coordination with the Stanford Center for Chicano Research, an organized research unit of the University. The principal interests of the SCCR, which recently became a founding member of the Inter-

University Program for Chicano and Puerto Rican Research, include urban-focused research on the social, political, and economic conditions of Mexican Americans; educational research centering on processes and policies to foster learning and promote educational equity for Mexican Americans; communication studies analyzing community information networks, the production and distribution of mass communications, and the impact of these media on Mexican Americans; and demographic analysis.

The Mexican American collections, of course, support the curricular and research needs of students as well as those of the SCCR and of scholars more generally. Stanford has a program for undergraduate studies on Chicano society and culture, and Stanford recruits nationally for doctoral students in the social sciences and humanities with particular interests in Mexican American scholarship. In a sense, the collections at Stanford support this scholarship within a series of concentric spheres. Local constituents include the SCCR, faculty, research associates, doctoral level graduate students, other graduate students, and an undergraduate curriculum. The audience then widens to incorporate visiting faculty and researchers. Finally, we serve scholars who simply need access to Stanford's unique primary source materials.

Although the collections at Stanford have only recently been developed, their scope and significance attract scholars from throughout the country. In the past two years, for example, both Mexican and United States scholars have visited for the purpose of studying the Mexican experience in the United States, and particularly Mexican immigration across the border.

With the institutional commitment demonstrated above, it is clear that Stanford perceives the need for research and instruction on the Mexican American experience. Since 1980, program development at Stanford in both academic structures and the library system has been quite remarkable. The programs came about from tremendous efforts on the part of individuals within the Chicano academic community, and the Stanford community in general. The early efforts of Chicano students, in 1971, forced attention upon library collections and services. Activities to develop manuscript collections began with Luis Nogales, who was Assistant to the President for Chicano Affairs and, later, a member of the University Libraries Visiting Committee; and through the late Dr. Ernesto Galarza's donation of his personal papers.

These efforts were reinforced by Cecilia Burciaga, also an Assistant to the President, who arranged for the acquisition of El Espectador, a Chicano newspaper published by Ignacio Lopez, who was one of the Chicano community's earliest and most articulate spokesmen from 1933 to 1960. The more recent efforts of Albert M. Camarillo, Director of the SCCR and Associate Professor of History at Stanford University, have brought us the

CASA and Bert Corona papers. Stanford's largest collection is the MALDEF archive, an acquisition involving the combined efforts of the Assistant Provost and Advisor to the President for Chicano Affairs, Fernando de Necochea; Professor Camarillo; myself; and library staff members including Director of Libraries David C. Weber, Associate Director Paul H. Mosher, Special Collections Curator Michael T. Ryan, and Manuscripts Librarian Carol Rudisell.

The current collections program is the result of many years of discussions, negotiations, proposals, collection reviews and evaluations, and education on the part of both library staff and Chicano students and scholars. Stanford's collection of secondary source material will continue to be maintained, and the direction of manuscript collections development will address new research efforts and interests, encompassing every kind of material. Books, videos, machine-readable data files, microtexts, journals, newspapers, manuscripts, and archives are all currently represented. Stanford has particular interests in urban social and political history and in literature. These two mainstays are likely to remain important to the entire field of Mexican American studies.

Between the late 1960s and the 1980s, we've seen some major landmarks in the writing of Chicano history. Recent publications by major university presses demonstrate a trend, and illustrate the need for increased access to primary source material pertaining to the population of Mexican origin. Mexican American research collections can and do support the publication of new histories and the development of new curricula. The Stanford collections are particularly significant insofar as research and subsequent publications on many aspects of the Mexican American experience must rely on papers now held at the University.

The Nature of Mexican American Collection Development

Today we face a dilemma in describing the development of research collections pertinent to the Mexican experience in the United States. Research materials on the Mexican American date from at least 1621, and they continue to the present. Many earlier primary source materials have already been preserved and, in some measure, organized for scholarly access. Such achievements have occurred quite apart from current collection development efforts for Mexican American materials. For example, the Spanish Archives of New Mexico, 1621 to 1821; the Mexican Archives of New Mexico, 1821 to 1846; and the Territorial Archives of New Mexico, 1846 to 1912, all contain background resources for contemporary Mexican American history. Organized and concerted collection development efforts for specifically "Mexican American" collections, however, only date from 1969, when the Chicano student movement forced major universities to address the curricular and scholarly needs of those interested in the Mexican American experience. Mexican American history, in other words, is not a phenomenon that began with the collection development efforts of the Chicano studies programs of the late 1960s.

The early materials on microform comprise an important core for the research collections developed since 1969. Even with recent collection development programs, which have made a distinct difference to researchers and students, Mexican American collections--collections based on secondary materials published since 1969--do not by themselves constitute comprehensive or independent research resources. No single Mexican American collection can function as a comprehensive research resource, because too many materials are unique. Only the secondary source materials are prevalent. Primary source materials are also, in many cases, beyond the service scope of "Mexican American" library programs functioning independently of larger library systems. And, again, many primary source collections predate the Chicano movement of the 1960s and 1970s, and the Chicano library programs then engendered.

The Network of Collections

The collections of materials pertaining to the Mexican American, taken together, comprise a network of research library resources that is increasingly relied upon by advanced students and scholars. This is particularly apparent for the libraries mentioned earlier--the University of California's Santa Barbara, Los Angeles, and Berkeley campuses, the University of Texas at Austin, and--now--Stanford University. Scholarship on the Mexican American will increasingly rely on both Chicano Studies library programs (that link comprehensive collections of secondary source materials with microformat archival and retrospective serial collections) and Chicano collection development programs (within university library structures as well as through quasi-independent branch or departmental libraries that develop original manuscript collections).

Secondary Sources

Secondary materials comprise the bulk of most "Mexican American" collections. Most of this material, perhaps as much as 75 to 80 percent, has been published since 1968. Maintaining secondary source collections is now beginning to take less time, relative to efforts to develop manuscript collections. This holds all the more for library programs that have not been part of university library operations.

Access to Collections

Stanford University is, of course, a member of the Research Libraries Group Inc., and participates in the Research Libraries Information Network (known as RLIN). The Libraries' Mexican

American holdings are included in the RLIN bibliographic data-base, in the Archives and Manuscripts, Films, Serials, Record-ings, and Books files. The Libraries' manuscript collections are open to researchers regardless of affiliation. Descriptive guides, as well as an author-title-subject card catalog, provide detailed information on the collections. Both the RLIN and the Socrates databases (the latter Stanford's computerized online catalog) provide access to manuscript collections. Given the recent vintage of Mexican American collection development at Stanford, virtually all these materials are on the computerized databases.

Future Development of the Collections

The Libraries are interested in expanding the scope of the Mexican American Manuscript Collections to document more fully the activities of the Mexican American population. The Libraries' primary interest is in unpublished materials--correspondence, diaries, speeches and writings, informal notes, interviews, reports, memoranda, research files, posters, photographs, films, videotapes, and sound recordings. Printed materials such as handbills, pamphlets, and small press publications are also collected. Personal papers are of inestimable value to scholars in that they provide significant insight into the activities of individuals and organizations who might otherwise be lost to history. Unanalyzed data of this kind are essential to the growth and development of such relatively young disciplines as Mexican American studies.

In sum, the collections at Stanford provide significant docu-mentation on the contemporary and historical condition of people of Mexican origin within the United States. The role played by individuals, groups, and indeed, by the Chicano movement itself, cannot be underestimated. The initiative taken by the University has of late been particularly impressive. The collections have been formed and shaped in response to scholars' activities and interests vis-à-vis the Mexican American experience. The Stanford Mexican American collections indeed reflect the masses and minorities. Their images and realities are preserved now, as they will always be, in ink as well as sweat.

37. "HOME OF LOST CAUSES": MASSES AND MINORITIES IN THE BODLEIAN

Robert A. McNeil

Beautiful city! So venerable, so lovely, so unravaged by the fierce intellectual life of our century, so serene! . . . Home of lost causes, and forsaken beliefs, and unpopular names, and impossible loyalties!

Matthew Arnold on Oxford
Essays in Criticism, 1865

When Matthew Arnold wrote his famous encomium on Oxford in the 1860s, he would probably have been surprised to learn that the last part, at least, of his remarks was as true when applied to the Latin American materials in the Bodleian as it was to the University as a whole. In fact, taken in toto, this description does not seem to me likely to be true of (or indeed complimentary to) any university. Like all comparable institutions, universities and libraries cannot survive on nostalgia alone: even ivory towers must have at least their foundations in the real world. Thus, large proportions of our collections naturally reflect current orthodoxy of belief in and about Hispanic America. It is also undeniable that the Bodleian holdings, in common with most of those to be found in non-Hispanic Europe, lack the breadth of coverage of South America available in the best U.S. research libraries. As I have explained elsewhere,[1] before about 1960 Oxford made no attempt at the systematic collection of Latin Americana. Much of the material that we did acquire came almost by chance, and was seen as being quite peripheral to the main concerns of the University. The Bodleian Library was, nonetheless, during the first three centuries of its existence, building up a significant Latin American collection by a process of serendipity. I should like to concentrate in this paper on three specific areas of the Library's holdings which nicely point up the truth of Matthew Arnold's dictum: "forsaken beliefs" as illustrated in the group of pre-Hispanic codices from Mexico; "impossible loyalties" shown during the Araucanian Wars in seventeenth-century Chile; and "unpopular names" featured in the war of pamphlets which characterized Mexico's struggle for independence in the 1820s.

To start, however, I should like to say a little about the beginnings of the Bodleian's Hispanic collections. At the time of Sir Thomas Bodley's reestablishment of the University Library in 1598, England was still engaged in a bitter military and ideological struggle with Hapsburg Spain, Portugal, and the Indies.   This struggle did not officially end until 1604, two years after the Library's opening.   Partly as a result, the Bodleian's Hispanic collections got off to a spectacular start, with the library of a Portuguese bishop seized as a prize of war.   In 1596 the Earl of Essex, returning from the sacking of Cadiz, landed at Faro in the Algarve and quartered himself in the Bishop's Palace.   While he was there, he liberated the 252 volumes which comprised the bishop's library, and subsequently passed them on to his friend Bodley.   This was, in fact, the earliest recorded donation of a complete collection of books to the new library.

The acquisition of these works obviously alerted Bodley to the importance of having a large selection of books from and about Spain and its empire, presumably on the principle of knowing one's enemy.   Even after the peace treaty was signed, Spain and England remained separated by a deep religious divide, and the privateers continued their own war against Spanish trade with the Indies for many years.   One of the earliest formal acquisition trips undertaken on behalf of the Bodleian was to Spain: in 1604 John Bill, a London bookseller, was travelling Europe in search of books, and went on to Seville on Bodley's behalf.   He did not stay there long, however: "The peoples' usage towards all of our nation is so cruel and malicious," Bodley wrote later.   He was nevertheless able to arrange for a con-siderable consignment of Spanish books to be sent to Oxford, including a first edition of the Quijote.   This acquisition field-trip (to use more modern terminology) seems to have been a model of its kind--leaving aside Bill's poor reception from the locals--and we might do worse today than work on the same principle. Bodley reported proudly that Bill "hath gotten everywhere what the place would afford, for his commission was large, his leisure very good, and his payment sure at home."[2]

It was during Bodley's lifetime that the Library received the nucleus of the collection which is probably still the most signifi-cant element in its Latin American holdings: the five Mexican codices.   Codices are perhaps the most important way that the civilizations of pre-Columbian America can communicate with us today, assuming that we can understand what they are saying. The Bodleian's five were for a very long time--and may still be-- the largest group in any library in the world.   I do not propose here to enter on the thorny topic of detailed interpretation of the texts themselves.   There is considerable divergence of opinion among codicologists and anthropologists as to the exact signifi-cance of most of them, and a new facsimile and interpretation of at least one of them is due to be published in the near future.[3] I think that it might be useful, however, to consider how each of them became part of the Bodleian Library between 1600 and 1640.

The first to arrive was the Codex Bodley, which seems to have reached the Library some time between 1600 and 1603.   It is

a deerskin screenfold, and is assumed to be a type of historical
or genealogical record. I wish I could tell you where it came to
Bodley from, but alas no record exists. Sir J. Eric Thompson,
the distinguished expert on the Maya, has conjectured that it was
part of the booty from the Earl of Essex's descent upon Cadiz
and Faro,[4] but such evidence as there is seems to tell against
this hypothesis. The same doubt surrounds the Codex Laud,
presented to the Library by Archbishop Laud (the Chancellor of
the University) in 1636. All that we can say is that, from
similarities with other extant codices, it probably came into the
Archbishop's possession from a European collection. It has been
suggested that it formed part of the first consignment of Mexican
treasures sent by Cortés to the Emperor Charles V. John Dee,
the Elizabethan occultist, might have brought it to England from
Bohemia, where he visited the Emperor Maximilian II in 1564; the
Prince of Wales or the Duke of Buckingham might have brought it
from Madrid after their abortive negotiation for the hand of a
Spanish princess in 1623.[5] It is certainly the most obscure of
the Bodleian codices, and from its elaborate portrayal of the
Mexican gods is normally regarded as being ritualistic or
divinatory.

The other three codices all came to the Bodleian under the
will of John Selden, in 1659. For one of them, at least, we have
a definite provenance: the story of the Codex Mendoza, probably
the most celebrated of all Mexican codices, is well-known.
Antonio de Mendoza, the first viceroy of Mexico, assembled the
three-part manuscript from a copy of the annals of the lords of
Tenochtitlan, a copy of the annual tribute paid by more than 400
communities to Montezuma, and a specially-commissioned account of
the everyday life of the people he governed. The whole was
annotated in Spanish by a sympathetic priest--who complained,
incidentally, that his Indian informants took so long to agree on
the interpretation of some of the glyphs that the codex nearly
missed the ship that was to carry it to Spain. It never reached
Spain, of course. In the words of Samuel Purchas (who later
owned the codex), "This historie thus written, sent to Charles
the fifth Emperour, was together with the shippe that carried it
taken by French men of war, from whom Andrew Thevet the
French King's geographer obtained the same."[6] Passing through
the hands of two other geographers, Richard Hakluyt and
Purchas himself, the manuscript eventually came into the collection of the learned antiquary John Selden. Selden had also
acquired two other codices, now known as the Codex Selden and
the Selden Roll. The Codex is a screenfold genealogical history,
sufficiently similar in style to the Codex Bodley to suggest some
common provenance; the Roll is an incomplete strip of <u>amatl</u> paper
which, it is thought, contains the pictorial account of a tribal
migration. The Selden Roll seems to be the latest of the five
Bodleian codices. Imaginative conjectures have, of course, been

made about its provenance, involving French pirates, Prince Charles' trip to the Spanish court, or English raiders on the Spanish Main.[7] The fact is that we have no idea where Selden got it.

Before we leave the Selden Collection, it might be instructive to those libraries that rely heavily on gifts and legacies to note that it very nearly failed to come to the Bodleian at all. Selden died in 1654, and by a 1653 codicil in his will intended to bequeath all his Oriental and Greek manuscripts to the Bodleian (the codices were at the time classed with Egyptian hieroglyphics). Unfortunately, by a curious omission neither the name of the Library nor, indeed, of the University, was mentioned in the drafting. It was nearly five years before Selden's executors could be prevailed upon to allow the collection to come to the Bodleian, and in the meantime a large number of Selden's other manuscripts had been destroyed by a fire in London.

The second area of the Bodleian's holdings I should like to consider here is the Yriarte Collection, which we acquired at a sale in 1835. More specifically, I would like to address the manuscript it contains of Francisco Núñez de Pineda y Bascuñán. Pineda was a seventeenth-century Chilean military leader who spoke up boldly for the rights of the Araucanian Indians through the interminable series of Indian wars and uprisings that form the history of the province. The son of a high-ranking colonial commander, he was serving as a captain in the Spanish army against the Araucanians in 1629 when he was captured by the Indians. His six months as a prisoner (he later called it his "Cautiverio feliz") completely changed his view of colonial life. He discovered that the Araucanians, notorious for their recalcitrance and savagery, were in fact an honourable people who only wished to be treated honourably by the Spaniards. (The parallel with the situation of some North American tribes in the nineteenth century is at times irresistible.) Pineda spent the rest of his life trying to change his compatriots' attitude and behaviour to the Indians--a lost cause, if ever there was one, in seventeenth-century Chile. He eventually prepared the Bodleian manuscript, an abridgement of a much longer text preserved in the Archivo Nacional in Santiago, as a plea to Spain's King Charles II for a reform of Chilean government.

As with the Mendoza Codex, the progress of the manuscript can be traced: prepared between 1675 and 1678, it was carried to Spain, it would seem, in 1680. In Madrid it dropped out of sight. It may have reached the court, but it seems never to have come before the Council of the Indies, for had it done so it would surely have come to rest in the Archivo General de Indias. In fact it only surfaced again in 1823, when the American dealer Obadiah Rich purchased the private library of Juan de Yriarte-- the Bodleian's Yriarte Collection. Yriarte was a classical scholar who worked for much of his life in the Royal Library in Madrid, and it is tempting to assume that the Pineda manuscript came from that library, which was formed originally from the personal collections of Philip IV and Charles II. Yriarte was certainly an avid reader and a collector of catholic tastes: the remainder of his library consists mainly of Spanish history and literature, and includes some interesting Calderón manuscripts. The importance of the Pineda manuscript was not in fact recognized until 1978, when it was fully identified. The text has now been published,[8] and can take its place as at once one of the major sources for the history of colonial Chile and a fascinating literary work in its own right.

The third collection I want to mention here had not yet reached Oxford when Arnold wrote the words quoted earlier. This is the small but rich selection of Mexican pamphlets acquired by the Bodleian in 1870 for the sum of £80. As is well known, the 1820s were the halcyon days of pamphleteering in Mexico. Freedom of the press had been introduced in 1820, and the intellectual ferment among the small group of educated creoles and Spaniards led to the appearance of thousands upon thousands of broadsides and pamphlets, covering a vast range of topics. It was also a crowded period of history--for the educated middle class, that is to say; the lives of the mass of the people continued virtually unchanged. Agustín de Iturbide claimed independence for Mexico with his Plan of Ayala, political parties formed and reformed, Iturbide was proclaimed Emperor, Santa Anna proclaimed a republic. Throughout it all the perennial debates continued, between centralists and federalists, Spaniards and creoles, anticlericals and the Church. All these events and viewpoints are faithfully reflected in the pamphlets of the time, sometimes painstaking and accurate, sometimes sensational and scurrilous. Pamphlets and broadsides have in the past been an under-used resource for Mexican history. Nowadays historians are beginning to look beneath the propagandizing and name-calling to discover more of the political development of the nation and the talents of the pamphleteers themselves--men like Joaquín Fernández de Lizardi, Pablo de Villavicencio, and Rafael Dávila, all of whom are heavily represented in the Bodleian holdings.

Collecting these pamphlets and assembling them into extensive archives seems to have been a popular pastime among antiquarians from around 1860, as reflected by the major collec-tions of such materials in Mexico, the United States, and Europe. The Bodleian material was brought together by Henry Ward Poole, the younger brother of William Frederick Poole, pioneer of the nineteenth-century library movement in the United States. Henry was commissioned by the American Antiquarian Society to collect books and manuscripts in Puebla and Mexico City during the suppression of the convents and monasteries, in 1861, under the anti-clericalist legislation of Juárez. While in Mexico City, he also assembled for his own purposes a selection of pamphlets from the independence period. This collection is thus one of the earliest of the major ones to be formed: Bancroft amassed his library from 1866 onwards, and Sutro did not start to form his until 1885. Poole continued his researches in Mexico until 1866, undaunted by a spell in prison under the French-backed regime of the Emperor Maximilian; and again from 1868 to 1870. Throughout this period he was selling much of the material he had found to Henry Stevens of Vermont, the leading specialist bookdealer of his time, and it was Stevens who brought the existence of the pamphlets to the attention of Bodley's Librarian, the Reverend H. O. Coxe. The collection as purchased consists of 41 volumes containing 1,446 separate pamphlets, in addition to several short runs of periodicals. The Bodleian was, in fact, slightly misled by its supplier: according to Stevens the number of separate works was between two and three thousand. They date from 1754 to 1841, though the vast majority of the pamphlets comes from the years 1820 to 1827. Regrettably, like the Pineda manuscript, they lay unrecognized and uncatalogued in the Bodleian bookstacks for nearly a century; happily, their rediscovery in the 1960s led to the preparation and publication of a detailed catalogue.[9] Small when compared to the Sutro and Bancroft libraries, the Bodleian collection of Mexican pamphlets is relatively homogenous, and is now recognized to constitute one of the major sources for the early political history of Mexico.

Looking at these three areas of Bodleian Latin American lost causes, it is difficult to point a specific moral for other libraries currently active in the same field. One obvious conclusion is the importance of making sure that any expected bequests are properly set down in the will of the potential donor. For the rest, I think the best course is to go back once more to the words of Sir Thomas Bodley. The four essential gifts for a librarian, he said, are Learning, Leisure, Money and Friends.[10] Learning and leisure enable us to identify the materials we need; money and friends help us to acquire them. For the money and the leisure, each of us has to look to our respective institutions. The learning and the friends we can find every year at SALALM.

NOTES

1. "Latin Americana in Oxford Libraries," in Latin American Studies in Europe: final report and working papers of the 23rd SALALM (Austin, TX, 1979), pp. 242-248.

2. Letters of Sir Thomas Bodley to Thomas James, ed. G. W. Wheeler (Oxford, 1972), pp. 90, 118.

3. A new edition of the Codex Mendoza, with commentaries based on papers given at the 44th International Congress of Americanists (Manchester, 1982) is projected by the University of New Mexico Press. The best general introduction to the other

four codices is the Bodleian pamphlet <u>Mexican pictorial manu-scripts</u> introduced by A. R. Pagden (Oxford, 1972).

    4.   The conjecture is reported by Alfonso Caso in <u>Inter-pretation of the Codex Bodley</u> (México, DF: 1960).

    5.   See C. A. Burland, <u>Codex Laud</u> (Graz, 1966).

    6.   <u>Purchas his Pilgrimes</u>, Part 3 (London, 1625), p. 1065.

    7.   See C. A. Burland, <u>The Selden Roll</u> (Berlin, 1955).

    8.   F. Núñez de Pineda y Bascuñán, <u>Suma y epílogo de lo más esencial que contiene el libro intitulado Cautiverio féliz</u>, ed. J. Anadón and R. A. McNeil (Santiago, 1984). See also J. Anadón, <u>Pineda y Bascuñán, defensor del araucano</u> (Santiago, 1977), and R. A. McNeil, "A 'Happy Captivity' in the Bodleian Library," in <u>Bodleian Library Record</u>, vol. 10, no. 5 (Oxford, 1981).

    9.   <u>Independent Mexico: A Collection of Mexican Pamphlets in the Bodleian Library</u>, ed. C. Steele and M. P. Costeloe (London, 1973).

    10. <u>The Life of Sir Thomas Bodley, Written by Himself</u> (Oxford, 1647, repr. in facs. 1983), p. 15.

38. LA COLECCION PERONISTA EN LA UNIVERSIDAD DE HARVARD

Margarita Anderson Imbert

El tema del Seminario que nos reúne este año es de veras importante: nada menos que la adquisición de materiales relativos al conflicto entre masas y minorías en Latinoamérica.

En la Argentina--que es el país que conozco mejor--ese conflicto se agudiza cuando a fines del siglo XIX llega una millonada de inmigrantes europeos. José Luis Romero, en Las ideas políticas en Argentina,[1] estudió el impacto de ese aluvión inmigratorio en la sociedad argentina. Distingue entre una "era criolla" y una "era aluvial." La "era criolla" culmina en 1880, con instituciones liberales y progresistas; en la "era aluvial" esa estructura empieza a desintegrarse. Dice Romero:

> El primer signo de esta era que se inicia (en 1880) es, en el campo político-social, un nuevo divorcio entre las masas y las élite. Las masas han cambiado su estructura y su fisonomía y, por reflejo, las élite han cambiado de significación y de actitud frente a ellas y frente a los problemas del país. Las consecuencias de este hecho fueron inmensas y perduran aún en el panorama argentino. . . . La tradición liberal adquirió, cada vez más, un carácter aristocrático y conservador en respuesta a los sentimientos confusos-- en parte retrógrados y en parte avanzados--de la nueva masa que se constituía debajo de la élite.[2]

Obsérvese que Romero habla de "masas y élite" en el sentido de "masas y minorías." No necesito aclarar que esta significación de minorías difiere del uso del término "minorities" en los Estados Unidos. El termino "minorías," sobre todo en Argentina, que es un país sin problemas raciales, se refiere a clases y grupos de personas que se consideran distinguidas. Son las élites de los "elegidos" entre la flor y nata de la sociedad; gente culta, con ideales responsables; élite política, intelectual, artística, etc.

Para Romero, la justa solución a la crisis argentina será la reconciliación de élite y masas. Sus palabras son de 1946, pero resultan más actuales ahora que entonces pues esa crisis se ha agravado con recientes tendencias populistas y "tercer mundistas".

Pues bien: del tema general que SALALM ha propuesto para este año--la adquisición de materiales relativos al conflicto entre masas y minorías--he escogido un aspecto muy particular: la

451

colección sobre el movimiento peronista en la Argentina, en la universidad de Harvard.

Este tema ofrece dos dimensiones: una cronológica y otra sociológica.

La dimensión cronológica de la bibliografía se refiere a hechos que se extienden desde la aparición de Perón en la vida política argentina hasta su desaparición. Esto es, desde el golpe militar del 4 de junio de 1943, que instauró un régimen fascista, con el coronel Perón al frente de la Secretaría de Trabajo y Previsión, hasta el 1º de julio de 1974 que es cuando muere, en ejercicio, por tercera vez, de la presidencia de su país.

Por supuesto que estos hitos (mojones) que marcan los límites no son fijos. Se pueden correr para atrás y para adelante. Después de todo, un período no es más que un corte arbitrario en el contínuo fluir de sucesos. La serie histórica que hoy calificamos como "peronista" podría comenzar con el cuartelazo del 6 de setiembre de 1930 que, por primera vez desde la Constitución de 1853, derrocó un gobierno legítimo. En esa dictadura nacionalista, oligárquica y fascistoide del general Uriburu participó el capitán Perón, aunque muy oscuramente. A partir de 1930 la Argentina ha sido regida por dictaduras militares o por presidentes que nunca terminaron su mandato constitucional porque fueron depuestos por el Ejército.

Así como se puede ampliar el período peronista adelantando la fecha de 1943 a 1930, también podríamos prolongarlo dando cuenta de los acontecimientos que siguen a la muerte de Perón en 1974. Esto es, la gestión presidencial de su mujer "Isabelita", la revuelta militar de 1976 que la metió en la cárcel, la represión del peronismo y finalmente las elecciones libres de 1983, en las que las fuerzas peronistas son derrotadas por el Partido Radical, que lleva al doctor Raúl Alfonsín a la Presidencia.

Esta es, pues, la dimensión cronológica de la realidad política; más de medio siglo de violencias políticas que interrumpen el imperio de la Constitución.

En cuanto a la dimensión sociológica, es mucho más complicada porque el peronismo no constituye un partido sino un movimiento.

Es importante señalar este distingo. Un partido es una organización política con cierta ideología y con un programa de acción. El peronismo, en cambio, fue un movimiento que obedeció ciegamente las órdenes de un dictador de extraordinaria personalidad carismática. Y este movimiento, a diferencia de un partido, que es más o menos homogéneo, fue absolutamente heterogéneo.

Lo más visible fue la adhesión a Perón de la clase trabajadora, pero lo cierto es que en el movimiento peronista hubo de todo: fascistas y comunistas, militares y sacerdotes, intelectuales y analfabetos, conservadores y radicales, proletarios resentidos, burgueses corruptos y aun almas candorosas. El peronismo representa uno de los primeros ejemplos de populismo, incorporando a las masas de pronto y sin revolución social. Por ser un movimiento mayoritario, el peronismo puso de manifiesto la falta de educación política de la nación entera. Sin embargo, Perón y sus peronistas no fueron más ineptos que sus opositores. Félix Luna, uno de los más serios historiadores del régimen peronista, ha señalado esta incapacidad política demostrada por los argentinos en las últimas décadas; "doble incapacidad",

> la incapacidad para establecer un sistema estable de poder que permita gobernar a la mayoría y garantice a la minoría sus legítimos derechos e intereses. Y la incapacidad para financiar nuestro desarrollo con nuestros propios recursos y según nuestros propios objetivos. Perón gobernó interpretando, en líneas generales, las aspiraciones mayoritarias. Pero vulneró los derechos de la minoría y terminó montando una estructura de poder compulsiva que provocó la desesperación de sus opositores. Y desde la caída de Perón para acá, la mayoría ha sido marginada, usada, proscripta o dividida. El resultado está a la vista: el pueblo no se ha sentido articulado a ninguna de las soluciones políticas que se han sucedido desde entonces.[3]

La heterogeneidad del movimiento peronista hace que los libros que tratan de caracterizarlo sean también heterogéneos pues sus autores representan niveles de la realidad social. Los bibliotecarios que coleccionan estudios sobre Perón deben tener en cuenta esta diversidad de perspectivas. Daré unos pocos ejemplos:

Obras Generales

Materiales Oficiales

Decretos, leyes, discursos oficiales, planes quinquenales, conferencias, correspondencia. En la Harvard Law Library hay quince gruesos volúmenes de más de mil páginas cada uno donde se recogen las leyes federales dictadas de 1945-1954.

Libros de Perón

Doctrina peronista filosófica y social, 1947; La fuerza es el derecho de las bestias, Habana, 1956; artículos bajo el pseudónimo "Descartes"; Los Estados Unidos de América del Sur, 1982 (es en realidad una recopilación de viejos artículos).

Libros de Eva Perón

La razón de mi vida, Buenos Aires, 1951 (libro de lectura obligatoria en el ciclo secundario); Historia del Peronismo (curso dictado en la Escuela Superior Peronista), 1952; La palabra, el pensamiento y la acción de Eva Perón, 1950?.

Propaganda Peronista

Por ser un movimiento heterogéneo, las voces vienen de distintos sectores: Partido Comunista: Jorge Abelardo Ramos, Perón, historia de su triunfo y su derrota (1959). Grupos marxistas: Rodolfo Puigross, "El peronismo" en Historia crítica de los partidos políticos argentinos, vol. 5 (1969). Radicales: Arturo Jáuretche, Política y economía (1977). Conservadores: Federico Pinedo, Porfiando hacia el buen camino; salida del remolino político e ideológico (1955). Nacionalistas: Julio Irazusta, Juan Perón y la crisis argentina (1956); y Mario Amadeo, Ayer, hoy y mañana (1956). En el libro citado dice Mario Amadeo, nacionalista nazi que luego cambió:

> Para los anti-peronistas de derecha el peronismo es fruto de la ignorancia como lo es la superstición o el curanderismo. Para los anti-peronistas de izquierda liberal, Perón y los peronistas eran nazis totalitarios que querían imponer en la Argentina el régimen de Hitler y Mussolini. Para la izquierda anti-liberal y marxista, que del peronismo sólo desaprueba la persona del Jefe, ve en ese movimiento una forma eficaz de lucha contra el imperialismo.[4]

Propaganda Anti-Peronista

Los socialistas: Americo Ghioldi, Los trabajadores, el señor Perón y el Partido Socialista (1951) y De la tiranía a la democracia (1956); y Milciades Peña, El peronismo. Selección de documentos para la historia (1951). Estos documentos se publicaron en distintos números de la revista Fichas de investigación. La intención de Peña al seleccionar estos documentos fue de desmistificar el peronismo. También Bernardo Rabinovitz, Sucedió en la Argentina (1945-56). Lo que no se dijo (1956).

Intentos de Evaluación Objetiva

El primero fue el de Ernesto Sábato: El otro rostro del peronismo. Carta abierta a Mario Amadeo (1956). Dice Sábato:

> Se habla mucho de que debe reeducarse a la masa peronista. Es hora de que comprendamos la urgencia de reeducar también a la masa anti-peronista. . . . todos somos culpables . . . directa o indirectamente, ligera o notablemente, de la funesta historia: las clases pudientes, por haber preparado el advenimiento del tirano; la Iglesia por haberlo apoyado hasta sus últimos momentos, hasta sufrir en carne propia el insulto y la opresión que los demás habíamos venido sufriendo durante diez años; los cuerpos armados, por haber soportado la tiranía, por haberla apuntalado con la fuerza de sus regimientos y por haber cedido en buena

medida a la corrupción general; la prensa, por haberse sumado en su casi totalidad al coro ditirámbico, más propensa a defender su negocio que a defender la verdad y la salud de la república; los profesores, por haber sido cómplices pasivos en su inmensa mayoría; los maestros, por haber enseñado los sofismas destinados a deformar el alma de nuestros niños; los escritores e intelectuales, porque no supimos comprender a los desposeídos, en nombre de la Ilustración; los grupos nacionalistas, en fin, porque en nombre de Dios y la Soberanía Nacional olvidaron o despreciaron la Libertad, ayudando así al fortalecimiento espiritual del dictador y a su fortalecimiento físico mediante las siniestras fuerzas de la Alianza, con el resultado de que ni siquiera sirvieron a Dios ni a la Soberanía, pues ni Dios quiere esclavos ni una nación de lacayos puede llegar a ser soberana.[5]

Con frecuencia la pretendida imparcialidad de un investigador es cuestionada por un colega que juzga con otra tabla de valores. Por ejemplo: Félix Luna, en Perón y su tiempo (1984) para equilibrar la balanza se esforzó en mostrar los aspectos menos desagradables de la dictadura pero al hacerlo volvió a desequilibrar los platillos pues, como bien le observó otro investigador, Luis Mario Lozzia (La Nación, 29-VII-1984) no denunció con bastante claridad la raíz fascista, cínica y cruel del reinado peronista.

Interpretaciones desde el Extranjero

Blanksten, George I. Peron's Argentina. Chicago, IL: The University of Chicago Press, 1974.
    (Dice el comentarista Milton Bracker, en el New York Times: "This is the most serious attempt so far to put the inflation-ridden, bomb-wracked Argentina of Juan Domingo Perón into one book, to explain peronismo and relate it to the hemisphere policy of the United States . . . Mr. Blanksten's work is timely, impressive . . . disturbing, heavily documented, and of essential interest to the specialist on Latin America.")
Gèze, François et Alain Labrousse. Argentina: révolution et contrerévolutions. Paris: Editions du Seuil, 1975.
Turner, Frederick C., and José Enrique Miguens, eds. Juan Perón and the Reshaping of Argentina. Pittsburgh, PA: University of Pittsburgh Press, 1983.
Vita-Finzi, Paolo. Perón mito e realità. Milano: Pan Editrice Milano, 1973.
Waldmann, Peter. Der Peronismus, 1943-1955. Hamburg: Hofflann und Campe Verlag, 1974.

Barnes, John. Evita First Lady: A Biography of Eva Perón.
New York, NY: Grove Press, 1978.
Bruce, George. Eva Perón. Geneva, 1970. (French translation)
Main, Mary. The Woman with the Whip: Eva Perón. Garden
City, NY: Doubleday, 1955.
Taylor, J. M. Eva Perón: The Myths of a Woman. Chicago, IL:
University of Chicago Press, 1979.

El Peronismo Visto como un Episodio Menor en la Historia
General de toda la América Española

Halperin Donghi, Tulio. Historia contemporánea de América
Latina. Madrid: Alianza Editorial, 1969.

  "En Historia contemporánea de América Latina, Tulio
Halperin Donghi reconstruye el curso de los acontecimientos que llevan desde el pasado de la América colonial
del siglo XVII al conflictivo presente de unos países que
se esfuerzan por romper el pacto neocolonial que les
condena al estancamiento económico y la dependencia
política. La inestabilidad gubernamental, la disgregación
social, los enormes contrastes de riqueza y penuria, la
explosión demográfica no acompañada por la creación
paralela de puestos escolares y de trabajo no son sino
consecuencias de la trágica suerte de un continente cuya
independencia del dominio español y portugués fue pronto
anulada en la práctica por la política expansionista de
Inglaterra y Estados Unidos. La explicación de ese
doloroso desarrollo culmina en una aguda descripción de la
realidad latinoamericana en nuestros días--el peronismo, el
desenlace de la revolución mexicana, la intervención
estadounidense en Guatemala y la República Dominicana, la
epidemia de golpes de estado, el castrismo y el movimiento
guerrillero, etc.--cuyas claves sociales, económicas y
políticas Tulio Halperin Donghi pone al descubierto."
(Nota del editor)

Publicaciones Periódicas (Selección de Títulos)

  Doctrina Peronista
  Mundo Peronista
  Perón el hombre del destino
  Re-eñcuentro peronista

  Lo que falta, o por lo menos yo no la conozco, es una buena
bibliografía crítica sobre el peronismo. He encontrado dos, ambas
mecanografiadas: Medina, Noemi, Bibliografía sobre el Peronismo
(1972); y Ferre, Dominique, Le Peronisme, Bibliographie (Rennes:
Centre d'etudes Hispaniques et Hispano-Americains. Sin fecha
pero probablemente de fines del 70). La segunda contiene 734
títulos de libros y artículos y, de las dos, es la más útil. La de
Medina es muy elemental.

Y ahora permítaseme hacer un poco de historia sobre los estudios latinoamericanos en Harvard.

En 1960 se organizó en Harvard "The Committee on Latin American Studies", cuyo objeto era considerar los métodos y recursos para el desarrollo de los estudios latinoamericanos a nivel graduado y subgraduado. Sin embargo, no fue éste el comienzo de los estudios latinoamericanos en Harvard. The Law Library contaba ya con una importante colección en esta área. En la Facultad de Artes y Ciencias, gracias a los prestigiosos historiadores Roger B. Merriman y Clarence H. Haring, Harvard era considerada como "leader" en la historia colonial de América Latina.

Después del retiro del Prof. Haring, en 1953, no hubo en la Facultad de Artes y Ciencias ningún profesor permanente interesado en América Latina. Además, en años anteriores Harvard no manifestó interés en diversificar los estudios de otras disciplinas en el campo latinoamericano. La primera reacción al retiro del Prof. Haring fue buscar un re-emplazante; pero después de siete años el Departmento de Historia informó que no había encontrado a nadie calificado para ocupar la cátedra vacante, aún cuando la búsqueda se había extendido al campo de los economistas.

Inmediatamente después de la revolución cubana, muchas universidades, fundaciones y el gobierno de los Estados Unidos, descubrieron que el conocimiento de los asuntos latinoamericanos en Estados Unidos era muy limitado. Se lanzaron nuevos programas de estudios por todas partes, y Harvard no fue una excepción. En 1962 la Ford Foundation estableció "a grant" de un millón de dólares para repartirlo entre seis universidades entre las que se contaba Harvard. La situación en Harvard mejoró muchísmo, y hacia mediados del 60 había cuatro profesores permanentes: un economista, un sociólogo, un historiador y un profesor de literatura.

No escapó a las autoridades de la Facultad de Artes y Ciencias la importancia de la biblioteca y la necesidad de desarrollar y mantener al día la colección latinoamericana como requisito primordial para el éxito de los nuevos programas de estudios. En 1965 se nombró a la primera persona encargada de la adquisición de materiales latinoamericanos. Tradicionalmente, el bibliotecario es en Harvard responsable de la colección a su cargo. Maneja sus propios fondos y goza de completa libertad para adquirir todo material que se ajuste al "Collection Development Policy". Los consejos y sugerencias de los profesores son, naturalmente, apreciados y tomados en cuenta, pero en última instancia la responsabilidad de la colección recae exclusivamente en el bibliotecario. Yo fui la primera Latin American bibliographer o Book Selector como se les llama, y conté no solamente con suficientes fondos sino también con el total apoyo de mis jefes. Y, con este nombramiento, ya empieza otra ponencia--por hacer--sobre la consolidación de una colección latinoamericana rica y diversa, dentro de la cual se ubican recursos importantes correspondientes a la época peronista en la Argentina.

NOTAS

1.   México, DF, 1946.
2.   Ibid., p. 167.
3.   <u>Argentina de Perón a Lanusse: 1943-1973</u> (Barcelona, 1972), p. 220.
4.   Pp. 91-92.
5.   Pp. 53-54.

39. THREE LATIN AMERICAN COLLECTIONS IN THE BRITISH LIBRARY, DEPARTMENT OF PRINTED BOOKS

Margaret H. Johnson

Although The British Library's collection of Latin American material is unrivaled in the British Isles, it has no separate Latin American library. Rather, this material is dispersed throughout its holdings in all its departments. For the purposes of this presentation, I have selected three particular groups of publications related to the theme of this meeting. All are held by the Library's Department of Printed Books, and I have used their description to give a brief overview of the Department's attitude to the acquisition of Latin Americana during the course of its history.

The foundation of the Department of Printed Books lay in the acquisition by purchase or donation of large private libraries, both general and specialised. These included the Cotton, Royal, King's, and Grenville collections and brought, almost by accident, many individual treasures to the Library. The Grenville bequest alone added items such as the extremely rare Rome 1493 edition of Leandro de Cosco's translation of Columbus' letter on the discovery of the New York; the first edition of Hernán Cortés' second Carta de Relación (Seville: J. Cromberger); the 1516 Alcalá edition of Pedro Mártir de Anglería's De orbe novo . . . Decades; the 1534 Seville edition of La Conquista del Perú, the earliest Spanish account of Pizarro's conquest of Peru; and Pero Magalhães de Gandavo's Historia da Provincia Santa Cruz a qui vulgarmente chamamos Brasil, published in Lisbon in 1576. However, it was not until later that a positive selection policy was established, and that holdings of Latin American interest grew in strength.

At the beginning of the nineteenth century, London was the home of many of the leaders of the independence movement, including San Martín, Bolívar, Miranda, Irisarri, Rivadavia, and Andrés Bello. The latter, who was a regular visitor to the British Museum Reading Room, said of his adopted country "en ninguna parte del globo son tan activas como en la Gran Bretaña las causas que vivifican y fecundan el espíritu humano; en ninguna parte es más audaz la investigación, más libre el vuelo del ingenio, más profundas las especulaciones científicas, más animosas las tentativas de las artes." From his contacts in Miranda's house, and with friends such as James Mill and Jeremy Bentham, came the inspiration for his and other émigré publications in London--for example, the Biblioteca Americana, the Censor Americano, the Repertorio Americano. The aim of these

was "la educación de la América Española," and the collection
provides a rich source for studying this group's ideals.   Its
members in turn inspired Rudolph Ackermann, a London publisher, to issue almost one hundred works in Spanish, intended
primarily for the newly independent peoples of Latin America.
They ranged from encyclopaedias, news journals, and travel
books to educational text-books and the first translations of the
works of Sir Walter Scott.   Although they at first claimed to be
non-political, by 1825 an Ackermann publication was referring to
Latin America as "having vegetated for centuries in the most
oppressive tutelage under the damnation of the blindest government in Europe."

The British had to be educated, too.   Examples of the
material issued to this end include Manuel Palacio Fajardo's
Outline of the Revolution in Spanish America (London, 1817), and
James Mill's articles in The Edinburgh Review.

The importance of the émigrés' publications, evidenced by
their sympathisers' support, was summarised by Blanco White.
To them, he said, "the Spanish-speaking public of America will
owe, in large part, the achievements for which political liberty
paves the way."

The Department of Printed Books, of course, acquired these
materials by way of copyright deposit rather than by positive
selection.   Sadly, however, there are gaps in the holdings, for at
that time legal deposit was not yet strictly enforced.

This was one of the shortcomings to which Antonio Panizzi
referred in his report of 1845--On the Collection of Printed Books
at the British Museum, Its Increase and Arrangement.   In this
report he mentions specifically the gaps in the Museum's holdings
of Latin Americana, which he describes as being "far inferior to
the libraries of other countries of Europe which have much less
connexion than Great Britain has with South America"--and this
in spite of some important recent purchases, among them a large
collection of Latin American items acquired at the sale of the
library of Monsieur Chaumette des Fosses, former French consul
at Lima.

Panizzi took steps to enforce legal deposit and to negotiate
an adequate purchase grant from Parliament.   His construction of
a new reading room and bookstacks meant that the library had
space as well as funds for increased foreign acquisitions and,
from the mid-nineteenth century, it enjoyed a period of expansion
in its collecting.   It was able, for example, to benefit from the
attentions of the bookseller Henry Stevens, who noted that
Panizzi realised "the necessity of collecting the literature of new
countries while there was a reasonable probability of securing it
with tolerable completeness."   Between 1857 and 1862, the
American collections doubled in size.   Moreover, when the library
of José María Andrade was offered for sale in Leipzig in January,
1869, the Museum was able to buy extensively.   It thus acquired

the foundation of an excellent collection of Mexican revolutionary pamphlets which forms the second group of publications which I should like to mention.

Andrade, a bookseller and collector, had built up his library over the course of forty years, intending that it should form the core of the Biblioteca Imperial de México. On Maximilian's downfall, however, the library was shipped to Europe and dispersed at the Leipzig sale.

The British Library's collection spans the years 1810 to 1860, being especially strong in the publications of 1820, and includes works issued by Iturbide, Santa Anna, and Lizardi. Unfortunately these items are not all kept together, although there is a record of the shelfmarks at which groups of them have been placed. Moreover, works in the Lizardi collection, originally entered in the General Catalogue simply as "A collection of pamphlets," have recently been brought together and individually catalogued.

More material was added to the Mexican pamphlet collection at the sale of the library of Maximilian's chaplain, Agustín Fischer, and at the 1880 sale of the library of José Fernando Ramírez (when Henry Stevens again acted as the Museum's agent). Further individual items have been added over the years, to form a most impressive collection documenting the Mexican struggle for independence.

Other important collections of Latin Americana were also acquired during the second half of the nineteenth century. They include a group of Guatemalan items dating from 1796 to 1851, purchased from Asher in 1870 for £4-4s; of early Peruvian and Colombian legal material; and a collection of Peruvian handbills advertising bullfights from 1760 to 1787, purchased from Henry Stevens in 1871 for six guineas.

The third special collection which I should like to describe, the Domínguez collection, was acquired in the twentieth century. The Museum had recovered from the difficulties of acquisition brought about by two world wars and their aftermath, and the Department of Printed Books was approaching its incorporation into The British Library. Its Language Sections as they now exist had not yet been formally established. Hispanic interests had nonetheless been protected, first by Sir Henry Thomas during his keepership of the Department; then by Harold Whitehead, who from 1947 until 1983 was specifically responsible for the acquisition of Spanish, Portuguese, and Latin American publications.

The Domínguez pamphlets were offered for sale at a London auction in the early 1960s, and the Department was thus able to acquire more than five hundred items documenting the struggle for and early days of Latin American independence. The collection is particularly strong in the publications of the River Plate countries. The items purchased were placed together and individually catalogued. Examples include a broadsheet bulletin issued by the gaucho leader Facundo Quiroga announcing his victory of 4th November 1831 at La Ciudadela de Tucumán against the "unitarios" led by General Lamadrid; two petitions addressed by Colonel Manuel Dorrego to the Buenos Aires Junta de Representantes, protesting his exile to Mendoza because of his sympathies with the Uruguayan insurgents; the Manifiesto del Congreso a los pueblos of 1st August 1816, appealing to the Argentinian people for unity and order, and ending with a decree proclaiming "fin a la revolución, principio al orden," together with many examples of the early output of the Imprenta de los Niños Expósitos.

The majority of the collection had been built up by the Argentinian Luis López Domínguez, author of the famous poem El Ombú. (Other items were added by his compatriot Lorenzo López.) Born in 1810, Domínguez was forced to take refuge in Montevideo in his youth because of his political views. There he became a journalist, and he founded the newspaper El Orden upon returning to Buenos Aires. He went on to serve as a deputy; as Minister for Economic Affairs for both the Province of Buenos Aires and the national government; and as Argentina's representative in the United States, Spain, and Great Britain.

These, then, have been but brief mentions of just three areas of special strength in the Library's holdings of Latin American material produced by or for masses or minorities. Over the years, the Library has been fortunate in acquiring this material, in many cases long after the events which prompted its publication. Indeed, we are still able to find individual items to build up our strengths.

As far as current works are concerned, we are no longer prepared to chance too much to future luck, but attempt to gather material as it is issued. In 1985, as in the early to mid-nineteenth century, émigré political groups are active publishers in Great Britain. Efforts must be made now as then to collect their publications, as they often prove to be less than active where legal deposit is concerned. For material issued in Latin America, success is dependent largely on the efforts of academics on field trips, research students studying in Latin America, journalists covering news stories, enlightened booksellers--in short, on any friends of the Library who will take the trouble to make representative collections of this ephemeral material and bring it back to us. Among collections recently acquired in this way are the publications of minority rights groups of several countries, and handbills gathered during the 1982 Brazilian and 1983 Argentinian election campaigns.

It is to be hoped that, by these continuing efforts, we can maintain the strength and traditions of the collections established by our predecessors.

SUGGESTIONS FOR FURTHER READING

Bello y Londres: segundo congreso del bicentenario.   2 vols.
Caracas: Fundación La Casa de Bello, 1980.

Esdaile, Arundell.   "The British Museum: The Collections."   In
The Uses of Libraries, ed. Ernest A. Baker.   Rev.   ed.
London: University of London Press, 1930.   Pp. 51-73.

_____.   The British Museum Library.   London: George
Allen & Unwin, 1946.

Ford, John.   Ackermann 1783-1983: The   Business   of   Art.
London: Ackermann, 1983.

Independent Mexico: A Collection of Mexican Pamphlets in the
Bodleian Library, ed. Colin Steele and Michael P. Costeloe.
London: Mansell, 1973.

Miller, Edward.   Prince of Librarians: The Life and Times of
Antonio Panizzi of the British Museum.   London: André
Deutsch, 1967.

_____.   That Noble Cabinet: A History of the British
Museum.   London: André Deutsch, 1973.

Judith Selakoff

Lambros Comitas's Caribbeana, 1900-1965, a large topical
bibliography on the non-Hispanic Caribbean covering materials
published between 1900 and 1965, appeared in 1966. Since then,
the output of published and unpublished resources, from both
inside and outside the Caribbean area, has increased by more
than 200 percent. The original Caribbeana consisted of only one
very large volume. The Complete Caribbeana, 1900-1975, which
added but ten years to the coverage, includes three very fat
volumes with a small separate volume of indexes. Were the work
now updated, to cover only the years 1976-1985, there would be
at least two additional volumes.

Such tremendous growth in the literature suggests the
importance of a library like that of the Research Institute for the
Study of Man, in New York City, which encompasses documentation on all aspects of life in both the non-Hispanic Caribbean and
its overseas communities. Since its founding, in 1955, the
Research Institute has been a major focal point for studies of the
non-Hispanic Caribbean. The library has developed along the
same lines, and now includes approximately 23,000 books and
bound periodicals, as well as a considerable body of vertical file
materials.

Since we are concerned with a geographic area outside the
United States, it is critical for me, the Research Institute's
librarian, to remain constantly aware of what's being published.
The task is comparatively easy for North American imprints, for
which I use the American librarian's standard tools. Monitoring
Caribbean output, however, can prove far more complicated.

Even this has become easier with the rise of specialized
library services dealing almost exclusively with the region's
publications. I make extensive use of two: Caribbean Books, of
Parkersburg, Iowa; and Caribbean Imprint Library Services of
West Falmouth, Massachusetts. And, of course, there are sources
within the Caribbean to which one can also apply, including both
the publishers themselves and such bookdealers as Alan Moss in
Barbados.

Even with all these sources, however, too many things slip
by: when you do find out about titles (some of which do not

Author's Note. The address of the Research Institute for
the Study of Man is 162 East 78th Street, New York, NY 10021.

really exist!), you still have to try to get them. A number of Latin American and Caribbean research institutes here in the United States, including those at New York University, Columbia University, and the University of Florida at Gainesville, also publish important materials.

Many journals are published in the Caribbean, and some of these are invaluable for serious research. The better-known titles include Social and Economic Studies, Caribbean Quarterly, The Bulletin of Eastern Caribbean Affairs, and Caribbean Studies. There are also some journals published in the United States that are devoted exclusively to Caribbean and/or Latin American subjects. These include Caribbean Review, The Journal of Caribbean Studies, and, in a more "popular" vein, Everybody's Magazine. However, many of the journals that come out of the Caribbean region are often published very late indeed, and some fairly frequently appear out of sequence. This produces a great deal of confusion. Letter-writing to obtain issues that may have been missed (even though you cannot always be sure), or to clarify the publication status of a particular journal, may do no good at all: there is frequently no response, even to a second or third communication. Even in 1985, it is not at all safe to assume that a journal is no longer being published just because the last issues received date from 1980 or 1981. When preparing journals for the bindery, this can be a serious and frustrating problem.

Having once obtained these specialized journals, however, the Research Institute works hard to make them both more valuable and more accessible to our users by preparing a periodical card index, with full author and subject cataloging. This is incorporated within our card catalog, which is yet one more item that is growing at an alarming rate.

Another problem area is of particular importance for our collection. The larger islands, such as Trinidad and Tobago, Jamaica, and Barbados, provide much of their statistical material either free of charge or at a very low cost. However, most of the smaller islands cannot afford such generosity. We must therefore look to some of our other sources, referred to earlier, to acquire these items. The prices can be very high, which is a major problem for a library--like ours--with a relatively small budget.

Yet another important source of information on the non-Hispanic Caribbean is the by-now practically limitless number of dissertations on life and culture in the Caribbean, and on Caribbean immigrant communities as well. Dissertations purchased from University Microfilms are quite expensive. Nevertheless, they are an invaluable resource, and we acquire as many as we possibly can. Information on such materials has most recently been compiled in UMI's relatively new catalog of dissertations concerning the Caribbean region.

There are also, of course, nonstatistical government publications to acquire from both the United States and the Caribbean, sometimes easily and sometimes not. Last, but by no means least, are materials that go into our vertical files: pamphlets, reprints, unpublished conference papers, and the like. These also involve a considerable effort to acquire and make accessible.

Before closing, I would like to add that we do, I think, a really first-rate job: our library at the Research Institute for the Study of Man is one of the foremost collections on the non-Hispanic Caribbean anywhere in the world.

*II.   Libraries as Gatekeepers in Latin American
Studies: Obstacles and Opportunities*

41. LIBRARIES AS GATEKEEPERS: SOME INTRODUCTORY REMARKS

Dan C. Hazen

Latin Americanist scholars and librarians face both opportunities and obstacles as we address the insights shared in these papers. Many of the presentations have suggested that we need new sorts of research tools, and new priorities for library acquisitions. Some such materials--regional imprints or women's writings, for instance--are natural complements to existing collections. Others, like chapbooks or fotonovelas, may entail more substantial challenges. And some--photographs, films, or music, for example-- remain alien to many of us. However problematic some of these resources may appear, all are needed. And so we must consider how, and whether, we can collect them.

One way to make sense of our needs is to ponder the impact of such acquisitions upon major library operations, particularly collection development and processing. In so doing, we must address the peculiar requirements posed by the fairly specialized materials that we have considered. We must likewise confront the broader relationship between Latin American (and other area studies) materials and more general trends in academic librarianship.

Contemporary research librarianship emphasizes a number of generic approaches to users' aspirations and needs. Some are obviously palliatives, others appear as panaceas. All, as we shall see, carry different impacts for different disciplines and research problems. The academic library context is dominated by efforts to stabilize acquisitions costs and rates, to implement cooperative plans based in essentially traditional delineations of materials and responsibilities, to develop new approaches to processing and bibliographic access, and to adapt and deploy the massively expensive technology of automation for both bibliographic and substantive information.

Though seldom addressed in an overt way, the changing nature of public service in the academic library is equally or perhaps more significant. In the past, the public service ("reference") function tended to center on specialists who would interpret a local collection to its users. As our information resources and needs have grown more complex, the public service function has expanded in both scope and the personnel it encompasses. Today, virtually all librarians are involved in the primordial task of mediating between the entire extension of discipline-defined knowledge--a range that includes local collections, but also goes far beyond them--and users both local and remote.

But the broad issue of reconceptualizing our public service
function must, for the moment, give way before more fully articulated agendas and possibilities. Cooperation and carefully
planned collection development have become generally accepted
responses to the straitened acquisitions budgets of the 1980s.
Yet the rhetoric has often been facile, and activity has centered
more on the instruments and instrumentalities of cooperation than
on tangible progress. Within the multidisciplinary context of
Latin American Studies, two dimensions of cooperation demand
particular scrutiny. The first involves cooperation and coordination within a single institution. As we have seen, Latin
Americanist scholarship does not recognize artificial distinctions
between types of materials, their provenance, or their format.
Yet such distinctions underlie both the organizational structures
and the assignments of selection responsibility within most
research libraries.

Our libraries often lack full internal coherence regarding
their own collection policies and priorities. To cite but one hypo-
thetical example, music materials are in many institutions handled
by music libraries. These music libraries, however, tend to be
located near and primarily accountable to the music department.
In most such departments, both performers and musicologists
emphasize Western art music. The scattered Latin Americanist
constituency for regional music resources is not immediately
apparent. Lack of coordination and conflicting demands upon
limited budgets too often mean that Latin American music
resources are collected only as an afterthought.

Internal coordination is also a key for ensuring congruent
priorities for processing and collection development. It is by now
an accepted truth that paraprofessional copy cataloging should
stress efficiency, through the rapid adaptation of online bibliographic records. Processing units often insist that they should
likewise establish priorities for original cataloging. Such
priorities may or may not conform to either bibliographers' inten-
tions or user needs. Once again, intra-institutional cooperation
comes into question.

Cooperation between institutions is, today, widely regarded
as the panacea for limited acquisitions budgets and possibilities.
The issues of interinstitutional cooperation, perhaps because such
sharing requires conscious analysis and decision making, may be
more obvious than those of intra-institutional coordination.
Nonetheless, interlibrary cooperation remains fraught with both
practical difficulties and conceptual inconsistencies.

Latin Americanist librarians have responded to the current
mandate for cooperation with a newly ramified SALALM committee
structure and a host of fledgling plans and commitments.
Perhaps inevitably at this early stage, efforts have tended to be
partial in coverage and simplistic in design. Our very limited
ability to ensure the timely processing of "priority" materials,

which reflects the organizational fragmentation common to most research libraries, exemplifies the gaps in existing efforts. The delineation of cooperative collecting responsibilities in terms of countries likewise suggests a rather crude level of analysis and action.

Instruments like the SALALM/RLG/ARL Conspectus for Latin American Library Collections should enable us to refine our cooperative efforts and emphases. Yet even the Conspectus will afford only partial and indirect evaluation of such "nonstandard" materials as sound recordings, ephemera, posters, motion pictures, and photographs and slides. Cooperative programs like those of the Latin American Microform Project (LAMP) and the Center for Research Libraries have not yet developed a consensus on whether and how to pursue "nonstandard" materials, given the special difficulties that these pose for acquisition, processing, bibliographic control, preservation, and storage. We seem reasonably close to effective cooperation in developing our collections of scholarly monographs--in which there has always been a substantial degree of overlap between institutions. We have not really addressed the perhaps more crucial resources, and formats, highlighted during this conference.

A third issue concerns the somewhat paradoxical relationship between the kind of resources needed to support Latin American Studies, particularly those nontraditional sorts that we have considered during this conference, and the new electronic tech-nologies. The latter, in one form or another, are garnering ever-increasing shares of most library budgets. On one level, the current distortion toward library automation may be partly redressed when, after another decade or two, most major reposi-tories can finally boast integrated systems with fully converted retrospective bibliographic files.

Nonetheless, Latin Americanists and other area studies specialists may appear retrograde and reactionary by emphasizing "outmoded" types of information, even as our institutions lurch into the electronic age. How can we defend and expand our efforts in an era when both area studies and the media we emphasize are so frequently perceived as behind the times? Alternatively, can we ourselves seize the new technologies for our own ends?

Two aspects of this broad issue merit particular attention. The emergence of online databases within research libraries has made various sorts of information immediately available. These resources have thus far clustered most heavily around abstracting and indexing services in the sciences and some professional disciplines. The nature of Latin Americanist scholarship, inquiry, and publication, in conjunction with the market-based economics of automation, have thus far limited the extension of online resources to our field. More generally, the research library community has not yet articulated a consistent response to online information.   Nonetheless, these services do appear to compete with book budgets for limited materials funds.   To what extent will such developments affect Latin American Studies? What role can Latin Americanist librarians play in shaping the field's electronic future?

A second aspect centers on bibliographic information, which is for the most part both produced and consumed within the library community.   Immense resources are now being poured into automated systems of bibliographic control.   Thus far, none of these systems has been able in practice to exploit fully the capabilities implicit in the MARC format--even though the creation of records conforming to MARC is itself very expensive.   The resources being devoted to bibliographic systems and library automation are quite clearly drawing against funds that might have otherwise been available for collection development.   The common argument has been that online bibliographic access will enable institutions to receive wanted materials through inter-library loan, particularly as formal cooperative collecting plans are put into place.

Automation has not yet met these promises.   Furthermore, considerations of cost and productivity have frequently relegated Latin American and other foreign-language imprints to the end of processing queues.   The promise of online bibliographic access has been used to reduce our individual and collective purchasing power, while contemporary processing constraints have produced mushrooming backlogs and have compromised possibilities for effective cooperation.   We thus become less and less able to monitor our current acquisitions, or to share the specific biblio-graphic information on which cooperative collection development might be based, or even to engage in rational arrangements for interlibrary loan.

Many current proposals to simplify, speed, and cheapen cataloging entail an inherent ethnocentrism.   "Minimal level cataloging," for instance, not only revolves around strictly local efforts to reduce backlogs, but targets foreign imprints for any cutbacks.   Its general implementation may well ratchet Latin American and other foreign language materials another notch down on the scale of research library priorities.

The papers in this section are all concerned with the research library's role in controlling the flow of information available to researchers.   The decisions, policies, and dogmas here discussed have all invoked considerations of economic prudence, administrative convenience, technological currency, and an indiscriminately phrased "better service to users."   As the papers indicate, though, one effect has been a consistent reduction in our capability to serve students and scholars of Latin America.   Perhaps the fundamental lessons are that disci-plines, the materials they use, and the questions they ask, are different; and that current library doctrine is frequently inimical to the needs and emphases of Latin Americanist scholarship. In fields such as ours, library technocracies are in danger of subverting the scholarly process. Despite them, and as our conference papers demonstrate, Latin Americanists demand increased research resources, in an increased array of forms and formats.

42.   THE NEED FOR COOPERATION AND RATIONALITY:
COLLECTION DEVELOPMENT IN THE SINGLE INSTITUTION

John R. Hébert

The need in the Library of Congress for cooperation in developing comprehensive Latin American collections of diverse materials,
encompassing both the book form and special formats, has been
ever more fully met in recent years. Official procedures,
seminars, and informal meetings have all played a part in this
essential process.

The Library of Congress is an institution with no academic
departments to appease, but whose most important user is the
Congress of the United States. Congressional concerns for
information on Latin America vary as different issues come to the
fore. Recent events in Latin America--Grenada in 1983, the
Falklands/Malvinas in 1982, the continuing eruptions in Central
America--have thrust the Congress of the United States into
decision making on issues that had not been considered before.
The Library's collections must meet the need for materials on
wide-ranging topics and in varied formats, and must anticipate
potential use as well as active consultation.

The Library of Congress, like other large research libraries,
has several approaches for collecting materials on Latin America.
The institution treats research materials in terms of their format
as well as their regional content. That is, materials are collected
for geographical coverage, by country, within broad collecting
guidelines which cover all disciplines, and also by format.
Clinical medicine and experimental/field test agriculture constitute
the only exceptions, and the Library has cooperative collecting
agreements with both the National Library of Medicine and the
National Agricultural Library. Furthermore, periodic meetings are
held with the collection development specialists in each of those
libraries to keep them up to date on current practice. Efforts
are made in those meetings to fill obvious current lacunae.

The geographic coverage of Latin American materials is
entrusted to the Library's Hispanic and Hispanic Law Divisions.
Recommending officers in both divisions deal exclusively with the

development of the Library's Latin American collection. But those two divisions are not alone in this responsibility, since the Library also collects materials in terms of format. Separate special collections--maps and atlases, manuscripts, rare books, prints, photographs, music, recordings, motion pictures, broadcasts, newspapers, microforms--possess rich sources for the study of Latin America. These special collections provide essential complementary materials.

The Library's Hispanic specialists, then, provide critical guidance to researchers seeking to employ fully the Library's Latin American resources. Most of the special collections rely on internal finding aids, or extremely knowledgeable reference specialists, to guide the researcher to pertinent data. One can already detect one source of internal cooperation within the Library, that is, among the specialists who service the Library's collections. In fact, for several years, a group of specialists formed a reference roundtable with periodic meetings to exchange problems and ideas on reference encounters.

Because the Library of Congress splits between collections defined by geography and those defined by format, a whole series of Acquisition Policy Statements have been developed through the Library's Collections Development Office. These documents provide guidance to recommending and collecting officials and cover all manner of materials, from official publications of non-United States entities at the state and city level to children's literature. These Acquisition Policy Statements are carefully reflected in the guidelines provided to the bookdealers with whom the Library contracts, and are likewise reflected in the types of materials acquired through exchange from the thousands of institutions worldwide who produce publications and other research materials related to the study of Latin America.

Acquisition Policy Statements are normally developed in consultation with Latin American specialists and other area studies representatives (Asian, African, Middle Eastern), to ensure that they truly reflect our interests in collection development. To cite one example, the Acquisition Policy Statement on agriculture was under discussion several years ago. Latin Americanist input on critical items related to land tenure, agrarian reform, the history of agriculture, and other pertinent topics was actively sought. The Hispanic Division's advice helped ensure that the Library continued to acquire items deemed important in understanding Latin American culture. Area studies responses to proposed changes in acquisition policy statements are usually coordinated through the Director for Area Studies, under whose aegis lies the Hispanic Division. These coordinated responses are usually quite broad ranging, and they endeavor to encompass the concerns of all the Library's foreign language and Third World collections.

Within the sphere of Latin American collection development, the Library possesses a number of acquisition sections in the

Processing Department to provide direct, close, and coordinated communication with its Latin American specialists. These sections include the Hispanic Acquisitions Program of the Exchange and Gift Division, which implements recommendations by physically acquiring materials through both purchase from blanket order dealers and exchange. This section handles the acquisition of all materials from Latin America less than five years old. Items of more venerable vintage are purchased through the Order Division's Special Order Section.

Finally, the Collections Development Office has sponsored a series of subregional seminars to discuss current acquisition situations and problems. All of Latin America, save Brazil, has thus far been reviewed. These formal discussions, while convened by the Collections Development Office, have for the most part been chaired by the Hispanic Division and considered our show. They have included representatives from the Hispanic Acquisitions Program, Hispanic Law Division, Order Division, various cataloging divisions, Serial and Government Publications Division, Motion Pictures, prints and photographs, science, and geography and maps. The difficulties of acquiring specific materials--underground publications of a political or social nature, for example--are discussed, and a strategy is advanced for acquiring and then housing the materials. Participation from the cataloging divisions helps to alert them of the types of special materials that may be acquired. One such meeting provoked an experiment to acquire Brazilian television programming. This is a pilot project, where we seek to acquire enough materials to assist us in reaching a policy on the types and quality of such materials to be acquired from throughout the Hispanic world.

Now I wish to digress. The call for papers for this session emphasized information on the internal, recognizable guidelines and formalities that encourage cooperation in developing our Latin American collection. The call further indicated that comments limited to the need for informal discussions or connections were too frequently given and too seldom substantiated. The terms of the call notwithstanding, I consider that collecting and agreement on collecting do occur through informal exchanges among divisions of the Library. In the final analysis, these informal agreements promote the development of stronger Latin American collections.

The Library does, for the most part, possess adequate resources for the acquisition of current research materials, and it has policy statements that provide for most types of resources. For current acquisitions, the more significant problem lies in identifying sources for such elusive materials as, for example, fugitive literature. Once acquired, the political pamphlet, the literary journal, or the variety of existing periodical literature will normally be saved for research use some place in the Library, whether as a hard copy work accessible through the catalog, or in a microform state, or in the Hispanic Division's reference collections.

The items that do cause acquisition problems are best described as expensive retrospective materials: rare books, manuscript collections, long runs of newspapers, and the like. The acquisition of these types of materials, should we initiate a request, requires coordination with the appropriate special format division: the Hispanic Division is in this case not acquiring a rare book collection for its own holdings but rather for the Library's collections. Such requests require strong justifications. Each Library division involved in retrospective acquisition recommendations must operate within a strict annual budget. Midyear budget corrections often release unused supplementary funds. Finally, if the item is very expensive, the request has to be routed through the highest level of the Library. But the Library has accommodated requests if the items sought are in keeping with established strengths and concerns.

What has helped in recent months has been the dollar's extremely strong position on the world market. Requests involving the Hispanic Division also may incorporate resource- or budget-sharing. For that matter, the acquisition of commercially produced retrospective microform collections, covering several regions of the world, frequently entails joint proposals. Many such collections have been considered during recent years.

I have thus far provided a brief overview of how materials are currently acquired at the Library of Congress. The discussion was particularly necessary insofar as our approaches to collecting may vary markedly from those of other research libraries. But now I must stand back to address the larger issue, whether research libraries can support the study of Latin America's masses and minorities through the information technology explosion.

This topic is quite suggestive, since it takes for granted that masses and minorities are poorly represented in the traditional research materials collected by research libraries. I would agree with this assumption: personal experience has highlighted the difficulties of finding historical materials, produced by the masses and minorities, in our research libraries. Consider, for example, the vast gaps of materials related to the study of early twentieth-century Argentine, Uruguayan, and Brazilian labor and political movements, especially anarchism, anarcho-syndicalism, and general labor organizations. The important newspapers, journals, and pamphlets of these groups are practically nonexistent in the United States, with the possible exception of a representative collection acquired by the University of California, Los Angeles several years ago. Serious research on topics related to early labor and political formations in the La Plata region would require travel to the Netherlands or Italy. And yet, were not research libraries collecting materials in the early years of this century? Why were these important items not acquired when they first appeared on the streets? These omissions evidently occurred because collecting policies did not allow acquisition of such ephemeral materials, or because bookdealers were unavailable to provide such politically sensitive materials to foreign libraries.

Perhaps the history of the development of our collections has not changed. It is still difficult to acquire similar materials, and even more difficult to make them available to the researcher due to inadequate bibliographic control. As I have indicated, the Library of Congress has identified similar fugitive literature as important. It has not, however, developed a totally successful system to ensure that such material is recovered from the field, or properly handled once it arrives. Furthermore, materials of this type are received haphazardly--perhaps in fair reflection of their distribution channels. This complex problem, from the standpoint of the individual institution, is solvable only through full internal cooperation. Accommodation, and a shared appreciation of the importance of these materials, must be reached by all segments of the Library's collection development system-- recommending official, acquisition specialists, selection officer, and cataloging divisions.

Future safekeeping of these types of materials may well require microfilming and group cataloging, simply to ensure research access. The memory of the reference specialist helps little when that specialist moves on to another position. We still depend greatly on information available only in the memories of specialists. Improved automated technologies should allow us to safely share such information. As items known to have been acquired are brought under control, frustration should diminish. We can hope that the research library is moving toward simple identification for such fugitive materials.

But it would be mistaken to believe that only materials on the masses or minorities are eluding our grasp. Some materials readily available for purchase are not acquired owing to large price tags or disagreement within the institution over their quality as objects or as documents. Recent, nonprofessional photographs of posters and billboards in contemporary Nicaragua were not acquired because the quality of the photographs did not meet collecting standards. But consider the dilemma: is it better to acquire the unique item regardless of quality? How do we address the preservation problems inherent in such a purchase? Such acquisitions clearly pose many problems whose solutions require cooperation.

I am not certain that we now possess more than seat-of-the-pants guidelines for collection development on the institutional level. When one weighs my comments concerning historical documents of similar ilk, the obvious question is whether we have really progressed. Or are we just discussing the same issues again? How do we provide research materials that do not conform to book standards, much less those that do conform? How do we ensure continuous, uninterrupted coverage of Latin America's periodical literature? These are the pressing issues today and the complex issues of the future, despite the advances in micro-filming and automation. And these issues are further exacerbated by increased publishing from and on the Latin American world. One can suggest greater selectivity in acquisition, but at the expense of what materials?

Collecting, identifying, and providing access to Latin American materials in any research library will depend entirely on that institution's commitment. Money for purchase and for cataloging is in too short supply for us to assume that all research materials will be acquired and identified. The demand for information on wide-ranging topics has increased markedly, especially since the comparative study of governments, organizations, peoples, and interest groups has become a major research topic for the late twentieth century. But no one possesses a budget sufficient to meet all these demands. Many of us seek to build on our strengths, further increasing the chasm of under-researched areas.

No single institution can today claim absolute comprehensiveness. For that matter, it would be extremely difficult to provide comprehensive coverage for even one Latin American country. The current quest for interinstitutional cooperation, through utilization of the SALALM/RLG Conspectus, marks a positive effort first to describe the varied fields of our cultural area, and then to identify strengths and weaknesses in our collections. But no single institution can provide comprehensive coverage, no matter how often we say it can be done. Depending on their specific mandates, many individual institutions will make every effort to acquire and to provide access for a fully representative sample of the literature, sufficient for concentrated research. Even when we are able to enlist the full support of those encharged with all of the varied formats within our institutions, our budgets will not permit truly comprehensive acquisitions or cataloging. The current project to prepare a national bibliography for Nicaragua has uncovered 20,000 titles for the period 1800 to 1978 alone, not including manuscripts, photographs, music, prints, maps, newspapers, and runs of official publications. If one broadens the potential scope to include radio and television broadcasts, movies, and computer-generated data, the body of material from Latin America becomes almost limitless.

I did not wish to leave the discussion on such a pessimistic note. It was intended, rather, to inject a sense of reality into the practice of assessing the comprehensiveness of collecting and the value of collections.

43. COOPERATION WITHIN THE ACADEMIC LIBRARY: RESPONSE AND ADDITIONAL REFLECTIONS

Carl Deal

The preceding paper serves two objectives. First, it presents an overview of how materials in Latin America are acquired by the Library of Congress in the multiple and complex formats in which they appear, and provides us with information on how the Library of Congress's approach to collection development may compare with those of other research libraries. Second, the paper looks at the larger issue of whether or not research libraries can support the study of Latin America's masses and minorities through the information technology explosion. If my comments focus on academic research libraries, that is because this is the environment I know best.

The Library of Congress first serves the needs of Congress. Academic libraries serve the teaching and research needs of university faculties and students. Other libraries have a more diverse or a more specialized clientele. But all types of libraries have an interest in the materials and the topics discussed during this conference.

Academic libraries are driven by and are responsible for specific academic disciplines and for meeting the needs of academic units like colleges, departments, and interdisciplinary programs. No academic library can match the Library of Congress in the resources that can be brought to bear on its Latin American collections, and academic institutions have too often approached internal cooperation in a manner significantly less sophisticated or organized. I know of only one academic library that, like the Library of Congress, brings all the area studies together into a single departmental unit which is administered by an area studies specialist. Thus, most of us here do not enjoy the opportunity to work closely with colleagues in other world areas. In some ways we are more conscious of competing with other area studies programs than of possibilities for cooperating with them. I think the Library of Congress's model of a director for area studies is one that should be more widely emulated by large academic libraries supporting several strong and well-funded area studies programs. This personal view, however, probably would not be shared by most academic research library directors.

My impression from this paper is that the Library of Congress houses a closer knit and larger extended professional family than is found in many if not most of our research libraries. To provide one supporting example, the libraries at

Harvard University are controlled by college deans rather than by a central library administration. The latter could unite library department heads within a cozy administrative structure, and focus librarians' loyalties on the broad mission of the library itself, rather than on the academic departments or units served. I also think it is true that the larger the number of departmental libraries in an academic library system, the stronger and more focused the departmental and disciplinary loyalties of librarians. Conversely, a smaller number of departmental libraries encourages communication and cooperation.

Whether or not I convince you that cooperation among units in the Library of Congress is easier to accomplish than in other research libraries, I do want to focus on one area where research libraries and the Library of Congress are or should be similarly focused. That area is the setting of collection goals in area-specific Latin American acquisition policy statements, instruments that I prefer to call collection development statements. These statements reflect the geographic parameters, formats, and language inclusions or exclusions for the library's subject collections, and provide a conspectus or map of library strengths and goals. Such statements enable us to track shared responsibilities for an area or subject, and thereby facilitate the identification of areas where cooperation may or should take place, of subjects in which this is desirable or should be required, and of languages and formats in which materials will or should be made available. Current work on a new, librarywide policy statement at my own institution, the University of Illinois at Urbana-Champaign, has done more than anything else to bring the area studies librarians and departmental librarians into closer contact. Participation by each librarian has clarified responsibilities for some areas needing greater attention, and shifted other collecting assignments to new and more appropriate fund managers.

In fact, as more and more libraries become committed to ARL's North American Collections Inventory Project (NCIP), now in its third stage of development and implementation, more people here may become involved in preparing those policy statements that must be consistent with the information on their collections which they will be entering and describing in the RLG/ARL Latin American Conspectus. The ARL conspectus will describe each institution's holdings, and our policy statements will describe their collecting goals and mission.

We can now proceed to the larger and perhaps more important issue in this paper: "Can research libraries support the study of Latin America's masses and minorities through the information explosion?" Here I find myself less comfortable, and greatly concerned. We, as Latin American specialists, are reminded of serious gaps in our collections not only in the standard formats of books and journals but also in the expanding areas of research formats like films and Machine Readable Data Files.

In dealing with this material, I am afraid we are faced with the same nagging and age-old problems. Responsibility to local research and to instructional needs comes first, and precious little funding is available to accommodate these newly identified topics and materials. The many different formats within which much of this material appears, the difficulty of obtaining much of the material we need even if staff and funding were available, and the preservation implications of acquiring materials with a short or predictable life span must surely convince us that cooperation is the only way for institutions to proceed. How many of our libraries are able to form vertical files on evangelical and pentecostal religious movements in Latin America? How many will assemble collections of photographs, field interviews, and recordings? How much of the Nicaraguan national bibliography for 1800-1978, cited by John Hébert, will we aspire to make available to our local scholars?

Cooperation has been extremely difficult and expensive to achieve. It has, too often, been short-lived as well. It will be no less costly in the future. But if the Association of Research Libraries' North American Collections Inventory Project is sub-scribed to in a forceful manner by ARL libraries, our expanded grasp of our collective holdings will certainly make cooperation, and collection development and management decisions, more possible. The more that can be done cooperatively, the greater the resources that we can concentrate on our primary institutional collecting concerns.

I hope that SALALM will adopt a resolution requesting ARL to elevate the Latin American Conspectus on its list of priorities for input into the North American Collections Inventory Project. With or without ARL's willingness to assign Latin America a higher priority, we should still undertake to utilize the con-spectus for our own collection development statements. These statements will help make us aware of special strengths that exist in our own institutions as well as at the regional and national levels. The conspectus has the potential to provide data that will encourage cooperative collection development and resource sharing at all levels of need and compatibility, that is, through agree-ments between departmental library units, and also between individual institutions, regional groups, and national consortia.

If there is a light at the end of the tunnel, it will focus on cooperation. I believe that light, which at the moment may be more imagery than reality, may be ignited by new cooperative opportunities that can emerge from our work with the RLG/ARL Latin American Conspectus. That instrument can illuminate better our individual collection strengths and weaknesses, and guide libraries in better meeting local needs and establishing cooperative goals.

44. AN OLD BOOK WITH A NEW COVER: NONSTANDARD LIBRARY MATERIALS IN THE NATIONAL CONTEXT

Laura Gutiérrez-Witt

In reviewing the literature on the theme of cooperation, I was struck by the repeated recurrence of many of the same ideas. Like new parents, librarians of each succeeding generation have again discovered the thrills of giving birth. The newborn has varied slightly each generation, but all have been sufficiently similar to be classed in the same species. The same holds true within our organization.

The cornerstone of Latin American bibliographical collecting endeavors was laid at Chinsegut Hill in 1956, and that cornerstone was cooperation, the sharing of information among the thirty-two participants at the first Seminar on the Acquisition of Latin American Library Materials. Yet that historic meeting was described by the organizers as "the latest link in the chain of cooperative efforts to resolve mutual acquisitions problems." And, in fact, the introduction to the published Final Report of the 1956 meeting enumerated at least seventeen conferences or projects underway designed to pool resources or knowledge, or both, in order to acquire Latin American materials.[1]

The first Seminar, in addition to establishing a dialog among Latin American library specialists, put in motion two important cooperative acquisitions programs: the extension of the Farmington Plan to Latin America and the establishment of LACAP, the Latin American Cooperative Acquisitions Program. A working paper on the "Experience of Farmington Plan in the Latin American Field," by Edwin E. Williams, was an integral part of the Chinsegut Hill program. Drafted in 1942 but put into operation only in 1947, the Farmington Plan was to ensure that "at least one copy of each new foreign book and pamphlet that might reasonably be expected to interest a research worker in the United States . . . be acquired by an American library, promptly listed in the Union Catalogue at the Library of Congress, and made available by inter-library loan or photographic reproduction." Williams concluded that, except for Mexico and the Caribbean, the Farmington Plan did not effectively cover Latin America.[2]

In 1958, the third Seminar finally drafted a resolution--to be conveyed to the Association of Research Libraries (ARL)--about extending Farmington Plan coverage to Latin America.[3] The following year, participants at the fourth Seminar received a reply and an invitation from ARL to join its newly established Latin American program.[4]

The Latin American Cooperative Acquisitions Program (LACAP) also had its genesis at the first SALALM meeting. That year's Resolution Three recommended "that interested libraries explore the possibilities and feasibility of maintaining on a cooperative basis one or more full time acquisition agents in Latin America."[5] The consequent organization, development, and eventual decline of LACAP are fully documented and well known to us. It is recognized that LACAP represented a solution suitable to the problems confronting institutions requiring Latin American materials during the 1950s and 1960s.[6]

The tradition of cooperation and of cooperative ventures was established early in SALALM. Early cooperation consisted, as we have seen, of the exchange of ideas and information about sources of materials and, later, of joint sponsorship of traveling agents or representatives. As a group and individually we continue to seek satisfactory solutions to current acquisition problems by comparing our successes as well as our failures.

But cooperative acquisition ventures have not been the only instances of cooperation among our institutions. Currently, many SALALM members, both personal and institutional, are involved in resource-sharing through the Latin American Microform Project (LAMP), based at the Center for Research Libraries (CRL). Formally launched in 1976, LAMP was the result of several years of study, research, planning, and lobbying by a number of SALALM members. The dues paid by LAMP members are used to "film or acquire film of unique, scarce, rare and/or bulky and voluminous research materials pertaining to Latin America and to make them available to subscribers to the project."[7]

Other forms of cooperation as well are known and used by our institutions: bibliographic databases, interlibrary loan, union lists, regional consortia, preservation microfilming, and so forth. The commitment of libraries as well as library professionals to cooperation is unquestioned. The broader availability of materials, increased cost effectiveness, and the avoidance of duplicative effort are recognized advantages of cooperative projects. Nonetheless, a recent study by ARL's Office of Management Studies concluded that few cooperative acquisitions programs--with the exception of the Farmington Plan and the Center for Research Libraries--have had "continuing, substantive impact."[8] Factors hindering cooperation, according to this study, have included user expectations of immediate access to materials, inefficient or slow interinstitutional delivery systems, the lack of a standard methodology for describing and comparing collections, and the lack of structures and procedures for cooperative acquisition decisions. The study pointed out, however, that developments in bibliographic networks, advances in telecommunications, improved document delivery systems, and better tools for describing and assessing collections are factors that will have substantial impacts on cooperative programs in the near future.

How then can we harness this momentum toward greater cooperation among libraries to ensure that nonstandard materials related to Latin America are identified, acquired, processed, and preserved? Again, let us consider our past. In 1956, Session III of the first SALALM was devoted to "Non-Book Materials," and included a working paper on "Mapping Services in Latin America."[9] The published summary report also noted concern among participants over the difficulty in locating "microfilm of special manuscripts and archival materials of Latin America now in the United States" and "information about private manuscript collections and their availability for microfilming," as well as "the problems involved in acquiring other nonbook materials, such as motion picture films, records, performance music, and art material."[10]

Whereas access to manuscript collections and microfilm of archival collections has been considerably enhanced by the National Union Catalog of Manuscript Collections (NUCMC),[11] the National Register of Microform Masters,[12] and SALALM's own Microfilming Projects Newsletter,[13] the acquisition of other nonbook materials remains problematic. As late as 1982, Carl Deal and   William Carter lamented "the chronic neglect of fugitive and/or poorly formatted materials that, in spite of their often excellent research content, can all too easily be dismissed as ephemera."[14]

Despite these pessimistic comments, we can all admit some success in identifying and gathering certain ephemeral materials: broadsides and posters, Brazilian street literature, sheet music, and maps all come to mind. But who is cataloging these materials? We view both popular and documentary films on our campuses and at conferences, but who is collecting and preserving them? Photographs and slides of monuments and art works are equally neglected: we tend to expect art department slide collections to acquire them, but do they? Collections of audio and video recordings, despite the existence of various programs and agencies, are not actively pursued by libraries collecting other Latin American materials.

Why? Because in trying to meet the needs of our local faculty and students, we are all collecting the same types of materials and usually the same titles. This situation has been pointed out time and again by scholars, librarians, and administrators, at SALALM and elsewhere. The result is a group of collections with superficial coverage of a number of countries or areas, with little depth in any of them. Support for the continuation of a Farmington Plan-type approach, with country specialties, has recently been reaffirmed by SALALM member institutions. But how many of us are committed to collecting more than books, serials, and government documents? What about other types of materials, such as posters, broadsides, films, photographs, audio and video recordings, slides, juvenile and street literature, sheet music, not to mention archival collections or microfilms of archives? The reality, unfortunately, is that there are few budgets that can support so comprehensive a collecting effort, even for one country.

Obviously, alternatives must be found if future generations are to find documentation about the "masses and minorities" on which this meeting has focused. Have we neglected to work with special libraries or collections such as those specializing in music, manuscripts, or films in the acquisition of Latin Americana? The most common reason given by special librarians for the paucity of Latin American materials in their collections is their lack of information on sources. A faculty member at my institution recently asked me to identify a librarian knowledgeable about Latin American theater archives who might participate on a panel for a Society of Theater History meeting. As Latin American bibliographic specialists, we are uniquely qualified to assist special libraries within our institutions and elsewhere, if we are not collecting these materials ourselves, to find Latin American sources of such nonstandard materials as playbills, posters, and other theater memorabilia. Special libraries often have the technical expertise and the equipment to catalog, preserve, and make accessible nonstandard materials in varying formats.

Another alternative is that LAMP could provide a model structure to preserve and share certain types of nonstandard materials, most obviously those which are paper-based and which could be microfilmed. But who would identify and collect these items if not the member libraries themselves? Original materials must first be acquired before LAMP, as it is presently constituted, can microfilm and service them.

But is it too farfetched to think about a centralized motion picture film archive (as opposed to microfilms), where pristine copies of popular as well as documentary films from and about Latin America could be made available for researchers' screenings? The same center could serve as a repository for unused film footage, scripts, sound recordings, and other items associated with the making of the films or videos. If expensive items such as films were acquired by a consortium of libraries, then individual institutions could consider, if not country-specific assignments related to ephemera, subject-specific assignments: theater memorabilia, or political propaganda, or feminist literature, or something else. Special funding from federal or private foundations could be sought to identify and process these collections of ephemera, particularly if the resulting materials were to be shared with other institutions through microfilm or similar means. In 1981, a federal grant to the University of Texas funded the identification of Latin American public and private corporations to be contacted for their annual reports, financial statements, and other business publications. The intensive letter-writing campaign yielded innumerable publications for the cost of identification, letter writing, and postage.

I am not suggesting that a LAMP clone be organized for the purposes of collecting films or any other type of material. However, we do need to think in group terms when considering the acquisition of costly materials such as films. But LAMP is evolving, and may be poised on the threshold of a new phase. It has survived its period of adolescence and successfully reached maturity. Its funding is assured through membership dues; the selection of materials to film or acquire is by majority decision; relationships with repositories holding materials to be filmed have generally been cordial and mutually satisfying. Currently LAMP is funding the preparation of a proposal to seek major support for a large microfilming project to which several institutions will contribute holdings. The organization is flexible and organic.

It is therefore not inconceivable that LAMP itself could embark on new ventures, if the membership so desires. But no one organization can be all things to all men/women, as we are all aware. Cooperation is not an easy undertaking, and it can be expensive. Bringing together institutions and organizations as well as individuals is a difficult task, but we are fortunate in having precedents to follow. If the study of "masses and minorities" in all of their facets is to be possible to future scholars, LAMP or a similar cooperative resource-sharing con-sortium will be essential in identifying, acquiring, processing, and preserving their documentation, whatever the format.

NOTES

1. Seminar on the Acquisition of Latin American Library Materials (SALALM), Final Report (Gainesville, FL: The Univer-sity of Florida Libraries, 1956).

2. Edwin E. Williams, "Experience of Farmington Plan in the Latin American Field," in ibid., working paper IIF.

3. "Resolutions and Recommendations of the Third Seminar [1958]," SALALM, Final Report and Papers (Berkeley, CA: General Library, University of California, 1959), p. 35.

4. SALALM, Final Report and Papers [1959]. Washington, DC: Library of Congress, 1960), p. 6.

5. SALALM, Final Report, 1956, p. 21.

6. M. J. Savary, The Latin American Cooperative Acquisi-tions Program . . . An Imaginative Venture (New York, NY: Hafner Publishing Co., 1968).

7. Carl W. Deal, "The Latin American Microform Project (LAMP) Is Inaugurated," SALALM Newsletter, 3 (March, 1976), 13.

8. Systems and Procedures Exchange Center, Cooperative Collection Development, Kit 111 (Washington, DC: Office of Management Studies, Association of Research Libraries, February, 1985.

9. Arch C. Gerlach, "Mapping Services in Latin America," in SALALM, Final Report, 1956, working paper IIIi.

10. SALALM, Final Report, 1956, p. 9.

11. National Union Catalog of Manuscript Collections (Washington, DC: Library of Congress, 1965--).

12. National Register of Microform Masters, 1959-- (Washington, DC: Library of Congress, 1965--).

13. SALALM Microfilming Projects Newsletter, in its Final Report and Papers, 1960--.

14. Carl W. Deal and William E. Carter, "The Implementation of a National Plan for Latin American Library Collections in the United States," in Public Policy Issues and Latin American Library Resources: Papers of the 27th Annual Meeting of SALALM (Washington, DC: March 2-5, 1982), p. 155.

45. OLD ATTITUDES AND NEW RESPONSES:
REFLECTIONS ON COOPERATION

Cecelia L. Shores

Laura Gutiérrez-Witt pointed out in the preceding paper what we have all heard many times before: despite years of purported effort to collaborate and cooperate, our institutions are all still individually collecting the same materials--books, serials, and government documents, with an emphasis on those that are "scholarly" in tone and content. Barbara Valk, in a later paper (see pp. 514-518, below), notes the reluctance of the U.S. commercial sector to take on responsibility for creating or marketing Latin American databases: "Sure, it's worthwhile stuff, but you have a limited audience, and we have to look at the bottom line. Sorry, there's no money in it." David Zubatsky, also in a later paper (pp. 519-523), acknowledges that Third World countries' materials are still a low priority for the bibliographic utilities.

This is only the second time I have attended SALALM in its entirety, but already I have in my head some recurring refrains, refrains heard more often in corridors than in the formal meetings:

> They don't really have a level four collection. . . .
> Who's gonna see that they really collect what they say
> they will? . . . What if five or ten years from now,
> nobody on their campus cares? . . . ILL takes too
> long--my researchers can't wait . . . my faculty
> members just HATE using microforms. . . . I know I
> agreed to work on that, but . . . . Maybe LC (or
> Texas, or Princeton) can afford to do that, but we
> can't. . . . What they're doing isn't of any interest to
> my institution.

Notice the us versus them attitude. In one way or another, these are all "poor me" or "me first" responses--very human, quite understandable, but basically counterproductive if cooperation is truly our goal.

Even when we have our positive-attitude and cooperative hats on, we talk about acquiring, providing bibliographic access to, and preserving materials here, in the United States. We talk to each other (the already committed), bemoaning our problems and congratulating ourselves on our purported successes. We speak of the need to expand our activities to the third-tier journals and to the nontraditional formats. All we need is more money.

But are we seeing it straight? Are we facing up to the harsh realities, or are we continuing to bury our heads in sand, afraid to acknowledge that what we are doing may be all we can reasonably expect to do? Will we admit that some of the materials our researchers clamor for may result in more outpourings of empty academic verbiage, serving no purpose but to secure or improve the rank and status of the so-called scholar? Can we face the fact that area studies (indeed, the humanities in general) are no longer in vogue in the United States, and that special funding from federal or private foundations may not be forthcoming to answer our needs? Do we see that even our cooperative accomplishments, such as the National Register of Microform Masters and SALALM's Microfilming Projects Newsletter, are and possibly will always be woefully incomplete as long as their content depends--as in our democracy, it should--on voluntary reporting? RLG's success in dividing up subject responsibility is a worthy cooperative model, but how many institutions can participate? Even those that meet the criteria for membership must and do question the cost-benefit ratio from year to year.

Returning for a moment to Laura Gutiérrez-Witt's concern for nontraditional materials, could LAMP extend itself into this area or serve as a model for a separate group that would do so? The latter, surely, if a number of libraries or their parent institutions can be persuaded to pony up still more dollars in support of Latin American materials. You know the answer to this better than I, but what I have been hearing suggests such a group would be small, indeed. And I feel I must disagree with Gutiérrez-Witt's statement that LAMP's funding is secure: any group dependent on annual membership dues for its revenue can scarcely be so considered. Moreover, there is a fundamental question still unanswered: are nontraditional materials (maps, broadsides, sheet music, and such) one of our priorities at this time? Can we afford to move into this area and still do the traditional thoroughly and well?

Is all this anything beyond more moaning? Should we accept certain defeat and abandon our efforts? Or adopt the attitude that little more than we are doing can be done? I think not. I do think, however, that progress may depend not only on money but also on personal and political activism, on extending our generosity and friendship, and on sharing our knowledge and skills.

Here are some questions to ponder anew; you have all heard them many times before. Is SALALM, or any other group, reaching all those who might contribute to our efforts to increase access to Latin American library materials? Are we as visible as we need to be, as we can be? Can we offset the declining interest in area studies by presenting our work and our materials in more discipline-specific terms (geography, history, political science), and by more actively involving the teaching faculties at our own and neighboring institutions? Would we be wise to urge that the Library of Congress be formally transformed into our national library, that it be charged with developing mechanisms to guarantee rapid access to Latin American materials in its collections? Would we trust LC or any other institution to do the job as we feel it should be done?

But involvement and cooperation need not and should not stop at our borders. The SALALM meeting in Berlin next year (indeed, all SALALM meetings held outside the United States) provides an opportunity to extend our cooperative efforts and to infect others with our zeal and our belief that both traditional and so-called ephemeral materials are potentially of value to research. We need to let the world know that we value acquisition and preservation of Latin American library materials wherever it may happen--that our goal is assistance to scholarship, not simply enhancement of U.S. libraries' volume counts.

As coordinator for all four of CRL's area studies microform projects, my greatest pleasure and satisfaction has come not when a project has acquired or preserved some particular item but when that project has made friends for itself in another country, when it has formed a bond with a foreign institution, when it has established a new source for future acquisition of research library material. In many cases, this has been accomplished through seemingly small deeds and gestures which ultimately benefit the project as well as the host institution or country. The best example currently comes from the Southeast Asia Microform Project (SEAM). With SEAM funding, a U.S. scholar is now working at the Indonesian National Library in Jakarta, selecting and having converted to microfilm serial runs of particular importance to North American researchers. Yes, SEAM is providing the raw film, which is available in Jakarta only at grossly inflated prices. But that kind of provision is common. As those of you connected with LAMP know, the Brazilian Relatórios project came to fruition only through LAMP's willingness to supply film, equipment, and even film cement. What SEAM is providing that is special is bibliographic and technical expertise: SEAM's representative is working with the Jakarta library staff, teaching them how to prepare runs for filming, how to create and insert filming targets, and how to use their equipment so the resultant product will be properly ordered, stable, and fully legible. Even if SEAM's collection interests were totally fulfilled with this one project (which is highly unlikely), the goodwill and credibility gained would benefit SEAM in other Southeast Asian ventures, both for traditional and nontraditional materials. Scholars from other parts of the world would likewise be able to ask for that library's films with confidence that they are well ordered and easily read.

This is no small accomplishment but, as you can see, it rests less on dollars and more on a willingness to offer time, assistance, and knowledge.   May I urge all of you, and ask you to urge those students and faculty who travel to (or even write to) other areas of the country, other areas of the world, to be generous with your time and your expertise?   The rewards to scholarship are incalculable and long-lasting.

46. MINIMAL LEVEL CATALOGING OF LATIN AMERICAN MATERIALS: SOME CONSIDERATIONS

Sharon A. Moynahan

Cataloging is one of the most expensive and labor-intensive library tasks. It has therefore often, and rightly, been the target of economizing schemes. The notable success of online shared cataloging encourages library administrators to look once again at the cataloging process to see whether there may be another way to save precious library funds. Modern technology offers the possibility of increased access to information without the stylized headings, the redundancy, and the cross references typical of the manual card catalog. At the same time, this technology demands complete accuracy and consistency since errors and "browsing" take on new meanings in the online environment. The phrases "minimal level cataloging" and "less than full level cataloging" raise eyebrows, tempers, or hopes, depending on the perspective of the librarian. Could less cataloging be the answer?

Almost everyone agrees that "something" must be done about the increasing backlogs of uncataloged materials in academic libraries. The nation's current conservative climate precludes any miracle cure from the Library of Congress or other governmental sources. While there is agreement on the need, the specifics of a cure and the materials to which such a cure might be applied remain sources of contention in many libraries.

How Did We Get into This Situation in the First Place?

In the 1960s, administrators and catalogers hailed the advent of technology and shared cataloging networks as solutions to the slow and expensive task of cataloging. Here was an opportunity to eliminate or reassign staff. College, junior college, and public libraries reaped the greatest benefits. The availability of copy for up to 95 percent of the titles they acquired meant that scarce personnel could be used elsewhere.

While research libraries experienced some of these benefits, they found that the networks lacked copy for large portions of their acquisitions. These items would thus require expensive original cataloging. As acquisitions budgets rose sharply during the boom years, and academic libraries' collections became more sophisticated and comprehensive, the work load for original cataloging units increased. I doubt that any cataloging unit experienced a parallel growth in personnel.

As resources became scarcer, many libraries concentrated their efforts on collection development: many materials, especially foreign imprints, would be available only once. Rising backlogs accompanied the shrinking processing funds. The impact of AACR2 on catalog departments is well documented in the litera-ture. Backlogs continued to grow as catalog departments both adapted to the new rules and assumed such new tasks as main-taining circulation databases and online catalogs.

A full MARC record, the standard bibliographic unit, suit-ably tagged and authenticated, is expensive. It is only natural to look for a shorter and more efficient version. However, the online environment requires that any move away from a full MARC record be very carefully considered. While the consequences of a false step vary from network to network, they could cause con-siderable and in some cases irreparable damage to a database.

What Is a Minimal Level Record?

Before deciding whether to use "less than full level" cataloging, it is necessary to define the term. Unfortunately, there is no absolute standard that can be applied to all cataloging and to all cataloging networks. While there are minimal require-ments for the inclusion of any cataloging record on individual networks, and while AACR2 outlines several levels, there is no national definition of a minimal level record. As long as basic network or database requirements are met, libraries may include as much or as little information as they wish. Since most of the institutions considering this procedure are research libraries, their users' needs are often considerable.

Among the items most often considered for exclusion in minimal level records are various elements in the fixed fields. Although of little use when card production was the only consideration, many of these codes are valuable in the online environment. Some provide the means for subdividing the databases, for limiting online search responses, or for providing access by such features as the language of a work--features that may not be evident from the record's text.

Several elements of cataloging description and classification are also frequently considered dispensable. Name added entries, series tracings, notes, and illustration and size notations lead the list. The possibilities of free-text and key-word searching are cited in proposals to eliminate subject headings, or at least multiple subject headings, and standardized series statements. In some cases, call numbers have also been targeted.

The next question to consider is which records these stream-lined procedures will affect. Should they only apply to original cataloging, and to the attendant authority control? These two operations are the most expensive tasks in the catalog depart-ment. But what about the cataloging copy obtained from a network's online database? If a research library conducts extensive checking and verification for its own copy, perhaps member-input copy should be subject to the same standards. When online copy is good and complete, should a particular library "waste" access points by reducing it to a minimal-level standard? What, if any, distinction should be made between cataloging for input into a national database and copy revised for inhouse use?

All these questions have to be considered both before and after we address the issue of which library materials will be given minimal, less than full, or base level cataloging.

Latin American Library Materials

Of primary concern to SALALM members is the effect that minimal level cataloging might have if applied to Latin American library materials. These materials are at risk. Foreign language materials are often at the top of the list for brief records. While Spanish is not usually considered an exotic foreign language, materials in Spanish and Portuguese often challenge even the experienced cataloger, and in most cases take extra time to process. Personnel with good language skills in Spanish and especially Portuguese are hard to find. And many academic libraries find that their backlogs of Spanish and Portuguese language materials are so large that only herculean efforts will reduce them to manageable proportions.

The decision to implement less than full level standards for cataloging is based on many factors, chief among them costs and the impact on users. While all the possibilities and ramifications cannot be determined in advance, the following points are among the most important to consider. As my own list suggests, it is important to keep the future in mind whenever a cataloging policy decision is made.

The loss of searching capabilities can affect the national community as well as the local user. While networks may accept several levels of cataloging standards, research libraries have traditionally provided the national community with complete, high-quality cataloging. Diminished standards will mean extra work for libraries who must upgrade the copy they use. This extra effort, repeated many times, defeats the purpose of shared cataloging networks. Furthermore, loss of added entries, subject headings, and other fields will mean fewer access points. While it might seem obvious that any work could be found by searching under the title and author, we should not forget the many materials--especially Latin American documents--whose titles are not immediately apparent, and whose authors could be any or all of several names on the piece. Locating existing copy can be difficult.

The local user is especially affected by the potential loss of subject headings. Words in titles do not always reflect subject content, and vocabularies change from year to year. Consider the terms "trailers," "trailer homes," "mobile homes," "modular homes," and "manufactured housing." The researcher who is working in Spanish, spoken in more than a dozen countries, likewise faces the challenge of idiomatic variety. Only a skilled linguist could successfully use keyword searching to full advantage. Subject headings using a controlled vocabulary are often essential to group materials on the same subject.

While some disciplines are adequately covered on a timely basis in commercial bibliographies and databases, this is not true for Latin American materials. The bibliographies that do exist are usually selective and delayed. Research on a current topic must be conducted with a database or an in-house catalog, and there are not yet any widely used databases that cover Latin American materials.

Cost considerations should be weighed carefully, since immediate savings sometimes result in future cleanup projects. How often is money available to systematically recatalog or upgrade records? A final consideration is purely speculative: whether either textual or coded cataloging information that now appears useless and expensive might be helpful or even critical for efficient online searching at some point in the future.

Clearly, many issues are involved in the decision to change cataloging standards. Minimal, or less than full, standards may not always be bad--just as complete, full level cataloging may be overkill for some online databases. High standards, and the corresponding expectations, can perpetuate large backlogs of uncataloged and hence unavailable material, and thus be a disservice to users. Latin American specialists and bibliographers are well advised to become acquainted with cataloging standards and to participate in their libraries' decision-making processes. Only those familiar with the particularities of Latin American bibliography can ensure easy and complete access to these materials.

Minimal Level Bibliographic Records

Definitions

"Minimal level" is a generic term used to define machine-readable bibliographic records that contain a basic set of data elements, the least number necessary to identify a work, and codes that allow a computer to identify those elements. Two things minimal level records are not are:

1. Acquisitions or in-process records. While such records are often minimal, they are impermanent. Minimal level records are permanently cataloged records.

2. Nonstandard records. Such records meet no commonly accepted standard. An example would be cataloging done by a specialized library which uses its own subject thesaurus rather than one of the standard lists, such as the Library of Congress Subject Headlines.

Individual institutions and bibliographic utilities have developed subcategories of minimal level records:

1.   AACR2 LEVEL 1

Rule 1.0.D1 defines a minimal level bibliographic description. Library of Congress full records are at second or third level (Anglo-American Cataloguing Rules, 2d ed. [1978], p. 15).

2.   NLBR MINIMAL LEVEL

After national consultation and consensus, National Level Bibliographic Record documents for the various formats were published to define two levels of machine-readable cataloging records that would be acceptable for a nationwide database. These levels are full and minimal (National Level Bibliographic Record: Books [Films, etc.] [1980--]).

3.   OCLC K LEVEL

OCLC has long had two levels of acceptable records, K level and I level. K level was designed for the small libraries in OCLC which neither need nor want extremely detailed catalog cards. The standard is now being considered for revision as some of the big libraries see possibilities for saving time and resources by cataloging with less detail (OCLC Bibliographic Input Standards, 2d ed. [1982]).

Editor's Note.   Adapted from a report prepared for Academic Assembly Meeting, Cornell University Libraries, September 11, 1984.

4.   RLG BASE LEVEL

The RLG base level standards are the NLBR standards adapted to the RLIN system. Guidelines for books and scores/ sound recordings have been issued; those for serials are now being developed. The Cataloging Category (CC) code for base level records is X55X (RLG Base-level Standard for Books [Scores, etc.] [1983--]).

5.   LC MINIMAL LEVEL (MLC)

The Library of Congress version of the NLBR standards. Distribution of MLC records through the MARC distribution service began in the fall of 1983. RLG began loading LC MLC tapes on RLIN in January, 1985.

Data Elements Required in an RLG Base-Level Books Record

Fixed Field Data

Bibliographic type and level code   (e.g., am = printed monograph)
Descriptive cataloging form code   (e.g., a = AACR2)
Date type code   (e.g., s = single date)
Date[s] of publication
Country of publication code
Language code
Cataloging source code   (e.g., d = other than LC)

Variable Field Data

Library of Congress card number, when available
International Standard Bibliographic Number, when available
Cataloging agency/Transcribing agency/Modifying agency codes

Name or uniform title main entry, when required by cataloging rules
Title
     Title proper
     Other title information, excluding parallel titles
     Statement of responsibility
Edition statement
Publication, distribution area
     First place of publication
     First publisher
     Date[s]
Physical description
     Extent of item (usually paging)
Series Statement

No notes, subjects, name, other titles or series added entries are
  included.

The list above gives the basic data set. In certain cases a few other data elements are required. For example, a record for microfilm also includes a General Material Designator, additional fixed field codes and a microform note.

Minimal Level Records: LC BOOKSM and NLBR

MARC Data Element	LC BOOKSM Minimal Level Record	NLBR Books Min. Lev.
LDR	M	M
/5 Record Status	M (n=new generated)	M
/6 Record Type	M (a=lang. mat. generated)	M
/7 Bib. Level	M (m=mono. generated)	M
/17 Encoding Level	M (7=prelim. cata. generated)	M
/18 Desc. Cat. Form.	M (a=AACR2 generated)	M
001 Control Number	M (generated)	M
005 Date/Time of Latest Transaction	(LC does not use)	M
007	MA	MA
/0 Microform	M	M
/1-12	M	0
008	M	M
/0-5 Date Entered on File	M (generated)	M
/6 Type of Publication Date	M	0
/7-10 Date 1	M	0
/11-14 Date 2	M	0
/15-17 Country of Publ.	M	0
/22 Intellectual Level	M	0
/35-37 Language Code	M	M
/39 Cataloging Source	M (b̸=LC generated)	M
/18-21 Illustration Codes	0 (generated from 300)	0
/23 Form of Reproduction	M (b̸=Not a repro. generated)	0
/24-27 Nature of Contents	0 (b̸b̸b̸b̸=Not specified gen.)	0
/28 Gov. Publication Code	0 (b̸=Not a gov. publ. gen.)	0
/29 Conf. Indicator	0 (0=Not a conf. generated)	0
/30 Festschrift Ind.	0 (0=Not a Fest. generated)	0
/31 Index Ind.	0 (0=No index generated)	0
/32 Main Entry in Body Ind.	0 (0=Not in body generated)	0
/33 Fiction Indicator	0 (0=Not fiction generated)	0
/34 Biography Code	0 (b̸=Not biography gen.)	0
/38 Mod. Record Code	0 (b̸=Not modified generated)	0
010 LC Control Number	(LC does not use)	MA
020 ISBN	R	R
$a ISBN	MA	MA
$c Terms of availability	MA	OD
$z Cancelled/Invalid ISBN	MA	MA
034 Cartographic Coded Data	MA	MA
039 Level of Control	M (generated)	M
040 Cataloging Source	(LC does not use for Minimal Level)	M

MARC Data Element	LC BOOKSM Minimal Level Record	NLBR Books Min. Lev.
050 LC Call Number	M (shelf sequence order)	OD
1XX Main Entry	MA	MA
100 (Main Entry--Personal Name)	MA	MA
110 (Main Entry--Corporate Name)	MA	MA
111 (Main Entry--Conference or Meeting)	MA	MA
130 (Main Entry--Uniform Title Heading)	MA	MA
245 Title Statement	M	M
$a Title proper	M	M
$b Remainder of title	MA	OD
$c Statement of responsibility	MA	MA
$n Number of part/section	MA	MA
$p Name of part/section (of a work)	MA	MA
$h Media qualifier	MA	OD
250 Edition Statement	MA	MA
$a Edition statement	M	M
$b Remainder of edition statement	MA	OD
255 Cartographic Textual Data	MA	MA
260 Imprint Statement (AACR2)	M	MA
$a Place of publ., distribution., etc.	MA	OD
$b Name of publisher, distrib., etc.	MA	MA
$c Date of publ., distrib., etc.	MA	MA
$e Place of manufacture	MA	OD
$f Manufacturer	MA	OD
$g Date of manufacture	MA	OD
300 Physical Description (AACR2)	M	M
$a Extent of item	M	M
$b Other physical details	MA	OD
$c Dimensions	M	OD
$e Accompanying material	MA	OD
440 Series Statement--Title (Traced)	MA	MA
$a Title	M	M
$n Number of part/section	MA	MA
$p Name of part/section of a work	MA	MA
$x International Standard Serial No.	MA	R
$v Volume or number	MA	MA
490 Series Untraced or Traced Differently	MA	MA
$a Title untraced or traced dif.	M	M
$x International Standard Serial No.	MA	R
$v Volume or number	MA	MA

MARC Data Element	LC BOOKSM Minimal Level Record	NLBR Books Min. Lev.
500/Earlier editions notes	MA	OD
/Translation notes	MA	OD
533 Reproduction Note	MA	MA
700 Added Entry--Personal Name	MA (if no main entry)	OD
710 Added Entry--Corporate Name	MA (if no main entry)	OD
711 Added Entry--Conf. Name	MA (if no main entry)	OD
730 Added Entry--Unif. Title Heading	MA (if no main entry)	OD
773 Host Item Entry	(LC does not use)	MA
800 Series Added Entry--Traced Dif.	MA	OD
810 Series Added Entry--Traced Dif.	MA	OD
811 Series Added Entry--Traded Dif.	MA	OD
830 Series Added Entry--Traced Dif.	MA	OD
850 Holdings	(LC does not use)	M

LDR, 007, 008

M = Mandatory (field must always be present; value other than
        fill must be used)

MA = Mandatory if Applicable (field must be present if appropriate)

O = Optional (value may either be fill or one of the defined values)

Other Fields

M = Mandatory (field or subfield must always be present)

MA = Mandatory if Applicable (field or subfield must be present
        if appropriate for the item being cataloged)

R = Required if Available (field or subfield must be present if
        data appears on the item being cataloged)

OD = Optional Data (field or subfield is optional for inclusion
        in the record)

Cataloging Example No. 1: Minimal Level Copy

```
PROD       Books       PAR        DCLC82142907-B        Search          NYCX-OCA
Cluster 46 of 57
+B
Benevides, Maria Victoria de Mesauita.
   O soverno J_anio Quadros / Maria Victoria de Mesauita Benevides. -- S~ao
Paulo-Brasil : Brasiliense, 1981.
   87 p. : ill. ; 16 cm. -- (Tudo _e hist_oria ; 30)

   Series.
   LCCN: 82142907
   L.C. CALL NO: MLCS 82/345/
   ID: DCLC82142907-B            CC: 9650        DCF: a
```

```
PROD       Books       FUL/BIB    DCLC82142907-B        Search          NYCX-OCA
Cluster 46 of 57
+B
  ID:DCLC82142907-B   RTYP:c    ST:p    FRN:      NLR:012001 MS:n EL:7 AD:04-14-82
  CC:9650  BLT:am      DCF:a    CSC:    MOD:      SNR:      ATC:      UD:01-01-01
  CP:???    L:por      INT:?    GPC:    BIO:?     FIC:?     CON:????
  PC:?      PD:1981/????        REP:?   CPI:?     FSI:?     ILC:???? MEI:? II:?
  MMD:      OR:   POL:    DM:     RR:             COL:      EML:      GEN: BSE:
  010       82142907
  020       #cCr$190.00
  040       #dCStRLIN
  050 0     MLCS 82/3457
  100 1     Benevides, Maria Victoria de Mesauita.
  245 12    O soverno J_anio Quadros /#cMaria Victoria de Mesauita Benevides.
  260       S~ao Paulo-Brasil :#bBrasiliense,#c1981.
  300       87 p. : ill. ; 16 cm.
  440       Tudo _e hist_oria ; 30
```

Cataloging Example No. 1: Full Cataloging Copy

```
PPOD       Books       PAR        NYCX82-B36224         Search          NYCX-OCA
Cluster 46 of 57
+B
Benevides, Maria Victoria de Mesauita.
   O soverno J_anio Quadros / Maria Victoria de Mesauita Benevides. -- S~ao
Paulo : Brasiliense, 1981.
   87 p. : ill. ; 16 cm. -- (Tudo _e hist_oria ; 30)

   Series: Tudo _e hist_oria (1981) ; 30.
   ID: NYCX82-B36224             CC: 9118        DCF: a
- - - - - - - - - - - - - - - - - - - - - - - - - - - - - - - - - - - -
OLIN   F2538.2.B46
   c.1   (CAT 03/14/85)
     Aca: 82-B36224-1.
- - - - - - - - - - - - - - - - - - - - - - - - - - - - - - - - - - - -
  UID 82-B36224-1      UTYP DB    LSI                   CPST CAT 03/12/85 UST P
```

```
PROD       Books       FUL/BIB    NYCX82-B36224         Search          NYCX-OCA
Cluster 46 of 57
+
  ID:NYCX82-B36224    RTYP:b    ST:p    FRN:     NLR:      MS:  EL:  AD:06-16-82
  CC:9118  BLT:am      DCF:a    CSC:d   MOD:     SNR:      ATC:      UD:03-14-85
  CP:bl     L:por      INT:     GPC:    BIO:     FIC:0     CON:
  PC:s      PD:1981/            REP:    CPI:0    FSI:0     ILC:a     MEI:1 II:0
  MMD:      OR:   POL:    DM:     RR:            COL:      EML:      GEN: BSE:
  040       NIC#cNIC
  043       s-bl---
  100 10    Benevides, Maria Victoria de Mesauita.
  245 10    O soverno J_anio Quadros /#cMaria Victoria de Mesauita Benevides.
  260 0     S~ao Paulo :#bBrasiliense,#c1981.
  300       87 p. :#bill. ;#c16 cm.
  490 1     Tudo _e hist_oria ;#v30
  600 10    Quadros, J_anio,#d1917-
  651 0     Brazil#xPolitics and sovernment#y1954-
  830 0     Tudo _e hist_oria (1981) ;#v30.
```

Cataloging Example No. 2: LC Minimal Level Copy

Cataloging Example No. 2: LC Minimal Level Copy

```
PROD      Books      PAR      DCLC82142925-B      Search      NYCX-OCA
Cluster 53 of 57
+B
Monteiro, Hamilton de Mattos.
   Nordeste insurgente : 1850-1890 / Hamilton de Mattos Monteiro. -- S~ao Paulo-
Brasil : Brasiliense, 1981.
   99 p. : ill. ; 16 cm. -- (Cole_c~ao Tudo _e hist_oria ; 10)


   Series.
   LCCN: 82142925
   L.C. CALL NO: MLCS 82/3454
   ID: DCLC82142925-B              CC: 9650        DCF: a
```

```
PROD      Books      FUL/BIB   DCLC82142925-B      Search      NYCX-OCA
Cluster 53 of 57
+B
   ID:DCLC82142925-B   RTYP:c    ST:p    FRN:    NLR:012001 MS:n EL:7 AD:04-14-82
   CC:9650   BLT:am     DCF:a    CSC:    MOD:    SNR:      ATC:       UD:01-01-01
   CP:???     L:por      INT:?   GPC:    BIO:?   FIC:?     CON:????
   PC:?      PD:1981/????        REP:?   CPI:?   FSI:?     ILC:????  MEI:?   II:?
   MMD:       OR:    POL:    DM:      RR:        COL:      EML:        GEN:  BSE:
   010        82142925
   020        #cCr$190.00
   040        #dCStRLIN
   050 0      MLCS 82/3454
   100 1      Monteiro, Hamilton de Mattos.
   245 10     Nordeste insurgente :#b1850-1890 /#cHamilton de Mattos Monteiro.
   260        S~ao Paulo-Brasil :#bBrasiliense,#c1981.
   300        99 p. : ill. ; 16 cm.
   440        Cole_c~ao Tudo _e hist_oria ; 10
```

Cataloging Example No. 2: Full Cataloging Copy

```
PROD      Books      PAR      UTBG82-B542      Search      NYCX-OCA
Cluster 53 of 57
+B
Monteiro, Hamilton de Mattos.
   Nordeste insurgente (1850-1890) / Hamilton de Mattos Monteiro. -- S~ao Paulo :
Brasiliense, 1981.
   99 p. : ill., maps ; 16 cm. -- (Tudo _e hist_oria ; 10)


   Series.
   ID: UTBG82-B542              CC: 9114        DCF: a
- - - - - - - - - - - - - - - - - - - - - - - - - - - - - - - - - - - - - - - - -
F2536.M657x


MAN
   c.1   (CAT 01/11/82)
     Circ: 6107632.
```

```
PROD      Books      FUL/BIB   UTBG82-B542      Search      NYCX-OCA
Cluster 53 of 57
+
   ID:UTBG82-B542      RTYP:c    ST:p    FRN:    NLR:      MS:  EL:  AD:01-11-82
   CC:9114   BLT:am     DCF:a    CSC:d   MOD:    SNR:      ATC:      UD:02-07-85
   CP:bl      L:por      INT:    GPC:    BIO:    FIC:0     CON:b
   PC:s      PD:1981/            REP:    CPI:0   FSI:0     ILC:ab    MEI:1   II:0
   MMD:       OR:    POL:    DM:      RR:        COL:      EML:        GEN:  BSE:
   040        UPB#cUPB#dUPB
   043        s-bl---
   100 10     Monteiro, Hamilton de Mattos.
   245 10     Nordeste insurgente (1850-1890) /#cHamilton de Mattos Monteiro.
   260 0      S~ao Paulo :#bBrasiliense,#c1981.
   300        99 p. :#bill., maps ;#c16 cm.
   440 0      Tudo _e hist_oria ;#v10
   504        Bibliography: p. 98-99.
   651 0      Brazil#xHistory#y1822-1889.
```

Cataloging Example No. 3: LC Minimal Level Copy

```
PROD       Books      PAR       DCLC82143047-B          Search          NYCX-OCA
Cluster 47 of 57
+B
Santos, Joel Rufino dos.
  Hist_oria pol_itica do futebol brasileiro / Joel Rufino dos Santos. -- S~ao
Paulo-Brasil : Brasiliense, 1981.
  93 p. : ill. ; 16 cm. -- (Cole_c~ao Tudo _e hist_oria ; 20)

  Series.
  LCCN: 82143047
  L.C. CALL NO: MLCS 82/5005
  ID: DCLC82143047-B               CC: 9650       DCF: a
```

```
PROD       Books      FUL/BIB   DCLC82143047-B          Search          NYCX-OCA
Cluster 47 of 57
+B
  ID:DCLC82143047-B   RTYP:c    ST:p    FRN:    NLR:012001 MS:n EL:7 AD:04-14-82
  CC:9650  BLT:am      DCF:a    CSC:    MOD:    SNR:    ATC:         UD:01-01-01
  CP:???     L:por      INT:?   GPC:    BIO:?   FIC:?   CON:????
  PC:?       PD:1981/????        REP:?  CPI:?   FSI:?   ILC:????  MEI:?   II:?
  MMD:       OR:   POL:    DM:      RR:          COL:    EML:     GEN:   BSE:
  010      82143047
  020      #cCr$190.00
  040      #dCStRLIN
  050 0    MLCS 82/5005
  100 1    Santos, Joel Rufino dos.
  245 10   Hist_oria pol_itica do futebol brasileiro /#cJoel Rufino dos Santos.
  260      S~ao Paulo-Brasil :#bBrasiliense,#c1981.
  300      93 p. : ill. ; 16 cm.
  440      Cole_c~ao Tudo _e hist_oria ; 20
```

Cataloging Example No. 3: Full Cataloging Copy

```
PROD       Books      PAR       NYCX82-B38275          Search          NYCX-OCA
Cluster 47 of 57
+B
Santos, Joel Rufino dos.
  Hist_oria pol_itica do futebol brasileiro / Joel Rufino dos Santos. -- S~ao
Paulo-Brasil : Brasiliense, 1981.
  93 p. : ill. ; 16 cm. -- (Cole_c_ao Tudo _e hist_oria ; 20)

  Series: Tudo e_ hist_oria (1981) ; 20.
  LCCN: 82143047
  L.C. CALL NO: MLCS 82/5005
  ID: NYCX82-B38275               CC: 9110       DCF: a
- - - - - - - - - - - - - - - - - - - - - - - - - - - - - - - - - -
OLIN   GV944.B7S23
  c.1   (CAT 05/24/85)
    Acq: 82-B38275-1.
- - - - - - - - - - - - - - - - - - - - - - - - - - - - - - - - - -
 UID 82-B38275-1      UTYP DB    LSI              CPST CAT 05/22/85  UST P
```

```
PROD       Books      FUL/BIB   NYCX82-B38275          Search          NYCX-OCA
Cluster 47 of 57
+
  ID:NYCX82-B38275   RTYP:b    ST:p    FRN:    NLR:012001 MS:  EL:7 AD:06-21-82
  CC:9110  BLT:am     DCF:a    CSC:d   MOD:    SNR:    ATC:         UD:05-24-85
  CP:b1     L:por      INT:    GPC:    BIO:    FIC:0   CON:
  PC:s       PD:1981/           REP:   CPI:0   FSI:0   ILC:a     MEI:1   II:0
  MMD:       OR:   POL:    DM:      RR:          COL:    EML:     GEN:   BSE:
  010      82143047
  020      #cCr$190.00
  040      #dCStRLIN#dNIC
  043      s-bl---
  050 0    MLCS 82/5005
  100 10   Santos, Joel Rufino dos.
  245 10   Hist_oria pol_itica do futebol brasileiro /#cJoel Rufino dos Santos.
  260 0    S~ao Paulo-Brasil :#bBrasiliense,#c1981.
  300      93 p. :#bill. ;#c16 cm.
  490 1    Cole_c_ao Tudo _e hist_oria ;#v20
  650  0   Soccer#zBrazil.
  830  0   Tudo e_ hist_oria (1981) ;#v20.
```

48. MINIMUM LEVEL CATALOGING: THE USER

Mark L. Grover

Catalog departments have the distinction of being both the most misunderstood and the most mistrusted area of the library. Very few patrons, or for that matter librarians, have an understanding or appreciation of the cataloging process. Cataloging terminology is difficult to understand, and the use of a seemingly unlimited number of acronyms frightens most from trying to comprehend what catalogers do. All of these factors contribute to the myth that important books lie hidden in the catalog department, completely unavailable to noncataloging personnel for months and years. Most of the problems of the library somehow, eventually, will be blamed on catalogers.

Yet there is no area in the library that over the past twenty years has been more responsive to the discoveries and innovations of automation. Unfortunately, the catalogers' ventures into areas where other librarians feared to tread have resulted in another problem for which cataloging departments are again being criticized: the inability to deliver on the many promises of automation. One such unrealized expectation is that automation and the creation of national library networks would simultaneously eliminate cataloging backlogs and decrease the number of personnel required for cataloging. These perceptions, held mostly by those outside of cataloging, have led to frustration and conflict as the library continues to experience not only backlogs but also the need for additional personnel to maintain traditional levels of cataloging excellence.

The areas most significantly affected by continued backlogs have been foreign language materials from Third World countries. Research needs for these materials are perceived as limited, so that they can be backlogged without causing serious problems. Some books from Latin America have been backlogged for years while they await full cataloging by some other library in the network. However, even though the value of these items may be limited for the individual library, they are extremely important on a national level. Books published by major university presses in the United States are available in all research libraries and are easily obtainable. Third World publications purchased by only a few libraries are of immense importance for researchers across the nation. Because of the lack of publicity, oftentimes the only way researchers become aware of these items is through the cataloging information available in the national bibliographic networks. This is a need and responsibility seldom recognized by library administrators.

Minimum level or "less than full cataloging" is being suggested as a time-saving alternative that would eliminate cataloging
backlogs and make these items immediately available in the
national networks. This is not a new concept, since archives and
manuscript libraries have a tradition of doing less than full
cataloging for a certain percentage of their collections. It is but
a matter of time before all national networking organizations adopt
some type of minimum level cataloging standards.

As organizations establish the rules and regulations for
minimum level cataloging, it is important that they remember the
purpose of these changes: to improve library service to the
patron. The adjustments must be done in such a way as to not
significantly decrease this level of service. Notice the following
comment by Joseph R. Matthews: "Of all the components of the
online catalog--hardware, software, data bases--arguably, the
most important and least understood is the user. . . . Hardware
can be upgraded, software rewritten and databases improved,
but the user cannot be redesigned to match the 'needs of the
system' . . . . System behavior must conform to and complement
user behavior" (Matthews et al., 1983:84). The needs of the
patrons must continually be considered as changes are made in
the catalog.

An examination of catalog use studies conducted over the
past twenty years leaves several questions still open. Most of
the studies were limited in scope, and their results tentative. We
still lack a comprehensive and definitive study of catalog use that
provides a clear understanding about how the patron utilizes the
catalog. However, by combining the results of the several
studies, we can develop a feeling for catalog use (Beckman,
1982).

Studies on the use of the paper card catalog date back
several decades, and we can glean some relevant user attributes
as we review the results (Atherton, 1980; Lancaster, 1977).
Patrons came to the catalog more often with titles or key words
than with the names of authors. Author searching required about
five times as long as title searches. Most users did not persist
in their use of the catalog if the desired item was not obtained
after the first or second attempt. Few patrons knew the accepted
subject headings, but they were able to find the desired item by
beginning with nonstandard subject headings. Subject headings
were not specific enough, nor did they include the right information for the user to know if the book would give them what they
wanted. These studies also showed that, for the patron,
84 percent of all card catalog use centered on five elements:
author, title, call number, date of publication, and subject
heading. With contents notes included, the percentage of satisfaction increased to 90 percent. Most of these studies pointed
out the need for redundancy and multiple-access routes to the
cataloged items (Atherton, 1980:107).

Recent studies of the use of online catalogs are more relevant for understanding catalog usage in the future. Although the number of such studies is small, they still provide important information on how automation has changed catalog use. Use of the online system is much higher, and these catalogs are regarded much more favorably than card files. In the words of Joseph Matthews: "As with overall attitudes toward the online catalog, user's preferences for the online or the card catalog are rather strongly related to the search satisfaction and retrieval results, but even those who had unsuccessful or unsatisfactory searches seem to prefer the online catalog" (Matthews, 1983:152).

Researchers found that a much higher percentage of patrons used the online system for subject related searches than occurred with the card catalog. Increased success and less frustration with the system encouraged usage. Most came to the catalog with incomplete or inaccurate information, and consequently needed multiple access points to obtain the desired information. Given a preference, most users employed the key word and term searching retrieval capabilities of the computer system rather than standard subject headings or a controlled vocabulary. However, combining a key word with the standard subject headings was an important search strategy. A key word or term search could lead to a relevant item that identified subject headings, which could then be employed to search for related materials. A significant percentage of all searches used multiple access points (ibid., pp. 91, 147).

Only 28 percent of all online users found exactly what they sought. This low success rate is partly because most of the libraries studied had split collections, in which a significant percentage of materials were not online. However, 85 percent of the users found some relevant materials that partly satisfied their needs. Over half discovered useful items they had not anticipated. In the words of Matthews: "The number of pleasant 'surprises' now found by users of the online catalog is indeed encouraging. And, the more frequently the online catalog is used, the more likely the user will find other things of interest" (ibid., p. 150).

The reasons for search failures are obvious, but important to a discussion of minimum level cataloging. The online system could fail for one of three reasons: (1) The desired item was in the catalog but not found owing either to a searching error by the user or a mistake in the catalog; (2) the book was not in the library owing to a failure in collection development; (3) the item was in the library, but not online, because it was either in process or in a collection not incorporated within the system (ibid., pp. 149-150).

Latin American User

A second area to examine centers on the attributes of patrons seeking Latin American materials published in Spanish or Portuguese. Very few published studies have examined the use of foreign language materials. We know, however, that under-graduates will generally use English-language materials whenever possible. Graduate students also use English-language items for curriculum-related library use, although the use of foreign language materials increases substantially in research projects such as theses and dissertations. Faculty in general also rely on English language publications for curriculum needs, but use foreign language materials for research (Grover, 1985).

The library's success in meeting faculty and student research needs varies by discipline and by subject. However, all disciplines have informal systems to disseminate information and research results. Those systems allow the researcher to obtain information, books, and help from colleagues much more quickly than the library can provide. Libraries often are used to reaffirm or substantiate information already obtained, or tap information not available through the informal system (Price, 1967).

The informal system is active for most disciplines in Latin American Studies in the United States. However, there is a surprising lack of contact between scholars in Latin America and their counterparts in the United States. Distance, language, and professional pride all contribute to the lack of communication. Since the informal communications system between Latin America and the United States is generally not effective, the library often becomes the North American scholar's primary source of informa-tion about research occurring in Latin America. Taking into account the time lag between research and publication, an addi-tional two or three years for processing and cataloging drastically decreases the value of Latin American publications to library patrons (Grover, 1984).

Minimum Level Cataloging

Consequently, it is important that library materials from Latin America be made available as soon as possible. Ideally, all items would receive full cataloging, with as many access points and as much descriptive information as possible. However, since this is not likely to occur, the task is to limit the amount of information processed for each individual item in a way that substantially reduces cataloging time without significantly affecting user service.

I would like to suggest that the amount of information on the cataloging record is not the most significant obstacle in getting library materials onto the shelf and into the hands of the user. Less than full cataloging may now seem a viable solution, but it will in fact do little to eliminate the real problem involved in making library materials available to the researcher. Unless changes are made in areas other than cataloging, significant backlogs will persist.

The problem of cataloging lies in the failure of administrators in major research libraries to accept and maintain a commitment to the goals of national library consortiums and organizations. This is evident in the way cooperative cataloging groups have developed within OCLC and RLG. Library directors and administrators, rather than using these networks to significantly improve cataloging, have reduced cataloging staffs or changed the direction of their activities. Some libraries actually stopped cataloging new Latin American books altogether. Instead of each major research library in the country contributing its fair share, the cataloging of Latin American materials has been left to the few whose size and commitment require them to carry on. This type of arrangement works only if the library doing the cataloging is willing and able to consistently maintain a high level of production. When problems arise, and the responsible library is unable to maintain its cataloging pace, the entire country suffers (Grover, 1984).

As a stopgap measure, some libraries have instituted their own programs of minimum level cataloging, in which basic bibliographic information about new books is placed into in-house computer systems. This allows local users access to the books until another library in the national network completes full cataloging. This is an unfortunate reversion to preautomation days, in which libraries cataloged items with little regard for the national community. Why spend the money for a national network if libraries are unwilling to fully support it?

The United States is unique in the world because it does not have a national library in the same sense that other countries have one very strong central library. We have several libraries with large collections that are unique and not duplicated in Washington. Together they form our national library; they are brought together through organizations such as OCLC and RLG. The libraries within these organizations must therefore act as part of the national library to ensure that, somewhere within the system, all relevant and important items are being collected and cataloged. It is unacceptable that close to a third of all newly published Latin American books in libraries in the United States have not been cataloged, anywhere, a full two years after their acquisition (ibid.).

For various reasons, most English language books get cataloged somewhere shortly after their publication. The assignment of cataloging responsibility for these items would seem neither necessary nor productive. For non-English materials, however, research libraries must accept specific cataloging responsibilities so that these materials do become available. Should libraries accept priority cataloging responsibilities, there would be no need for less than full cataloging. Instead of each individual library duplicating minimum level cataloging, the item would be cataloged once or twice and become available to the rest of the country, as national-level cooperation originally promised.

My fear is that the acceptance of minimal level cataloging as a legitimate practice will lead us along the same path followed with automation à la OCLC or RLIN. Rather than allowing catalog departments to process more material, processing units will again be seen as candidates for budget and personnel cuts. The ultimate result of minimum level cataloging will not be a significant reduction of backlogs, or any increased availability of newly purchased materials to the user. Rather, we can only expect further degradation in the quality of cataloging. Whether we like it or not, backlogs protect what we have. Their absence makes us vulnerable to cutbacks.

Conclusion

History, however, has taught us that consistent national level cooperation, and the acceptance by individual libraries of full national responsibility, will probably never happen. We need to accept the reality of what is going to happen. Right now, that reality is one of less than full cataloging. Most users could live with minimum level cataloging as long as systems incorporate capabilities for key word or term searching. Without these attributes, the disruption of service will simply be too great.

BIBLIOGRAPHY

Atherton, Pauline. "Catalog Users' Access from the Researcher's Viewpoint: Past and Present Research Which Could Affect Library Catalog Design," in Closing the Catalog: Proceedings of the 1978 and 1979 Library and Information Technology Association Institutes. D. Kaye Gapen and Bonnie Juergens, eds. Phoenix, AZ: Oryx Press, 1980. Pp. 105-122.

Beckman, Margaret M. "Online Catalogs and Library Users," Library Journal, 107 (Nov. 1, 1982), 2043-2047.

Grover, Mark L. "Cataloging Comparison of OCLC and RLIN Systems: A Preliminary Report," SALALM Newsletter, 12 (Dec., 1984), 6-7.

_____. "Latin American History: Concerns and Conflicts." Unpublished paper, 1985.

Lancaster, F. W. The Measurement and Evaluation of Library Services. Washington, DC: Information Resources Press, 1977.

Matthews, Joseph R., et al., eds. Using Online Catalogs: A Nationwide Survey, A Report of a Study Sponsored by the Council of Library Resources. New York, NY: Neal-Schuman Publishers Inc., 1983.

Price, Derek J. de Solla. "Communication in Science: The Ends:
   Philosophy and Forecast," in Communication in Science: Docu-
   mentation and Automation. Anthony de Reuck and Julie
   Knight, eds. Boston, MA: Little, Brown and Co., 1967.
   Pp. 199-209.

49. THIRD WORLD DATABASES AND
THE NEW INFORMATION AGE

Barbara G. Valk

Within the last ten to fifteen years, computer technology has
revolutionized the production of basic bibliographic reference
sources much as it has altered nearly every aspect of our daily
lives, from the way we cook our food to the way we pay our
bills. Pioneered by the sciences in the 1960s, the trend toward
automation of bibliographic resources expanded rapidly to the
social sciences and the humanities in the 1970s. Today, nearly
all commercially published indexes and abstracting services, as
well as many ongoing bibliographies, are produced by computer.

The overwhelming growth in the use of automation to
generate bibliographic reference works has been made possible, of
course, by major technological advances which have at once
lowered costs, expanded text editing and database management
capabilities, and made computers far easier to use. Inexpensive
microcomputers and a plethora of commercially available software
now bring the advantages of computerized production within the
reach of more researchers than ever before. The obvious
efficiencies and concomitant reduction in staffing needs achieved
by the computer's abilities to sort and format complex data, to
replicate citations as often as necessary, to generate indexes and
create authority files, to store information indefinitely in machine-
readable form, and to produce formatted tapes for photocomposed
output (to itemize but a few of the advantages), clearly make this
mode of production the most logical and economical choice for
preparing any bibliographic publication.

Latin Americanist sources are no exception. In addition to
HAPI, automated indexes and bibliographies related to our field
include the Chicano Periodical Index; the California Spanish
Language Database, now known as the Hispanic Information
Exchange or HISPANEX; the PAIS Foreign Language Index; and
G. K. Hall's Bibliographic Guide to Latin American Studies,
produced by the University of Texas at Austin. The Handbook
of Latin American Studies, while not yet fully computerized, is
well along the road, having been selected several years ago to
serve as the pilot for automating all the bibliographies prepared
by the Library of Congress.

The question at hand, therefore, is not really whether automation is appropriate or economically feasible for the production
of subject specific Latin American bibliographic tools. Clearly
it is. Rather, we might more fruitfully examine the broader
economic issue of whether the market for specialized research

materials in the field of Latin American studies is sufficiently large or influential to support the cost of publishing even the most efficiently produced of the information sources we need. I would argue that, on its own, it is not. To publish our research resources successfully, on an ongoing basis, requires not only maximum efficiency but also substantial subsidies supplied either by the producer's institution, an outside source, or both.

HAPI is a case in point. This annual index to the contents of 250 Latin Americanist journals could never have been produced without the support of the thirty-five to forty volunteer indexers who supply the basic data for the work, ongoing financial help from UCLA, and major funding assistance from the National Endowment for the Humanities. Two initial NEH grants, covering most of the period from July, 1976 through September, 1980, fully subsidized the expense of subcontracting an off-campus vendor to develop an automated indexing system. The grants also supported basic staffing costs, providing HAPI the wherewithal to become financially established through the sales of three annual volumes.

Two more large grants were received from NEH for the period between February, 1981 and April, 1983, to support a three-volume set of retrospective HAPI indexes covering the years 1970-1974. That assistance supplied both additional staff and a programmer to rewrite the HAPI automated system for more efficient in-house operation on the University's mainframe computer. Through this investment HAPI has been able to reduce computer production costs by an impressive 80 percent, while shortening production time by one to two months per year and greatly increasing editorial control over the accuracy of the database.

While HAPI is no longer supported by federal grants, subsidies for processing and connect time are awarded annually by the University's Office of Academic Computing, virtually eliminating all technical production costs except for those associated with photocomposition, printing, and binding. Moreover, the UCLA Latin American Center continues to provide HAPI with some salary assistance, as well as office space, computer terminals, and basic supplies. Without these cost savings, an index the size and complexity of HAPI 1970-1974 could never have been produced, nor would the annual index have continued until now.

Still, the future remains uncertain. Salaries and printing costs continue to rise each year, while the market for the index remains determinedly inelastic. Nor does it appear that online access, as presently available, will provide a solution to HAPI's financial problems.

Today, online access represents the state-of-the-art technology for disseminating bibliographic information. Two relatively distinct types of services have emerged to provide this access.

In the first, MARC-formatted records for standard library materials are supplied to institutions by large-scale library information networks such as OCLC and RLIN. Although the primary function of these services is to facilitate cooperative cataloging and acquisitions efforts, they have recently begun to offer appropriately formatted specialized bibliographies as well.

Indexes, abstracts, and other nonstandard bibliographic sources are most commonly accessed online through private vendors of computer search services, such as DIALOG, BRS, Systems Development Corporation, and others. These firms standardize diverse database formats and market the files to information agencies on a subscription basis. Royalties are paid to producers on a percentage of usage.

Most indexes and abstracts in the sciences and social sciences are available through these vendors. Even some major humanities sources, such as the MLA Bibliography, can now be searched via a computer terminal. With the exception of the PAIS Foreign Language Index, however, this is not possible for materials in the field of Latin American studies.

A number of attempts have been made over the years to convince vendors that HAPI and other Hispanic databases should be ushered into the new information age through online access. All efforts to date have failed, however, owing to the demonstrated lack of market for specialized databases in small, interdisciplinary, humanities-oriented fields such as ours. No vendor will go to the expense of mounting and marketing a file, regardless of how valuable it may be to a particular interest group, unless the company is convinced that the data will be used enough to generate a profit. For the same reason, we as producers are unwilling to offer up our products as so-called "private databases," whereby the vendor makes the file available online, but the owner of the database assumes the risk of success or failure by paying all of the costs of mounting and maintaining the information. To this extent, therefore, there are indeed limitations to the accessibility of the "new technology" to Latin American studies.

It is questionable, however, whether this level of sophistication is really essential, or even perhaps desirable, to our information needs. Would we in fact use online access if it were available, or do we wish to have it simply because it does represent the state of the art? Many Latin Americanists still prefer to consult books rather than a computer terminal, and they can certainly do so far less expensively. Moreover, libraries have been known to cancel subscriptions to printed works if the information is available online through a vendor to which they subscribe. This is particularly true of highly specialized and relatively expensive sources, such as HAPI, for which there is limited perceived patronage.

It is doubtful that royalties from online usage would fully compensate for lost income from sales of the printed work. In HAPI's case, in consequence, online access through a commercial vendor would be a potentially mixed blessing at best. Producers of more widely marketed databases have speculated on this issue . . . and can afford to do so. HAPI cannot. Any reduction in sales at this time would be fatal.

This is not to say, however, that online access to Latin American materials is either wholly undesirable, or totally beyond the realm of possibility. In 1981, the UCLA Latin American Center began to explore the feasibility of developing a cooperative bibliographic database that would become self-sufficient solely on the basis of online usage and the sale of offline printouts on specific research topics. No competitive printed publication was planned.

Known as BorderLine, the database contains full MARC record citations to library materials in all formats and all disciplines related to the U.S./Mexican border region. It is maintained as a subfile of the University of California, Los Angeles, Library's online cataloging and acquisitions system, ORION, and as such is fully searchable by author, LC subject heading, and key word in title or series, as well as by a unique subject classification number designed specifically for the project.

With the assistance of a two-year NEH grant, awarded in May, 1984, BorderLine has grown to more than 5,000 items, and is now adding about 250 records per month. Although the project is still in its developmental stage, demand for the information is strong. Thirteen universities and research institutions in both the United States and Mexico have joined a UCLA-based consortium to collect appropriate data for the file in exchange for access to the database. A number of other institutions have inquired about paying for search-only access, and more and more individuals are writing or calling to request searches on specific topics.

Inexpensive online access to BorderLine is at present somewhat limited geographically by UCLA's lack of a satellite telecommunications system. A system of this kind, however, should become available within the next few years. In the meantime, possibilities are being explored to make the file accessible to a wider audience through RLIN and/or OCLC, or perhaps, because of its broad scope, even through a commercial vendor.

Whether BorderLine's constituency will prove adequate to support the rather substantial costs of staffing and maintaining an in-house database after the initial funding period ends remains unclear. Nonetheless, a second substantial grant, recently received from the Atlantic Richfield Foundation, lends hope that the concept is one enjoying enough appeal to attract additional support from other funding sources during the project's developmental period. In the future, conversion to a more flexible and

less expensive database management system, now under consideration by the University, would help to ensure BorderLine's
long-term continuation on an independent basis.

   At the very least, the BorderLine experiment represents a
major step toward harnessing the newest of the new technologies
to advance research in Latin American studies. If it proves
successful, the concept of maintaining an institutionally sponsored
online database, for which all revenues from usage would accrue
to the producer, may also hold the key to economically feasible
online access to HAPI at some time in the not-too-distant future.

50. EMERGING TECHNOLOGIES, BIBLIOGRAPHIC NETWORKS, AND AREA STUDIES PROGRAMS

David Zubatsky

Many Latin American bibliographers began their careers, like myself, in the 1960s and early 1970s--an era in which there may have been more national cooperative collection development activities than previously thought.

What do we have today to match LACAP and its associated activities, book stock, and publications; the Farmington Plan; priority cataloging of Latin American materials by the Library of Congress; an activist and economically viable OAS library support program; an internationally oriented USBE; major microfilming programs by a large number of institutions; and a variety of active but informal agreements among institutions on the local or regional levels?

Much of what I have mentioned above certainly seems to contradict the usual view that cooperative programs only can be justifiable and viable during times of budgetary stringency. Not being a specialist in any other field of area studies librarianship, I am not sure if Latin America represented the one exception to the rule.

Sure, there were problems with all of these cooperative activities; but again, how do these programs compare with what we have today? And how have the multitude of local, regional, and national automation projects today helped or hindered us in acquiring, processing, storing, and preserving Latin American materials?

Scott Bennett of Northwestern University argues in a recent article that the bibliographic utilities' accomplishments in the area of cooperative collective management have been quite modest.[1] Although Bennett is "optimistic that use of the [RLG] Conspectus will enable libraries to plan better for cooperative action on their collections," he is, at the same time, very concerned that "there is as yet little cooperative activity that meaningfully engages the priorities and resources of the partner libraries," and that "individually, the RLG libraries have done little in the management of their collections to reduce their autonomy and increase their dependence on one another."[2] Some of these issues are being studied under a Conoco, Inc. grant received by RLG. According to Bennett: "The Conoco project will allow us to get inside the Conspectus and address the financial issues involved in cooperation."[3] OCLC member libraries have not even taken some of the preliminary steps that RLG institutions have, although that may change in the future.

519

There is one statement with which we could all probably agree. It appears in the Association of the American Universities' Beyond Growth: The Next Stage in Language and Area Studies, and it reads as follows: "Few matters have come up with such regularity and with such a sense of impending crisis on our individual campuses, in various sections of government, and in the private foundations as has the condition of our national resources base for language and area studies."[4]

The report's title is controversial but, in today's world, it may be the most realistic one for both Latin American area programs and the libraries and their dedicated staffs that must support the teaching and research needs of program participants. Would you and/or your library and university administrators, therefore, agree with the report's assertion "that the period of expansion in programs of international and foreign area studies is over and that the main goal of policy be to sustain the base and improve its quality in various ways"?[5] I suppose we all could guess what the faculty concerned would say.

With the above perspective in mind, what did the authors have to say about library resource-sharing on the national level? They succinctly state their case by noting that "redundancy in area-related collections, coupled with rising costs and increases in the volume of materials to be acquired and stored, make it urgent that plans be developed for complementarity and shared resources among universities."[6]

The report recommended the following "strategy for collaboration and complementarity of resources":

> Language and area specialists must participate actively in the ongoing efforts of the national library networks to develop mechanisms for a division of labor and collaboration in the development of collections; and they must make their own supplemental plans. To these ends, a special task force ought to be created within each area studies group to engage in such planning. Preceding that planning, a number of studies of patterns of use of the collections could be undertaken.[7]

Certainly, SALALM has for several years had two separate committees that have been concerned with the activities of OCLC and RLG as they affect Latin American collections. Both RLG and OCLC have East Asian Advisory Committees. As far as I know, no committee or task force from the Latin American Studies Association, or any regional Latin American specialist's group, has approached OCLC. Such groups may have established contact with RLG.

All of the national bibliographic utilities were presumably established by individuals who believed that such organizations would best support the movement away from local self-sufficiency to nationwide interdependence in many endeavors. Increasing the availability of library resources to individual library patrons and limiting the growth of per unit costs, as well as enhancing access to and use of the ever-expanding body of knowledge and information worldwide, have certainly been major goals of our bibliographic utilities. The Research Libraries Group has developed along more programmatic lines than the other utilities, although OCLC's research library members appear more and more to want the same.

Even with the above goals and objectives in mind, have the national library networks met the needs of area studies librarians and the scholarly communities they serve? Are they now, or will they be, organized to allow for what the authors of Beyond Growth recommend? Can one area studies group (including librarians), or even several of them, have that much influence on things national or international, or even on the bibliographic utilities? Will we once again see the special needs and problems faced by any area studies collection submerged, as per the following recommendation in Beyond Growth: "A major review of problems with the area-related collections should be made, but from the perspective of the universities and general librarians in addition to the specialists attached to those collections"? Or are the authors just being realistic?

What about the emerging technologies and their impact upon bibliographic utilities and their members? Will these alleviate the special problems encountered by area studies librarians? If so, how? Maurice Line, a noted English information technology specialist, has suggested on several occasions that

> electronic technology will not provide more resources, of money, of stock, or of staff. It would be foolish not to use technology where it can be useful--always looking at the costs as well as the benefits--but it would be even more foolish to devote excessive attention to costly applications that will bear little fruit or to lose sight of faults in systems that require quite different solutions. Otherwise we are in danger of trying to automate a pantomime horse: costs will increase, performance will not improve, audiences will decline, and the horse may be electrocuted.

Like RLG, OCLC is moving outward from the centralized network now in place to a distributed network of cooperating computer systems. Both bibliographic utilities are developing intelligent work stations which will serve individual scholars and researchers. The decentralization will be accomplished through new system architectures, various interfaces, the Linked Systems Project, new optical disk and terminal technologies, intelligent gateways (both national and international), electronic document delivery systems, true international interlibrary loan agreements, and the like. In addition, OCLC is continuing to explore other ways that it can cooperate with all bibliographic utilities in order to improve its members' access to worldwide information.

But when will Latin American specialists see any payoff for your collections and their constituents for the money being used to develop these systems and these approaches to resource sharing? I very much doubt that it will be soon. The private and nonprofit sectors both place little emphasis on current cataloging standards and processes, bibliographic or nonbibliographic database creation, universal availability of information programs, local systems development, telecommunications links, and the like as they apply to Third World countries.

This is not to say that there has been no progress in attempting to provide unimpeded access to information being produced in developing countries. For example, OCLC has been negotiating with various East Asian and Middle Eastern libraries and governmental agencies to exchange bibliographic data. We have sent staff to Latin America to advise on local systems and telecommunications development. A few Latin American countries have sent automation specialists to OCLC, and an experiment with the University of the West Indies is now under way. Northwestern University's NOTIS Project has successfully sold its software to several Latin American countries. The Library of Congress is exchanging retrospective MARC records for Chilean commercial publications with the National Library of Chile. There is also hope that the renewed efforts now being planned for UNIMARC will be successful. But all these projects will take years to bear fruit. What can be done now? My personal view is that, instead of relying on automation and bibliographic networks to accomplish everything, Latin American specialists should take the bull by the horns--as was the case in the golden age of cooperative Latin American library projects--in order to carry out their agenda.

We all know, for example, that the Association of Research Libraries would like to see the Conspectus not only become a national standard for the description of collections but also be used in building national agreements for cooperative collection development. Maybe SALALM, through its membership and perhaps with added support from the Latin American Studies Association and the bibliographic utilities, could take the lead to see that Latin American studies is among the first fields in which ARL will implement both the regional and national collection development by-products of the Conspectus. Unlike any other area studies group, SALALM has had the successes that should impress ARL, the bibliographic utilities, and the funding agencies. Planning can never be too early. The success of such a program would no doubt reduce somewhat the autonomy of individual institutions in the management of their collections, as it would increase their dependence on one another. Will Latin American specialists and their institutions agree to that?

For the last several years, OCLC has had its own successful "UK CIP," or Cataloging-in-Publication, program. Possibly, arrangements can be made to incorporate a few other countries as well.

Maybe SALALM, with cooperation from various agencies, can also seek funding for retrospective conversion projects that would convert large amounts of specific Latin American material. (The recent ARL-proposed "Plan for a North American Program for Coordinated Retrospective Conversion" recommends Latin Americana as one of four priority areas for Phase I. One hopes that SALALM will have a role in any implementation.) Should there not be a larger role for area studies in the current cooperative authority and cataloging arrangements with the Library of Congress? Can we get HAPI more current, and then established as part of a national database vendor's offerings?

Of course, there are many other potential projects that you all can think of. The idea, however, will be for SALALM to work with other groups in order to implement its agenda. This will require compromise as well as a strong SALALM leadership to identify where SALALM's interests must be synchronized with those of other groups, including bibliographic utilities, for SALALM's agenda to succeed. Bibliographic utilities can provide the technology, but SALALM will have to provide the leadership and the agenda.

NOTES

1.   "Current Initiatives and Issues in Collection Management," Journal of Academic Librarianship, 10 (1984), 257-261.

2.   Ibid., p. 258.

3.   RLG News, 5 (1984), 13.

4.   Washington, DC, April, 1984, p. ix.

5.   Ibid., p. xi.

6.   Ibid., p. 251.

7.   Ibid., p. 253.

Part Five

The Tools of Understanding:
Bibliographies, Research Guides, and Finding Aids
for Latin American Masses and Minorities

INTRODUCTION

This final section of our <u>Papers</u> incorporates the various bibliographies and guides, sometimes compiled independently and sometimes as appendixes to narrative presentations, which were prepared for the conference. Using these bibliographies to conclude our volumes has been a deliberate choice. As we have considered Latin American masses and minorities, in their interrelated dimensions of image and reality, we have progressed from very broad philosophical and paradigmatic questions, to narrower analyses of particular phenomena and research problems, to the overt consideration of libraries' roles in Latin Americanist scholarship. In a sense, our sequence of topics has recapitulated the research process.

Now, as we present papers that detail the structures of particular literatures, and describe the resources apposite to specific research concerns, we bring the discussion full circle. Here images and realities, as captured in the existing documentation, are at last brought together. Bibliographies and guides allow us to summarize and evaluate past scholarship, and also to phrase new questions. As we employ these resources to contrapose existing assumptions, interpretations, and conclusions, we are inevitably drawn back into the dialectical cycle of research. Here, thus, we find works which are at one and the same time the culmination of the scholarly process and the starting point for new endeavors.

D.C.H.

51. WOMEN IN LATIN AMERICA: A PATHFINDER

Mina Jane Grothey

Scope

This bibliography reflects the areas of research used for my paper "Latin American Women and Liberation Theology" (Volume I, pp. 215-226). Emphasis has therefore been placed on sources about women under the assumption that the researcher has a basic familiarity with Latin American sources. Two other areas, women in development and in religion, are also emphasized. I have not included any country-specific works. Research on women in Latin America is still a relatively new field and this is reflected in the tools available. The items included here are only starting points.

Library of Congress Subject Headings

Women (Indirect)
Women--Developing countries (earlier Women--Underdeveloped areas)
Women--Latin America (earlier Women in Latin America)
Women--(name of country) (earlier Women in (name of country)

Feminism (Indirect)
Sex discrimination against women (Indirect)
Women's rights (Indirect)

Woman (Christian theology)
Woman (Theology)
Women in Christianity
Women and religion (Indirect)
Women--Religious life
Women in the Bible
Women clergy (earlier Women as ministers)
Ordination of women
Women's rights--Religious aspects

Bibliographies

Buvinic, Mayra. Women and World Development: An Annotated Bibliography. Washington, DC: Overseas Development Council, 1976.

Knaster, Meri. Women in Spanish America: An Annotated Bibliography from Pre-conquest to Contemporary Times. Boston, MA: G. K. Hall, 1977.

The standard in the field, although getting dated. Covers primarily secondary sources, and was compiled between late

529

1972 and 1974. It includes books, separate chapters, articles, pamphlets, and dissertations. Does not include fiction and poetry. Geographic coverage includes the Spanish-speaking countries of the Caribbean, Spanish America, and Middle America.

Grau, Ilda Elena. "La mujer en la sociedad latinoamericana: Su papel y su situación, bibliografía comentada." América Indígena, 38:2 (April-June, 1978), 475-511.

Saulniers, Suzanne Smith, and Cathy A. Rakowski. Women in the Development Process: A Select Bibliography on Women in Sub-Saharan Africa and Latin America. Austin, TX: Institute of Latin American Studies, University of Texas, 1977.

Searing, Susan. "Women and Politics in Latin America: A Selective Bibliography." Madison, WI: University of Wisconsin, Women's Studies Librarian-at-Large, 1984.

Women and Religion: A Bibliography Selected from the ATLA Religion Database. 3d rev. ed. Chicago, IL: American Theological Association, 1983.

Literature Reviews

General

Knaster, Meri. "Women in Latin America: The State of Research." Latin American Research Review, 11:1 (1976), 3-74.

Navarro, Marysa. "Research on Latin American Women: Review Essay." Signs, 5:1 (Autumn, 1979), 111-120.

Pescatello, Ann M. "The Female in Ibero-America: An Essay on Research Bibliography and Research Directions." Latin American Research Review, 7:2 (Summer, 1972), 125-141.

Soeiro, Susan A. "Recent Work on Latin American Women: A Review Essay." Journal of Interamerican Studies and World Affairs, 17:4 (Nov., 1975), 497-516.

Feminist Theology

Christ, Carol P. "The New Feminist Theology: A Review of the Literature." Religious Studies Review, 3 (1977), 203-212.

Summarizes and analyzes major works in the field. Excellent general overview.

Patrick, Anne E. "Women and Religion: A Survey of Significant Literature, 1965-1974." Theological Studies, 36 (1975), 737-765.

Miscellaneous

Boulding, Elise. Handbook of International Data on Women. New York, NY: Halstead Press, Sage, 1976.

Chaney, Elsa M. Women of the World: Latin America and the Caribbean. Washington, DC: U.S. Department of Commerce, Bureau of the Census, 1984.

Information derived from the WID database, which was started in 1977. Chapters include both narrative and statistical information on subjects such as population, economic activity, and literacy. For sale by Supt. of Docs., U.S. G.P.O.

Women in Development: A Resource Guide for Organization and Action. Geneva: ISIS International Women's Information and Communication Services, 1983.

Essays overlap in their coverage of various aspects of development. Each chapter usually includes bibliographical references and information on organizations in the area.

Indexes and Abstracts

In this section I only give detailed information on those for religion and women's studies. The special indexes for Latin America, the Handbook of Latin American Studies and HAPI, are necessary starting places. The general indexes, such as those from the H. W. Wilson Company, and the citation indexes should also be consulted.

Religious Indexes

Catholic Periodical and Literature Index. Haverford, PA: Catholic Library Association.

Provides an author and subject index to a selected list of Catholic periodicals on currently significant subjects. Also includes an annotated author-title-subject bibliography of adult books by Catholics and books of interest to Catholics by other authors.

Religion Index One: Periodicals. Chicago, IL: American Theological Library Association, 1977--.

Covers more than three hundred journals with preference given to those published in North America and to English-language journals from other countries. Also covers scholarly journals in Western European languages. In 1981 increased its coverage of Latin American sources.

Religion Index Two: Multi-Author Works. Chicago, IL: American Theological Library Association, 1976--.

Coverage for earlier dates provided by two companion volumes; Festschriften 1960-1969 and Multi-Author Works, 1970-1975. The whole set complements Religion Index One. Both parts are available online. Besides the special bibliography on women listed under Bibliographies, above, this group has also compiled one on liberation theology.

Bibliografía teológica comentada del area iberoamericana. Buenos
Aires: Instituto Superior Evangélico de Estudios Teológicos de
la Asociación Inter-Confesional de Estudios Teológicos, 1973--.

Has a very broad coverage of subjects for works published not
only in Latin America but also in Spain and Portugal. There
is a subject index and an author index for added access. An
additional feature is the Biblical citation index. Abbreviations
are used for journal titles, and the list of these abbreviations
includes addresses for new titles. Many sections are preceded
by a brief introductory essay.

Indexes on Women

Women Studies Abstracts. Rush, NY: Rush Publishing, 1972--.

Arranged by broad subject categories, though not every issue
includes a section on religion. Most recently, the heading has
become "Religion, Philosophy, and Ethics." The format and
indexing have varied over the years. There is supposed to be
an annual cumulative index for each volume, though the latest
available is for volume 7. The indexes allow one to search by
specific subjects, including the names of countries. Many
times the index will refer users from Latin America or South
America to the individual countries.

Women's Annual (1980--): The Year in Review. Boston, MA:
G. K. Hall, 1981--.

The first two volumes include separate chapters on religion,
while the third discussed the subject as part of the section on
humanities. Each volume consists of narrative essays followed
by a bibliography. The first two volumes also include a
chapter called "Third World Women in America."

Journals

The following is a brief list of journals in the area of
women's studies.

Fem. México, DF: Nueva Cultura Feminista, 1976--.

One of many magazines from Latin America.

Journal of Women and Religion. Berkeley, CA: Center for Women
and Religion, Graduate Theological Union, 1981--.

Off Our Backs. Washington, DC, 1970--.

"A women's news journal." Often contains information on
feminist activities in Latin America.

Resources for Feminist Research. Toronto: Ontario Institute for
Studies in Education, 1972--.

"A Canadian journal for Feminist scholarship."

Signs.   Chicago, IL: University of Chicago Press, 1975--.

"Journal of women in culture and society." Probably the top journal in the field.

Other Resources

Many libraries, as at the University of New Mexico, have a women's studies librarian. One repository with an active publications program is:

Susan E. Searing
Women's Studies Librarian-at-Large
The University of Wisconsin
712A Memorial Library
728 State Street
Madison, WI 53706

Another source on many campuses is the women's center. An example of one with an emphasis on development issues is:

Office of Women in International Development
Michigan State University
202 International Center
East Lansing, MI 48824-1035

There are in addition many other types of resources which can be located through some of the works listed earlier.

52. SOURCES ON THE THEOLOGY OF LIBERATION IN LATIN AMERICA: JOURNALS, NEWSLETTERS, PERIODICALS, RESEARCH INSTITUTES

John Blazo

Publications Focusing on Social Issues

Central America Report
Inforpress Centro-Americana
9a Calle "A", 3-56
Zona 1, Guatemala

Weekly. Independent, analytical

Central American Update
P.O. Box 2207
Station P
Toronto, Ontario
Canada M5S 2T2

Alternate press

Denuncia
P.O. Box 134
Times Square Station
New York, NY 10108-0134

Alternate press

LARU Studies
Box 673
Adelaide St. P.O.
Toronto, Ontario
Canada M5C 2J8

2-3 per year. Alternate press

Latinamerica Press
Apartado 5594
Lima 100
Peru

Weekly. Independent

Latin America Weekly Report
91-93 Charterhouse St.
London EC1 M6LN
England

Weekly. Political, economic
analysis

LAWG Letter
Latin America Working Group
Box 2207, Sta. P
Toronto, Ontario
Canada M5S 2T2

4 per year. Alternate press

Mesoamérica
Inst. for Central American
Studies
Apartado 300
1002 San José
Costa Rica

Update--Latin America
Washington Office on Latin
America (WOLA)
110 Maryland Ave.
Washington, DC 20002

Alternate press

Washington Report on the
Hemisphere
The Council on Hemispheric
Affairs (COHA)
1900 L Street
Washington, DC 20036

Alternate press

Publications on Latin America and the Caribbean
Specializing in Theology, Church, and Social Issues

Amanecer
Apartado Postal 3205
Managua
Nicaragua

From Centro Valdivieso in
 Managua

Boletín CELAM
Consejo Episcopal
 Latinoamericano
Apartado Aéreo 51086
Bogotá, D.C.
Colombia

Monthly

Cadernos do CEAS
Centro de Estudos e Ação Social
Rua Aristides Novis, 101
40,000 Salvador
Bahia, Brazil

Bimonthly

Caribbean Contact
Caribbean Conference of Churches
P.O. Box 616
Bridgetown
Barbados, W.I.

Caribbean Journal of
 Religious Studies
The United Theological College
 of the West Indies
P.O. Box 136
Golding Avenue
Mona, Kingston 7
Jamaica, W.I.

Centro Puebla
Apartado 30.522
Caracas 1030 "A"
Venezuela

10 per year

Christus
Apartado Postal 19-213
Colonia Mixcoac
Delegación Benito Juárez 03910
México, DF
México

Comunidad
SERPAC
J.B. Justo 33
(8300) Neuquén
Argentina

Diocesan magazine on
 church and social issues

Criterio
Alsina 840
Buenos Aires
Argentina

Cultura Popular
CELADEC
General Garzón 2267
Lima 11
Peru

4 per year. Popular education

De Pie
Diócesis de Viedma
Irigoyen 71
(8500) Viedma
Río Negro
Argentina

Diocesan magazine on
 church and social issues

Envío
Instituto Histórico Centro
 Americano
Apartado A-194
Managua
Nicaragua

Focus on Catholic church in
 current Nicaragua

Envío subscriptions to:
Central American Historical
  Institute
Intercultural Center
Georgetown University
Washington, DC 20057

IDOC Bulletin
Via S. Maria dell'Anima 30
00166 Rome
Italy

Monthly

Informes de Pro Mundi Vita:
  América Latina
Pro Mundi Vita
Rue de la Limite 6
B-1030 Brussels
Belgium

Occasional

International Inter-
  communication, COELI
Rue du Boulet 31
B-1000 Brussels
Belgium

LADOC (Latin American
  Documentation)
LADOC
Apartado 5594
Lima 100
Peru

Medellín
Apartado Aéreo 1931
Medellín
Colombia

4 per year

Mensaje
Almirante Barroso 24
Casilla 10445
Santiago
Chile

Monthly

New Blackfriars
New Blackfriars
Oxford
England

Monthly. Occasional articles
  on theology of liberation

Overview
Thomas More Association
223 West Erie Street
Chicago, IL 60610

11 per year

Páginas
Centro de Estudios y
  Publicaciones (CEP)
Apartado 6118
Lima
Peru

Monthly. Related to Gustavo
  Gutiérrez and reflection team

Pastoral Popular
Centro Ecuménico Diego
  de Medellín
Casilla 386-V
Santiago 21
Chile

Focus from basic Christian
  communities

Puebla
Editora Vozes
25600 Petrópolis
Rio de Janeiro
Brazil

Revista Eclesiástica
  Brasileira (REB)
Editora Vozes Limitada
Rua Frei Luis 100
25600 Petrópolis
Rio de Janeiro
Brazil

4 per year. Church issues,
  theology of liberation

Revista Latinoamericana
  de Teología
Universidad Centroamericana
  José Simeón Canas
Apartado (01) 668
San Salvador
El Salvador

4 per year

Selecciones de Teología
Rosellón, 223
Barcelona 8
Spain

4 per year

Servir
Apartado Postal 334
9100 Jalapa
Veracruz
Mexico

4 per year

SIC
Centro Gumilla
Av. Berrizbeitia 14
El Paraíso
Apartado 29056
Caracas
Venezuela

Solidaridad
Solidaridad
Casilla 26-D
Santiago
Chile

Santiago Archdiocese. Biweekly.
  Focus on human rights

The Tablet
48 Great Peter Street
London SW1 P2HB
England

Catholic weekly

Teología y Vida
Diagonal Oriente 3300
Casilla 114-D
Santiago
Chile

4 per year

Tiempo Latinoamericano
Obispo Trejo 772
(5000) Córdoba
Argentina

Vozes
Editora Vozes
Caixa Postal 23
25600 Petrópolis
Rio de Janeiro
Brazil

Research Institutes

Instituto Latino Americano de
  Doctrina y Estudios Sociales
  (ILADES)
Almirante Barrosa 6
Casilla 14446. C21
Santiago
Chile

Research projects on recent
  evolution of theology of
  liberation, 1984. (F. Moreno,
  Raúl Vergara, J. Donoso)

53. PROTESTANTISM IN LATIN AMERICA AND THE CARIBBEAN: A PRELIMINARY LIST OF MOSTLY POST-1975 MATERIALS

Sonia M. Merubia

General Titles

Alliende Luco, Joaquín. "Reflexiones sobre religiosidad popular en América Latina." Criterio, 50:1763 (12 May 1977), 228-233.

Bastian, Jean Pierre. "Protestantismos latinoamericanos entre la resistencia y la sumisión, 1961-1983." Cristianismo y sociedad, 12:82 (1984), 49-68.

Clawson, David L. "Religious Allegiance and Economic Development in Rural Latin America." Journal of Inter-American Studies and World Affairs, 26:4 (Nov., 1984), 499-521.

Consejo de Iglesias Evangélicas Metodistas de América Latina. Boletín. La Paz, 1978--.

Cultura popular. Lima: Consejo Evangélico Latino Americano de Educación Cristiana, 1976--.

Glazier, Stephen D., ed. Perspectives on Pentecostalism: Case Studies from the Caribbean and Latin America. Washington, DC: University Press of America, 1980. Reviewed by Carol L. Dow in Americas, 33 (June-July, 1981), 23-24, and by André Droogers in Boletín de Estudios Latinoamericanos y del Caribe, 36 (June, 1984), 151-152.

Indice de materias de publicaciones periódicas bautistas. San Antonio, TX: Instituto Bíblico Bautista, 1975--.

Millet, Richard L. "The Perils of Success: Post-World War II Latin American Protestantism." In L. Brown, ed., Religion in Latin American Life. Waco, TX: Markham Press Fund, 1980. Pp. 52-66.

Montgomery, T. S. "Latin American Evangelicals: Oaxtepec and Beyond." In Daniel H. Levine, ed., Churches and Politics in Latin America. Beverly Hills, CA: Sage, 1980. Pp. 87-107.

Nelson, Wilton M. "Bosquejo y bibliografía para una historia del protestantismo en América Latina." In B. Melia, ed., Para una historia de la evangelización. Barcelona: Editora Nueva Tierra, 1977. Pp. 179-189.

Norman, Edward. Christianity in the Southern Hemisphere: The Churches in Latin America and South Africa. Oxford: Clarendon Press, 1981.

Oaxtepec un año después; aportes y documentos. Lima: Comisión Evangélica Latino Americana de Educación Cristiana, 1981.

Orr, J. Edwin. Evangelical Awakenings in Latin America. Minneapolis, MN: Bethany Fellowship, Inc., 1978. Reviewed by Cornelia Butler Flora in Hispanic American Historical Review, 59 (Aug., 1979), 569-570.

Prien, Hans-Jürgen. "Der Protestantismus in Lateinamerika von der Herausforderungen der Entwicklungsproblematik." Zeitschrift für Lateinamerika (Wien), 20 (1981), 21-41.

Suess, Pablo. Culturas indígenas y evangelización. Lima: Centro de Estudios y Publicaciones, 1983.

Vargas, Bertha. "Cristianas protestantes en América Latina." Fem, 5:20 (Aug., 1981-Jan., 1982), 85-89.

Ecumenical Titles

Carta mensual de evangelización. La Paz: Comisión Mundial de Misión y Evangelización, 1978--.

Christian Action. Bridgetown: Caribbean Conference of Churches, 1974--.

Christian Action for Development in the Caribbean. CADEC-ARC Annual Report. Bridgetown: Caribbean Conference of Churches, 1981--.

Hutt, Maurice Bateman. "Windows to the Sea": A Report to CADEC on the Establishment of Coastal Facilities along the South and West Coasts of Barbados. . . . Bridgetown: The Cedar Press, 1980.

Men of Vision. Kingston: The Jamaica Council of Churches, 1981.

Paz y justicia. Buenos Aires: 1983--.

Smith, Ashley A., and Michael De Verteuil. Renewal and Ecumenism in the Caribbean. [Bridgetown?]: CADEC, [197_?].

Missiology

Arias, Mortimer. "That the World May Believe." Mission Trends, 3 (1976), 84-103.

Costas, Orlando E. Theology of the Crossroads in Contemporary Latin America: Missiology in Mainline Protestantism, 1969-1974. Amsterdam: Rodopi, 1976.

_____. "Tradition and Reconstruction in Mission: A Latin American Protestant Analysis." Occasional Bulletin of Missionary Research, 1 (Jan., 1979), 4-8.

Elliot, Elisabeth. Through Gates of Splendor. Rev. ed. Wheaton, IL: Living Books, Tyndale House Publishers, 1981.

Goff, James, and Margaret Goff. In Every Person Who Hopes . . . The Lord Is Born Every Day. New York, NY: Friendship Press, 1980.

In Other Words. Huntington Beach, CA: Wycliffe Bible Translators, 1975--.

Keyes, Lawrence E. "The New Age of Missions: A Study of Third World Missionary Societies." Ph.D. diss., Fuller Theological Seminary, 1981.

Küng, Andrés. Bruce Olson: Missionary or Colonizer. Chappaqua, NY: Christian Herald Books, 1981.

El mensajero luterano. El Paso, TX: Wisconsin Evangelical Lutheran Synod, 1975--.

Niklaus, Robert. "Latin America: Counter-evangelism." Evangelical Missions Quarterly, 19 (July, 1983), 259-270.

Ninomiya, Tadahiro. Pastorale Missiologie; Die Protestantische Theologie in Latein-Amerika am Beispiel Emilio Castro. Europäiche Hochschulschriften/Publications Universitaires Européennes, Reihe XXIII Theologie. Frankfurt-am-Main: Peter D. Lang, 1980.

Olson, Bruce. Bruchko. Carol Stream, IL: Creation House, 1978.

Tambo Newsletter. Cochabamba: New Tribes Mission School, 1979--.

Theology: General

Arias, Esther, and Mortimer Arias. The Cry of My People. New York, NY: Friendship Press, 1980.

Arias, Mortimer. Venga Tu Reino. La memoria subversiva de Jesús. México, DF: Casa Unida de Publicaciones, 1980. Engl. trans., Philadelpha, PA: Fortress Press, 1984.

Duque, José, ed. La tradición protestante en la teología latino-americana. Primer intento, lecturas de la tradición metodista. San José: Departamento Ecuménico de Investigaciones, 1983. Reviewed by Juan Stam in Anuario de Estudios Centro-americanos, 9 (1983), 169-170.

Echegaray, Hugo. Anunciar el reino. Lima: Centro de Estudios y Publicaciones, 1981.

Furter, Pierre. "Nouvelles Perspectives sur le Role des Croyances dans le Developpement de l'Amérique Latine." Revue d'Histoire et de Philosophie Religieuses, 57 (1977), 523-532.

Gibellini, Rosino, ed. Frontiers of Theology in Latin America. Maryknoll, NY: Orbis Books, 1979.

Melano Couch, Beatriz. "New Visions of the Church in Latin America: A Protestant View." In S. Torres, ed., The Emergent Gospel. Maryknoll, NY: Orbis Books, 1978. Pp. 193-226.

Míguez Bonino, José. Ama y haz lo que quieras. Hacia una ética del hombre nuevo. Buenos Aires: Escatón, 1976.

_____. Room To Be People: An Interpretation of the Message of the Bible for Today's World. Wickie Leach, trans. Philadelphia, PA: Fortress Press, 1979.

Míguez Bonino, José, ed. Jésus. Ni vencido ni monarca celestial (imágenes de Jesucristo en América Latina). Buenos Aires: Tierra Nueva, 1977. Engl. trans., Maryknoll, NY: Orbis Books, 1983.

Reconozcamos al Señor. Una espiritualidad evangélica desde América Latina. Colección "Por los frutos los conocerán." 4-6. San José: Departamento de Publicaciones, Seminario Bíblico Latinoamericano, 1983.

Vida y pensamiento. San José: Seminario Bíblico Latinoamericano, 1981--.

Wagner, C. Peter. What Are We Missing? Carol Stream, IL: Creation House, 1978.

Liberation Theology

Alvarez, Carmelo E. "Latin American Protestantism, 1969-1978." In S. Torres, ed., The Challenge of the Basic Christian Communities. Maryknoll, NY: Orbis Books, 1981. Pp. 103-106.

Bonnín, Eduardo, ed. Espiritualidad y liberación en América Latina. San José: Departamento Ecuménico de Investigaciones, 1982.

Davis, Kortright, ed. Moving into Freedom. Bridgetown: The Cedar Press, 1977.

Encuentro Latinoamericano de Mujeres. Comunidad de mujeres y hombres en la iglesia. San José: Seminario Bíblico Latinoamericano, 1981.

Escobar, Samuel. "Search for Freedom, Justice and Fulfillment." Mission Trends, 3 (1976), 104-110.

Farré, Luis. Libertad y riesgo, en una teología del hombre y el mundo. Buenos Aires: Editorial La Aurora, 1976.

Galilea, Segundo. "Evangelization and Cultural Liberation." Mission Trends, 3 (1976), 70-76.

Kirk, J. Andrew. Liberation Theology: An Evangelical View from the Third World. Atlanta, GA: John Knox Press, 1979.

Míguez Bonino, José. Christians and Marxists: The Mutual Challenge to Revolution. Grand Rapids, MI: Eerdmans, 1976.

Movimientos populares por la liberación. Lima: Comisión Evangélica Latino Americana de Educación Cristiana; Geneva: Comisión para la Participación de las Iglesias en el Desarrollo, 1981.

Neely, Alan Preston. "Protestant Antecedents of the Latin American Theology of Liberation." Ph.D. diss., American University, 1977.

Participación de los cristianos en el desarrollo en contextos socialistas. Lima: Comisión Evangélica Latino Americana de Educación Cristiana; Geneva: Comisión para la Participación de las Iglesias en el Desarrollo, 1980.

Robb, Carol Sue. "Integration of Marxist Constructs into the Theology of Liberation." Ph.D. diss., Boston University, 1978.

Santa Ana, Julio de. El desafío de los pobres a la iglesia. San José: EDUCA, 1977.

Silva Gotay, Samuel. El pensamiento cristiano revolucionario en América Latina y el Caribe. Implicaciones de la teología de la liberación para la sociología de la religión. 2a ed. Río Piedras: Cordillera Ediciones Sígueme, 1983.

Sobrino, Jon. "La promoción de la justicia como exigencia esencial del mensaje evangélico." Estudios Centroamericanos, 34:371 (Sept., 1979), 779-792.

Stähli, Martin Johann. Reich Gottes und Revolution: Christliche Theorie und Praxis für die Armen dieser Welt. Die Theologie des Religiösen Sozialismus bei Leonhard Ragaz und die Theologie der Revolution in Latein-Amerika. Hamburg-Bergstedt: Herbert Reich Evangelischer Verlag, 1976.

Winter, Derek. Hope in Captivity: The Prophetic Church in Latin America. London: Epworth Press, 1977.

Protestantism in the Caribbean

Archer, Colin Baltron. Poverty, the Church's Abandoned Revolution: A Scientific, Biblical and Theological Commentary. Nassau: Colmar Publications, 1980.

Baytop, Adrianne. "James Baldwin and Roger Mais: The Pentecostal Theme." Jamaica Journal, 42 (n.d.), 14-21.

Chevannes, Barrington. "Revivalism: A Disappearing Religion." Caribbean Quarterly, 24:3-4 (Sept.-Dec., 1978), 1-17.

Conway, Frederick James. "Pentecostalism in the Context of Haitian Religion and Health Practice." Ph.D. diss., American University, 1978.

Cornevin, Robert. "A propos du pasteur François Ledin, 1825-1892, missionaire á Jeremie et pasteur d'Oran." Conjonction, 141-142 (Feb., 1979), 53-61.

Cristo vivo en Cuba. Reflexiones teológicas cubanas. San José: Departamento Ecuménico de Investigaciones, 1978.

Glazier, Stephen Davey. "Leadership Roles, Church Organization, and Ritual Change among the Spiritual Baptists of Trinidad." Ph.D. diss., University of Connecticut, 1981.

Goodridge, Sehon S. Facing the Challenge of Emancipation: A Study of the Ministry of William Hart Coleridge, First Bishop of Barbados, 1824-1842. Bridgetown: The Cedar Press, 1981.

Hastings, Selvin U. Seedtime and Harvest: A Brief History of the Moravian Church in Jamaica, 1754-1979. N.p.: Moravian Church Corp., 1979.

Hilty, Hiram H. Friends in Cuba. Richmond, IN: Friends United Press, 1977.

Hopkin, John Barton. "Music in the Jamaican Pentecostal Churches." Jamaica Journal, 42 (n.d.), 23-40.

Lefleur, Gerard. Présence protestante en Guadeloupe au XVIIe siècle. Pointe-a-Pitre: Centre Documental de Documentation Pédagogique de la Guadeloupe, 1980.

Lockward, George A. El protestantismo en Dominicana. 2a ed. Publicaciones de la Universidad CETEC, Serie Historia, III. Santo Domingo: Editora Educativa Dominicana, 1982.

Manning, Frank E. "Religion and Politics in Bermuda: Revivalist Politics and the Language of Power." Caribbean Review, 8:4 (Fall, 1979), 18-21.

Mount, Graeme Stewart. "The Canadian Presbyterian Mission to Trinidad, 1868-1912." Revista Interamericana, 7:1 (Spring, 1977), 30-45.

Pérez-Torres, Rubén. "The Pastor's Role in Educational Ministry in the Pentecostal Church of God in Puerto Rico." Ph.D. diss., School of Theology at Claremont, 1979.

Pottinger, George. "Analysis and Evaluation of the Contribution of the Methodist Missionary Society of Jamaica, 1938-1967." Ph.D. diss., Boston University, 1977.

Puig Ortiz, José Augusto. Emigración de libertos norteamericanos a Puerto Rico en la primera mitad del siglo XIX. La Iglesia Metodista Wesleyana. Santo Domingo: Puig Ortiz, 1978.

Romain, Charles Poisset. "Introduction à la sociologie du protestantisme en Haïti." Conjonction, 141-142 (Feb., 1979), 35-48.

Rooke, Patricia T. "Evangelical Missionaries, Apprentices and Freedmen: The Psycho-Sociological Shifts of Racial Attitudes in British West Indies." Caribbean Quarterly, 25:1-2 (March-June, 1979), 1-14.

Smith, Ashley A. "Pentecostalism in Jamaica." Jamaica Journal, 42 (n.d.), 3-13.

Symonette, Michael C., and Antonina Cazoneri. Baptists in the Bahamas: An Historical Review. Nassau: Symonette and Cazoneri, 1977.

Tindall, John. Correspondencia de Tindall, primer misionero protestante en Dominicana. George A. Lockward, ed. Publicaciones de la Universidad CETEC, Serie Historia, I. Santo Domingo: Editora Educativa Dominicana, 1981.

Tschuy, Theo. Hundert Jahre Kubanischer Protestantismus (1868-1961): Versuch e. Kirchengeschichtl. Deitung. Frankfurt-am-Main: Lang, 1978.

Turner, Mary. Slaves and Missionaries: The Disintegration of Jamaican Slave Society, 1787-1834. Urbana, IL: University of Illinois Press, 1982.

Villalón, José Ramón. "Ser cristiano en Cuba." Areito, 5:18 (1979), 5-10.

White, Tom. Missiles Over Cuba. Diamond Bar, CA: Uplift Books, 1981.

Williams, Colbert. The Methodist Contribution to Education in the Bahamas, Circa 1790 to 1975. Gloucester: Alan Sutton, 1982.

Winkelman, Winnifred. "Barbadian Cross-Currents: Church-State Confrontation with Quaker and Negro, 1660-1689." Ph.D. diss., Loyola University of Chicago, 1976.

Protestantism in Central America

Belli P., Humberto. Persecution of Protestants in Nicaragua: The Neglected Story. N.p.: 1983.

Los Cristianos en la revolución nicaragüense. Lima: Consejo Evangélico Latinoamericano de Educación Cristiana, 1980.

Domínguez, Enrique. "The Great Commission." NACLA Report on the Americas, 18:1 (Jan.-Feb., 1984), 12-33.

Ferris, George Irwin, Jr. "Protestantism in Nicaragua: Its Historical Roots and Influences Affecting Its Growth." Ph.D. diss., Temple University, 1981.

Huntington, Deborah. "God's Saving Plan." NACLA Report on the Americas, 18:1 (Jan.-Feb., 1984), 23-34.

_____. "The Prophet Motive." NACLA Report on the Americas, 18:1 (Jan.-Feb., 1984), 2-11.

Instituto Histórico Centroamericano. El evangelio en la revolución. Managua: Instituto Histórico Centroamericano, 1979.

Minnery, Tom. "Why the Gospel Grows in Socialist Nicaragua: The Revolution Turned Against Capitalism but not Christianity." Christianity Today, 27 (April, 1983), 34-42.

Mulholland, Kenneth. Adventures in Training the Ministry: A Honduran Case Study in Theological Education by Extension. N.p.: Presbyterian and Reformed Publishing Company, 1976.

Nelson, Wilton M. El protestantismo en Centro América. Miami, FL: Editorial Caribe, 1982.

Reflexión cristiana y revolución sandinista. Lima: Comisión Evangélica Latino Americana de Educación Cristiana, 1979.

Sider, Ronald J. "Who Is My Neighbor: Nicaraguan Evangelicals Host U.S. Evangelicals." T.S.F. Bulletin, 6:4 (March-April, 1983), 11-13.

Taylor, William David. "Worlds in Conflict: The Impact of the University Social Structure on Protestant Students in the National University of Guatemala." Ph.D. diss., University of Texas at Austin, 1976.

Wilson, Everett A. "Sanguine Saints: Pentecostalism in El Salvador." Church History, 52 (June, 1983), 186-198.

Protestantism in Mexico

Barabas, Alicia M. "Mesianismo chinanteco. Una respuesta político-religiosa ante la crisis." Revista Mexicana de Ciencias Políticas y Sociales, 23:88 (April-June, 1977), 53-85.

Berninger, Dieter. "Immigration and Religious Toleration: A Mexican Dilemma, 1821-1860." The Americas, 32:4 (April, 1976), 549-565.

Boletín teológico. Cuernavaca: La Fraternidad Teológica Latino-americana, 1980--.

Bridges, Julian C. "Evangelical Expansion in Mexico: A Study of the Number, Distribution, and Growth of the Protestant Population, 1857-1970." In L. Brown, ed., Religion in Latin American Life. Waco, TX: Markham Press Fund, 1980. Pp. 150-168.

Clawson, David Leslie. "Religion and Change in a Mexican Village." Ph.D. diss., University of Florida, 1976.

Dorantes, Alma. Intolerancia religiosa en Jalisco. Centro Regional de Occidente, 29. Guadalajara: Instituto Nacional de Antropología e Historia, Dirección de Centros Regionales, 1976.

Garma Navarro, Carlos. "Liderazgo protestante en una lucha campesina en México." América Indígena, 44:1 (Jan.-March, 1984), 127-141.

El Instituto Lingüístico de Verano. México, DF: Revista Proceso, 1981.

Patterson, Frank W. A Century of Baptist Work in Mexico. El Paso, TX: Baptist Spanish Publishing House, 1979.

Rus, Jan, and Robert Wasserstrom. "Evangelización y control político: El Instituto Lingüístico de Verano (ILV) en México." Revista Mexicana de Ciencias Políticas y Sociales, 25:97 (July-Sept., 1979), 141-159.

Protestantism in South America

Argentina

Canclini, Arnoldo. Allen F. Gardiner, marino, misionero, mártir. Buenos Aires: Ediciones Marymar, 1979.

_____. Cómo fue civilizado el sur patagónico. Buenos Aires: Editorial Plus Ultra, 1977.

_____. "La correspondencia de John Armstrong, primer pastor anglicano en la Argentina." Investigaciones y ensayos, 28 (Jan.-June, 1980), 357-368.

_____. Jorge A. Humble, médico y misionero patagónico. Buenos Aires: Ediciones Marymar, 1980.

_____. Tomás Bridges, pionero en Ushuaia. Buenos Aires: Ediciones Marymar, 1980.

_____. Waite H. Stirling, el centinela de Dios en Ushuaia. Buenos Aires: Ediciones Marymar, 1980.

Miller, Elmer S. Los tobas argentinos: Armonía y disonancia en una sociedad. México, DF: Siglo Veintiuno, 1979.

Montes de Oca, Alba. Mi Dios y mis tobas. Buenos Aires: Junta Bautista de Publicaciones, 1976.

Monti, Daniel P. Ubicación del metodismo en el Río de la Plata. Buenos Aires: Editorial La Aurora, 1976.

Ruggiero, Kristin. "Italians in Argentina: The Valdenses at Colonia San Gustavo, 1850-1910." Ph.D. diss., Indiana University, 1979.

Sinclair, Maurice. Green Finger of God. Exeter: Paternoster Press, 1980.

Vox evangelii. 2a serie. Buenos Aires: Facultad de Teología, Instituto Superior Evangélico de Estudios Teológicos, 1984--.

Brazil

Alves, Rubem A. Protestantismo e repressão. São Paulo: Editora Attica, 1979. Reviewed by Geraldo Bonadio in Convivium, 23:1 (Jan.-Feb., 1980), 96-100; by Pedro Demo in Vozes, 73:8 (Oct., 1979), 73-74; and by Paulo José Krischke in Hispanic American Historical Review, 60:4 (Nov., 1980), 728-730.

Brandão, Carlos Rodrigues. Os deuses do povo. Un estudo sobre a religião popular. São Paulo: Livraria Brasiliense Editora, S.A., 1980.

Brown, George P. "Secularization and Modernization in Imperial Brazil: The Question of Non-Catholic Marriage." Revista de Historia de América, 83 (Jan.-June, 1977), 121-133.

Dreher, Martin Norberto. Kirche und Deutschtum in der Entwicklung der Evangelischen Kirche Lutherischen Bekenntnisses in Brasilien. Göttingen: Vandenhoeck und Ruprecht, 1978. Reviewed by Horst Drechsler in Hispanic American Historical Review, 60:3 (Aug., 1980), 541-542.

Grijp, Klaus van der. História do protestantismo brasileiro. Texto preparado como contribuição a história geral da Igreja na América Latina. São Leopoldo: Faculdade de Teologia da IECLB, 1976.

Hoffnagel, Judith Chambliss. "The Believers: Pentecostalism in a Brazilian City." Ph.D. diss., Indiana University, 1978.

Hunsche, Carlos Henrique. Pastor Heinrich Wilhelm Hunsche e os começos da Igreja Evangélica no sul do Brasil. São Leopoldo: Editora Rotermund, 1981.

A Igreja dos pobres na América Latina. São Paulo: Livraria Brasiliense Editora, 1980.

Mizuki, John. The Growth of Japanese Churches in Brazil. South Pasadena, CA: William Carey Library, 1978.

Oliveira, Pedro A. Ribeiro de. "Coexistência das religiões no Brasil." Vozes, 71:7 (Sept., 1977), 23-34.

Religião e sociedade. São Paulo: 1977--.

Robinson, John L. "Sources of Brazilian Protestantism: Historical or Contemporary." In L. Brown, ed., Religion in Latin American Life. Waco, TX: Markham Press Fund, 1980. Pp. 385-393.

Rolim, Francisco. "Religion and Poverty: Brazil." In G. Baum, ed., Work and Religion. Edinburgh: T. & T. Clark, 1980. Pp. 43-50.

Vieira, David Gueiros. O protestantismo, a maçonaria e a questão religiosa no Brasil. Brasília: Editora Universidade de Brasília, 1980. Reviewed by Eul-Soo Pang in Hispanic American Historical Review, 62:4 (Nov., 1982), 689-691.

Wedemann, Walter. "A History of Protestant Missions to Brazil, 1850-1914." Ph.D. diss., Southern Baptist Theological Seminary, 1977.

Chile

Lalive d'Epinay, Christian. "Régimes politiques et millenarisme dans une société dépendante (Réflexions á propos du pentecôstisme au Chile)." In Religion et politique. 15e Conference Internationale de Sociologie Religieuse, Venice, 1979. Lille: Secretariat CISR, 1979. Pp. 71-93.

Vives Pérez-Cotapos, Christian, and Katherine Gilfeather. Diagnóstico socio-religioso en poblaciones de San Bernardo. Santiago: Centro Bellarmino, Departamento de Investigaciones Sociológicas, 1982.

Colombia

Flora, Cornelia Butler. Pentecostalism in Colombia: Baptism by Fire and Spirit. Rutherford, NJ: Fairleigh Dickinson University Press, 1976. Reviewed by Wilkins B. Winn in Hispanic American Historical Review, 58:1 (Feb., 1978), 157-158.

Osorio G., Héctor K. El Instituto Lingüístico de Verano. El gran desconocido. Bogotá: Editoriales de Lomalinda, 1981.

Rappaport, Joanne. "Las misiones protestantes y la resistencia indígena en el sur de Colombia." América Indígena, 44:1 (Jan.-March, 1984), 111-126.

Thornton, W. Philip. "Resocialization: Roman Catholics Becoming Protestants in Colombia, South America." Anthropological Quarterly, 57 (Jan., 1984), 28-37.

Ecuador

Maynard, Kent Arthur. "Christianity and Religion: Evangelical Identity and Sociocultural Organization in Urban Ecuador." Ph.D. diss., Indiana University, 1981.

Muratorio, Blanca. Etnicidad, evangelización y protesta en el Ecuador. Una perspectiva antropológica. Quito: Ediciones CIESE, 1981.

Paraguay

Hack, Hendrick. Indianer und Mennoniten im Paraguayischer Chaco. Amsterdam: CEDLA Incidentele Publicaties, 1976.

Kaputi mennonita (Arados y fusiles en la Guerra del Chaco). Asunción: Imprenta Modelo, 1976.

Plett, Rudolf. Presencia menonita en el Paraguay. Asunción: Instituto Bíblico Asunción, 1979. Reviewed in Revista Paraguaya de Sociología, 17:47 (Jan.-April, 1980), 149.

Redekop, Calvin. Strangers Become Neighbors: Mennonite and Indigenous Relations in the Paraguayan Chaco. Studies in Anabaptist and Mennonite History, 22. Scottsdale, PA: Herald Press, 1980.

Ryckman, Lucile Damon. Paid in Full: The Story of Harold Ryckman, Missionary Pioneer to Paraguay and Brazil. Winona Lake, IN: Light and Life Press, 1979.

Stahl, Wilmar. Escenario indígena chaqueño pasado y presente. Filadelfia, Paraguay: Asociación de Servicios de Cooperación Indígena-Menonita, 1982.

Peru

Aranda de los Ríos, Ramón. Marankiari, una comunidad campa de la selva peruana. Lima: Universidad Nacional Mayor de San

Marcos, Departamento Académico de Ciencias Histórico Sociales, Programa de Trabajo Social, 1978.

Jofré, Rosa del Carmen. "Social Gospel, the Committee on Cooperation in Latin America, and the APRA: The Case of the American Methodist Mission, 1920-1930." NorthSouth, 9:18 (1984), 75-110.

Misión Nuevas Tribus, ¿Evangelización o colonialismo? Servicio Documental, 12. Lima: Comisión Latino Americana de Educación Cristiana, 1980.

Palomino, Cebero. El Instituto Lingüístico de Verano, un fraude. Lima: Ediciones Rupa Rupa, 1980.

Venezuela

Ayerra, Jacinto. Los protestantes en Venezuela: Quiénes son, qué hacen. Caracas: Ediciones Trípode, 1980.

El caso Nuevas Tribus. Caracas: Editorial Ateneo de Caracas, 1981.

54. PUERTO RICAN STUDIES: RESOURCES IN THE UNITED STATES AND PUERTO RICO

United States
New York

CENTRO DE ESTUDIOS PUERTORRIQUEÑOS
Hunter College, CUNY
695 Park Avenue
New York, NY 10021
(212) 772-5689
Director: Frank Bonilla

A research center that focuses on the interpretation of the Puerto Rican migration process and its social, cultural, and linguistic dimensions. In the twelve years since its creation, the Centro has published widely on this theme. Research teams composed of specialists in the areas of history and migration, language, culture, and higher education have produced books, articles, and a series of working papers. In recent years, a film and an oral history work group were integrated into the Centro. Their productions, which complement written research, include a film on Operation Bootstrap, traveling exhibits, slide and radio programs, and a series of oral history tapes which are available for use by the public.

CENTRO LIBRARY
Information: (212) 772-4197
Library Staff: Nélida Pérez, Amilcar Tirado, and Félix Rivera

An integral part of the Centro is its library, which contains a growing collection of materials encompassing all aspects of the experience of Puerto Ricans both in the United States and in Puerto Rico. In addition to a book collection of more than 5,000 volumes, special features include nearly 1,000 doctoral dissertations on Puerto Rican topics; nineteenth- and twentieth-century newspapers, journals, and documents on microfilm; and a vertical file of clippings and pamphlets now mostly on microfiche. The library is developing an archival component to document Puerto Rican community history in the United States, and has already received two important donations: the Jesús Colón Collection of manuscripts dating from 1917 to 1974; and the Justo Martí Collection, a large

---

Editor's Note. This list was distributed during the workshop session on Puerto Rico.

collection of photographs dating from 1950. The library is open to the public. However, with the exception of films, materials do not circulate.

HISPANIC RESEARCH CENTER
Fordham University, Rose Hill Campus
Thebaud Hall, 2d floor
Bronx, NY 10458
(212) 579-2628
Director: Lloyd H. Rogler

A Center that conducts research on mental health issues affecting the Hispanic population in the United States. Its research is geared toward other professionals engaged in similar work, and toward policy-makers. Publications include a monograph series and a quarterly research bulletin.

INSTITUTE FOR PUERTO RICAN POLICY
114 East 28th Street, 3d floor
New York, NY 10016
(212) 689-6331
Director: Angelo Falcón

In its statement of purpose, the Institute cites the empowerment of the Puerto Rican community as its primary objective. To this end it publishes issue-oriented, timely reports, working papers, a newsletter, and research notes that analyze how national and local policies affect Puerto Ricans in the United States and Puerto Rico.

PUERTO RICAN STUDIES INSTITUTE
Brooklyn College, CUNY
Bedford Avenue and Avenue H
Brooklyn, NY 11210
(718) 780-5561
Director: María E. Sanchez

Primarily concerned with curriculum and educational development in the area of Puerto Rican Studies. It publishes occasionally, and houses a small library.

THE NEW YORK PUBLIC LIBRARY
42d Street and Fifth Avenue
New York, NY 10018

THE HUNTS POINT BRANCH
877 Southern Boulevard
Bronx, NY 10459

Both contain extensive holdings on Puerto Rico and Puerto Ricans.

Illinois

LATINO INSTITUTE
53 West Jackson Boulevard, Suite 940
Chicago, IL 60604
(312) 663-3603
Director: María Aranda

Conducts research on population and specifically focuses on demographic data on Latinos in Illinois. Its publications include a newsletter and a monograph series.

Connecticut

UNIVERSITY OF CONNECTICUT LIBRARY
Special Collections
Homer Babbidge Library
U-5 SC
Storrs, CT 06903
(203) 486-2524

In 1982, the library purchased the private collection of the Geigel family of Puerto Rico. The Geigel Collection consists of 2,200 titles including books, pamphlets, periodicals, and government documents covering 150 years of Puerto Rican historical and cultural development. It is particularly strong for nineteenth-century materials, but also covers important political and social developments of the twentieth century. It is part of a broader Puerto Rican Collection which the library is continuing to develop. Although not fully cataloged, the Geigel Collection is accessible for use. Hours of the Special Collections area are 9-12 and 1-5, Monday through Friday.

Puerto Rico

CENTRO DE ESTUDIOS DE LA REALIDAD
PUERTORRIQUEÑA (CEREP)
Apartado 22200, Estación de Correos
Universidad de Puerto Rico
San Juan, PR 00931
Director: Juan Manuel Carrión

Founded in 1970 by an interdisciplinary group including historians, economists, sociologists, and culture theorists, CEREP's members carry out research projects in a variety of areas. Chief among these are working-class history, women in the labor force, development of the Puerto Rican labor market, the sugar industry, slaves, the electoral process, and militarism. CEREP has published various books and "cuadernos" and also put out a newsletter. In 1981, it initiated

"El plan de divulgación," in order to produce and disseminate materials written in a simpler language, and in formats accessible to the general public. The results include radio programs, photographic exhibits, posters, illustrated cuadernos, and a newsletter. CEREP's latest production is a book (1985) on the history of the Puerto Rican working class, composed mainly of photographs.

CENTRO DE ESTUDIOS AVANZADOS DE PUERTO RICO Y EL CARIBE
San Sebastián, num. 1
Old San Juan, PR 00904
(809) 723-8772/4481
Director: Ricardo Alegría

Primarily an institute for graduate studies (M.A.). It publishes an occasional journal, as well as other materials on Puerto Rican and Caribbean history and culture.

CENTRO DE INVESTIGACIONES HISTORICAS
Facultad de Humanidades
Universidad de Puerto Rico
Recinto de Río Piedras, PR 00931
(809) 764-2400
Director: María de los Angeles Castro Arroyo

This center was founded in 1946 to stimulate historical research about Puerto Rico. Its subsequent activities have centered on collecting documents and conducting special research projects. Among its holdings are numerous microform or photocopied archival documents from repositories outside Puerto Rico. The Centro has played an important role in facilitating research for historians who would otherwise have had to travel to Spain and elsewhere for material unavailable in Puerto Rico. In recent years, efforts have been directed toward accessioning or microfilming historically significant collections in private hands. The Centro has produced and continues to publish an historical documents series.

CENTRO DE ESTUDIOS DEMOGRAFICOS
Universidad de Puerto Rico
Recinto de Ciencias Médicas
Facultad de Ciencias Biosociales y
   Escuela Graduada de Salud Pública
G.P.O. Box 5067
San Juan, PR 00936
(809) 753-5253
Director: José L. Vázquez Calzada

In addition to conducting population research, which is published in journals as well as in a yearly monograph series, this center collects and interprets census data. It provides reference service on Puerto Rican vital statistics to the public.

CENTRO DE INVESTIGACIONES SOCIALES (CIS)
Facultad de Ciencias Sociales
Universidad de Puerto Rico
Recinto de Río Piedras, PR   00931
Director: Celia Fernández de Cintrón

The CIS, since its 1945 foundation, has focused its research on Puerto Rican social issues. Its initial research agenda was determined by such North American sociologists and anthropologists as Clarence Senior, Julian Steward, and Melvin Tumin. Now Puerto Rican scholars define the problems and conduct the research. Research concerns include urban studies, women, income distribution and economic dependency, crime, and migration. The CIS publishes a journal, La Revista de Ciencias Sociales, and numerous studies.

MISION INDUSTRIAL
Apartado 376
Hato Rey, PR   00919
(809) 765-4303

Conducts research and coordinates and promotes community efforts aimed at protecting the environment and Puerto Rico's natural resources. It publishes an environmental newsletter, articles, and reports on various topics, mostly concerning pollution and the exploitation of natural resources.

PROYECTO CARIBEÑO DE JUSTICIA Y PAZ
Calle Navarro, num. 53
Hato Rey, PR   00919
(809) 763-2451

A project comprised of workers, professors, and students who seek peace and a more just social order for the Caribbean region. The project promotes educational and research activities concerning Caribbean issues and focuses on two principal areas of work: human rights and militarism. Among its publications are a series of Dossiers, each on a specific topic. Recent issues examined the U.S. military build-up in the Caribbean, the invasion of Grenada, and the Caribbean Basin Initiative. Puerto Rico's role within the Caribbean is always central to these discussions.

Special Puerto Rican Collections

ARCHIVO GENERAL DE PUERTO RICO
Ponce de León, num. 500
Puerta de Tierra (Edificio Bacardi)
San Juan, PR 00901
(809) 724-2680
Director: Miguel Angel Nieves

The national archives of Puerto Rico, established in 1955, is the official depository for records from all branches of government and from the municipalities. It contains approximately 36,000 cubic feet of materials, about half of which dates from the nineteenth century. In addition to public records, the archive accepts and seeks out private collections judged to be of research value or historical significance. The archive provides reference services for governmental agencies, researchers, and the general public.

BIBLIOTECA GENERAL DE PUERTO RICO
Ponce de León, num. 500
Puerta de Tierra, PR 00901

A library inaugurated in 1973, to complement the Archivo General by becoming a comprehensive collection of published Puerto Rican materials. It was initiated with 30,000 volumes which originally belonged to the Instituto de Cultura Puertorriqueña. Although it has not developed as planned, it does contain valuable titles.

BIBLIOTECA DEL COLEGIO REGIONAL DE PONCE
Centro de Estudios Puertorriqueños
Universidad de Puerto Rico
Apartado 7186
Ponce, PR 00732
(809) 844-8181, ext. 138/139
Bibliotecario: Roberto Colón

Center that focuses on materials concerning the Southern region of Puerto Rico. At present its holdings include 7,000 books and numerous pamphlets, magazines, and journals. It is open to researchers and to the general public.

BIBLIOTECA PUBLICA CARNEGIE
Avenida Ponce de León
Parada 2
San Juan, PR 00901
(809) 724-1046

Library containing an important Puerto Rican collection which includes rare books, pamphlets, newspapers, and valuable manuscript and archival materials.

LA COLECCION PUERTORRIQUEÑA
Biblioteca General
Universidad de Puerto Rico
Recinto de Río Piedras
Río Piedras, PR   00931
(809) 764-0000, ext. 3463
Director: Carmen Mí Costa de Ramos

The most complete Puerto Rican collection anywhere. Since the early 1930s, when Puerto Rican materials began to be kept apart from the University Library's general collection, the collection has grown steadily by way of donations and pur- chases. It houses books, magazines, journals, government documents, manuscripts, and audiovisual materials on all topics of Puerto Rican studies.

A rare books section contains books published in Puerto Rico during the nineteenth century. The collection of retrospective and current newspapers is comprehensive and invaluable. Special library projects include indexing the newspaper El Mundo, as well as various journals. La Colección is a reference collection with closed stacks. It mainly serves the University community but is also accessible to others outside the institution.

Other Institutions Housing Significant
Puerto Rican Collections

BIBLIOTECA CENTRO DE DOCUMENTACION Y
PROMOCION CULTURAL
Recinto Universitario de Mayagüez
Mayagüez, PR   00708
(809) 832-4040

BIBLIOTECA UNIVERSIDAD INTERAMERICANA
Recinto de San Juan, Edificio Ocasio
Avenida Ponce de León, num. 405
Hato Rey, PR   00919
(809) 753-8008

55. BORICUAS EN EL NORTE: A SELECTED BIBLIOGRAPHY ON PUERTO RICANS IN THE UNITED STATES

Algarín, Miguel, and Miguel Piñero, eds. Nuyorican Poetry: An Anthology of Puerto Rican Words and Feelings. New York, NY: William Morrow and Co., 1975. 185 pp.

Berle, Beatrice B. 80 Puerto Rican Families in New York City. New York, NY: Arno Press, 1975. 331 pp. (Repr. of 1958 ed.)

Camacho Souza, Blase. Boricua Hawaiiana: Puerto Ricans of Hawaii, Reflections of the Past and Mirror of the Future, A Catalog. Honolulu, HI: Puerto Rican Heritage Society of Hawaii, 1982. 28 pp.

Centro de Estudios Puertorriqueños. History Task Force. Labor Migration under Capitalism: The Puerto Rican Experience. New York, NY: Monthly Review, 1979. 287 pp.

_____. Sources for the Study of Puerto Rican Migration, 1879-1930. New York, NY: 1982. 224 pp.

Chenault, Lawrence R. The Puerto Rican Migrant in New York City. New York, NY: Russell and Russell, 1970. 190 pp. (Repr. of 1938 ed.)

Chicago. Mayor's Committee on New Residents. Puerto Rican Americans in Chicago: A Study. Chicago, IL: 1960. 154 pp.

Colón, Jesús. A Puerto Rican in New York, and Other Sketches. New York, NY: International Publishers, 1982. 202 pp.

Colón, Ramón. Carlos Tapia: A Puerto Rican Hero in New York. New York, NY: Vantage Press, 1976. 89 pp.

Cordasco, Francesco, and Eugene Bucchioni, eds. The Puerto Rican Community and Its Children on the Mainland: A Source Book for Teachers, Social Workers, and Other Professionals. Metuchen, NJ: Scarecrow Press, 1982. 465 pp.

_____. The Puerto Rican Experience: A Sociological Sourcebook. Totowa, NJ: Rowman and Littlefield, 1973. 370 pp.

Cotto-Thorner, Guillermo. Trópico en Manhattan. San Juan, PR: Editorial Cordillera, 1969. 186 pp.

Díaz Ramírez, Ana María. "The Roman Catholic Archdiocese of New York and the Puerto Rican Migration, 1950-1973: A Sociological and Historical Analysis." Ph.D. diss., Fordham University, 1983. 384 pp.

Editor's Note. This bibliography was distributed during the workshop session on Puerto Rico.

Donahue, Frances M. "Study of the Original Puerto Rican Colony in Brooklyn, 1938-1943." M.A. thesis, Fordham University, 1945. 88 pp.

Estades, Rosa. Patterns of Political Participation of Puerto Ricans in New York City. Río Piedras, PR: Editorial Universidad de Puerto Rico, 1978. 94 pp.

Falcón-Meléndez, Angel Rafael. "La emigración puertorriqueña a Nueva York en los cuentos de José Luis González, Pedro Juan Soto y José Luis Vivas Maldonado." Ph.D. diss., University of Iowa, 1981. 409 pp.

Fitzpatrick, Joseph P. Puerto Rican Americans: The Meaning of Migration to the Mainland. Englewood Cliffs, NJ: Prentice-Hall, 1971. 192 pp.

Garza, Catarino, ed. Puerto Ricans in the United States: The Struggle for Freedom. New York, NY: Pathfinder Press, 1977. 64 pp.

Glazer, Nathan, and Daniel Moynihan. Beyond the Melting Pot: The Negroes, Puerto Ricans, Jews, Italians, and Irish of New York City. Cambridge, MA: M.I.T. Press, 1970. 363 pp.

González, Jóse Luis. En Nueva York y otras desgracias. México, DF: Siglo Veintiuno Editores, 1973. 140 pp.

Gosnell, Patria Aran. "The Puerto Ricans in New York City." Ph.D. diss., New York University, 1945. 647 pp.

Handlin, Oscar. The Newcomers: Negroes and Puerto Ricans in a Changing Metropolis. Cambridge, MA: Harvard University Press, 1971. 171 pp. (Repr. of 1959 ed.)

Hernández, José. Puerto Rican Youth Employment. Maplewood, NJ: Waterfront Press, 1983. 155 pp.

Jaffe, Abram J., ed. Puerto Rican Population of New York City. New York, NY: Arno Press, 1975. 61 pp. (Repr. of 1954 ed.)

Jaffe, Abram J., and Zaida Carreras Carleton. Some Demographic and Economic Characteristics of the Puerto Rican Population Living on the Mainland, U.S.A. New York, NY: Columbia University, 1974. 76 pp.

Jennings, James. Puerto Rican Politics in New York City. Washington, DC: University Press of America, 1977. 275 pp.

Jennings, James, and Monte Rivera. Puerto Rican Politics in Urban America. Westport, CT: Greenwood Press, 1984. 167 pp.

Levine, Barry B. Benjy López: A Picaresque Tale of Emigration and Return. New York, NY: Basic Books, Inc., 1979. 202 pp.

Lewis, Oscar. La Vida: A Puerto Rican Family in the Culture of Poverty--San Juan and New York. New York, NY: Random House, 1965. 671 pp.

_____. A Study of Slum Culture: Backgrounds for La Vida. New York, NY: Random House, 1968. 240 pp.

Llamas, Frank Robert. "Puerto Rican Migrant Farmworkers in Massachusetts and Connecticut: A Case Study of Perceived Training and Service Needs." Ed.D. diss., University of Massachusetts, 1977. 196 pp.

López, Adalberto, ed. The Puerto Ricans: Their History, Culture, and Society. Cambridge, MA: Schenkman Publishing Co., 1980. 490 pp.

López, Adalberto, and James Petras, eds. Puerto Rico and Puerto Ricans: Studies in History and Society. New York, NY: John Wiley and Sons, 1974. 499 pp.

López, Alfredo. The Puerto Rican Papers: Notes on the Re-Emergence of a Nation. New York, NY: The Bobbs-Merrill Company, 1973. 383 pp.

Maldonado Denis, Manuel. Puerto Rico y Estados Unidos: emigración y colonialismo. México, DF: Siglo Veintiuno Editores, 1976. 197 pp.

_____. The Emigration Dialectic: Puerto Rico and the U.S.A.. New York, NY: International Publishers, 1980. 156 pp.

Marcantonio, Vito. I Vote My Conscience: Debates, Speeches and Writings of Vito Marcantonio, 1935-1950. New York, NY: Vito Marcantonio Memorial, 1956. 494 pp.

Mills, C. Wright, Clarence Senior, and Rose Kohn Goldsen. The Puerto Rican Journey: New York's Newest Migrants. New York, NY: Harper and Brothers Publishers, 1950. 238 pp.

Mohr, Eugene V. The Nuyorican Experience: Literature of the Puerto Rican Minority. Westport, CT: Greenwood Press, 1982. 139 pp.

Mohr, Nicholasa. El Bronx Remembered. New York, NY: Harper and Row Publishers, 1975. 179 pp.

_____. In Nueva York. New York, NY: The Dial Press, 1977. 194 pp.

Morales, Jr., Julio. "Puerto Rican Poverty and the Migration to Elsewhere: Waltham, Massachusetts, A Case Study." Ph.D. diss., Brandeis University, 1979. 474 pp.

New York City. Department of City Planning. Puerto Rican Population and Households, New York City and Boroughs, 1980. New York, NY, 1982. 144 pp.

_____ . The Puerto Rican New Yorkers: A Recent History of Their Distribution and Population and Household Characteristics. New York, NY, 1982. 114 pp.

_____ . Mayor's Committee on Puerto Rican Affairs. Interim Report of the Mayor's Committee on Puerto Rican Affairs in New York City. New York, NY, 1983. 49 pp.

Nieves Falcón, Luis. El emigrante puertorriqueño. Río Piedras, PR: Editorial Edil, 1975. 200 pp.

O'Brien, Robert William. A Survey of the Puerto Ricans in Lorain, Ohio. Lorain, OH: Neighborhood House Association of Lorain, 1954. 85 pp.

Ojeda, Félix. Vito Marcantonio y Puerto Rico: por los trabajadores y por la nación. Río Piedras, PR: Ediciones Huracán, 1978. 154 pp.

Padilla, Elena. Up from Puerto Rico. New York, NY: Columbia University Press, 1958. 317 pp.

Powers, Mary, and John J. Macisco, Jr. Los puertorriqueños en Nueva York: un análisis de su participación laboral y experiencia migratoria, 1970. Río Piedras, PR: Centro de Investigaciones Sociales, Universidad de Puerto Rico, 1982. 201 pp.

Puerto Rican Forum. The Puerto Rican Community Development Project. New York, NY: Arno Press, 1975. 145 pp. (Repr. of 1964 ed.)

Quintero Rivera, Angel G., et al. Puerto Rico: identidad nacional y clases sociales. Coloquio de Princeton. Río Piedras, PR: Ediciones Huracán, 1979. 147 pp.

Ribes Tovar, Federico. Enciclopedia puertorriqueña ilustrada. The Puerto Rican Heritage Encyclopedia. San Juan, PR: Plus Ultra Educational Publishers, 1970. 3 vols.

Rivera, Edward. Family Installments: Memories of Growing Up Hispanic. New York, NY: Morrow, 1982. 300 pp.

Rodríguez, Clara. "The Ethnic Queue in the United States: The Case of Puerto Ricans." Ph.D. diss., Washington University, 1973. 349 pp.

Rodríguez, Clara, Virginia Sánchez Korrol, and José Oscar, eds. The Puerto Rican Struggle: Essays on Survival in the U.S. New York, NY: Puerto Rican Migration Research Consortium, Inc., 1980. 151 pp.

Rogler, Lloyd. Migrant in the City: The Life of a Puerto Rican Action Group. New York, NY: Basic Books, 1972. 251 pp.

Rosario Natal, Carmelo. Exodo puertorriqueño (Las emigraciones al Caribe y Hawaii: 1900-1915. San Juan, PR: I. C. Rosario Natal, 1983. 136 pp.

Rosenberg, Terry J. Residence, Employment and Mobility of Puerto Ricans in New York City. Chicago, IL: University of Chicago, 1974. 230 pp.

Sánchez Korrol, Virginia. From Colonia to Community: The History of Puerto Ricans in New York City, 1917-1948. Westport, CT: Greenwood Press, 1983. 242 pp.

Santiago Hernández, Sonia Margarita. "Acculturation and Biculturalism among Puerto Ricans in Lamont, California." Ph.D. diss., United States International University, San Diego, CA, 1981. 114 pp.

Schaffer, Alan. Vito Marcantonio: Radical in Congress. New York, NY: Syracuse University Press, 1966. 256 pp.

Senior, Clarence. Puerto Rican Emigration. Río Piedras, PR: Social Science Research Center, University of Puerto Rico, 1947. 166 pp.

Soto, Pedro Juan. Spiks. Río Piedras, PR: Editorial Cultural, 1973. 109 pp. Engl. trans., New York, NY: Monthly Review Press, 1973. 92 pp.

Thomas, Piri. Down These Mean Streets. New York, NY: Alfred A. Knopf, 1967. 336 pp.

_____. Seven Long Times. New York, NY: Praeger Publishers, 1974. 246 pp.

_____. Stories from El Barrio. New York, NY: Alfred A. Knopf, 1978. 143 pp.

Turner, Faythe Elaine. "Puerto Rican Writers on the Mainland: The Neoricans, A Thematic Study." Ph.D. diss., University of Massachusetts, 1978. 181 pp.

United States Commission on Civil Rights. Puerto Ricans in California: A Staff Report. Washington, DC: Government Printing Office, 1980. 19 pp.

_____. Puerto Ricans in the Continental United States: An Uncertain Future. Washington, DC: Government Printing Office, 1976. 157 pp.

_____. Connecticut State Advisory Committee. El Boricua: The Puerto Rican Community in Bridgeport and New Haven. Hartford, CT: The Advisory Committee, 1973. 87 pp.

_____. Massachusetts Advisory Committee. Issues of Concern to Puerto Ricans in Boston and Springfield. Boston, MA: The Advisory Committee, 1972. 104 pp.

_____. Pennsylvania State Advisory Committee. In Search of a Better Life: The Education and Housing Problems of Puerto Ricans in Philadelphia. Washington, DC: Government Printing Office, 1974. 51 pp.

United States. Department of Commerce. Bureau of the Census. Puerto Ricans in the United States: 1970 Census of Population. Washington, DC: Government Printing Office, 1973. 148 pp.

_____. Department of Labor. Bureau of Labor Statistics. A Socio-Economic Profile of Puerto Rican New Yorkers. New York, NY: Regional Report no. 46, July 1975. 138 pp.

_____. Labor Force Experience of the Puerto Rican Worker. New York, NY: Regional Report no. 9, June 1968. 31 pp.

Vega, Bernardo. Memoirs of Bernardo Vega: A Contribution to the History of the Puerto Rican Community in New York. New York, NY: Monthly Review, 1984. 243 pp.

_____. Memorias de Bernardo Vega: una contribución a la historia de la comunidad puertorriqueña en Nueva York. San Juan, PR: Ediciones Huracán, 1977. 282 pp.

Wagenheim, Kal. A Survey of Puerto Ricans on the U.S. Mainland in the 1970s. New York, NY: Praeger Publishers, 1975. 135 pp.

Wagenheim, Kal, and Olga Jimenez de Wagenheim, eds. The Puerto Ricans: A Documentary History. New York, NY: Praeger Publishers, 1973. 332 pp.

Wakefield, Dan. Island in the City: The World of Spanish Harlem. New York, NY: Arno Press, 1975. 278 pp. (Repr. of 1959 ed.)

Welfare Council of New York City. Committee on Puerto Ricans in New York City. Puerto Ricans in New York City. New York, NY: Arno Press, 1975. 60 pp. (Repr. of 1948 ed.)

56. BIBLIOGRAPHIC SOURCES ON PUERTO RICANS
IN THE UNITED STATES

American Library Association. Sourcebook of Hispanic Culture in the United States. Chicago, IL: ALA, 1982. 352 pp. "Continental Puerto Ricans," pp. 133-200.

Berry-Cabán, Cristobál S., comp. Hispanics in Wisconsin: A Bibliography of Resource Materials. Madison, WI: The State Historical Society of Wisconsin, 1981. 258 pp.

Bobson, Sarah. The Education of Puerto Ricans on the Mainland: An Annotated Bibliography. New York, NY: ERIC Clearing House on Urban Education, Institute for Urban and Minority Education, 1975. 81 pp.

Brooklyn College. Institute of Puerto Rican Studies. The Puerto Rican People: A Selected Bibliography for Use in Social Work Education. New York, NY: Council on Social Work Education, 1973. 54 pp.

Cordasco, Francesco. The People of Puerto Rico: A Bibliography. New York, NY: S.E., 1968. 45 pp. (Repr. in The Puerto Ricans: Migration and General Bibliography. New York, NY: Arno Press, 1975.)

Cordasco, Francesco, Eugene Bucchioni, and Diego Castellanos. Puerto Ricans on the United States Mainland: A Bibliography of Reports, Texts, Critical Studies and Related Materials. Totowa, NJ: Rowman and Littlefield, 1972. 146 pp.

Cordasco, Francesco, and Leonard Covello. "Studies of Puerto Rican Children in American Schools: A Preliminary Bibliography." Journal of Human Relations, 16:2 (1968), 264-285. (Repr. in The Puerto Ricans: Migration and General Bibliography. New York, NY: Arno Press, 1975.)

Dossick, Jesse J. Doctoral Research on Puerto Rico and Puerto Ricans. New York, NY: New York University, 1967. 34 pp. (Repr. in The Puerto Ricans: Migration and General Bibliography. New York, NY: Arno Press, 1975.)

Hadgis, Diana, comp. Puerto Rican Heritage: An Annotated Bibliography of the Puerto Rican Experience. New York, NY: BCC (Bronx Community College), 1979. 26 pp.

Herrera, Diane. Puerto Ricans and Other Minority Groups in the Continental United States: An Annotated Bibliography. Detroit, MI: Blaine Ethridge-Books, 1979. 397 pp. Originally

---

Editor's Note. This list was distributed during the workshop session on Puerto Rico.

published as Puerto Ricans in the United States: A Review of the Literature. Austin, TX: Dissemination Center for Bilingual Bicultural Education, 1973. 397 pp.

Indiana University. Libraries. Pueblo Latino, Vol. II. The Puerto Ricans. Bloomington, IN: Indiana University, 1975. 107 pp.

Miller, Wayne Charles. A Comprehensive Bibliography for the Study of American Minorities. New York, NY: New York University Press, 1976. "Puerto Rican Americans," pp. 757-771.

New York. State Education Department. An Annotated Bibliography of Materials on the Puerto Rican and Mexican Cultures. Albany, NY: 1972. 110 pp.

New York, N.Y. Municipal Reference Library. "The Puerto Rican New Yorkers: A Guide to Available Materials at the Municipal Reference Library," Notes, 7 (Sept., 1967), 81-87.

Parker, Franklin, and Betty June Parker. Education in Puerto Rico and of Puerto Ricans in the United States: Abstracts of American Doctoral Dissertations. San Juan, PR: Inter-American University Press, 1978. 603 pp.

"Puerto Rican Migrants on the Mainland of the United States." IRCD Bulletin (ERIC Information Retrieval Center on the Disadvantaged), 4:1 (Jan., 1968), 12 pp. (Repr. in The Puerto Ricans: Migration and General Bibliography. New York, NY: Arno Press, 1975.)

Puerto Rico. Department of Labor. Migration Division. The People of Puerto Rico: A Bibliography. New York, NY: 1968. 45 pp.

_____ _____. Bibliography on Puerto Ricans in the United States. Clarence Senior, ed. New York, NY: 1959. 37 pp.

_____ _____. A Selected Bibliography on Puerto Rico and the Puerto Ricans. Clarence Senior and Josefina de Roman, comps. New York, NY: 1951. 32 pp. (Repr. of 1951 ed. in The Puerto Ricans: Migration and General Bibliography. New York, NY: Arno Press, 1975.)

Teschner, Richard V., Garland D. Bills, and Jerry R. Craddock, eds. Spanish and English of United States Hispanos: A Critical, Annotated Linguistic Bibliography. Arlington, VA: Center for Applied Linguistics, 1975. 352 pp. "Puerto Ricans on the United States Mainland," pp. 258-301.

Vivo, Paquita, ed. The Puerto Ricans: An Annotated Bibliography. New York, NY: R. R. Bowker Co., 1973. 299 pp.

Acosta Belén, Edna, ed. The Puerto Rican Woman. New York,
NY: Praeger, 1979. 169 pp.
_____. La mujer en la sociedad puertorriqueña.
Río Piedras, PR: Huracán, 1981. 237 pp.

Alegría, Ricardo E. Descubrimiento, conquista y colonización de
Puerto Rico, 1493-1599. San Juan, PR: Colección de Estudios
Puertorriqueños, 1971. 179 pp.
_____. Discovery, Conquest and Colonization of Puerto
Rico, 1493-1599. San Juan, PR: Colección de Estudios Puerto-
rriqueños, 1971. 165 pp.

Anderson, Robert William. Party Politics in Puerto Rico.
Stanford, CA: Stanford University Press, 1972. 269 pp.
(Repr. of 1965 ed.)
_____. Gobierno y partidos políticos en Puerto Rico.
Madrid: Tecnos, 1973. 293 pp.

Campos, Ricardo, and Juan Flores. National Culture and
Migration: Perspectives from the Puerto Rican Working Class.
New York: NY: Centro de Estudios Puertorriqueños, 1978.
49 pp.
_____. "Migración y cultura nacional puertorriqueñas:
perspectivas proletarias." In Puerto Rico: identidad nacional y
clases sociales (Coloquio de Princeton). Río Piedras, PR:
Huracán, 1979. Pp. 81-146.

Cordova, Gonzalo. "Resident Commissioner Santiago Iglesias and
His Times." Ph.D. diss., Georgetown University, 1982.
3 vols. 797 pp.
_____. Santiago Iglesias: creador del movimiento obrero de
Puerto Rico. Río Piedras, PR: Editorial Universitaria,
Universidad de Puerto Rico, 1980. 231 pp.

Corretjer, Juan Antonio. "Albizú Campos y la Masacre de
Ponce." In Albizú Campos. Montevideo: El Siglo Ilustrado,
1969. Pp. 61-98. (Repr. of 1965 ed.)
_____. Albizú Campos and the Ponce Massacre. New
York, NY: World View Publishers, 1965. 25 pp.

_____

Editor's Note. This list was distributed during the workshop
session on Puerto Rico.

Díaz Valcárcel, Emilio. Figuraciones en el mes de marzo. Barcelona: Seix Barral, 1972. 329 pp.
_____. Schemes in the Month of March. New York, NY: Bilingual Press, 1979. 285 pp.

Estades, Rosa. Patterns of Political Participation of Puerto Ricans in New York City. Río Piedras, PR: Editorial Universitaria, Universidad de Puerto Rico, 1978. 94 pp.
_____. Patrones de participación política de los puertorriqueños en la ciudad de Nueva York. Río Piedras, PR: Editorial Universitaria, Universidad de Puerto Rico, 1978. 94 pp.

Farr, Kenneth R. Personalism and Party Politics: Institutionalization of the Popular Democratic Party of Puerto Rico. Hato Rey, PR: Inter-American University, 1973. 143 pp.
_____. Personalismo y política de partidos: la institucionalización del Partido Popular Democrático de Puerto Rico. Hato Rey, PR: Inter-American University, 1975. 268 pp.

Figueroa de Thompson, Annie. An Annotated Bibliography of Writings about Music in Puerto Rico. Ann Arbor, MI: Music Library Association, 1975. 34 pp.
_____. Bibliografía anotada sobre la música en Puerto Rico. San Juan, PR: Instituto de Cultura Puertorriqueña, 1977. 70 pp.

Figueroa, Loida. Breve historia de Puerto Rico. Río Piedras, PR: Edil, 1971. 2 vols.
_____. History of Puerto Rico from the Beginning to 1892. New York, NY: Anaya Book Co., 1972. 474 pp.

Flores, Juan. The Insular Vision: Pedreira's Interpretation of Puerto Rican Culture. Rev. ed. New York, NY: Centro de Estudios Puertorriqueños, 1980. 94 pp.
_____. Insularismo e ideología burguesa: nueva lectura de A. S. Pereira. Río Piedras, PR: Ediciones Huracán, 1979. 127 pp.

Gould, Lyman J. "The Foraker Act: The Roots of American Colonial Policy." Ph.D. diss., University of Michigan, 1958. 254 pp.
_____. La ley Foraker: raíces de la política colonial de los Estados Unidos. 2d ed. Río Piedras, PR: Editorial Universitaria, Universidad de Puerto Rico, 1975. (1st ed., 1969.) 186 pp.

Jiménez de Wagenheim, Olga. "El Grito de Lares: A Socio-Historic Interpretation of Puerto Rico's Uprising against Spain in 1868." Ph.D. diss., Rutgers University, 1981. 340 pp.
_____. El Grito de Lares. Sus causas y sus hombres. Río Piedras, PR: Huracán, 1985. 231 pp.

Laguerre, Enrique A. El laberinto. In Obras completas.
San Juan, PR: Instituto de Cultura Puertorriqueña, 1964.
Vol. III, pp. 9-211.
_____. The Labyrinth. Maplewood, NJ: Waterfront, 1984.
275 pp.

Lewis, Gordon K. Puerto Rico: Freedom and Power in the
Caribbean. New York, NY: Monthly Review, 1974. 626 pp.
_____. Puerto Rico: libertad y poder en el Caribe.
Río Piedras, PR: Edil, 1969. 752 pp.

Lewis, Oscar. La Vida: A Puerto Rican Family in the Culture of
Poverty--San Juan and New York. New York, NY: Random
House, 1966. 669 pp.
_____. La Vida: una familia puertorriqueña en la cultura
de la pobreza--San Juan y Nueva York. México, DF: Joaquín
Mortiz, 1969. 646 pp.

Maldonado Denis, Manuel. Puerto Rico: una interpretación
histórico-social. 2d ed. México, DF: Siglo XXI, 1973. (1st
ed., 1969.) 303 pp.
_____. Puerto Rico: A Socio-Historic Interpretation.
New York, NY: Vintage, 1972. 336 pp.

_____. Puerto Rico y Estados Unidos: emigración y
colonialismo: un análisis sociohistórico de la emigración
puertorriqueña. México, DF: Siglo XXI, 1976. 197 pp.

_____. The Emigration Dialectic: Puerto Rico and the
U.S.A. New York, NY: International Publishers, 1980.
156 pp.

Marqués, René. La carreta. Río Piedras, PR: Cultural, 1973.
172 pp.
_____. The Oxcart. New York, NY: Scribner's, 1969.
155 pp.

_____. "El puertorriqueño dócil (literatura y realidad
psicológica)." In El puertorriqueño dócil y otros ensayos.
Barcelona: Antillana, 1977. Pp. 151-215.
_____. The Docile Puerto Rican. Philadelphia, PA:
Temple University, 1976. 137 pp.

Negrón de Montilla, Aida. Americanization in Puerto Rico and the
Public School System, 1900-1930. Río Piedras, PR: Edil, 1970.
282 pp.

_____. La americanización de Puerto Rico y el sistema de
instrucción pública, 1900-1930. Río Piedras, PR: Editorial
Universitaria, Universidad de Puerto Rico, 1977. 290 pp.

Negrón Portillo, Mariano. "A Study of the Newspaper 'La
Democracia,'" Puerto Rico, 1895-1914: A Historical Analysis."
Ph.D. diss., State University of New York at Stony Brook,
1980. 278 pp.

_____. El autonomismo puertorriqueño: su transformation ideológica (1895-1914): la prensa en el análisis social: "La Democracia" de Puerto Rico. Río Piedras, PR: Huracán, 1981. 95 pp.

Partido Socialista Puertorriqueño. La alternativa socialista: tesis política del Partido Socialista Puertorriqueño. Río Piedras, PR: Puerto Rico, 1974. 216 pp.

_____. Political Thesis of the Puerto Rican Socialist Party: The Socialist Alternative. New York, NY: NACLA, 1975. 74 pp.

_____. Seccional de Estados Unidos. Desde las entrañas . . .: declaración política de la seccional de Estados Unidos del Partido Socialista Puertorriqueño. New York, NY: El Partido, 1973. 121 pp.

_____. "Desde las entrañas . . .": Political Declaration of the United States Branch of the Puerto Rican Socialist Party. New York, NY: The Party, 1973. 41 pp.

Pico, Rafael. The Geography of Puerto Rico. Chicago, IL: Aldine, 1974. 439 pp.

_____. Nueva geografía de Puerto Rico: física, economíca y social. Río Piedras, PR: Editorial Universitaria, Universidad de Puerto Rico, 1969. 460 pp.

Pietri, Pedro. Puerto Rican Obituary. New York, NY: Monthly Review, 1974. 109 pp.

_____. Obituario puertorriqueño (Selección). San Juan, PR: Instituto de Cultura Puertorriqueña, 1977. 139 pp.

Presser, Harriet B. "Sterilization and Fertility Decline in Puerto Rico." Ph.D. diss., University of California, Berkeley, 1970. 327 pp.

_____. La esterilización y el descenso de la fecundidad en Puerto Rico. Berkeley, CA: Instituto de Estudios Internacionales, Universidad de California, 1974. 215 pp.

Quintero Rivera, Angel G., comp. Lucha obrera: antología de grandes documentos en la historia obrera puertorriqueña. Río Piedras, PR: Centro de Estudios de la Realidad Puertorriqueña, 1972. 165 pp.

_____. Workers' Struggle in Puerto Rico: A Documentary History. New York, NY: Monthly Review, 1976. 236 pp.

Ribes Tovar, Federico. Albizú Campos: el revolucionario. New York, NY: Plus Ultra Educational Publishers, 1971. 252 pp.

_____. Albizú Campos: Puerto Rican Revolutionary. New York, NY: Plus Ultra Educational Publishers, 1971. 252 pp.

_____. La mujer puertorriqueña: su vida y evolución a través de la historia. New York, NY: Plus Ultra Educational Publishers, 1972. 251 pp.

_____. The Puerto Rican Woman: Her Life and Evolution throughout History. New York, NY: Plus Ultra Educational Publishers, 1972. 256 pp.

Safa, Helen Icken. The Urban Poor of Puerto Rico: A Study in Development and Inequality. New York, NY: Holt, Rinehart, and Winston, 1974. 116 pp.

_____. Familias del arrabal: un estudio sobre desarrollo y desigualdad. Río Piedras, PR: Editorial Universitaria, Universidad de Puerto Rico, 1980. 158 pp.

Sánchez, Luis Rafael. La guaracha del Macho Camacho. Buenos Aires: Ediciones de la Flor, 1976. 256 pp.

_____. Macho Camacho's Beat. New York, NY: Pantheon, 1980. 213 pp.

Seda Bonilla, Eduardo. Interacción social y personalidad en una comunidad de Puerto Rico. San Juan, PR: Juan Ponce de León, 1969. 190 pp.

_____. Social Change and Personality in a Puerto Rican Agrarian Reform Community. Evanston, IL: Northwestern University, 1973. 187 pp.

Senior, Clarence Ollson. Santiago Iglesias: Labor Crusader. Hato Rey, PR: Inter-American University, 1972. 98 pp.

_____. Santiago Iglesias: apóstol de los trabajadores. Hato Rey, PR: Inter-American University, 1972. 110 pp.

Silén, Juan Angel. Hacia una visión positiva del puertorriqueño. Río Piedras, PR: Antillana, 1976. 246 pp. (1st ed., 1970.)

_____. We, the Puerto Rican People: A Story of Oppression and Resistance. New York, NY: Monthly Review, 1971. 134 pp.

Soto, Pedro Juan. Ardiente suelo, fría estación. Xalapa, Mexico: Universidad Veracruzana, 1961. 258 pp.

_____. Hot Land, Cold Season. New York, NY: Dell, 1971.

_____. Spiks. Río Piedras, PR: Cultural, 1970. 78 pp.

_____. Spiks. New York, NY: Monthly Review, 1976. 92 pp.

Tuck, Jay Nelson, and Norma C. Vergara. Heroes of Puerto Rico. New York, NY: Fleet Press Corp., 1969. 141 pp.

_____. Héroes de Puerto Rico. New York, NY: Fleet Press Corp., 1974. 142 pp.

United States. Commission on Civil Rights. A Better Chance to Learn: Bilingual Bicultural Education. Washington, DC: Government Printing Office, 1975. 254 pp.

_____. Una mejor oportunidad para aprender: la educación bilingüe bicultural. Washington, DC: Government Printing Office, 1975. 289 pp.

_____. Counting the Forgotten: The 1970 Census Count of Persons of Spanish Speaking Background in the United States. Washington, DC: Government Printing Office, 1974. 112 pp.

_____. Enumerando los olvidados: el recuento del Censo de 1970 de personas de descendencia hispana en los Estados Unidos. Washington, DC: Government Printing Office, 1974. 123 pp.

_____. Puerto Ricans in the Continental United States: An Uncertain Future. Washington, DC: Government Printing Office, 1976. 157 pp.

_____. Puertorriqueños en los Estados Unidos continentales: un futuro incierto. Washington, DC: Government Printing Office, 1976. 179 pp.

Vega, Bernardo. Memorias de Bernardo Vega: contribución a la historia de la comunidad puertorriqueña en Nueva York. Río Piedras, PR: Ediciones Huracán, 1977. 282 pp.

_____. Memoirs of Bernardo Vega: A Contribution to the History of the Puerto Rican Community in New York. New York, NY: Monthly Review Press, 1984. 243 pp.

Wells, Henry. The Modernization of Puerto Rico: A Political Study of Changing Values and Institutions. Cambridge, MA: Harvard University Press, 1969. 440 pp.

_____. La modernización de Puerto Rico: un análisis político de valores e instituciones en proceso de cambio. Río Piedras, PR: Editorial Universitaria, Universidad de Puerto Rico, 1972. 465 pp.

Zeno Gandia, Manuel. La Charca. In Obras completas. San Juan, PR: Instituto de Cultura Puertorriqueña, 1973. Pp. 4-168.

_____. La Charca. Maplewood, NJ: Waterfront, 1982. 216 pp.

58. PUBLISHERS AND DISTRIBUTORS OF PUERTO RICAN BOOKS

Current

Editorial Cultural
Calle El Roble #51
Río Piedras, PR   00925

Editorial Interamericana
GPO Box 3255
San Juan, PR   00936

Editorial Universitaria
Universidad de Puerto Rico
Río Piedras, PR   00931

Eliseo Torres & Sons
1164 Garrison Avenue
Bronx, NY   10474

Librería Hispanoamericana
Avenida Ponce de León #1013
Apartado 20830
Río Piedras, PR   00928

Librería La Tertulia
Amalia Marín esquina Avenida
    González
Santa Rita
Río Piedras, PR   00925

Waterfront Press
52 Maple Street
Maplewood, NJ   07040

Current and Reprints

Instituto de Cultura Puertorriqueña
Oficina Programa de Publicaciones
San Juan, PR   00901

Old Puerto Rican Books

Brennan Books
Box 9002
Salt Lake City, UT   84109

Ms. María Carrasco
Centro de Reproducción de
    Materiales
Biblioteca José M. Lázaro
Sistema de Bibliotecas
Universidad de Puerto Rico
Río Piedras, PR   00931

Fernández-Gatell
P.O. Box 896
Santa Monica, CA   90406

The Jenkins Company
Box 2085
Austin, TX   78768

Howard Karno
P.O. Box 431
Santa Monica, CA   90406

Editor's Note.   This   list   was   distributed   during   the workshop session on Puerto Rico.

Frances Klennet
13 Cranberry Street
Brooklyn, NY   11201

Out-of-State Book Service
Box 3253
San Clemente, CA   92672

Libros Latinos
P.O. Box 1103
Redlands, CA   92373

Parnassus Books
Route 6A
Yarmouth Port, MA   02675

McBlain Books
P.O. Box 5062
Hamden, CT   06618

Tainter's
Temple, NH   03084

José R. Olmo-Olmo
65 West 106 Street, 3-C
New York, NY   10025

Copy Services

Centro de Reproducción de Materiales
Sistema de Bibliotecas
Apartado Postal C
Estación de la Universidad
Río Piedras, PR   00931

Duplicados de documentos; reproducciones de libros; copias por ambos lados del papel; compaginación; reducciones; duplicados de microformas a papel; transparencias

Centro de Reproducción de Materiales
Biblioteca José M. Lázaro
Segundo Piso, ala Este
(809) 764-0000 ext. 3437

Horario

Lunes a viernes   8:00 a.m. - 12:00 m.
1:00 p.m. - 4:30 p.m.

Descripción

El Centro de Reproducción de Materiales es un área de trabajo que se especializa en duplicar materiales impresos o en microformas, a papel. Cuenta con un equipo sofisticado que responde a las exigencias de nuestros usuarios. Dentro de los propósitos generales del Centro, se destacan: mantener una servicio de reproducción de materiales con una alta calidad del duplicado; participar activamente en el enriquecimiento de las colecciones del Sistema de Bibliotecas, mediante la reproducción de materiales; mejorar y facilitar la obtención del servicio de duplicado de documentos.

Servicios

- Duplicado de documentos de papel a papel
- Duplicado de microformas a papel
- Preparación de transparencias
- Coordinar el mantenimiento y cuidado del equipo de reproducción existente en las Colecciones del Sistema de Bibliotecas
- Duplicar el material solicitado mediante préstamo interbibliotecario a las diferentes colecciones y originar el procedimiento de facturar el servicio
- Preparar cotizaciones para las solicitudes de servicios de aquellos usuarios que desconocen la tarifa total de la reproducción solicitada

Acceso al Servicio

El usuario tendrá acceso a nuestros servicios después que haya localizado e identificado el material que desea reproducir.

Normas para Solicitar el Servicio

Una vez el usuario haya realizado la búsqueda, identificación y solicitud de autorización para la reproducción del material, éste será recibido por el personal del Centro para asignarle el turno correspondiente y el tipo de reproducción que conlleva.

En el caso de servicios para pago directo, el usuario recibe la factura en el Centro y efectua el pago en la Oficina del Tesorero de la Universidad de Puerto Rico, Recinto de Río Piedras. Al presentar la factura sellada, se entregará el material duplicado.

Los servicios solicitados para dependencias del Recinto de Río Piedras y usuarios con cuentas personales, son facturados al finalizar el mes en curso.

El equipo de reproducción es manejado exclusivamente por el personal del Centro.

El servicio puede ser solicitado por la Comunidad Universitaria y el público en general.

Tarifas

El importe a pagar por cada reproducción es de diez centavos ($0.10). En las copiadoras de las salas y/o colecciónes del Sistema de Bibliotecas, el cargo es el mismo. Cuando un usuario obtiene una copia de pobre calidad, el Centro de Reproducción de Materiales le provee otra copia sin cargo adicional. Para poder efectuar esta transacción, el usuario debe solicitar al bibliotecario de turno la forma de copia gratis.

59. THE HISTORICAL ARCHIVES OF PUERTO RICO

María de los Angeles Castro

I. Guías Generales

Están dirigidas a los que se inician como investigadores en la historia de Puerto Rico, particularmente estudiantes. Indican los repositorios más importantes y las guías que existen para cada uno.

Castro, María de los Angeles, María Dolores Luque, y Gervasio Luis García. Los primeros pasos. Una bibliografía para empezar a investigar la historia de Puerto Rico. Universidad de Puerto Rico. Recinto de Río Piedras: Centro de Investigaciones Históricas, Oficina de Publicaciones de la Facultad de Humanidades, 1984. 80 pp.

Silvestrini-Pacheco, Blanca, y María de los Angeles Castro Arroyo. "Sources for the Study of Puerto Rican History: A Challenge to the Historian's Imagination," Latin American Research Review, 16:2 (1981), 156-171.

II. Archivos y Bibliotecas Principales

Archivo General de Puerto Rico (AGPR)

Es el archivo insular más importante por ser el custodio de los documentos públicos. Tiene escasa documentación de la segunda mitad del siglo XVIII pero es sumamente rico en documentación del XIX y XX. Está en preparación una guía nueva.

de la Rosa Martínez, Luis. "Los fondos documentales en el Archivo General de Puerto Rico." Anales de Investigación Histórica, Universidad de Puerto Rico, Recinto de Río Piedras, 4:1-2 (1977), 1-20.

Guía al Archivo General de Puerto Rico. San Juan de Puerto Rico: Instituto de Cultura Puertorriqueña, Archivo General de Puerto Rico, 1964.

Centro de Investigaciones Históricas (CIH). Universidad de Puerto Rico, Recinto de Río Piedras, Facultad de Humanidades

Es depósito documental y centro propulsor de investigaciones. Como archivo, su caudal principal reside en la colección de micropelículas, fotocopias, fotografías y transcripciones procedentes de archivos del extranjero: España, Inglaterra, Estados Unidos, Francia, Dinamarca, México, Cuba y Suecia.

Los fondos del Archivo General de Indias (Sevilla) y del Archivo General de la Nación (México), suplen la casi total ausencia de documentos de los siglos XVI al XVIII en los archivos del país. Igualmente importantes son la correspondencia de los cónsules extranjeros, los números de periódicos y otros impresos y las fotografías de mapas y planos, casi todos del siglo XIX. Existen inventarios para todas las colecciones.

Recientemente se inició un programa para la microfilmación de colecciones privadas que se encuentran dispersas por la Isla. A pesar de que se han localizado algunas muy importantes, pocas han podido microfilmarse por falta de recursos.

Su biblioteca, aunque pequeña, es importante. Se especializa en Puerto Rico y la América Colonial con una sección de metodología para la investigación histórica. Custodia los originales de todas las tesis presentadas para obtener el grado de Maestría en la Escuela Graduada de Historia de la Universidad de Puerto Rico y copia de algunos trabajos inéditos sobre la historia insular.

Como centro de investigaciones ha concentrado sus esfuerzos en la localización, edición y publicación de colecciones documentales. Algunas de éstas han jugado un papel importante en la renovación reciente de la historiografía puertorriqueña. Además, publica periódicamente cuadernos y boletines orientados hacia la metodología y el conocimiento y manejo de fuentes en la investigación de la historia de Puerto Rico.

Caro Costas, Aída R. "Los fondos documentales del Centro de Investigaciones Históricas." Anales de Investigación Histórica, Universidad de Puerto Rico, Recinto de Río Piedras, 4:1-2 (1977), 36-42.

Castro, María de los Angeles. "En busca de los orígenes perdidos: los documentos del siglo XVI al siglo XVIII en el Centro de Investigaciones Históricas." Cuadernos de la Facultad de Humanidades, Universidad de Puerto Rico, Recinto de Río Piedras, 10 (1983), 55-73.

_____. Guía descriptiva de los fondos documentales existentes en el Centro de Investigaciones Históricas. Universidad de Puerto Rico, Recinto de Río Piedras: Oficina de Publicaciones de la Facultad de Humanidades, 1984.

Documentos de la Real Hacienda de Puerto Rico (1510-1519). Transcriptos y compilados por Aurelio Tanodi. Universidad de Puerto Rico, Editorial Universitaria y Centro de Investigaciones Históricas, 1971.

El proceso abolicionista en Puerto Rico. Documentos para su estudio. San Juan de Puerto Rico: Centro de Investigaciones

Históricas e Instituto de Cultura Puertorriqueña, 1974 y 1978. 2 vols.

Tirado, Dulce María. "Colonialismo, revolución y reformismo: Puerto Rico en los archivos cubanos." Cuadernos de la Facultad de Humanidades, Universidad de Puerto Rico, Recinto de Río Piedras, 10 (1983), 73-91.

Biblioteca José M. Lázaro (BJML). Universidad de Puerto Rico, Recinto de Río Piedras

Es la biblioteca principal de Puerto Rico. Las secciones más importantes para la investigación, por sus ricos fondos documentales son: La Biblioteca y Hemeroteca Puertorriqueña (Colección Puertorriqueña), la Sección de Documentos y la Biblioteca Regional del Caribe. Una breve descripción de éstas y otras secciones aparece en Castro et al., Los primeros pasos . . ., pp. 10-13.

"La biblioteca; su organización, recursos y servicios." Folleto mimeografiado, 1977.

Museo de Antropología, Historia y Arte (MAHA). Universidad de Puerto Rico, Recinto de Río Piedras

Aunque su colección de manuscritos es reducida, deben tenerse en cuenta los documentos de Eugenio María de Hostos y, en menor grado, los de otros próceres puertorriqueños.

Su importantísima colección de riles de haciendas complementa los estudios económicos y sociales sobre éstas.

III. Archivos Privados

Archivo Eclesiástico de Puerto Rico (AEPR)

Es el más importante para la historia de la iglesia católica en Puerto Rico durante los siglos XIX y XX, aunque contiene algunos documentos del XVIII. Actualmente no se permite su consulta pero está en proceso el inventario y la catalogación de sus fondos con miras a abrirse pronto para los investigadores. El Centro de Investigaciones Históricas asesora y colabora en este importante proyecto. Al terminar el inventario y la catalogación se publicarán las guías oportunas.

Gómez Canedo, Lino. Los archivos históricos de Puerto Rico. Apuntes de una visita (enero-mayo 1960). San Juan de Puerto Rico: Instituto de Cultura Puertorriqueña, 1964.

Archivos Parroquiales

Se custodian en las distintas parroquias de la Isla y el tiempo que cubre la documentación varía. Los más completos incluyen desde mediados del siglo XVIII. Además de su importancia para estudiar la iglesia católica en Puerto Rico, son fundamentales para la historia social y demográfica. Los libros de bautismo, confirmación, matrimonios y entierros hicieron las veces de registro demográfico hasta que éste se fundó en 1885.

Cuadro de los registros parroquiales de Puerto Rico. Compilado en febrero y marzo de 1973 por la Sociedad Genealógica de la Iglesia de Jesucristo de los Santos de los Ultimos Días. Puede consultarse una copia en el CIH.

Gutiérrez del Arroyo, Isabel. "Los libros parroquiales como fuentes de la historia social." Anales de Investigación Histórica. Universidad de Puerto Rico, Recinto de Río Piedras, 4:1-2 (1977), 20-36.

Rodríguez León, Mario. "Los registros parroquiales y la microhistoria demográfica en Puerto Rico." Tesis de M.A. presentada al Centro de Estudios Avanzados de Puerto Rico y el Caribe, 1983.

Százdi, Adam. "Los registros del siglo XVIII en la parroquia de San Germán." Historia, Universidad de Puerto Rico, 1:1, nueva serie (enero, 1962), 51-63.

IV. Colecciones Particulares

Las integran documentos que se conservan—o se han conservado hasta fechas recientes—en custodia privada, bien sea de una familia o de una corporación. El AGPR, la BJML y el CIH han adquirido muchas de estas colecciones pero un sinnúmero de ellas quedan en manos particulares. Para una lista de las que están en los archivos véase la sección de Guías Generales, arriba.

Se presentan algunos ejemplos que por haber servido de apoyo a alguna publicación o algunas tesis evidencian el alcance de estas colecciones.

Propietarios y Corporaciones Agrícolas

Empresas Serrallés y la Central Mercedita (Ponce). Libros de contabilidad: 1861-1900.

Ramos Mattei, Andrés A. La hacienda azucarera. Su crecimiento y crisis en Puerto Rico (siglo XIX). San Juan de Puerto Rico: CEREP, 1981.

Sociedad Agrícola Fantauzzi Hnos. y la Central Lafayette (Arroyo). Mediados del siglo XIX a la tercera década del siglo XX. Colección extensa y variada respecto al tipo de documentos: escrituras de fundación, otorgación de poderes, liquidación y disolución de la sociedad, escrituras de compraventa, copiadores de cartas, diarios de gastos, libros mayores, libros de asientos, libros de balances, libros de cajas, trámites relacionados con el muelle en el puerto de Arroyo, etc.

Tapia Ríos, Gloria E. "Origen y desarrollo de la Central Lafayette (1850-1910)." Tesis de M.A. en progreso para ser presentada al Departamento de Historia de la Universidad de Puerto Rico, Recinto de Río Piedras.

Familia Lluberas y la Central San Francisco (Guayanilla). Ultimo tercio del siglo XIX a primer cuarto del XX. La familia Lluberas mantiene los libros mayores de Francisco, Jerónimo y Arturo Lluberas (1873-1914), mientras que la Central conserva los copiadores de cartas (1912-1919) y los libros de jornales (1904-1920).

Caraballo Ramón, Eurípides. "Origen y fundación de la Central San Francisco." Tesis de M.A. presentada al Departamento de Historia de la Universidad de Puerto Rico, Recinto de Río Piedras, 1983.

Colección Jaime y Federico Calaf Collazo y la Central Monserrate (Manatí). Escrituras de compra de tierras y otros útiles, a partir de 1869. Esta colección está en proceso de microfilmarse para el CIH.

Medina Vázquez, Angel. "La Central Monserrate, desarrollo, declive y desaparición." Tesis de M.A. en progreso para ser presentada al Centro de Estudios Avanzados de Puerto Rico y el Caribe.

Colección Pietri-Mariani y la Hacienda Pietri (Adjuntas). Desde mediados hasta fines del siglo XIX. Contiene correspondencia, libros de contabilidad, documentos notariales, etc. Fue depositada en el AGPR (Fondo Pietri-Mariani).

Buitrago Ortíz, Carlos. Los orígenes históricos de la sociedad precapitalista. Río Piedras: Ediciones Huracán, 1976.

_____. Haciendas cafetaleras y clases terratenientes en el Puerto Rico decimonónico. Río Piedras: Editorial de la Universidad de Puerto Rico, 1982.

Carro Figueroa, Vivian. "Descripción del proceso de adquisición de tierras de la familia Pietri, de Adjuntas, 1858-1898." Anales de Investigación Histórica, Universidad de Puerto Rico. Recinto de Río Piedras, 2:1 (enero-junio, 1975). 111 pp.

Hacienda Castañer (Lares). 1868-1928. Contiene copiadores de cartas, diarios de cuentas, correspondencia, libros de inventario, etc.

Díaz Hernández, Luis Edgardo. Castañer. Una hacienda cafetalera en Puerto Rico (1868-1930). Ponce: Academia de Artes, Historia y Arqueología de Puerto Rico, 1982.

Colección Asociación de Agricultores de Puerto Rico. Incluye los libros de actas desde su fundación en 1924 hasta diciembre 1950 y la serie completa de la revista El Agricultor Puertorriqueño (julio 1926 a 1941). Fue cedida al CIH.

Alvarez Curbelo, Silvia. "La polémica agraria en Puerto Rico: 1924-1928." Tesis de M.A. en progreso para ser presentada al Departamento de Historia de la Universidad de Puerto Rico, Recinto de Río Piedras.

Firmas Comerciales

Colección José Víctor Oliver Ledesma. Mediados del siglo XIX al primer cuarto del siglo XX. Incluye libros mayores, libros diarios, cuentas corrientes, libros auxiliares, facturas, registro de clientes, mercancías recibidas, etc. de la Casa Roses y Co. de Arecibo, la más importante del distrito durante el período que cubre la documentación. Fue donada al CIH por el Sr. José Víctor Oliver Ledesma.

Cubano Iguina, Astrid Teresa. "Comercio y hegemonía social. Los comerciantes de Arecibo, 1857-1887." Tesis de M.A. presentada al Departamento de Historia de la Universidad de Puerto Rico, Recinto de Río Piedras, 1979. (La autora continúa trabajando el tema para su tesis doctoral en la Universidad de Princeton, NJ.)

Casa Pintueles (Ciales). Ultimo tercio del siglo XIX a la década de los '50 del siglo XX. Consta de libros mayores de cuentas, diarios de caja, diarios de cuentas, estados de cuentas, libros de recibos, libros de hipotecas, libros de ventas de café, libros de ventas de tabaco y libros de socios y transacciones de la cooperativa de agricultores.

González, Libia M. "Agricultura, comercio y poder local de Ciales: 1885-1895." Tesis de M.A. en progreso para ser presentada al Departamento de Historia de la Universidad de Puerto Rico, Recinto de Río Piedras.

Políticos y Otras Personalidades

Santiago Iglesias Pantín. Archivo particular conservado por Igualdad Iglesias vda. de Pagán.

Córdova, Gonzalo F. Santiago Iglesias, creador del movimiento obrero en Puerto Rico. Río Piedras: Editorial Universitaria, 1979.

José Celso Barbosa. Archivo particular conservado por Pilar Barbosa vda. de Rosario.

Barbosa de Rosario, Pilar. La obra de José Celso Barbosa. Parte II. Historia del autonomismo puertorriqueño. 4 vols. San Juan de Puerto Rico, 1957-1978. Parte III. Documentos para la historia política puertorriqueña. 4 vols. San Juan de Puerto Rico, 1981-1983.

_____. Manuel F. Rossy y Calderón. Ciudadano cabal (1861-1932). San Juan de Puerto Rico, 1981.

Muñiz de Barbosa, Carmen, y René Torres Delgado. José Gómez Brioso (1855-1930). Nada menos que todo un hombre. San Juan de Puerto Rico, 1982.

Torres Delgado, René. Dos filántropos puertorriqueños, Santiago Veve Calzada y Federico Degetau González. San Juan de Puerto Rico, 1983.

Colección María del Pilar Acosta Velarde de Legrand. Papeles de José Julián Acosta, Angel Acosta Quintero, Federico Acosta Velarde y Federico Legrand. Incluye algunos libros. Micropelículas depositadas en el CIH y la CP de la BJML.

Acosta Quintero, Angel. José Julián Acosta y su tiempo. San Juan de Puerto Rico, Instituto de Cultura Puertorriqueña, 1965.

Colección Ruby Black. Contiene los papeles acumulados por la periodista norteamericana durante los años en que actuó como corresponsal del periódico La Democracia en Washington y como enlace de Luis Muñoz Marín con la administración del presidente Franklin D. Roosevelt (1926 a 1948). Se encuentra en el CIH.

Estades Font, María Eugenia. "La Colección Ruby Black como fuente para el estudio del siglo XX puertorriqueño." Se publicará próximamente en el Boletín del Centro de Investigaciones Históricas.

Mathews, Thomas. La política puertorriqueña y el nuevo trato. Trans. Antonio J. Colorado. Universidad de Puerto Rico, Editorial Universitaria, 1975.

60. SELECT BIBLIOGRAPHY OF LATIN AMERICAN PUBLICATIONS DEALING WITH HOMOSEXUALITY

Robert Howes

Works of imaginative literature where homosexuality is the central theme are marked with an asterisk * . Gay movement serials are so irregular and ephemeral that it is not usually possible to give full bibliographical details. Issues I have actually seen are shown in parentheses. Serials held by the Canadian Gay Archives are annotated with "CGA," and those held by the Labadie Collection with "Lab."

Latin America in General and Spanish America

Nonfiction

Acevedo, Zelmar. Homosexualidad: hacia la destrucción de los mitos. Buenos Aires: Del Sur, 1985.

Argüelles, Lourdes, and B. Ruby Rich. "Homosexuality, Homophobia, and Revolution: Notes toward an Understanding of the Cuban Lesbian and Gay Male Experience." Signs: Journal of Women in Culture and Society, 9:4 (Summer, 1984), 683-699.

Blanco, José Joaquín. "Des yeux dont on a peur de rêver." Masques; Revue des homosexualités (Paris), 5 (Summer, 1980), 68-73.

Cabrera Infante, Guillermo. "El amor que (no) se atreve a decir su nombre." Vuelta, 2:13 (Dec., 1977), 49-50.

_____. "Bites from the bearded crocodile." London Review of Books, 3:10 (June 4-17, 1981), 3-8.

Cardín, Alberto. Guerreros, chamanes y travestís. Indicios de homosexualidad entre los exóticos. Barcelona: Tusquets, 1984.

Carrier, Joseph Michel. "Urban Mexican Male Homosexual Encounters: An Analysis of Participants and Coping Strategies." Ph.D. diss., University of California, Irvine, 1972. (72-32339.)

"Los cubanos y el homosexualismo." Mariel; Revista de literatura y arte, 2:5 (Spring, 1984), 8-15.

Da Gris, Carlos A. El homosexual en la Argentina. Buenos Aires: Continental, 1965.

Editor's Note. This bibliography was prepared to accompany the author's "The Literature of Outsiders: The Literature of the Gay Community in Latin America" (Volume I, pp. 288-304).

"Dossier: Argentine, exil et répression." Masques, 11 (Autumn, 1981), 18-38.

Estévez, María Elena, et al. "Síndrome de inmunodeficiencia adquirida (AIDS) con sarcoma de Kaposi en homosexuales en la Argentina." Medicina. Buenos Aires, 43:4 (1983), 477.

Fernbach, David. "Gay Liberation in Central America." Gay Left (London), no. 10, pp. 19-21.

Frente de Liberación Homosexual de la Argentina. "Argentina: Gay Manifesto." Trans. Allen Young. Gay Sunshine (San Francisco), 15 (Oct.-Nov., 1972), 7.

_____. "Male Homosexuality and Machismo." Gay Sunshine, 23 (Nov.-Dec., 1974), 21, 26.

Garbi. "Cuba: primer 'territorio libre de América Latina' (ven y verás . . .)." Gay hotsa (Bilbao), 26 (Feb.-March, 1985), unpaginated.

González Almaguer, Rodolfo. "Western." El caimán barbudo, (Dec., 1981), 18-19.

Guerra, Francisco. The Pre-Columbian Mind. A Study into the Aberrant Nature of Sexual Drives, Drugs Affecting Behaviour, and the Attitude Towards Life and Death, with a Survey of Psychotherapy, in Pre-Columbian America. London, New York: Seminar, 1971.

Hernández, Juan Jakobo, and Ignacio Sánchez. "Le mouvement homosexual mexicain: le FHAR." Masques, 5 (Summer, 1980), 87-92.

Hidalgo, Hilda A., and Elia Hidalgo Christensen. "The Puerto Rican Lesbian and the Puerto Rican Community." Journal of Homosexuality, 2:2 (Winter, 1976-77), 109-121.

Jamandreu, Paco. La cabeza contra el suelo. Memorias. Buenos Aires: Flor, 1975.

Lacey, E. A. "Latin America: Myths and Realities." Gay Sunshine, 40/41 (Summer/Fall, 1979), 22-31.

Lane, Erskine. Game-texts: A Guatemalan Journal. San Francisco: Gay Sunshine, 1978.

Leicht, Anton. "Argentine: la dictature contre les homosexuels. Reportage." Masques, 11 (Autumn, 1981), 19-28.

Lucena Salmoral, Manuel. "Bardaje en una tribu Guahibo del Tomo." Revista colombiana de antropología, 14 (1966-1969), 261-266.

Mario, José. "Allen Ginsberg en La Habana." Mundo nuevo, 34 (April, 1969), 48-54.

Martínez Z., Lisandro. Derecho penal sexual. 2a ed. Bogotá: Temis, 1977.

Maya Chumu. Salir a la luz como lesbianas de color / Coming out colored. Traducido por / Translated by Emiliana Carera. Seattle, WA: Tsunami, 1980.

Montaner, Carlos Alberto. Informe secreto sobre la Revolución Cubana. Madrid: Sedmay, 1976.

Nelly. "'We Have Our Ways.' The 'Modern Lesbian' in Peru." Rites for Lesbian and Gay Liberation, 2:4 (Oct., 1985), 12-13.

"Riksförbundet för Sexuellt Likaberättigande." A First Report on the Situation of Gays in Chile. Prepared and Researched by RFSL, Sweden, IGA 2nd annual conference, Barcelona, Spain, 4th-7th April 1980." Stockholm, 1980. Mimeographed.

Salas, Luis. Social Control and Deviance in Cuba. New York, NY: Praeger, 1979.

"Sufoco na Argentina." Lampião, 21 (Feb., 1980), 14-15.

Taylor, Jr., Clark Louis. "El ambiente: Male Homosexual Social Life in Mexico City." Ph.D. diss., University of California, Berkeley, 1978. (79-04623.)

Torres de Tolosa, Alvaro, and Luis Fontana. "El mundo gay." Perfil (Buenos Aires), 2 (Nov. 27, 1982), 148-153.

Valdiosera Bermán, Ramón. El lesbianismo en México. México: Eds. Asociados, 1973.

Young, Allen. "The Cuban Revolution and Gay Liberation." In Karla Jay and Allen Young, eds. Out of the Closet: Voices of Gay Liberation. New York, NY: Pyramid, 1974. Pp. 206-228.

_____. Gays under the Cuban Revolution. San Francisco, CA: Grey Fox, 1981.

Young, Allen, and Nick Benton. "¿Cuba sí?" Gay Sunshine, 13 (June, 1972), 11, 6.

Imaginative Literature

Alvarez Gardeazábal, Gustavo. El bazar de los idiotas. Bogotá: Plaza & Janes, 1974.

_____. La tara del papa. Buenos Aires: Compañía General Fabril, 1972.

*Arenas, Reinaldo. Arturo, la estrella más brillante. Barcelona: Montesinos, 1984.

Arévalo Martínez, Rafael. El hombre que parecía un caballo . . . Quetzaltenango, Guatemala: Tip. Arte Nuevo, 1915; San José, Costa Rica, 1918.

_____. Hondura. Novela. Guatemala, 1946 [i.e., 1947].

_____. Las noches en el palacio de la nunciatura. Guatemala: Tipografía Sánchez & De Guise, 1927.

Arlt, Roberto. El juguete rabioso. Novela. Buenos Aires: Editorial Latina, 1926.

Arraíz, Antonio. Puros hombres. [Caracas]: Cooperativa de Artes Gráficas, 1938.

Barba Jacob, Porfirio (pseud. of Miguel Angel Osorio Benítez). Poesías completas. [Bogotá?]: Compañía Grancolombiana de Ediciones, [1944].

Benedetti, Mario. Gracias por el fuego. Novela. Montevideo: Alfa, [1965].

Brunet, Marta. Amasijo. [Santiago de Chile]: Zig-Zag, [1962].

Cabrera Infante, Guillermo. Tres tristes tigres. Barcelona: Seix Barral, 1967.

Cardona, Jenaro. La esfinge del sendero. Buenos Aires: Impr. de J. Tragant, 1916.

Carrillo, Hugo. La calle del sexo verde, y El corazón del espantapájaros. Guatemala: Editorial de la Municipalidad, 1973.

Chocrón, Isaac. Pájaro de mar por tierra. Novela. Caracas: Tiempo Nuevo, 1972.

Cortázar, Julio. 62; modelo para armar. Buenos Aires: Sudamericana, [1968].

Cuentos: Stories by Latinas. Alma Gómez, Cherríe Moraga, and Mariana Romo-Carmona, eds. New York, NY: Kitchen Table Women of Color Press, 1983.

Darío, Rubén. El hombre de oro. [Novela inédita]. [Santiago de Chile]: Zig-Zag, [1938?].

Díaz Rodríguez, Manuel. Idolos rotos. Novela. Paris: Garnier, 1901.

Diez Canseco, José. "Duque". Novela. Santiago de Chile: Ercilla, 1934.

*Donoso, José. El lugar sin límites. México, DF: Joaquín Mortiz, 1966.

Foster, Stephen Wayne. "Latin American Studies. I. Homosexuality in Central American Fiction, 1894-1927. II. Augusto d'Halmar and 'El amor oscuro'." The Cabirion and Gay Books Bulletin, 11 (Fall/Winter, 1984), 2-7, 29.

Fuentes, Norberto. Condenados de Condado. [La Habana]: Casa de las Américas, 1968.

Gómez Carrillo, Enrique. Tres novelas inmorales. Madrid: Mundo Latino, [1920].

*González de Alba, Luis. El vino de los bravos. México, DF: Katún, 1981.

Gregorich, Luis. Literatura y homosexualidad, y otros ensayos. Buenos Aires: Legasa, 1985.

Gunn, Rufus. Something for Sergio. London: GMP, 1985.

Halmar, Augusto d' (pseud. of Augusto Goeminne Thomson). Los alucinados. Santiago de Chile: Ercilla, 1935.

_____. Christian y yo. [Santiago de Chile]: Nascimento, 1946.

_____. Mi otro yo: de la doble vida en la India. Novela. Madrid: Prensa Gráfica, 1924.

* _____. La pasión y muerte del cura Deusto. Berlin, Madrid, Buenos Aires: Editora Internacional, [1924]; 2d ed., Santiago de Chile: Nascimento, 1938; 3d ed., Santiago de Chile: Nascimento, 1969.

_____. La sombra del humo en el espejo. Madrid: Ed. Internacional, [1924].

Hernández, Luisa Josefina. La memoria de Amadís. México, DF: Joaquín Mortiz, 1967.

_____. La noche exquisita. Novela. Xalapa, México: Universidad Veracruzana, 1965.

*Hernández Catá, Alfonso. El ángel de Sodoma. Novela. Madrid: Mundo Latino, [1928]; 2d ed., Madrid: Mundo Latino, [1929]; Valparaíso: El Callao, [1929?].

Jaramillo Levi, Enrique, ed. El cuento erótico en México. México, DF: Diana, 1975.

*Leyland, Winston, ed. My Deep Dark Pain Is Love: A Collection of Latin American Gay Fiction. Trans. from Spanish and Portuguese by E. A. Lacey. San Francisco, CA: Gay Sunshine, 1983.

* _____. Now the Volcano: An Anthology of Latin American Gay Literature. Trans. Erskine Lane, Franklin D. Blanton, and Simon Karlinsky. San Francisco, CA: Gay Sunshine, 1979.

Lezama Lima, José. Paradiso. La Habana: UNEAC, 1966; Engl. trans. Gregory Rabassa, London: Secker & Warburg, 1974; Edición de Eloísa Lezama Lima, Madrid: Cátedra, 1980.

Marqués, René. La mirada. Río Piedras, PR: Antillana, 1975.

Montenegro, Carlos. Hombres sin mujer. [México, DF]: Masas, 1938.

Moraga, Cherríe. Loving in the War Years; lo que nunca pasó por sus labios. Boston, MA: South End, 1983.

Mujica Láinez, Manuel. Bomarzo. 6th ed. Buenos Aires: Sudamericana, 1968.

Muñoz, Elias Miguel. "La utopia sexual en 'El beso de la mujer araña' de Manuel Puig." Alba de América. Revista literaria, 2:2-3 (July-Dec., 1984), 49-60.

Murena, H. A. Las leyes de la noche. Buenos Aires: Sur, [1958].

Onetti, Juan Carlos. Para esta noche. Buenos Aires: Poseidón, [1943].

Pareja Diez-Canseco, Alfredo. Hombres sin tiempo. Novela. Buenos Aires: Losada, [1941].

Pellegrini, Renato. Asfalto. Novela. Buenos Aires: Tirso, [1964].

*Puig, Manuel. El beso de la mujer araña. Barcelona: Seix Barral, 1976; Engl. trans. Thomas Colchie, Kiss of the Spider Woman, New York, NY: Alfred A. Knopf, 1979.

*Rechy, John. City of Night. New York, NY: Grove, 1963.

*_____. Numbers. New York, NY: Grove, 1967.

*_____. Rushes. New York, NY: Grove, 1979.

*_____. The Sexual Outlaw. New York, NY: Grove, 1977.

Reinhardt, Karl J. "The Image of Gays in Chicano Prose Fiction." Explorations in Ethnic Studies, 4:2 (July, 1981), 41-55.

Revueltas, José. Los errores; Novela. [México, DF]: Fondo de Cultura Económica, [1964].

Reyes, Salvador. Valparaíso, puerto de nostalgia. [Santiago de Chile]: Zig-Zag, [1955].

Reynoso, Oswaldo. En octubre no hay milagros; Novela. [Lima]: Wuaman Puma, [1965].

Salas, Floyd. Tattoo the Wicked Cross. New York, NY: Grove, [1967].

Sarduy, Severo. Cobra. 3d ed. Buenos Aires: Sudamericana, 1974.

Schwartz, Kessel. "Homosexuality as a Theme in Representative Contemporary Spanish American Novels." Kentucky Romance Quarterly, 22:2 (1975), 247-257.

Shaw, D. L. "Notes on the Presentation of Sexuality in the Modern Spanish-American Novel." Bulletin of Hispanic Studies, 59:3 (July, 1982), 275-282.

"Sobre el 'Paradiso' de Lezama" [Two letters by Mario Vargas Llosa and Emir Rodríguez Monegal]. Mundo nuevo, 16 (Oct., 1967), 89-95.

Vargas Llosa, Mario. Conversación en la catedral. Barcelona: Seix Barral, [1969].

_____. Historia de Mayta. Barcelona: Seix Barral, 1984.

Villanueva, Alfredo. "Machismo vs Gayness: Latin American Fiction." Gay Sunshine, 29/30 (Summer/Fall, 1976), 22.

Viñas, David. Hombres de a caballo. Barcelona: Bruguera, 1981.

Zalamea Borda, Eduardo. 4 años a bordo de mi mismo: diario de los 5 sentidos. Novela. [Bogotá]: Santa Fe, 1934.

*Zapata, Luis. Las aventuras, desventuras y sueños de Adonis García, el vampiro de la Colonia Roma. 2d ed. México, DF: Grijalbo, 1979; Engl. trans., E. A. Lacey, Adonis García: A Picaresque Novel, San Francisco, CA: Gay Sunshine, 1981.

Gay Movement Serials

(CGA = Canadian Gay Archives, Toronto, Ontario; Lab = Labadie Collection, University of Michigan, Ann Arbor, MI)

Al margen: Boletín bimestral editado por GALF. Grupo de Autoconciencia de Lesbianas Feministas, Lima. (1:2, June 1985.)

Amazona. Colectivo de lesbianas del FHAR (Frente Homosexual de Acción Revolucionaria), México, DF. ([1979]). CGA.

Crisálida: Organo de difusión del GOHL. Grupo Orgullo Homosexual de Liberación, Guadalajara, Jalisco. (5, Dec., 1983; 7, Feb., 1984; 8, June, 1984; Sept., 1984.) CGA; Lab.

De ambiente: Informativo de lesbianas y homosexuales. Colectivo de Orgullo Gay, Bogotá. (1:1, Feb., 1985 – 1:5, June, 1985.)

Diferentes. Buenos Aires. (1:1, July, 1984.)

Entendido. Revista mensual de homosexualidades. Caracas. (2:5, March/April, 1981; 2:6, 1981; 7, 1983; 8.) CGA; Lab.

FHAR informa. Frente Homosexual de Acción Revolucionaria, México, DF. (1, Sept. 24, [1979].) CGA; Lab.

Fidelidad. Grupo Fidelidad, México, DF. (1, [1980?].) CGA.

Gay. Tubreviario Samizdat. San Martín, Argentina. (2 issues: 12 and unnumbered.) CGA.

Homosexuales. Frente de Liberación Homosexual de la Argentina, Buenos Aires. (6, July, 1973.) CGA.

Grupo Entendido. Boletín informativo del Grupo Entendido. Caracas. (1, Feb./March, 1982; 2, April, 1982.) CGA.

Nuestro cuerpo: información homosexual. Colectivo Mariposas Negras del Frente Homosexual de Acción Revolucionaria, México, DF. (1, May, 1979.) CGA.

Nuevo ambiente. Organo informativo del Grupo Lambda de Liberación Homosexual. México, DF. (1, June, 1979 – 5, June/July, 1983.) CGA, Lab.

El Otro. Medellín. (2, Feb., 1978; 4, Aug.-Sept., 1978; [5, 1979]; 6, [1979?].) CGA.

Pa' fuera. Publicación oficial de la Comunidad de Orgullo Gay. San Juan, PR. (1:3, Nov., 1974 - 2:3, April, 1975; May, 1975; Aug./Sept., 1975; Dec., 1975.) CGA.

Paz y liberación. Hollywood, CA, and Houston, TX. (1, May, 1979 - 7, March, 1985.)

Política sexual. Cuadernos del Frente Homosexual de Acción Revolucionaria. México, DF. (1:1 [1979?].) CGA.

Secretariado Latino-Americano de Grupos Homosexuales. Informativo del S.L.A.G.H. Salvador, Bahia, Brazil. (2, Feb. 1, 1985.)

Sin fronteras. A journal. Denver, CO. (2, Winter, 1985.)

Somos. Frente de Liberación Homosexual de la Argentina, c/o Comunidad de Orgullo Gay, San Juan, PR. (2, Feb., 1974; 5.) CGA.

Unidad. Gay and Lesbian Latinos Unidos, Los Angeles, CA. (4:4, June/July, 1985; 4:5, Oct.-Nov., 1985.)

Ventana gay. Bogotá. (1, Aug., 1980 - 16, March, 1983.) CGA; Lab.

¡Y qué! Boletín para la comunidad homosexual/lesbiana. Tijuana, Baja California, México. (5, Trimestre Sept./Nov., [1984?] - 9, Período Sept./Oct., 1985.) CGA.

Brazil

Nonfiction

Almeida, José Ricardo Pires de. Homossexualismo: a libertinagem no Rio de Janeiro. Estudo sobre as perversões e inversões do instinto genital. Rio de Janeiro: Laemmert, 1906.

Caminhos cruzados. Linguagem, antropologia e ciências naturais. São Paulo: Brasiliense, 1982.

Castro, Francisco José Viveiros de. Attentados ao pudor. Rio de Janeiro: D. de Magalhães, Livraria Moderna, 1895.

Colaço, Rita. Uma conversa informal sobre homossexualismo. Duque de Caxias, Rio de Janeiro: Edição do Autor, 1984.

Corrêa, Mariza. "Antropologia & medicina legal: variações em torno de um mito." In Caminhos cruzados (1982). Pp. 53-63.

Daniel, Herbert. Passagem para o próximo sonho: um possível romance autocrítico. Rio de Janeiro: Codecri, 1982.

Detrez, Conrad. "Jésus, les machos et le guérilleros. Entretien avec Conrad Detrez." Masques, 2 (Autumn, 1979), 115-124.

Feitosa, Reuel P. O avesso do amor. 2d ed. Venda Nova, Minas Gerais: Peniel, 1978.

Fichte, Hubert. "The Razor Blade and the Hermaphrodite." Gay Sunshine, 33/34 (Summer/Fall, 1977), 13-14.

_____. Xango. Die afroamerikanischen Religionen. II. Bahia, Haiti, Trinidad. Frankfurt am Main: S. Fischer, 1976.

Fry, Peter. "Da hierarquia à igualdade: a contrução histórica da homossexualidade no Brasil." In his Para inglês ver (1982). Pp. 87-115.

_____. "Febrônio Índio do Brasil: onde cruzam a psiquiatria, a profecia a homossexualidade e a lei." In Caminhos cruzados (1982). Pp. 65-80.

_____. "Homossexualidade masculina e cultos afro-brasileiros." In his Para inglês ver (1982). Pp. 54-86.

_____. Para inglês ver: identidade e política na cultura brasileira. Rio de Janeiro: Zahar, 1982.

Fry, Peter, and Edward Macrae. O que é homossexualidade. São Paulo: Brasiliense, 1983.

Grupo Outra Coisa. O bandeirante destemido: um guia gay de São Paulo. São Paulo, 1981.

Herzer. A queda para o alto. 3d ed. Petrópolis: Vozes, 1982.

"Homossexualidade e repressão." In Guido Mantega, ed. Sexo e poder (1979). Pp. 137-155.

Jaime, Jorge. Homossexualismo masculino. 2d ed. N.p., 1953.

Laurenti, Ruy. "Editorial. Homossexualismo e a Classificação Internacional de Doenças." Revista de saúde pública, 18:5 (Oct., 1984), 344-347.

Lima, Délcio Monteiro de. Os homoeróticos. Rio de Janeiro: Francisco Alves, 1983.

Macrae, Edward. "Os respeitáveis militantes e as bichas loucas." In Caminhos cruzados (1982). Pp. 99-111.

Mantega, Guido, ed. Sexo e poder. São Paulo: Brasiliense, 1979.

Míccolis, Leila, and Herbert Daniel. Jacarés e lobisomens: dois ensaios sobre a homossexualidade. Rio de Janeiro: Achiamé, 1983.

"As minorias sexuais." In Guido Mantega, ed. Sexo e poder (1979). Pp. 127-136.

Mott, Luiz. "A homossexualidade no Brasil: bibliografia." Salvador, Bahia, n.d. Mimeographed.

_____. "Report from Brazil." The Cabirion and Gay Books Bulletin, 11 (Fall-Winter, 1984), 14.

Okita, Hiro. Homossexualismo: da opressão a libertação. São Paulo: Proposta, [1981?].

Ribeiro, Leonidio. "Etiologia e tratamento da homosexualidade. Conferencia realizada na Universidade de Coimbra [. . .] em 24 de abril de 1937." Archivos de medicina legal e identificação, 8:15 (Jan. 1938), lx-lxxxv.

_____. "Homosexualité et glandes endocrines." Archivos de medicina legal e identificação, 8:15 (Jan. 1938), xcviii-c.

_____. "O problema medico-legal do homo-sexualismo sob o ponto de vista endocrinico." Archivos de medicina legal e identificação, 5:12 (Oct., 1935), 145-160.

Ribeiro, René. "Personality and the Psychosexual Adjustment of Afro-Brazilian Cult Members." Journal de la Société des Américanistes. Tome LVIII. Les Amériques noires. Paris, 1969. Pp. 109-120.

Rizzini, Jorge. O sexo nas prisões. São Paulo: Nova Época, 1976.

Tito Filho, A. "Homossexualismo." In his Sermões aos peixes. Rio de Janeiro: Artenova, 1975. Pp. 115-118.

Imaginative Literature

Abreu, Caio Fernando. Morangos mofados. 4th ed. São Paulo: Brasiliense, 1983.

Andrade, Mário de. Os contos de Belazarte. 7th ed. Belo Horizonte: Livraria Martins/Itatiaia, 1980.

*Ayala, Walmir. Um animal de Deus. Romance. Rio de Janeiro: Lidador, 1967.

* _____. Nosso filho vai ser mãe. Quem matou Caim? Rio de Janeiro: Letras e Artes, 1965.

Azevedo, Aluísio. O cortiço. Rio de Janeiro: Garnier, 1890.

*Caminha, Adolfo. Bom-Crioulo. Rio de Janeiro: Domingos de Magalhães--Livraria Moderna, 1895; 3d ed., Rio de Janeiro: Organização Simões, 1956; Engl. trans. E. A. Lacey, Bom-Crioulo: The Black Man and the Cabin Boy, San Francisco, CA: Gay Sunshine, 1982.

Canales, Luis. "O homossexualismo como tema no moderno teatro brasileiro." Luso-Brazilian Review, 18:1 (Summer, 1981), 173-181.

Coutinho, Edilberto, ed. Erotismo no conto brasileiro. Antologia. Rio de Janeiro: Civilização Brasileira, 1980.

_____. Zero zero sexo: o erotismo no romance brasileiro contemporaneo. Antologia. Rio de Janeiro: Récord, 1967.

*Damata, Gasparino. Os solteirões. Rio de Janeiro: Pallas, 1976.

590   Robert Howes

*Damata, Gasparino, ed. Histórias do amor maldito. Rio de Janeiro: Récord, 1967.

*Damata, Gasparino, and Walmir Ayala, eds. Poemas do amor maldito. Brasília: Coordenada Editora de Brasília, 1969.

Detrez, Conrad. L'herbe à brûler. Roman. Paris: Calmann-Lévy, 1978.

*Domingos, Jorge. Balu. Petrópolis, 1980.

Figueiredo, André de. Labirinto. Rio de Janeiro: Expressão e Cultura, 1971.

*Freire, Roberto. Travesti. São Paulo: Símbolo, 1978.
*Hecker Filho, Paulo. Internato. Novela. [Porto Alegre?]: Fronteira, 1951.

Mautner, Jorge. Sexo do crepúsculo. São Paulo: Global Ground, 1983.

*Penteado, Darcy. Crescilda, e os Espartanos. São Paulo: Símbolo, 1977.

*_____. A meta. 2d ed. São Paulo: Símbolo, 1977.

*_____. Nivaldo e Jerônimo. Rio de Janeiro: Codecri, 1981.

*_____. Teoremambo: delito delirante para coro e orquestra. São Paulo: Livraria Cultura, 1979.

Pompeia, Raul. O Atheneu. Rio de Janeiro: Tip. Gazeta de Notícias, 1888.

Rio, João do. Histórias da gente alegre. Contos, crônicas e reportagens da "Belle-Epoque" carioca. Seleção, introdução e notas: João Carlos Rodrigues. Rio de Janeiro: José Olympio, 1981.

Rodrigues, Nélson. Teatro quase completo. Rio de Janeiro: Tempo Brasileiro, 1965-66, 4 vols.

Silva, Aguinaldo. Cristo partido ao meio. Rio de Janeiro: Civilização Brasileira, 1965.

*_____. No país das sombras. Novela. Rio de Janeiro: Civilização Brasileira, 1979.

_____. República dos assassinos. Romance. Rio de Janeiro: Civilização Brasileira, 1976.

*Trevisan, João Silvério. Testamento do Jônatas deixado a David. São Paulo: Brasiliense, 1976.

Velho, Gilberto. "Literatura e desvio: questões para a antropologia." In Caminhos cruzados (1982). Pp. 81-88.

*24 poemas gays. Salvador: Grupo Gay da Bahia, 1982.

*Wilde, Zeno, and Wanderley Aguiar Bragança. Blue Jeans: uma peça sórdida. [Rio de Janeiro?], 1980.

Gay Movement Serials

CGI. Orgão informativo da Central Gay de Informações. Círculo Corydon. São Paulo. (2 [1979].) CGA

Chanacomchana. Grupo Ação Lésbica Feminista. São Paulo. (4, Jan., 1981.) CGA; Lab.

O Corpo. Grupo Somos. São Paulo. (0, Experimental, Nov., 1980; 4, Mar./April, 1983; 5, Oct., 1983; one unnumbered, undated issue.) CGA; Lab.

Coverboy. São Paulo: Editora Acti-Vita. (4;5.)

Grupo Gay da Bahia. Boletim do Grupo Gay da Bahia. Salvador. (2:4, Sept., 1982--5:11, June, 1985.) CGA; Lab.

Jornal do gay. Noticiário do mundo entendido. Publicação mensal do Círculo Corydon. São Paulo. (3, 1979; 4, 1979; 5.) CGA; Lab.

Jornal gay internacional. Publicação mensal da Liga Eloinista. São Paulo. (1, Feb., 1980; 2, 1980; 3; 4.) CGA; Lab.

Lampião. Rio de Janeiro (Edição experimental, No. zero, April, 1978--3:37, June, 1981.) CGA; Lab.

Pleiguei: o jornal do Homo. Rio de Janeiro. ([1], Nov., 1981--4, 1982.) CGA.

61. A HOMOSSEXUALIDADE NO BRASIL: BIBLIOGRAFIA

Luiz Mott

Em 1906, o Dr. Pires de Lima, um dos precursores dos estudos sobre a homossexualidade no Brasil, no seu livro Homossexualismo: A Libertinagem no Rio de Janeiro:, fazia a seguinte observação: "Excluida de objeto de estudo até o presente, a pederastia no Brasil tem atravessado quatro séculos de nossa história, não obstante carecer de observação e pesquisa."

De fato, enquanto em outros paises, notadamente na Alemanha, Inglaterra e Estados Unidos, já nos fins do século XIX existia uma rica e diversificada produção científica consagrada ao homossexualismo, no Brasil, o preceito do Apóstolo Paulo e o espectro da Inquisição--destruida somente em 1821!--continuavam imperantes inclusive dentro da Academia: "Que essas coisas não sejam sequer nomeadas entre vós!" Ainda em 1935, Capistrano de Abreu, ao editar as Confissões da Visitação do Santo Ofício na Bahia em 1591-1592, referia-se às confissões do "pecado contra a natura" como "assunto melindroso que exige habilidade singular em quem o aborda," indicando previamente as 40 páginas relativas ao "abominável pecado de sodomia" para o leitor "evitá-las ou procurá-las a seu talante . . ."

Prova de nosso atrazo nos estudos sobre a homofilia, é o pequeno número de referências bibliográficas e o fato de ser esta a primeira vez que no Brasil se publica uma bibliografia específica sobre a homossexualidade. Contudo, melhores ventos parecem soprar nos últimos anos em nosso país: não apenas prescenciamos um auspicioso incremento na produção científica sobre os homossexuais, como também, devido à emergente organizaçao do Movimento de Liberação Homossexual Brasileiro, os gays passam a constituir-se não apenas passivos objetos de estudo de médicos, legistas, e outros, para tornarem-se eles próprios estudiosos de suas preferências sexuais, pressionando inclusive a comunidade científica brasileira a ampliar suas pesquisas no campo da sexualidade humana en geral e da homossexualidade em particular, como se patenteia através de seis moções-resoluções aprovadas entre 1981-1984, todas de nossa iniciativa e autoria, pelas seguintes associações acadêmicas: Sociedade Brasileira para o Progresso da Ciência (duas moções), Associação Brasileira de Antropologia, Associação Brasileira de Estudos Populacionais, Associação Brasileira de Psiquiatria e Associação Nacional de Pós-Graduação em Ciências Sociais.

Esta bibliografia é um primeiro passo para futuros trabalhos mais completos e analíticos sobre a evolução ideológica dos estudos sobre a homossexualidade no Brasil: nosso próximo trabalho será publicar algumas páginas mais significativas destes autores, algo do estilio do Gay American History, de J. Katz. Para tanto, esperamos receber críticas, correções e novas indicações bibliográficas. Como o leitor notará, incluimos nesta Bibliografia títulos de livros, artigos, teses, comunicações e projetos de pesquisa que versam sobre a questão homossexual no Brasil, ou sobre o homossexualismo em geral porém publicados no Brasil originalmente. Encontrará igualmente indicações de artigos sobre os homossexuais do Brasil publicados no exterior. Além de trabalhos tratando especificamente da homossexualidade em geral e das diferentes manifestações do homossexualismo masculino e feminino no Brasil, tivemos por bem incluir trabalhos relativos ao travestismo, transexualismo e hermafroditismo: temas que embora não se relacionem obrigatoriamente à homossexualidade, por vezes e em certos casos particulares esta relação soe acontecer. Preferimos, por conseguinte, pecar por excesso e não por omissão. Não incluimos a produção literária abordando a temática homossexual: trabalho importante mas que foge a nosso interesse imediato--fica nosso estímulo para que outros pesquisadores brindem-nos com este futuro trabalho.

Concluo convidando os intelectuais brasileiros e estrangeiros a virem pesquisar temas relativos à homossexualidade no Brasil: campo fértil, cheio de surpresas e variações regionais, quer no nível linguístico quer no da sociologia do comportamento, hão de encontrar grande facilidade em obter informações junto às diferentes categorias de gays hoje existentes neste país. Agradeço finalmente ao antropólogo Aroldo Assunção, devotado companheiro que muito ajudou-me na seleção, ordenação e correção desta bibliografia. Ao Professor Wayne Dynes, muito obrigado pelo estímulo, tradução e ordenamento destas páginas.

BIBLIOGRAFIA

Adé-Dudu. "Diga aí, bicha! Depoimentos de activistas homossexuais." Salvador, Bahia, 1981. 22 pp. Mimeo.

_____. "Negros homossexuais." Salvador, Bahia, 1981. 18 pp. Mimeo.

_____. "O Brasil de 1964 a 1984 e o surgimento do movimento homossexual." Comunicação apresentada no 2[0] Encontro do Movimento Homossexual Brasileiro. Salvador, Bahia, Janeiro, 1984. 13 pp. Mimeo.

_____. "A participação dos homossexuais no Movimento Negro Brasileiro." Salvador, Bahia, 1984. 49 pp. Mimeo.

Adrados, Isabel. "Estudo da homossexualidade mediante o teste de Rorschach." Arquivo Brasileiro de Psicotécnica, 16 (March, 1964), 65-74.

Aguiar, Flávio. "Homossexualidade e repressão." In Guido Mantega, coord., Sexo e poder. São Paulo: Editora Brasiliense, 1979. Pp. 137-156.

Albuquerque, José. Da Impotência sexual no homem. Rio de Janeiro: Jornal de Andrologia Editora, 1933. 73 pp.

Almeida, Narceu. "Homossexualismo: a hora da verdade." Manchete, 1231, Nov. 22, 1975, pp. 18-23.

Almeida, Nélson Guilherme. Esboço médico-jurídico dos delinquentes sexuais. Salvador, Bahia: Imprensa Oficial do Estado da Bahia, 1924. 35 pp.

Almeida Júnior, A., and J. B. Costa Júnior. Lições de medicine legal. São Paulo: Companhia Editora Nacional, 1978. 337 pp.

Altman, Denis. "Down Rio a Way." Christopher Street, 4:8, 22-27.

Alves de Almeida, Sérgio. "Michê." Tese de Mestrado em Psicologia Social, Pontifícia Universidade Católica de São Paulo, 1984. 220 pp.

Alves, E. S. "Sexologia forense e moral contemporânea." Anais do I Congresso de Medicina Legal. Rio de Janeiro, 1968.

"A Minoria Sexual." Veja, April 25, 1979, 82-83.

Amoroso Lima, José B. "Dos sistemas penitenciários em relação à higiene." Tese da Faculdade de Medicina do Rio de Janeiro, 1880. Pp. 33-35.

Armonde, Amaro Ferreira. "Da educação física, intelectual e moral da mocidade no Rio de Janeiro e sua influencia sobre a saúde." Tese da Faculdade de Medicina do Rio de Janeiro, 1874. Pp. 60.

Assunção, Lino. Narrativas do Brasil. Rio de Janeiro: Livraria Contemporânea, 1881. Pp. 85-98.

Aufderheide, Patricia. "True Confessions: The Inquisition and Social Attitudes in Brazil at the Turn of the XVI Century." Luso-Brazilian Review, 10:2 (1973), 208-240.

Baptista, V. "Pseudo-Hermafroditismo." Arquivo da Assistência geral a psicopatas do Estado de São Paulo, 1 (1936), 127-148.

Bastos, José C. "Homossexualidade masculina." Jornal Brasileiro de Psiquiatria, 28:1-4 (1979), 7-11.

Bello da Mota, Antonio. "Homossexualismo em medicina legal." Tese de Concurso à Catedra da Faculdade de Direito do Ceará, Tipografia do Jornal do Comércio, 1937.

Beni Carvalho. Sexualidade anômala no direito criminal. São Paulo, n.p.

Benedetti, G. "Transexualismo e travestismo." Revista geográfica universal, 62, Documento Roche 1 (Jan., 1980), 87-94.

Bicudo, V. "O papel das figuras de pais combinados e ego combinado na homossexualidade e no acting out." Comunicação apresentada na 1ª Jornada Brasileira de Psicoanálise, São Paulo, maio, 1967.

Bittencourt, Francisco. A Bicha que ri. Rio de Janeiro: Esquina Editora, 1981.

Bivar, Antonio. "Revolução sexual à paulista." Ele-Ela, 9:93 (Jan., 1977), 50-57; 96 (April, 1977), 50-52.

Bragaglia, G. "A fascinação dos castrados." Revista Anhembi, Dec., 1959.

Brito, José G. L. A questão sexual nas prisões. Jacinto R. Santos, Editor. Rio de Janeiro, n.d.

Brito, Marinômio F. "Dissertação sobre a libertinagem e os seus perigos relativamente ao físico e moral do homem." Tese da Faculdade de Medicina da Bahia, Tipografia V.C.O. Chaves, 1853.

Cardoso, P. B. Oscar Wilde: estudo bibliográfico. Porto Alegre: Livraria Globo, 1935.

Cardoso, Evandro. A teatralidade do sexo à luz de uma análise biológica. Feira de Santana, Bahia: n.p., 1974. Pp. 126-130.

Carneiro de Cunha, Maria. "Sobre definições sexuais e classificações: a retórica do universo homossexual." Unicamp, Biblioteca do IFCH, 1975. Mimeo.

Carrilho, H. "Laudo do exame médico-psicológico procedido no acusado Febrônio Indio do Brasil." Arquivo do Manicômio Judiciário do Rio de Janeiro, 1 (1930).

Carrilho, H., and Manuel C. do Rego Barros. "A curiosa mentalidade de um deliquente. Laudo do exame médico-psicológico de Febrônio do Brasil." Pandectas brasileiras (Rio de Janeiro), 6, 5ª parte (1929), 442.

Carvalho, Manuel F. A. "Corpos extranhos no reto e seu tratamento." Tese da Faculdade de Medicina da Bahia, 1882. Pp. 21-25.

Carvalho, Rodrigo U. Relatório sobre a saúde mental de Febrônio Indio do Brasil. Rio de Janeiro, n.d.

Castelo Branco, Vitorino. O Advogado diante dos crimes sexuais. São Paulo: Sugestões Literárias, 1977. Pp. 391, 413-414.

Castro Neto, Alfredo. "O que os pais precisam saber sobre homossexualismo infantil." Estarbem, Aug., 1979.

Chalub, Miguel. "Homossexualismo infantil: um processo normal de conhecimento do próprio corpo." Pais e filhos, 12 (Aug., 1974), 106.

Chinelli, Filipina. "Acusação de desvio em uma minoria." In
Gilberto Velho, org., Desvio e divergência. Rio de Janeiro:
Zahar Editores, 1981.

Clestres, Pierre. "Vie et mort d'un pederaste." In Chronique
des Indiens Guayaki. Paris: Plon, 1972.

_____. "O arco e o cesto." In Sociedade contra o estado.
Rio de Janeiro: Livraria Francisco Alves, 1978.

Coelho Neto, Paulo. Perversão sexual e câncer. Rio de Janeiro:
Oficina Gráfica do Jornal do Brasil, 1944.

Colaço, Rita. Uma conversa informal sobre homossexualismo.
Duque de Caxias, Rio de Janeiro: Edição do Autor, 1984.
75 pp.

Cruz Neto, Otávio. Sexualidade: relações de produção, busca de
prazer, luta de classes, corpo e poder--A homossexualidade
neste contexto. Monografia de conclusão do curso de
Sociologia e Política, Pontifícia Universidade Católica do Rio de
Janeiro, 1980.

Cunha, Marcos V. "Homossexualismo infantil: um processo normal
de conhecimento do corpo." Pais e Filhos, 6:12 (Aug., 1974),
106-110.

Cunha, Persivo. Sexologia forense. São Paulo: Sugestões
Literárias S.A., 1977. 50 pp.

Cury, Ricardo. "As ciências da saúde mental, Direito e Homossexualismo." Comunicação, Resumos da 34a Reunião Anual da
Sociedade Brasileira para o Progresso da Ciência. Campinas,
julho, 1982. P. 890.

Daguer, Pedro J. "Transexualismo masculino." Tese de Mestrado
em Psiquiatria na Universidade Federal do Rio de Janeiro,
1977.

De Lamare, Rinaldo. A Vida de nossos filhos de 2 a 16 anos.
Rio de Janeiro: Editora Bloch, 1982. Pp. 408-428.

Dias, Astor Guimarães. A questão sexual nas prisões.
São Paulo: Saraiva Editora, 1965.

Dias, Mário. Sexualidade atormentada: o problema sexual nas
prisões. São Paulo: Secretaria de Segurança Pública, 1962.

Dourado, Luiz Angelo. Homossexualismo masculino e feminino e
delinquência. Rio de Janeiro: n.p., 1956. 402 pp.

Doyle, Iracy. Contribução ao Estudo da Homossexualidade
Feminina. Rio de Janeiro: n.p., 1956. 402 pp.

Dumbar, J., et al. "Attitudes toward Homosexuality among
Brazilian and Canadian College Students." Journal of Social
Psychology, 90 (1973), 174-175.

"Ele & Ele: uma relação normal?" Ele & Ela, 4:40 (Aug., 1972),
110-115.

Erdemann, Regina Maria. "Reis e Rainhas do Desterro: um estudo de caso." Tese de Mestrado da Universidade Federal de Santa Catarina, Florianópolis, 1981.

Espinheira, Carlos G. A. "Divergência e Prostituição: Uma análise sociológica da Comunidade Prostitucional do Maciel." Dissertação de Mestrado em Ciências Sociais da Universidade Federal da Bahia, 1975.

Eston, Alvaro. "Preâmbulo, tradução e notas." In Havelock Ellis, Inversão Sexual. São Paulo: Companhia Editora Nacional, 1933.

Fabri dos Anjos, Padre Márcio. "Homossexualismo: pistas para uma reeducação." Revista Familia Cristã, (March, 1980), 43-45.

Faury, Mara L. Uma flor para os malditos: A homossexualidade na literatura. Campinas: Papirus, 1983.

Fávero, Flamínio, and Athayde Pereira. "Considerações clínicas e médico-legais sobre um caso de pseudo-hermafroditismo (tubularia feminninus externus)." São Paulo Médico, 1:14 (Aug., 1928), 407-419.

Fávero, Flamínio, et al. "Considerações médico-legais sobre um raro caso de homossexualidade feminina. Interessantes aspectos do ponto de vista da deotologia e da psicopatologia forense." Anais do II Congresso Brasileiro de Medicina Legal e Criminalidade, Recife, julho, 1956. Pp. 563-586.

Fernandes, Albino G. Elementos de psicopatologia criminal. Recife: Ed. Diário da Manhã, 1942.

Fernandes, Florestan. Organização Social dos Tupinambá. São Paulo: Difusão Européia do Livro, 1963. Pp. 159-161.

Ferrão, L. M. "Homossexualidade e defesas maníacas." Revista Brasileira de Psicanálise, 1:1 (1967), 85.

Ferraz de Macedo, Francisco. "Da prostituição em geral e em particular em relação ao Rio de Janeiro. Tese da Faculdade de Medicina da Universidade do Rio de Janeiro, 1872. 115 pp.

Ferreira, A. A. "Sobre um caso de pseudo-hermafroditismo ginandroide irregular ou hipostático." Boletim do Instituto Oscar Freire, 3 (Jan.-Dec., 1936), 11-14.

Ferreira, A. A., and L. Santos. "Sobre um caso de pseudo-hermafroditismo ginandroide irregular ou hipostático." Boletim do Instituto Oscar Freire, 5 (Jan.-Dec., 1934), 11-14.

Figueiroa, Lúcia. "O diagnóstico da homossexualidade: Modificações ocorridas no nosso código." Jornal Brasileiro de Psiquiatria, 31:1 (1982), 19-23.

_____. "A questão psiquiátrica da homossexualidade."
Comunicação apresentada no 8º Congresso da Associação
Brasileira de Psiquiatria, Recife, outubre, 1984. 14 pp.
Mimeo.

Fock, Nina. Dicionário sexual. Curitiba: Grafipar, 1981.

Fonseca, Guido. "A prostituição masculina em São Paulo."
Arquivos da Polícia Civil de São Paulo, 30 (July-Dec., 1977),
65-87.

_____. "Prostituição masculina." In História da
Prostituição em São Paulo. São Paulo: Editora Resenha
Universitária, 1982. Pp. 217-237.

Foster, Robert. "O sombrio mundo dos amores proibidos."
Ele & Ela, 40 (Aug., 1972), 28; 49 (May, 1973), 28.

Foster, Stephen W. "Homosexuality and the Inquisition in Brazil:
1591-1592." Gay Sunshine, 38-39 (Winter, 1979), 17-18.

_____. "Notes on the Gay History of Brazil." 1979.
5 pp. (Dactilo).

Fraga, A. "Um caso de hermafroditismo." Revista brasileira de
cirurgia, 3:8 (Aug., 1934), 333-342.

Freitas, Franklin. Taras Sexuais. Rio de Janeiro: Irmãos
Giorgio Editores, n.d. 67 pp.

Freitas Júnior, Otàvio. A prostituição é necessária? Rio de
Janeiro: Civilização Brasileira, 1966.

Fry, Peter. "Homossexualidade masculina e cultos afro-
brasileiros." In Para Inglês ver. Rio de Janeiro: Zahar
Editores, 1982. Pp. 54-86.

_____. "Da Hierarquia à Igualdade: a construção histórica
da homossexualidade no Brasil." In Para Inglês ver. Rio de
Janeiro: Zahar Editores, 1982. Pp. 87-115.

_____. "Leonie, Pombinha, Amaro e Aleixo: prostituição,
homossexualidade e raça em dois romances naturalistas." In
Alexandre Eulálio et al., Caminhos Cruzados. São Paulo:
Editora Brasiliense, 1982. Pp. 33-52.

_____. "Febrônio Indio do Brasil: Onde cruzam a
psiquiatria, a profecia, a homossexualidade e a lei. In
Alexandre Eulálio et al., Caminhos Cruzados. São Paulo:
Editora Brasiliense, 1982. Pp. 65-80.

Fry, Peter, and Edward MacRae. O que é homossexualidade.
São Paulo: Editora Brasiliense, 1983. 126 pp.

Gabriel Nós-Também. "Baltazar da Lomba." Paraíba: João
Pessoa, 1982. 20 pp. Mimeo.

Gaiarsa, José A. A Juventude diante do sexo. São Paulo:
Editora Brasiliense, 1967. Pp. 283-297.

Garcia, J. Alves. Psicopatologia forense. Rio de Janeiro: Editora Forense, 1979. Pp. 221-222.

Gauderer, E. C. "Homossexualidade masculina e lesbianismo." Medicina de hoje (June, 1980), 236-242.

_____. "Homossexualidade masculina e lesbianismo." Jornal de Pediatria, 56:3 (1984), 123-125.

"Gays, uma expressão americana." Manchete, 28:1416 (July 9, 1979), 120-127.

Gikovate, Flávio. Sexo e amor para jovens. São Paulo: Editora MG, 1980. 212 pp.

_____. O Instinto sexual. São Paulo: Editora MG, 1980. 124 pp.

_____. "Homossexualidade." Comunicação no 1º Seminário sobre Sexualidade Humana, São Paulo, setembro, 1983. P. 24.

Goldberg, Maria A. A. Educação sexual: uma proposta, um desafio. São Paulo: Editora Aruanda, 1982. Pp. 71-78.

Goldkorn, Roberto. As melhores piadas de bicha. São Paulo: Global Editora, 1981.

Gomes, Hélio. Medicina legal. Rio de Janeiro: Livraria Freitas Bastos, 1980. Pp. 412-418.

Gomes, Júlio. A Homossexualidade no mundo. Lisboa: Edição do Autor, 1979. Pp. 153-192.

Gonçalves, L. "Considerações sobre um pseudo-hermafroditismo." Arquivo Riograndense de Medicina, 17:4 (April, 1930), 145-182.

Guimarães, Carmen Dora. "O Homossexual visto por entendidos." Tese de Mestrado, Museu Nacional da Universidade Federal do Rio de Janeiro, 1977.

_____. "O Homossexual face à norma familiar: Desvios e convergências." Comunicação apresentada na Reunião do Grupo de Trabalho sobre Reprodução da População, Teresópolis, 1980.

_____. "Um discurso de retorno: A reconstrução da identidade homossexual." Comunicação apresentada na XIII Reunião da Associação Brasileira de Antropologia, São Paulo, abril, 1982. 7 pp. Mimeo.

_____. "Casos e acasos." Comunicação apresentada na Reunião da Associação Brasileira de Estudos Populacionais, Aguas de São Pedro, 1984. 15 pp.

Hecker, Paulo. "Que é homossexualismo." Revista Zero Hora, Porto Alegre, Sept. 23, 1979.

Heilborn, Maria Luiza. "Grades do Parentesco." Comunicação apresentada na Reunião da Associação Brasileira de Antropologia, Rio de Janeiro, 1980. Mimeo.

Homossexualismo em questão: cartas comoventes e respostas esclarecedoras. Edição Especial de "Confissões." Curitiba: Grafipar, n.d. 63 pp.

"Homossexualismo: Do gueto para o debate pública." Mesa Redonda, Folhetim da Folha de São Paulo, Jan. 10, 1982.

"Homossexualismo: hora da verdade." Manchete, 21:1231 (Nov. 22, 1975), 18-20.

Hutz, A. "Homossexualismo." Comunicação no 1º Seminário sobre Sexualidade Humana, São Paulo, Sept., 1983. Pp. 22-23.

Irajá, Ernani. Psicoses do Amor: Estudo sobre as alterações do instinto sexual. Rio de Janeiro: Livraria Editora Freitas Bastos, 1931.

_____. Psicopatologia da sexualidade. Rio de Janeiro: Edição Getúlio Costa, 1946.

Klabin, Aracy A. L. "Aspectos jurídicos do transsexualismo." Tese de Mestrado da Faculdade de Direito da Universidade de São Paulo, 1977. 53 pp.

Kosinski, Cavalcanti J. "Homossexual: Onde está a diferença." Istoé, Oct., 1976. Pp. 114-117.

Kotscho, R. "Homossexualismo, um debate descontraído." Folha de São Paulo, Oct. 23, 1981.

Jaime, Jorge. "Homossexualismo masculino." Tese de Medicina Legal, Universidade do Brasil, Rio de Janeiro, 1947. 205 pp.

Jurth, Max. "L'Homophilie au Brésil." Arcadie, 83 (Nov., 1960), 654-665.

Junqueira, José N. "Estudo de um caso de intersexualidade." Arquivos da Sociedade de Medicina Legal e Criminologia de São Paulo (1954), 73-74.

Landes, Ruth. A cidade das mulheres. Rio de Janeiro: Editora Civilização Brasileira, 1967. Pp. 283-296.

_____. "A Cult Matriarchate and Male Homosexuality." Journal of Abnormal and Social Psychology, 35 (1940), 386-397.

Lembruger, Maria Julia. "Cemitério dos Vivos." Tese de Mestrado, Museu Nacional da Universidade Federal do Rio de Janeiro, 1979.

Lemos de Britto, José G. A Questão sexual nas prisões. Rio de Janeiro: Livraria Jacintho, n.d.

Lima, Délcio. O Comportamento sexual do Brasileiro. São Paulo: Editora Francisco Alves, 1978.

_____. Os Homoeróticos. Rio de Janeiro: Editora Francisco Alves, 1983. 200 pp.

Lima, Estácio. A Inversão sexual feminina. Bahia: Livraria Científica, 1934. 66 pp.

_____. A Inversão dos Sexos. Rio de Janeiro: Editora Guanabara, n.d. 250 pp.

Lordy, C. "Hermafroditismo verdadeiro e pseudo-hermafroditismo." Revista de Obstetrícia e Ginecologia, 1:4 (Dec., 1935), 247-256.

Lutz, Adolfo G. "Auto-acusação, homossexualismo e transvestismo. Contribuição à prática da Criminologia Psicoanalítica. Tese da Faculdade Nacional de Medicina da Universidade do Brasil, 1939.

Machado, Alberto. "O pensamento duro (e polêmico) de um homem da lei." Revista Jurídica LEMI, 12:139 (June, 1979), 4-20.

Machado, Luiz Carlos. Descansa em paz, Oscar Wilde. Rio de Janeiro: Pasquim, Editora Codecri, 1982. 134 pp.

Maciel, Francisco L. "Ser homossexual depende dos astros?" Fatos e Fotos, 17 (Jan. 22, 1979), 4-7.

MacRae, Edward. "A Afirmação Homossexual." Comunicação apresentada na 13ª Reunião da Associação Brasileira de Antropologia, São Paulo, 1982. 8 pp. Mimeo.

_____. "Homossexualidade e Individualismo." Comunicação apresentada na Reunião da Associação Brasileira de Estudos Populacionais, Aguas de São Pedro, 1984. 12 pp. Mimeo.

_____. "A Homossexualidade e os usos políticos da ciência." 1984. 35 pp. Mimeo.

_____. "Os respeitáveis militantes e as bichas loucas." In Alexandre Eulálio, et al., Caminhos Cruzados. São Paulo: Editora Brasiliense, 1982. Pp. 99-112.

Magalhães, Henrique. "Cinema e Homossexualismo." Plano Geral, Oficina de Comunicação, Universidade Federal da Paraiba, julho, 1981. Pp. 13-31.

Mantega, Guido, ed. Sexo e Poder. São Paulo: Editora Brasiliense, 1979. 218 pp.

Marañón, Gregorio. "Una clasificación de los homosexuales desde el punto de vista médico-legal." Arquivo de Medicina Legal e de Identificação, 7 (Jan., 1937), 90-100.

_____. "Prefacio." In Leonídio Ribeiro, Homossexualismo e Endocrinologia. Rio de Janeiro: Livraria Francisco Alves, 1938. Pp. 9-22.

Marone, Sílvio. Missexualidade e Arte. São Paulo: n.p., 1947.

_____. "Leonardo da Vinci, o artista cientista." Prêmio da Associação Paulista de Medicina (inédito), 1941.

_____. "Considerações em torno de uma nova classificação de missexuais." Arquivos da Polícia Civil de São Paulo, 10 (2ª semestre, 1945).

Marra, Heloisa. "Homossexualidade: O que eles querem e pelo que lutam?" Fatos e Fotos, 17:919 (April 2, 1979), 12-13.

Medeiros, Maurício, and J. Manfredini. Casamento: Psiquiatria forense. Rio de Janeiro: José Olympio Editora, 1950. Pp. 118-121.

Menezes, Holdemar O. "Transexualismo." Arquivos da Polícia Civil de São Paulo, 28 (July-Dec., 1976), 85-94.

Mesonero Romanos, Eugênio. Vida sexual normal e patológica. São Paulo: Piratininga, n.d. 186 pp.

Miccolis, Leila, and Herbert Daniel. Jacarés e Lobisomens: Dois ensaios sobre a homossexualidade. Rio de Janeiro: Achiamé, 1983.

Misse, Michel. O estigma do passivo sexual. Rio de Janeiro: Achiamé, 1979. 72 pp.

Moncorvo, Laurindo M. A. Algumas considerações higiênicas e médico-legais sobre o casamento e seus casos de nulidade. Tese da Faculdade de Medicina do Rio de Janeiro, 1848. Pp. 12-17.

Monteiro, Arlindo C. Amor Sáfico e Socrático. Separata dos Arquivos do Instituto de Medicina Legal de Lisboa, 1922.

Morais, M. L. S. "Homossexualidade: doença ou opção?" 6 pp. Mimeo.

Moreira, Rita. "Lésbicas: O alto preço de uma opção de vida." Revista Espacial, 5 (April, 1980), 36-39.

Mott, Luiz R. B. "Somitigos, tibiro e jimbandaa: A prática do homossexualismo entre brancos, índios e negros na Bahia e em Pernambuco, séculos XVI e XVII." Comunicação apresentada na 32ª Reunião Anual da Sociedade Brasileira para o Progresso da Ciência, Salvador, julho, 1981. 147 pp. Mimeo.

_____. "Dez Viados em questão. Tipologia dos homossexuais da cidade do Salvador." Comunicação apresentada na 13ª Reunião da Associação Brasileira de Antropologia, São Paulo, abril, 1982. Mimeo.

_____. "Relações raciais entre homossexuais no Brasil Colonial." Comunicação apresentada no Instituto Universitário de Pesquisas do Rio de Janeiro, setembro, 1982. Mimeo.

_____. "Escravidão e Homossexualidade." Comunicação apresentada no 3º Congresso Afro-Brasileiro--Fundação Joaquim Nabuco, Recife, outubro, 1982. Mimeo.

_____. "A homossexualidade: Uma variável esquecida pela demografia histórica. Os sodomitas no Brasil Colonial." Comunicação apresentada no 3º Encontro Nacional da Associação Brasileira de Estudos Populacionais, Vitória, outubro, 1982. Mimeo.

_____. "Antropologia, população e sexualidade." Gente (Revista do Departmento de Antropologia e Etnologia da Faculdade de Filosofia da Universidade Federal da Bahia, 1:1 (June-Dec., 1984), 89-103.

_____. "Slavery and Homosexuality." Black and White Men Together Quarterly (Colingwood), (Winter, 1984).

_____. "Report from Brazil." The Cabirion and Gay Books Bulletin, (Fall/Winter, 1984), 14.

Mott, Luiz R. B., and Aroldo H. F. Assunção. "Gilete na carne: Etnografia das automutilações corporais entre os homossexuais do Pelourinho, Salvador, Bahia." Comunicação apresentada na 32ª Reunião Anual da Sociedade Brasileira para o Progresso da Ciência, Salvador, julho, 1981. Pp. 102-103.

_____. "Os gays e as doençassexualmente transmisíveis." Comunicação apresentada na 33ª Reunião Anual da Sociedade Brasileira para o Progresso da Ciência, Campinas, julho, 1982. Mimeo.

_____. "A Gay Atheist of the XVIIth Century." Gay Atheist League of America Review, 7:2 (April, 1984), 8-10.

Nahoum, Jean C. "O Homossexualismo visto por um médico." Revista Vozes, 12 (Dec., 1967), 1087-1095.

Nava, José. Uma tragédia anti-florentina. Belo Horizonte: Imprensa Oficial, 1968.

Negrão, A. "Falso hermafroditismo." Publicação Médica, 7:10 (May, 1937), 27-33.

Nelino de Melo, J. Dicionário de assuntos sexuais. Rio de Janeiro: Organização Simões, 1954. 125 pp.

Nerici, I. G. Seus filhos, o sexo e você! Rio de Janeiro: Editora Fundo de Cultura, 1958.

Neto, Paulo Jr. Perversãosexual e câncer. Rio de Janeiro: Jornal do Brasil, 1944.

Novinsky, Ilana. "Heresia, mulher e sexualidade. Algumas notas sobre o Nordeste nos séculos XVI e XVII." Fundação Carlos Chagas (1983).

Nunes, Viriato F. "As perversões sexuais em Medicina Legal." Tese Inaugural da Faculdade de Direito de São Paulo, 1928. Pp. 11-13.

"O gay feminino." Folhetim da Folha de São Paulo, 73 (Aug. 20, 1983).

Okita,   Hiro.   Homossexualismo: Da   opressão   à   Libertação.
São Paulo: Proposta Editorial, 1981.

Olavarrieta, J. B.   Hygiene Sexual.   São Paulo: A. C. Martin
Editora, 1929. 96 pp.

Oliveira, José Lima.   "Homossexualismo: Aspectos éticos no mundo
atual." Arquivos da Polícia Civil de São Paulo, 28 (July-Dec.,
1976), 28-95.

_____. Violência Presumida: Estudo Médico Legal. Bahia:
Editora S. A. Artes Gráficas, 1959.

Oliveira, Neuza Maria.   "Travesti: Falo de tres atitudes diante do
falo." Jornal Maria-Maria, (July-Aug., 1984), 3.

Pacheco e Silva, A. C.   "Um interessante caso de homossexualismo
feminino." Arquivos da Sociedade de Medicina Legal e
Criminologia de São Paulo, 10 (1939), 69-81.

_____.   "As orígens psicológicas da Homossexualidade
Masculina." Tese de Doutoramento do Departamento de Neuro-
psiquiatria da Universidade de São Paulo, 1971. 165 pp.

_____.   "Terceiro Sexo? Sob a Luz da Psiquiatria."
Anhembi (São Paulo), (1963), 166.

Pacheco e Silva, A. C., and Olinto Mattos.   "Um interessante
caso de homossexualismo feminino." Revista de Direito Penal,
31 (Oct., 1940), 29-39.

Panasco, Wanderley L.   Medicina Legal face aos códigos penais.
Rio de Janeiro: Eldorado, 1969.

Peixoto, Afrânio.   "Los missexuales." Archivos de Medicina Legal
(Buenos Aires), (1931).

_____.   "Missexualismo." Arquivos de Medicina Legal e
Identificação, 3:6 (Feb., 1933), 67-73.

_____.   Sexologia Forense.   Rio de Janeiro: Editora
Guanabara, 1934.

Pereira, Armando.   "Adaptação cirúrgica de um pseudo-
hermafrodita ao verdadeiro sexo." Revista Urologia, 4:3
(May-June, 1937), 169-177.

_____.   "Considerações clínicas e médico-legistas sobre um
caso de pseudo-hermafroditismo." São Paulo Médico, 1:4
(Aug., 1928), 407-419.

_____.   Sexo e Prostituição.   Rio de Janeiro: Gráfica
Record Editora, 1967. P. 107.

Pereira, Carlos A. M.   "Desvio e/ou reprodução." In Testemunha
Ocular, Textos de Antropologia Social do Cotidiano. Rio de
Janeiro: Editora Tempo Literário, 1979.

Pereira da Silva, Mário. Medicina Legal. Rio de Janeiro: Gráfica Editora Itambé, 1974. P. 39.

Pereira, Ricardo Calheiros. "Causas históricas e sociais do preconceito contra homossexuais." Projeto de Pesquisa, apresentado ao Concurso de Seleção para o Mestrado em Ciências Sociais da Universidade Federal da Bahia, novembro, 1982. 13 pp. Mimeo.

Perlonger, Nestor. "Amor e comércio na prostituição viril." Comunicação apresentada na Reunião da Associação Brasileira de Estudos Populacionais, Aguas de São Pedro, 1984. 19 pp. Mimeo.

_____. "O Contrato da prostituição viril." Comunicação apresentada na 36ª Reunião da Sociedade Brasileira para o Progresso da Ciência, São Paulo, julho, 1984. 13 pp. Mimeo.

_____. "Prostitución Homosexual: El negocio del deseo." Comunicação apresentada na 13ª Reunião da Associação Brasileira de Antropologia, São Paulo, abril, 1982. 8 pp. Mimeo.

Petri, Valéria. "Observações preliminares sobre a ocorrência da AIDS no Brasil." Comunicação apresentada no 1º Seminário sobre Sexualidade Humana, São Paulo, setembro, 1983. 18 pp. Mimeo.

Pinheiro, Domingo F. O Androfilismo. Bahia: Imprensa Econômica, 1898. 216 pp.

Pires de Almeida, José Ricardo. Homossexualismo: A Liber- tinagem no Rio de Janeiro. Rio de Janeiro: Laemmert Editores, 1906.

Pires, Washington F. "Taras sexuais e falsa identidade." Anais do II Congresso de Medicina Legal em Criminologia, Recife, julho, 1956. Pp. 217-232.

Porchat, Ieda. "O terapeuta e o paciente homossexual." Psicologia Atual, 5:26 (June, 1982), 20-24.

Quintela, Glória F. "Estudo de um caso de hermafroditismo." Arquivo Brasileiro de Psicologia Aplicada (Rio de Janeiro), 30:3 (July-Sept., 1978), 139-145.

Ramos, Arthur. A criança problema: a higiene mental na escola primária. Rio de Janeiro: Livraria Editora Casa do Estudante do Brasil, 1951.

Ribas, J. C. "Oscar Wilde à luz da psiquiatria." Arquivos da Polícia Civil de São Paulo, 16 (2ª semestre, 1948).

Ribeiro, G. M. "Sobre um caso de hermafroditismo ginandroide." Bahia Médica, 5 (June, 1934), 236.

Ribeiro, Leonídio. "Aspectos Médico-Legais da Homossexualidade." Arquivos de Antropologia Criminal, 56 (1936), 425-436.

_____. "Aspectos Médico-Legais da Homossexualidade."
Arquivos de Medicina Legal e Identificação, 5 (1935), 12;
7 (1937), 808-815.

_____. Criminologia. 2 vols. Rio de Janeiro: F. Bastos
Editora, 1957.

_____. De médico a criminalista. Rio de Janeiro: Livraria
São José, 1967. Pp. 219-236.

_____. "Erro de pessoa por defeito físico." Revista Penal
e Penitenciária (São Paulo), 1 (1940), 173.

_____. "Etiologia e tratamento da homossexualidade."
Arquivos de Medicina Legal e Identificação, 1ª parte, 1938,
p. lx-lxxxv; xcvii-c.

_____. "Homossexualismo e Endocrinologia." Arquivos da
Medicina Legal e Identificação, 1937. P. 167.

_____. "Homossexualismo e Endocrinologia." Revista
Brasileira (Rio de Janeiro), 5 (1935), 155.

_____. Homossexualismo e Endocrinologia. Rio de Janeiro:
Livraria Francisco Alves, 1938. 246 pp.

_____. "Homosexuality: Etiology and Therapy." Arquivos
de Medicina Legal e Identificação, 1938, pp. 8-15; lx-lxxxv.

_____. "Homossexualité et Glandes Endocrines." Arquivos
de Medicina Legal e Identificação, 1ª parte, 1938, p. 98.

_____. Medicina Legal. São Paulo: Companhia Editora
Nacional, 1933. Pp. 342-361.

_____. O Novo Código Penal e a medicina legal. Rio de
Janeiro: Livraria Jacintho Editora, 1942. Pp. 86-147.

_____. "Omosessualitá ed Endocrinologia." La Giustizia
Penale (Rome), 44:1 (1938), 527,758; 45:1, 45,228,296.

_____. "O problema medico-legal do homossexualismo."
Arquivos da Medicina Legal e Identificação (Rio de Janeiro), 5
(1936), 145-160.

_____. "O problema medico-legal do homossexualismo sob o
ponto de vista endocrinológico." Revista Jurídica (Rio de
Janeiro), 3 (1935), 185.

_____. "El problema medicolegal del Homosexualismo.
Contribución a su estudio bajo el punto de vista endrocrino-
lógico." Archivos de Medicina Legal (Buenos Aires), 1935.
P. 362.

_____. "Um caso de grande sadismo." Arquivo do
Instituto Médico Legal e do Gabinete de Identificação, 5 (July,
1932), 90-105.

Ribeiro da Silva, Athayde. "Um caso de homossexualismo psiquico." Arquivos Brasileiros de Psicotécnica, 1:19 (March, 1967), 89-93.

Ribeiro, Sérgio N. Crimes Passionais. Rio de Janeiro: Editora Itambé, 1975.

Rizzini, Jorge T. O sexo nas prisões. São Paulo: Nossa Época, 1976. 109 pp.

Rocha, Vaz. "Aspectos clínicos da intersexualidade." Arquivos de Medicina Legal e Identificição, 3:7 (Aug., 1933).

Rodrigues, Armando C. "Transexualismo, transvestismo, homossexualismo e fetichismo." Comunicação apresentada no X Congresso Brasileiro de Medicina Legal, São Paulo, dezembro, 1974.

Rodrigues, Armando C., and Luiz M. Paiva. "Transexualismo, transvestismo, homossexualismo." Arquivos da Policia Civil de São Paulo, 26 (July-Dec., 1976), 7-39.

Rodrigues de Alcântara, Hermes. Perícia médica judicial. Rio de Janeiro: Guanabara Dois, 1982. Pp. 102-103.

Saldanha, P. H., and Luzia C. Olazabal. "Valor do estudo cito-genético no transexualismo." Comunicação apresentada no Simpósio do Departamento de Urologia da Associação Paulista de Medicina, São Paulo, 1975.

Salgado, Murilo R. "O transexual e a cirurgia para a pretendida mudança de sexo." Revista dos Tribunais, 491/241.

Santana, N. "Os delitos sexuais: Aspectos jurídicos e médicos sociais no Brasil." II Congresso Brasileiro de Medicina Legal, Curitiba, 1968.

Santos, Carlos N. "Bichas e entendidos, a sauna como lugar de confronto." Programa de Pós-Graduação em Antropologia Social, Museu Nacional da Universidade Federal do Rio de Janeiro, 1976. Mimeo.

Santos, M. "Sobre um caso de pseudo-hermafroditismo andro-ginóide." Brasil Médico 36 (1922), 89-91.

Santos, Roberto. Caracteres sexuais neutros e intersexualidade. Rio de Janeiro: Tipografia Artes Gráficas, 1931. Pp. 161-186.

Serpa, Fernando. "Androginia." Ele & Ela, 7:79 (Nov., 1975), 27-34.

Silva, José F. Barbosa. "Aspectos sociológicos do homossexualismo em São Paulo." Sociologia, 21:4 (Oct., 1959), 350-360.

Sinisgalli, Aldo. "Observações sobre hábitos, costumes e condições de vida dos homossexuais (pederastas passivos) de São Paulo." Arquivos da Polícia de Identificação, 2:1 (1938), 39.

Siqueira, A. R., and V. Baptista. "Pseudo-hermafroditismo."
Arquivo da Associação de Psicop. do Estado de São Paulo, 1
(1936), 127-138.

Snoek, Jaime. "Eles também são da nossa estirpe: Considerações
sobre a homofilia." Revista Vozes, 9 (Sept., 1967), 792-802.

_____. "Emancipação dos homossexuais e valores positivos
da homossexualidade." II Congresso Católico de Medicina. In
A. G. Mattos, Relatório sobre o II Congresso Católico
Brasileiro de Medicina, Rio de Janeiro, 1967.

_____. Ensaio de Etica Sexual. Edições Paulinas, 1982.

Souto Maior, Mário. Dicionário do Palavrão e termos afins.
Recife: Editora Guararapes, 1980.

Studart, Heloneida, and Wilson Cunha. A primeira vez à
brasileira. Rio de Janeiro: Edição Nosso Tempo, 1977. 35 pp.

Suplicy, Marta. Conversando sobre sexo. São Paulo: Edição do
Autor, 1983. 367 pp.

Sznick, Valdir. Aspectos jurídicos da operação de mudança de
sexo. São Paulo: Editora Sugestões Literárias, 1979. 65 pp.

Teixeira, N. Juventude transviada. Limeira: Editora Letras da
Província, 1966.

Thomas de Aquino, J. "Gênese dos caracteres sexuais
secundários no pseudo-hermafroditismo." Revista de
Obstetrícia e Ginecologia de São Paulo, 1 (Feb. 5, 1936).

"Um 'gay power' à brasileira." Veja, 468 (Aug. 24, 1977), 66-70.

Varjão, Marilda. "Quase tudo que você sempre quis saber sobre
homossexualismo e nunca ousou perguntar." Manchete, 21:1234
(Dec. 13, 1975), 16-19.

Vasconcelos, Gerardo. Lições de Medicina Legal. Rio de Janeiro:
Forense, 1976. P. 263.

Vasconcelos, Naumi. Resposta sexual brasileira. Rio de Janeiro:
Paz e Terra, 1973.

Veiga, Hilário C., and Marco Silva. Compêndio de Medicina
Legal. São Paulo: Saraiva, 1978. 202 pp.

Veloso de França, G. Medicina Legal. Rio de Janeiro: Guanabara
Koogan, 1977. 160 pp.

Vieira Filho, Joaquim. "Contribuição para o estudo clínico e
médico legal do hermafroditismo." Tese de livre-docencia na
Escola Paulista de Medicina, 1941.

Viera Filho, Joaquim, and Otávio Toledo. "Sobre um raríssimo
caso de pseudo-hermafroditismo interno masculino." Arquivos
da Polícia Civil de São Paulo, 2 (1941), 329-344.

Viveiros de Castro, F. J. <u>Atentados ao pudor: Estudos sobre as</u> <u>aberações do instinto sexual</u>. Rio de Janeiro: Livraria Editora Freitas Bastos, 1934.

Xavier, Francisco Cândido. <u>Vida e Sexo</u>. Rio de Janeiro: Federação Espírita Brasileira, n.d. 92 pp.

Young, Alen. "Gays in Brazil: 24/Veado." <u>Gay Sunshine</u>, 13 (June, 1972), 4.

_____. "Gay gringo in Brazil." <u>The Gay Liberation Book</u>. San Francisco, CA: Ramparts Press, 1973. Pp. 60-67.

Whitaker, E. A. "Contribuição ao estudo dos homossexuais." <u>Arquivos da Sociedade de Medicina Legal e Criminologia de São Paulo</u>, 8 (1938), 217-222.

Whitaker, E. A., et al. "Estudo biográfico dos homossexuais (pederastas passivos) da capital de São Paulo. Aspectos de sua atividade social (costumes, hábitos, apelidos e gírias)." <u>Arquivos de Polícia e Identificação</u>, 2 (1938-1939), 244-262.

Whitam, Frederick L. "The Entendidos: Middle Class Gay Life in São Paulo." <u>Gay Sunshine</u>, 38-39 (1979), 16-17.

_____. "The Prehomosexual Male Child in Three Societies: The United States, Guatemala, Brazil." <u>Archives of Sexual Behavior</u>, 9:2 (1980), 87-99.

_____. "Culturally Invariable Properties of Male Homosexuality: Tentative Conclusions from Cross-cultural Research." <u>Archives of Sexual Behavior</u>, 12:3 (1983), 207-226.

_____. "A Cross-cultural Assessment of Early Cross-Gender Behavior and Familial Patterns in Male Homosexuality." <u>Archives of Sexual Behavior</u>, 13:5 (1984), 427-438.

Martha Davidson

Historical Photography

Banco Central del Ecuador. Colección Imágenes. 5 vols. Quito: Banco Central del Ecuador, 1980-1984.

Pictorial history of Ecuador in five volumes: Imágenes de la Vida Política del Ecuador; Grabados sobre el Ecuador en el Siglo XIX; Quito en el Tiempo; Cuenca Tradicional; and Paisajes del Ecuador.

Bequer Casaballe, Amado, and Miguel Angel Cuarterolo. Imágenes del Río de la Plata. Buenos Aires: 1983.

Brief, illustrated history of photography from Argentina.

Billeter, Erika, ed. Fotografía latinoamericana. Madrid: Ediciones El Viso, 1982.

Translated from Fotografie Lateinamerika (Bern, 1981), the catalog of a major exhibition of historical and contemporary Latin American photography (1860-1981) held at the Kunsthaus, Zurich. Introduction to Latin American photography, brief biographies of photographers, full-page reproductions of photos.

Canales, Claudia. Romualdo García--un fotógrafo, una ciudad, una época. Guanajuato: Gobierno del Estado de Guanajuato, 1980.

Biographical study of Mexican studio photographer Romualdo García (1852-1930) and his role in the life of Guanajuato.

Ferrez, Gilberto, and Weston J. Naef. Pioneer Photographers of Brazil, 1840-1920. New York, NY: The Center for Inter-American Relations, 1976.

Early history of photography in Brazil, portfolios of fifteen photographers, portraits of the Imperial family.

Fondo del Sol Visual Arts and Media Center. The World of Agustín Víctor Casasola, Mexico: 1900-1938. Washington, DC: Fondo del Sol, 1984.

Photographs by Mexico's great press photographer during the period of the Revolution and its aftermath, with essays concerning Casasola's contribution to Mexico's historical consciousness and the influence of photography on other forms of art.

Fontcuberta, Joan, ed. Photovisión. No. 3 (January-March). Madrid: Photovisión, S.A., 1982.

Includes portfolios of photographs by Martín Chambi (Peru, 1891-1973), Romualdo García (Mexico, 1852-1930), and Fernando Paillet (Argentina, 1880-1967).

Hoffenberg, H. L. Nineteenth-Century South America in Photographs. New York, NY: Dover, 1982.

South American historical photographs from a private New York collection.

Kozloff, Max. "Chambi of Cuzco." Art in America (Dec., 1979), 107-111.

Biographical and critical essay on Peruvian photographer.

McElroy, Douglas Keith. "The History of Photography in Peru in the Nineteenth Century, 1839-1876." Ph.D. diss., the University of New Mexico, 1977. Ann Arbor, MI: Xerox University Microfilms, 1977.

Chronological development of photography in nineteenth-century Peru and an examination of the role of photography in society. Includes biographies of daguerreotypists.

_____. "Montage or Reportage?" History of Photography Journal, 3 (July, 1979), 232.

Brief analysis of photograph purporting to depict the hanging of the Gutiérrez brothers from the Cathedral in Lima, 1872.

Museo Nacional de Historia and Museo Nacional de Antropología. Imagen histórica de la fotografía en México. México, DF: Instituto Nacional de Antropología e Historia, 1978.

Essays on social significance of photography in Mexico, development of themes and styles in nineteenth- and twentieth-century Mexican photography.

Newhall, Beaumont. The History of Photography. New York,
NY: Museum of Modern Art, 1964.

History of photography, 1839-1964, from a North American/
European perspective.

Rosenblum, Naomi. World History of Photography. New York,
NY: Abbeville Press, 1984.

History of photography from its origins to the present day,
including Latin American photography.

Serrano, Eduardo. Historia de la fotografía en Colombia.
Bogotá: Museo de Arte Moderno/Op Gráficas, 1983.

Authoritative history of photography in Colombia, 1840-
1950. Lavishly illustrated in black and white and in color.

Contemporary Photography

Conger, Amy. "The Second Latin American Photography Colloquium." Obscura: The Journal of the Los Angeles Center for
Photographic Studies, 2 (Dec.-Feb., 1981-82), 6.

Critique of the Second Colloquium and its accompanying
exhibitions of contemporary Latin American photography.

Freund, Giselle. "Mexico Hosts First Latin American Conference
on Photography." AfterImage, 6 (Oct., 1978), 4.

Report on the First Colloquium on Latin American
Photography.

García, Wifredo. Fotografía: Un arte para nuestro siglo. Santo
Domingo, Dominican Republic, 1981.

Book by leading photographer of the Dominican Republic,
including regional history of photography.

Instituto Nacional de Bellas Artes and Fondo Nacional para
Actividades Sociales. Hecho en Latinoamérica 2. México, DF:
Consejo Mexicano de Fotografía, 1981.

Proceedings of the Second Colloquium on Latin American
Photography, with reproductions of photos exhibited and a
directory of participants.

Manuel Alvarez Bravo. México, DF: Academia de Artes, 1980.

Tribute to Mexico's greatest photographer, with portfolio of
his work.

Museo de Arte Moderno. Hecho en Latinoamérica. México, DF: Consejo Mexicano de Fotografía, 1978.

Proceedings of the First Colloquium on Latin American Photography, with reproductions of photos from the exhibition and brief statements by participating photographers.

Neal, Avon, and Ann Parker. Los Ambulantes: The Itinerant Photographers of Guatemala. Cambridge, MA: The MIT Press, 1982.

Informative account of contemporary itinerant photographers of Guatemala, their way of life and role in society.

Orive, María Cristina. Libros fotográficos de autores latino-americanos. México, DF, 1981.

First attempt at a bibliography of Latin American photography, prepared for the Second Colloquium on Latin American Photography.

Parada, Esther. "Notes on Latin American Photography." AfterImage, 9 (Nov., 1981), 10.

Examination of the Second Colloquium on Latin American Photography and its larger social and political contexts.

"Reflections on Latin American Photography." AfterImage, 12 (March, 1985), 4-5.

Reports by seven North American participants on the Third Colloquium on Latin American Photography, held in Cuba in November, 1984.

Taller la Huella. Fotografía colombiana contemporánea. Bogotá: Carlos Valencia Editores, 1978.

Brief introduction to the contemporary documentary photography, art photography, and photojournalism of Colombia.

Photography as a Research Tool

Blacklow, Laura, and David Bonetti. "The Uses and Abuses of Photojournalism." Art New England, 6 (Feb., 1985), 10.

Comments on the manipulation of photographs by the news media.

Collier, Jr., John. Visual Anthropology: Photography as a Research Method. New York, NY: Holt, Rinehart and Winston, 1967.

Applications of photography to research in the social sciences.

Dorronsoro, Josune. Significación histórica de la fotografía. Caracas: Equinoccio/Universidad Simón Bolívar, n.d.

Significance of photographs as historical documents. Includes extensive bibliography.

Freund, Giselle. La fotografía como documento social. Barcelona: Editorial Gustavo, 1976.

Hockings, Paul, ed. Principles of Visual Anthropology. The Hague: Mouton Publishers, 1975.

Essays by Edmund Carpenter, Sol Worth, John Collier, David MacDougall and others concerning the use of photography in cross-cultural studies.

Ivins, Jr., William M. Prints and Visual Communication. Cambridge, MA: The MIT Press, 1969.

A history of printmaking, from woodcuts to photography; comments on the effect of repeatable images on human perception and communication.

Weinstein, Robert A., and Larry Booth. Collection, Use, and Care of Historical Photographs. Nashville, TN: American Association for State and Local History, 1977.

Comprehensive guide to the use and care of photographs, including preservation techniques, archival methods, and methods of dating and identifying photographic images.

Worth, Sol. "Margaret Mead and the Shift from 'Visual Anthropology' to the 'Anthropology of Visual Communication.'" Studies in Visual Communication, 6 (Spring, 1980), 15-21.

Comments on the distinction between photographs as records about culture and photographs as records of culture.

63. TOWARD A COMPREHENSIVE APPROACH TO LATIN AMERICAN MUSIC BIBLIOGRAPHY: THEORETICAL FOUNDATIONS FOR REFERENCE SOURCES AND RESEARCH MATERIALS

Malena Kuss

Introduction

In 1963, the distinguished Chilean musicologist Eugenio Pereira Salas (1904-1979) wrote in a letter to Samuel Claro Valdés: "What is needed before other work begins are: 1) a methodical bibliography of printed music and musical literature; 2) a systematic survey of unpublished materials already deposited in public and private libraries and archives; and 3) the gathering of copies of these varied published and unpublished sources into one center where they can then serve the investigator."[1] While this utopian centralization of resources may one day materialize in a single data bank fed internationally, and accessible through terminals from any library around the world at a minimal cost, neither a "bibliographie imaginaire" of that scope nor a "musée bibliographique" à la Malraux may prove possible in the foreseeable future, especially in those Third World countries without technological resources. Reduced to feasible proportions, two projects conceived in the spirit of Pereira Salas's first two "visions" are presently underway: (1) a comprehensive enumerative bibliography of printed primary and secondary sources that would integrate materials for the study of Latin America's written and oral traditions within a single taxonomical system;[2] and (2) a Directory of Music Research Libraries: South America, Central America, Mexico and the Caribbean, Volume VII in Series C of RISM,[3] which is a census-catalog of music holdings that qualify as research collections in public and private Latin American and Caribbean libraries, archives, museums, or any other type of repository of manuscript, printed, and recorded music.

Regarding Pereira Salas's third "vision," the "gathering of copies of these varied published and unpublished sources into one center where they can then serve the investigator," one may conceive of a central microfilm archive of the printed and manuscript holdings surveyed in the RISM C Directory of Music Research Libraries, modeled after similar massive microfilm projects such as the Hill Monastic Manuscript Library at St. John's Abbey and University in Collegeville, Minnesota,[4] or the Census-Catalogue of Manuscript Sources of Polyphonic Music

Editor's Note. Item numbers in parentheses refer to the bibliography on pp. 625-661 of this paper.

1400-1550 at the Urbana-Champaign campus of the University of Illinois.[5]   Latin American collections already available in microfilm include the baroque holdings of eleven Brazilian archives,[6] and the Mexico City Cathedral Archives, microfilmed in 1969 by Lincoln Spiess and Thomas Stanford.[7]   In a far more modest undertaking--since it only represents about 5 percent of the total repertory of operas written by Latin Americans-- I microfilmed forty-eight operas by Argentine composers in 1976, with support from the Library of Congress.[8]   These "drops in an ocean" address the problem not only of making these resources centrally available but also of their preservation.   Important initiatives such as the Brazilian and Mexican microfilm collections should be bibliographically controlled through SALALM, and also reported to the International Association of Music Libraries' Project Group on the Universal Availability of Publications (Printed Music), which eventually should turn its attention to manuscript sources.[9]

The problem of access to musical materials hinges on centralization.   For the preparation of the first type of tool, Pereira Salas envisioned "a methodical bibliography of printed music and music literature."   Certain criteria must be met to ensure maximum centralization within the limitations that the vast amount of existing resources impose upon such an undertaking.   As Latin America's cultural predicament is the integration and coexistence of its native and transplanted musical traditions--what Alejo Carpentier called "su confluencia de coordenadas históricas" in a seminal essay[10]--the taxonomical complexities implied in this predicament require: (1) the integration of resources for the study of written and oral traditions into a single taxonomical system; and (2) the application of culture-specific criteria to the periodization of history.   In a discussion of his approach to what became an unprecedented coverage of Latin America in The New Grove (under the area editorship of Gerard Béhague), Stanley Sadie recognized these requirements when he noted that the boundaries between art and folk music are less defined in Latin America than in Europe or in East and Southeast Asia.   He also noted that the historico-cultural strata, that is, the varying degrees of interaction among the aboriginal, Ibero-American, and Afro-American musical traditions, complicate the taxonomy of history-- or bibliography--even further.[11]   For my forthcoming Latin American Music: An Annotated Bibliography of Reference Sources and Research Materials   (see   n. 2),   I   have adopted the RILM classification[12] (see Appendix, below) with modifications that mainly affect historical periodization.   Retaining RILM numbers, conventional European historical periods are replaced by: (22/23) Music   in   pre-Columbian   cultures; (24/26) Colonial   period,   post-Conquest   to   Independence; (27) Nationalism,   19th   and   20th   centuries;   and   (28) Post-Nationalism, 20th century.

Background

I shall now discuss the degree to which Latin American music materials have already been integrated into the international music information network and into interdisciplinary bibliographies that control information in the field of Latin American Studies. I focus particularly on some remarkable achievements in three categories of tools from the RILM classification: (03) Encyclopedias, dictionaries, and literature about lexicographical coverage of Latin America (Bibliography, items 1-55); History, of the discipline (20) and under the heading "General, collected biography, chronologies" (21) (Bibliography, items 56-170); and (08) Bibliographies of music literature (discipline-specific and interdisciplinary) (Bibliography, items 171-255).[13]

03   Encylopedias, dictionaries, and literature about lexicographical coverage of Latin America

As is often pointed out by scholars surveying the available literature, there is no recent or definitive encyclopedia of Latin American music. Coverage of Latin America in The New Grove (item 33), the most comprehensive in any discipline-specific reference work to date, should be revised and expanded into a LatinoAmeriGrove that would replace the still useful Música y músicos de Latinoamérica (item 30) and the uneven but also useful biobibliographical coverage of composers in the Composers of the Americas series (item 10). However, Marcos Antônio Marcondes' Enciclopedia da Música Brasileira (item 28) sets high lexicographical standards and can be used as a model for the type of coverage needed for other countries.

The coverage of Latin America in The New Grove, under the area editorship of Gerard Béhague, represents a giant step toward integration of present knowledge of Latin American music in European encyclopedias. Coverage of Latin America in general European and United State music encyclopedias and dictionaries before 1980 (date of publication of The New Grove) is documented by me in Latin American Music in Contemporary Reference Sources: A Study Session (item 25) and by Robert Stevenson in Peru in International Music Encyclopedias (item 48). With few exceptions that reflect the limitations of individual contributors, the coverage of Latin America in The New Grove is comprehensive and reliable. Not the least attractive feature of this coverage is the extensive bibliography accompanying each entry. According to Stanley Sadie, Gerard Béhague, and Robert Stevenson,[14] this unprecedented coverage, which assigned 120,000 words for entries on folk music of South America alone, includes regional entries ("Latin America"); subject entries ("Aztec music," "Inca music," and "Maya music"); entries on individual countries and cities; 250 biographical entries on composers, performers, and musicologists; and 70 entries on dances and other local forms (i.e., "bossa nova," "milonga," "sanjuanito," "tango"). This coverage

contrasts sharply with the total of 99 entries for Latin America in
Grove's 5th and 43 entries in the main body of Die Musik in
Geschichte und Gegenwart (vols. 1-14).[15] MGG's supplement
(vols. 15-16) includes many definitive entries by Robert
Stevenson and other Latin American scholars.

Besides specific coverage, the inclusion of Latin America
in general New Grove entries such as "Dictionaries and encyclopedias," "Education in music," "Instrument collections,"
"Libraries," "Periodicals," and "Private collections" is of special
significance since one of our pressing needs is precisely to
integrate existing information into the bibliographic mainstream.
While sections that deal with Latin America in these general
entries remain unsatisfactory--James Coover's brilliant coverage of
"Dictionaries and encyclopedias" in The New Grove omits
Marcondes' Enciclopedia da Música Brasileira (item 28), for
instance--Coover's coverage is a dramatic improvement over Alec
Hyatt King's attention to the region in "Dictionaries and encyclopedias" for Grove's 5th, where he only mentions Felipe Pedrell's
1897 Diccionario biográfico y bibliográfico de músicos y escritores
de música españoles, portugueses, e hispano-americanos of which
only Vol. I (A-F) and part of II (G-GAZ) were published in
Barcelona.   Regarding reviews of the coverage of Latin America
in The New Grove, Robert Stevenson displays his usual virtuoso
command of factual information by itemizing errors in entries on
the Americas, both North and South (item 45).   Also important
for lexicographical coverage prior to the publication of The New
Grove is Stevenson's "Nuevos recursos para el estudio de la
música latinoamericana" in Heterofonía (item 47), the second part
of which itemizes entries on Latin America in La enciclopedia de
México; Carl Dahlhaus's edition of Riemann Musik Lexikon
(item 39); the supplement of MGG, edited by Ruth Blume; John
Vinton's Dictionary of Contemporary Music (item 51); Helen
Delpar's Encyclopedia of Latin America (item 16); and The New
Catholic Encyclopedia (item 46).   Two more items deserve
mention: the Diccionario de la música cubana (item 34) which,
despite its inaccuracies, still provides comprehensive coverage of
Cuban music and musicians and can serve as the basis for future
revisions; and Luis Merino's excellent biobibliographical studies of
Chilean composers (item 31), a model for the groundwork needed
for that utopian, definitive encyclopedia of Latin American music
that, as Coover pointed out, is sorely needed.   In spite of some
limitations in scope and quality, the list of existing encyclopedias
and dictionaries that include or specifically cover Latin America is
vast.

HISTORY

My modified RILM classification for the History Category is as follows (cf. Appendix).

20   The discipline
21   History, general; collected biography; chronologies
22/23   Music in pre-Columbian cultures
24/26   Colonial period, post-Conquest to Independence
27   Nationalism, 19th and 20th centuries
28   Post-nationalism, 20th century
29a   Individual biographies

20   The discipline

Latin America shares with Europe its concept of music history, rooted in the music itself and following the broad chronology established through general historiography. Latin America, like the United States and Canada, is also forced to reconstruct and gauge the impact of its Amerindian past. I here concentrate on historical studies that emphasize coverage of the art music tradition, since John Schechter's contributions to this conference (see Volume I, pp. 334-345) deal specifically with bibliographic resources for research in ethnomusicology and discuss major repositories of both recorded sound and ethno-musicological literature.

Very few music historiographies match Pola Suárez Urtubey's "Antecedentes de la musicología en la Argentina. Documentación y exégesis," a Ph.D. dissertation completed in 1971 which should serve as model for the music historiography of other countries.[16] Until such thoroughly documented accounts of attitudes toward music history are undertaken and published, it will remain premature to seek a theory or philosophy of music historiography for the entire region. However, while recognizing Latin America as a European-related culture, several distinguished scholars have stressed the need to rely on different value systems than those that underlie approaches to European music history.

Gilbert Chase, in a paper delivered at the annual meeting of the American Musicological Society in Urbana, Illinois, on December 30, 1956, pioneered a cultural-historical view when he wrote that "some of the best musical historians of Latin America are also poets. Particularly Alejo Carpentier and Mario de Andrade. In the broader field of cultural history, I would say that such prose writers as Ricardo Rojas of Argentina and Gilberto Freyre of Brazil are essentially poets; for what is Rojas's concept of 'Eurindia' but a metaphor enveloping a dialectic of the universal and the particular?"[17] Samuel Claro Valdés has called attention to the neglected Arabic influence in Latin American music. Luiz Heitor Corrêa de Azevedo, that elegant intellect of Brazilian music history, observed, in the lectures that inaugurated the Ph.D. Program in Music at City University of

New York in 1968, that "before World War II, archival research was almost non-existent and musicologists in Latin America seemed to believe that only primitive and folk music were worthy of their efforts, an attitude that may be interpreted as a late reflection of a colonial mentality."[18]

At the present time, the two fields that stand investigated by the better equipped scholars are the ethnomusic of most countries and the art music tradition of the colonial period. Many studies of the art music tradition have sought to demonstrate that composers born or writing in Latin America have fared as well as their European counterparts. While this was a necessary stage in Latin America's music historiography, the approach also reflects a colonial mentality. If carefully documented historical surveys of genres, biographies of composers, comprehensive period histories, and other such building blocks of general history can concentrate on what is idiosyncratic, the music historiography of Latin America in the 1980s should shed its last trace of cultural dependency. It should also vivify the prophetic vitality of Ricardo Rojas's metaphor, and seek "the identity of this new, 'magic' America not in the revival of its aboriginal past, nor in a recreation of its adopted Europe, but in the welding of a new myth, nurtured by both."

21   History, general; collected biography; chronologies

The most reliable and comprehensive history of the region as a whole is Gerard Béhague's Music in Latin America: An Introduction (item 70). The taxonomical complexities inherent in the need to account both for the variety of acculturative components and for the early syntheses of art and ethnic musics are reflected in Béhague's book, as they will be in any other attempt to engulf the totality of art music expressions in as diversified a musical culture as Latin America.

Besides the monumental contribution of Robert Stevenson (items 154-162), who plowed the field in all directions and produced the indispensable, exhaustively documented and detailed building blocks of history, an important collection of essays that adopts a culture-specific approach is Isabel Aretz's América Latina en su música (item 67), sponsored by UNESCO as part of its series América Latina en su Cultura. None is more brilliant than Alejo Carpentier's synthesis of the elusive soul of Latin America's idiosyncratic music ("América Latina en la confluencia de coordenadas históricas y su repercusión en la música") (item 67).

Without intending to present an organic view of the region, Music in the Americas, edited by George List and Juan Orrego-Salas (item 114), is also an important collection of essays by ethnomusicologists and composers which includes Charles Seeger's seminal statement on "Tradition and the [North] American Composer."

Also country-specific is La música de México edited by Julio Estrada (item 98), the most recent history of music in Mexico, whose second volume is a Guía bibliográfica. The definitive, culture-specific history of Latin American music, however, remains to be written.

08   Bibliographies of music literature (written and oral traditions)

This list includes national bibliographies that contain items on music; index issues of journals, such as the 1975 retrospective index issue of Revista Musical Chilena, commemorating the 30th anniversary of that distinguished publication (item 245); articles that list partial or complete bibliographies of musicologists, such as Robert Stevenson (item 206), Lauro Ayestarán (item 181), and Carlos Lavín (item 213); and bibliographies of literature about the written and oral musical traditions.

Well known to Latin Americanists is Carl Deal's excellent bibliography of dissertations (item 215) and Marian C. Walters's 1979 supplement. Stevenson's "Nuevos recursos para el estudio de la música latinoamericana" in Heterofonía (item 250) lists both recent dissertations and lexicographical coverage of Latin America in reference sources before the publication of The New Grove. Of the extensive bibliographies included in Stevenson's publications, the most formidable appears in both editions of Music in Aztec and Inca Territory (1968, revised 1976).[19] His Guide to Caribbean Music History (item 248) is also a definitive bibliographic source for the study of that region's music.

Gilbert Chase's monumental bibliographic achievement in the 1962 edition of A Guide to the Music of Latin America (item 203) has not been surpassed; any bibliographic tool attempting to match the scope of Chase's Guide must be conceived to supplement it, not to replace it.

Specifically within the field of Latin American Studies, two tools of bibliographic control must be mentioned, although Latin Americanists are well acquainted with them. The Handbook of Latin American Studies, published since 1936 by the Hispanic Division of the Library of Congress and presently under the general editorship of Dolores Moyano Martin (item 225), remains the main tool of bibliographic control of publications on Latin America in the humanities and social sciences. Although the coverage of music has been entrusted to the most distinguished editors (William Berrien, no. 5, 1939; Gilbert Chase, nos. 6-8, 1940-1942; Charles Seeger, nos. 9-16, 1943-1950; Richard A. Waterman, nos. 17-20, 1952-1957; Bruno Nettl, nos. 21-25, 1958-1962; Gilbert Chase, nos. 26-30, 1964-1968; Gerard Béhague, nos. 32-36, 1970-1974; and Robert Stevenson, nos. 38--, 1976--), the selective nature of the lists cannot but reflect interests of each individual editor. Only surpassed by the holdings of the Library of Congress (although there not separately cataloged) is

the Nettie Lee Benson Latin American Collection at the University
of Texas at Austin, which presently holds approximately 450,000
volumes. The 39-volume Catalog of the Latin American Collection
(1969-1977) and its four supplements list materials accessed to
1974 (item 202a). The Bibliographic Guide to Latin American
Studies (1978--) (item 196a) serves as an annual supplement to
the main Catalog. There is, however, a four-year gap (1974-
1978) between these two complementary sources.

To conclude, and because I have made so strong a case for
the usefulness of single, comprehensive tools of bibliographic
control, I must also add that such tools can only alleviate but not
permanently solve the problem of control. The computer, in
particular, may render them obsolete--albeit only after some delay
for Latin American materials.

NOTES

1.   Letter to Samuel Claro Valdés dated Nov. 5, 1963.   See
Samuel Claro Valdés, "Eugenio Pereira Salas (1904-1979), In
Memoriam," Inter-American Music Review, 2:2 (Spring-Summer,
1980), 146.
2.   Malena Kuss, Latin American Music: An Annotated
Bibliography of Reference Sources and Research Materials
(New York, NY: Garland Publishing Co., in press), approxi-
mately 3,000 entries. A preliminary version of this bibliography,
with 1,093 entries, was published as Volume IV in the Work in
Progress series of Music in the Life of Man: A World History
(Paris: International Music Council, UNESCO, 1984). 133 pp.
3.   Series C of the Répertoire International des Sources
Musicales is a multivolume directory of music research libraries
(Kassel: Bärenreiter Verlag, in preparation, publication projected
1988). Described by the eminent British bibliographer Alec Hyatt
King as "one of the boldest pieces of long-term planning ever
undertaken for the source material of any subject in the human-
istic field," RISM is a project of the International Musicological
Society and the International Association of Music Libraries,
Archives and Documentation Centers. Volume VII is in prepara-
tion by me, with the collaboration of Donald Thompson.
4.   In 1977, the holdings of the Hill Monastic Manuscript
Library exceeded 50,000 codices and scrolls. See Peter Jeffery,
"Music Manuscripts in Microfilm in the Hill Monastic Library at
St. John's Abbey and University," Notes of the Music Library
Association, 35 (1978), 7-30; Julian G. Plante, "The Hill Monastic
Manuscript Library as a Resource for Musicologists and Musi-
cians," Sacred Music, 105 (Fall, 1978), 7-11; J. Evan Kreider,
"Austrian Graduals, Antiphoners and Noted Missals on Microfilm in
the Hill Monastic Manuscript Library at St. John's Abbey and
University," Notes, 36 (1980), 849-863; and William Liddell Smith,

"An Inventory of pre-1600 Manuscripts Pertaining to Music in the Bundesstaatliche Studienbibliothek (Linz, Austria)," Fontes artis musicae, 27 (1980), 162-171.

5. Compiled by the University of Illinois Musicological Archives for Renaissance Manuscript Studies. Renaissance Manuscript Studies, 1. Vol. I, A-J; Vol. II, K-O; Vol. III, P-U (Neuhausen-Stuttgart: Hänssler Verlag, for the American Institute of Musicology, 1979, 1982, 1984, respectively). Most of the sources listed are available in microfilm at that university's library.

6. Elmer Cypriano Corrêa de Barbosa, comp., O ciclo do ouro: o tempo e a música do barroco católico. Catálogo de um Arquivo de Microfilmes. Elementos para uma História da Arte do Brasil (Rio de Janeiro: Pontificia Universidade Católica, 1979), 454 pp., 269 musical examples. Microfilms are housed at the Library of the Pontificia Universidade Católica do Rio de Janeiro. Reviewed by Robert Stevenson in Inter-American Music Review, 3:1 (1980), 115-116.

7. Lincoln Spiess and Thomas Stanford, An Introduction to Certain Mexican Archives (Detroit, MI: Information Coordinators, 1969), 90 pp. Microfilms are presently housed at the Museo de Antropología, Mexico City.

8. Malena Kuss, "Argentine Operas in Microfilm at the Music Division of the Library of Congress" (1976), 30 pp., an unpublished, annotated list of forty-eight opera scores microfilmed for the Music Division, Library of Congress, and the Biblioteca Nacional, Buenos Aires, with copies at UCLA's Music Library. Annotations in English and Spanish. Copy of the typescript available from Music Division, Library of Congress.

9. The Project Group on the Universal Availability of Publications (Printed Music) of the International Association of Music Libraries, Archives and Documentation Centers, is presently dealing with availability of rental materials from music publishers which are, essentially, manuscript scores. Reports on the ongoing work of this project group may be found in Fontes artis musicae, 33:1 (Jan.-March, 1986), 77-79, and forthcoming issues.

10. Alejo Carpentier, "América Latina en la confluencia de coordenadas históricas y su repercusión en la música," in Isabel Aretz, ed., América Latina en su música (Paris and Mexico City: Siglo Veintiuno Editores for UNESCO, 1977), pp. 7-19.

11. Stanley Sadie, "Latinoamérica en el Nuevo Grove," Revista Musical Chilena, 30:134 (April-Sept., 1976), 69-74.

12. Barry S. Brook, editor in chief, Répertoire International de Littérature Musicale (RILM) (New York, NY: International RILM Center, City University of New York, 1967--). RILM was established in 1966 by the International Musicological Society and the International Association of Music Libraries. RILM Abstracts, the official journal of RILM, publishes abstracts

indexed by computer of all significant literature on music that has appeared since January 1, 1967. Included are abstracts of books, articles, essays, reviews, dissertations, catalogs, iconographies, etc. (see Classification, appended). A quarterly journal, each fourth issue is a cumulative index. National RILM committees are responsible for sending abstracts of all significant literature published in their respective countries to the International RILM Center. Coverage of Latin America in RILM would greatly improve if committees in each country would more aggressively feed this information into this central data bank, which is accessible via Dialog Information Services, Inc., through all major libraries. While the contribution of area editors (Gerard Béhague and presently John Schechter) has considerably improved the coverage of Latin America in RILM, comprehensive indexing of all significant literature can only be achieved through the cooperation of active national committees.

13. Selected list of items to be included in my forthcoming bibliography (see n. 2).

14. See Sadie, "Latinoamérica en el Nuevo Grove"; comments by Béhague in Malena Kuss, Latin American Music in Contemporary Reference Sources (Paramount, CA: Academy Printing and Publishing, 1976), pp. 3-4; and Robert Stevenson, "Music Section," Handbook of Latin American Studies, 38 (1976), 549.

15. Friedrich Blume, ed., Die Musik in Geschichte und Gegenwart, 14 vols. (Kassel und Basel: Bärenreiter Verlag, 1949-1967). Supplement, vols. 15-16, 1973, 1979.

16. Pola Suárez Urtubey, "Antecedentes de la musicología en la Argentina. Documentación y exégesis," Ph.D. diss., Universidad Católica Argentina, Buenos Aires, 1971.

17. An abridged version of this paper, "A Dialectical Approach to Music History," was published in Ethnomusicology, 2:2 (Jan., 1958), 1-9.

18. Luiz Heitor Corrêa de Azevedo, "The Present State and Potential of Music Research in Latin America," in Barry S. Brook, Edward O. D. Downes, and Sherman van Solkema, eds., Perspectives in Musicology (New York, NY: W. W. Norton, 1972), p. 250.

19. Robert Stevenson, Music in Aztec and Inca Territory (Berkeley and Los Angeles, CA: University of California Press, 1968; 2d rev. ed., 1976).

BIBLIOGRAPHY

[Annotations quoted from Marco, Garfield, and Ferris, Information on Music: A Handbook of Reference Sources in European Languages, Vol. II. The Americas (item 236), are indicated by an M in parentheses. References to Duckles are to Vincent Duckles, comp., Music Reference and Research Materials: An Annotated Bibliography, 3d ed., New York, NY: The Free Press, 1974; 4th ed., Schirmer Books, 1985.]

I.   Encyclopedias, dictionaries, and literature about lexicographical coverage of Latin America (03)

1   Alvarez Coral, Juan. Compositores mexicanos. México, DF: Editores Asociados, 1971. 195 pp.

Twenty-five biographies, focus on 19th- and 20th-century composers, includes composers of popular music.

2   Arizaga, Rodolfo. Enciclopedia de la música argentina. Buenos Aires: Fondo Nacional de las Artes, 1971. 358 pp.

Comprehensive coverage, biographical and terminological. Institutions, theaters, good chronological tables. Selected list of works, at times biased information on composers. Reviewed by Kuss in Yearbook for Inter-American Musical Research, 10 (1974), 208-211. Listed in Duckles, 103.

3   Barbacci, Rodolfo. "Apuntes para un diccionario biográfico musical peruano." Fénix, Revista de la Biblioteca Nacional, 6 (1949), 414-510.

Standard biographical source on Peruvian musicians, includes information from primary sources which were subsequently destroyed by fire. Fénix is a cultural annual which began publication in 1944. Four of the volumes published in the 15-year period between 1949 and 1964 contain articles on music. (M)

4   Boettner, Juan Max. Música y músicos del Paraguay. Asunción, Paraguay: Edición de Autores Paraguayos, 1956. 294 pp.

This history contains a 28-page dictionary of Paraguayan composers.

5   Callejo Ferrer, Fernando. Música y músicos portorriqueños.
     San Juan, PR: Editorial Coquí, 1971. 283 pp.

     Reprint of first, 1915 edition. Historical survey that
     includes a 200-page biographical dictionary of
     musicians. (M)

6   Cardoso, Sylvio Tullio. Dicionário biográfico da música
     popular. Rio de Janeiro: Empresa Gráfica Ouvidor, 1965.
     351 pp.

     Biographical dictionary of popular musicians covering
     Brazilians on pp. 11-164.

7   Carvalho Neto, Paulo de. Diccionario del folklore
     ecuatoriano. Quito, Ecuador: Editorial Casa de la Cultura
     Ecuatoriana, 1964. 488 pp.

     Folklore terms, songs, dances, instruments, numerous
     indexes, a 10-page bibliography.

8   Cascudo, Luís da Câmara. Dicionário do Folclore Brasileiro.
     5th ed. São Paulo: Edições Melhoramentos, 1979. 811 pp.

     One of the seminal sources on Brazilian folk music.

9   Coluccio, Félix. Diccionario folklórico argentino. Buenos
     Aires: El Ateneo, 1948. 203 pp.

     Served as basis for Arizaga's folk music entries (item 2).
     More literary than musical, Coluccio's dictionary is not a
     scholarly tool but is useful for legends and myths. Exten-
     sive bibliography.

10   Composers of the Americas. 19 vols. Washington, DC: Pan
     American Union, Music Section--presently Department of
     Cultural Affairs, Organization of American States, 1955-1983.

     The only source that attempts to list complete works by
     composers of all the Americas. Accuracy varies, short
     biographical prefaces are included. Volume 19 is also index
     volume. Listed in Duckles, 156.

11   Compositores Brasileiros. Brazil: Ministerio de Relações
     Exteriores, 1975-1978. Serial, 35 booklets, each 8 to 64 pp.

     Each booklet contains catalog of complete works and brief
     biography. I am grateful to Robert Stevenson for this
     reference.

12   Entry deleted.

13   Cortés, José Domingo. Diccionário biográfico americano. Paris: Tipografía Lahure, 1875.

Luis Merino remarks that this is an important source for 19th-century Chilean biography (item 31).

14   Cosme, Luiz. Dicionário musical. Rio de Janeiro: Ministério da Educação e Cultura, Instituto Nacional do Livro, 1957.

Reference to this source in Coover, "Dictionaries and encyclopedias," The New Grove (item 33).

15   Davidson, Harry C. Diccionario folclórico de Colombia; músicos, instrumentos y danzas. 3 vols. Bogotá: Banco de la República, Departamento de Talleres Gráficos, 1970.

16   Delpar, Helen, ed. Encyclopedia of Latin America. New York, NY: McGraw-Hill Book Co., 1974.

For music coverage see Stevenson, "Nuevos rumbos para el estudio de la música latinoamericana" in Heterofonía, 52:10(1) (Dec., 1976/Jan.-Feb., 1977), 20-24.

17   Domínguez, Franklin. "Biografía de los compositores dominicanos." Revista de Educación, 29 (Jan.-April, 1959), 38-85.

Biographical information on ten composers.

18   La Enciclopedia de Cuba. San Juan, PR: Enciclopedia y Clásicos Cubanos, 1974.

19   Figueroa, Pedro Pablo. Diccionario biográfico chileno (1550-1887). Santiago: Imprenta de Chile, 1887.

Comments on this source by Merino (item 31).

20   _____ . Diccionario biográfico de Chile. 4th ed. Santiago: Imprenta Barcelona, 1897.

Comments and evaluation of this source for Chilean biography by Merino (item 31).

21   _____ . Diccionario biográfico de extranjeros en Chile. Santiago: Imprenta Moderna, 1900.

Comments on this source by Merino (item 31).

22   Figueroa, Virgilio. <u>Diccionario histórico y biográfico de
      Chile</u>. Vol. I (Santiago: Imprenta y Litografía La Ilustra-
      ción, 1925); Vol. II (Santiago: Calcells, 1928); Vols. III,
      IV, and V (1931).

      Evaluation of this source by Merino (item 31).

23   Foppa, Tito Livio. <u>Diccionario teatral del Río de la Plata</u>.
      Buenos Aires: Argentores [Ediciones del Carro de Tespis],
      1962. 1,046 pp.

      Very valuable tool for dramatic music, plays, composers,
      librettists, theaters, and forms of popular music theater.

24   Grial, Hugo de. <u>Músicos mexicanos</u>, 4th ed. México, DF:
      Editorial Diana, 1965. 275 pp.

      Not a scholarly tool but useful for list of names; includes
      250 short biographies of musicians.

25   Kuss, Malena. <u>Latin American Music in Contemporary
      Reference Sources: A Study Section</u>. Paramount, CA:
      Academy Printing and Publishing Co., 1976. 19 pp.

      Report of a study session on lexicographical coverage of
      Latin America chaired by Robert Stevenson at the National
      Meeting of the American Musicological Society in Washington,
      DC, Nov. 2, 1974. Participants included Charles Seeger,
      Gilbert Chase, Carleton Sprague Smith, Gerard Béhague,
      Isabel Pope Conant, Donald Thompson, Arthur La Brew,
      Lester Brothers, Luis Merino, and Malena Kuss. Review by
      Stevenson in "Music Section," <u>Handbook of Latin American
      Studies</u>, 40 (1978), 537.

26   Lagarmilla, Roberto. <u>Músicos uruguayos</u>. Montevideo:
      Editorial Medina, 1970. 91 pp.

      Biographies of 40 Uruguayan composers with lists of works
      and name index. Also a 28-item bibliography. (M)

27   Manzanares, Rafael. "Músicos de Honduras." <u>Boletín Inter-
      americano de Música</u>, 81 (July-Oct., 1971), 26-28.

      Biographical information on five prominent Honduran
      musicians.

28   Marcondes, Marcos Antônio, ed. Enciclopédia da Música
      Brasileira. Erudita, folclórica, popular. 2 vols. São Paulo:
      Art Editora, 1977. 1,190 pp.

      Excellent coverage of Brazilian music by a team of Brazilian
      experts. Appendixes include a discography of Brazilian art
      music (pp. 835-881); a complete list of Brazilian operas
      (pp. 883-886); a list of symphony orchestras (p. 887); a list
      of music journals (pp. 889-890); Brazilian theaters (pp. 891-
      892); and an index of all the musical scores, in alphabetical
      order, that are listed in each individual entry in the body of
      the encyclopedia (pp. 895-1159).   Also, a bibliography
      (pp. 1163-1190). Review by Luiz Heitor Corrêa de Azevedo
      in Latin American Music Review, 4:2 (1983).

29   Mariz, Vasco. Dicionário bio-bibliográfico musical (brasileiro
      e internacional). Rio de Janeiro: Livraria Kosmos, 1948.

      Listed in Duckles, 154.

30   Mayer-Serra, Otto. Música y músicos de Latinoamérica.
      2 vols. México, DF: Editorial Atlante, 1947.

      Still the only biographical and terminological source for the
      entire region. Listed in Duckles, 155.

31   Merino, Luis. Very important biobibliographical studies of
      Chilean composers in recent issues of Revista Musical
      Chilena, of which Merino is present editor. See extensive
      biography and list of works of Juan Orrego-Salas and
      Domingo Santa Cruz in Revista Musical Chilena, 146-147
      (April-Sept., 1979), 5-14 and 15-79, respectively.

32   Moncada García, Francisco. Pequeñas biografías de grandes
      músicos mexicanos. México, DF: Ediciones Framong, 1966.
      291 pp.

      Sixty biographical sketches, not scholarly, no works listed,
      includes name index. (M)

33   The New Grove. Stanley Sadie, general editor; Gerard
      Béhague, area editor for Latin America. 20 vols. London:
      Macmillan Publishers Limited, 1980.

      For discussion of coverage of Latin America in The New
      Grove see pp. 617-618, above; Sadie's "Latinoamérica en el
      Nuevo Grove" in Revista Musical Chilena, 30:134 (April-
      Sept., 1976), 69-74; and Stevenson, "The Americas in
      European Music Encyclopedias, Part I: England, France,
      Portugal." Inter-American Music Review, 3:2 (Spring-
      Summer, 1981), 159-207.

34 Orovio, Helio, ed. <u>Diccionario de la música cubana</u>.
    La Habana: Editorial Letras Cubanas, 1981. 442 pp.

    Cuban composers expressed some reservations about accuracy
    of information. Still, comprehensive coverage of Cuban
    music and musicians; can serve as basis for future
    revisions.

35 Pinto Durán, Carlos, ed. <u>Diccionario personal de Chile</u>.
    Santiago: Imprenta Claret, 1921.

    Comments by Merino on value of this source for music
    biography in Chile.

36 Poblete, Carlos. <u>Diccionario de la música</u>. Valparaíso,
    Chile: Ediciones Universitarias de Valparaíso, 1972.

    Evaluation of this source for Chilean music by Merino.

37 Ramírez, Serafín. <u>La Habana artística; apuntes históricos</u>.
    La Habana: Imprenta del E. M. de la Capitanía General,
    1891. 687 pp.

    Early attempt to record activity in 19th-century Cuba,
    includes notes on 19th-century Cuban dances. Very impor-
    tant is the 200-page dictionary of composers.

38 Raygada, Carlos. "Guía musical del Perú." <u>Fénix</u>, 12
    (1956-1957), 3-77; 13 (1963), 1-32; and 14 (1964), 3-95.

    With Barbacci, standard reference work on Peruvian music
    and musicians. Biographical entries include lists of works.
    Also included are institutions, periodicals, all entries
    arranged alphabetically.

39 <u>Riemann Musik Lexikon</u>. Carl Dahlhaus, ed. Ergänzungs-
    band Personenteil A-K, L-Z. Mainz: B. Schott's Söhne,
    1972, 1975.

    A list of Latin American composers whose biographies appear
    in <u>Riemann</u> is included in Stevenson, "Nuevos recursos para
    el estudio de la música latinoamericana," <u>Heterofonía</u>,
    52:10(1) (Dec., 1976; Jan.-Feb., 1977), 23-24.

40 Rubertis, V. de. <u>Pequeño diccionario musical, tecnológico y
    biográfico</u>. 6th ed. Buenos Aires, 1962.

    Listed by Coover in "Dictionaries and encyclopedias," <u>The
    New Grove</u>.

41   Sadie, Stanley. "Latinoamérica en el Nuevo Grove." Revista
      Músical Chilena, 30:134 (April-Sept., 1976), 69-74.

      Important statement by the general editor of The New Grove
      on approach to coverage of Latin America.

42   Sás, Andrés. La música en la Catedral de Lima. Lima:
      1970-1972.

      This work includes a two-volume biographical dictionary.
      Listed by Coover in "Dictionaries and encyclopedias," The
      New Grove.

43   Senillosa, Mabel. Compositores argentinos. 2d ed.,
      expanded. Buenos Aires: Casa Lottermoser, 1956. 451 pp.

      First edition, 1947. Valuable for some entries provided by
      the composers themselves.

44   Slonimsky, Nicolas, ed. Baker's Biographical Dictionary of
      Musicians. 6th ed. New York, NY: G. Schirmer, 1978.

      Slonimsky's life-long interest in Latin American composers
      and his tireless quest for accuracy of information make this
      an important source for Latin American biography.

45   Stevenson, Robert. "The Americas in European Music
      Encyclopedias. Part I: England, France, Portugal." Inter-
      American Music Review, 3:2 (Spring-Summer, 1981), 159-207.

      Brilliant review of lexicographical coverage of Latin America.
      Pages 185-194 deal specifically with coverage in The New
      Grove. Wealth of information, should be consulted for
      errors in individual entries in The New Grove.

46   _____. "Latin America" (and other entries) in The
      New Catholic Encyclopedia. New York, NY: McGraw Hill,
      1967.

      Entries listed in item 47, pp. 22-23.

47   _____. "Nuevos recursos para el estudio de la música
      latinoamericana." Heterofonía, 52:10(1) (Dec., 1976;
      Jan.-Feb., 1977), 15-24.

      Coverage of Latin America in dictionaries and encyclopedias
      itemized. Lists composers included in Riemann Musik
      Lexikon, 1972, 1975, and in Delpar's Encyclopedia of Latin
      America.

48 _____ . Peru in International Music Ecyclopedias.
Lima: Pacific Press, 1973.

49 Uzcátegui García, Emilio. Músicos chilenos contemporáneos
(datos biográficos e impresiones sobre sus obras). Santiago:
Imprenta y Encuadernación América, 1919. 236 pp.

Biographies of 23 Chilean musicians, composers, and
performers.

50 Vásquez Messmer, Peter. Compositores bolivianos. La Paz,
1975. 96 pp.

Biographical sketches of 36 musicians, grouped by locality.
Includes lists of selected works. (M)

51 Vinton, John, ed. Dictionary of Contemporary Music.
New York, NY: E. P. Dutton, 1974.

Excellent coverage of 20th-century Latin American com-
posers, especially those from Argentina, Brazil, Chile, and
Mexico. Contributors were mainly composers, including Juan
Orrego-Salas, Alcides Lanza, and Marlos Nobre. Of 891
composers entered, 505 are Europeans, 296 from the United
States, and 90 from Latin America.

52 Zapata Cuencar, Heriberto. Compositores antioqueños.
Medellín: Editorial Granamérica, 1973. 130 pp.

Colombian composers, source listed by Coover in "Dictionaries and encyclopedias," The New Grove.

53 _____ . Compositores colombianos. Medellín: Editorial
Carpel, 1962. 180 pp.

Severely criticized by Andrés Pardo Tovar for inadequate
information. Can provide basis for later revisions.

54 _____ . Compositores nariñenses. Medellín: Editorial
Granamérica, 1973. 41 pp.

55 _____ . Compositores vallecaucanos. Medellín: Editorial
Granamérica, 1968. 96 pp.

II. History, general; collected biography; chronologies (21)

56 Adalid y Gamero, Manuel de. "La música en Honduras."
Revista del archivo de la Biblioteca Nacional, 17:5 (Nov. 30,

1938), 299-301; 17:7 (Jan. 31, 1939), 500-501; and 17:8 (Feb. 28, 1939), 594-596.

57 Almeida, Renato. História da Música Brasileira. 2d ed. Rio de Janeiro, F. Briguiet e Comp., 1942. 529 pp.

First edition, 1926; second edition, broader coverage of 20th century. According to Luiz Heitor, Almeida's is the standard history of Brazilian music.

58 Alvarez Coral, Juan. Compositories mexicanos. México, DF: Editores Asociados, 1971. 195 pp.

59 Andrade, Mário de. Aspectos da Música Brasileira. São Paulo: Livraria Martins, 1964. 247 pp.

Includes an essay on the origins of the lundu and modinha, and a 90-page survey of the samba. In Oneyda Alvarenga, ed., Obras Completas de Mário de Andrade, Aspectos . . . is Vol. XI (1965).

60 _____. Ensaio Sôbre a Música Brasileira, 3d ed. São Paulo: Livraria Martins, 1972. 188 pp.

In Obras Completas, Ensaio is Vol. VI (1962).

61 _____. Música del Brasil, trans. Delia Berrabó. Buenos Aires: Editorial Shapire, 1944. 128 pp.

Contains Mário de Andrade's important essay "Danças dramaticas iberobrasileiras" (1939).

62 _____. Pequena História da Música, 6th ed. São Paulo: Livraria Martins, 1967. 245 pp.

In Obras Completas, Pequena História is Vol. VIII.

63 Appleby, David P. The Music of Brazil. Austin, TX: University of Texas Press, 1983. 209 pp.

64 Araya, José Rafael. Vida musical de Costa Rica. San José, Costa Rica: Imprenta Nacional, 1957. 142 pp.

An updated expansion of a previous version.

65 _____. "Vida musical de Costa Rica." Educación, 16:96-97 (Nov.-Dec., 1942), 3-79.

66 Ardévol, José. Introducción a Cuba: la música. La Habana: Instituto del Libro, 1969. 195 pp.

67   Aretz, Isabel, relatora. <u>América Latina en su música</u>.
      UNESCO Series, América Latina en su Cultura. Paris:
      UNESCO, and México, DF: Siglo Veintiuno Editores, 1977.
      344 pp.

      An extraordinary collection of essays focusing on issues.
      Contributors to this essential source are all distinguished
      scholars. Among them, the ethnomusicologists Isabel Aretz
      (Argentina-Venezuela) and her husband Luis Felipe Ramón y
      Rivera (Venezuela); Argeliers León and his wife María
      Teresa Linares (Cuba); Luiz Heitor Corrêa de Azevedo and
      Rafael José de Menezes Bastos (Brazil); Ana María Locatelli
      de Pérgamo (Argentina); Daniel Devoto (Argentina-Paris);
      and the composers Roque Cordero (Panama) and Juan
      Orrego-Salas (Chile). No specific scores are discussed, as
      the approach tends to summarize rather than discover.
      Unsurpassed for his mastery of the pen and the relevance of
      his thought is the opening essay by Alejo Carpentier (1904-
      1980), the literary giant who produced novels à la Joyce and
      music criticism à la Shaw, and the author of the pioneer <u>La
      música en Cuba</u> (1946). (Item 83)

68   Auza León, Atiliano. <u>Dinámica musical en Bolivia</u>. La Paz:
      Cooperativa de Artes Gráficas E. Burillo, 1967. 116 pp.

      General survey of art and folk music. Information on organ-
      izations and institutions, biographical information on
      composers, illustrations and musical examples. Two-page
      bibliography, no index. (M)

69   Ayestarán, Lauro. <u>La música en el Uruguay</u>. Vol. I.
      Montevideo: S.O.D.R.E., 1953. 817 pp. Vol. II not
      published.

      Outstanding history of music in Uruguay to 1860. It
      includes traditional music.

70   Béhague, Gerard. <u>Music in Latin America: An Introduction</u>.
      Englewood Cliffs, NJ: Prentice-Hall, 1979. 369 pp.

      The most comprehensive and reliable general history of Latin
      American music written to date. Folk music not stressed
      because the author had already contributed chapters on
      Latin America to Bruno Nettl's <u>Folk and Traditional Music of
      the Western Continents</u> (1973) for the same Prentice-Hall
      series. Review by Juan Orrego-Salas in <u>Latin American
      Music Review</u>, 1:1 (Spring-Summer, 1980), 114-117.

71   Boettner, Juan Max. Música y músicos del Paraguay.
       Asunción, Paraguay: Editorial de Autores Paraguayos
       Asociados, 1957. 294 pp.

       Standard source for the music of Paraguay, from the pre-
       Columbian period to the present. The final section of the
       book contains a 28-page biographical dictionary of
       Paraguayan musicians and a 294-page bibliography. (M)

72   Bosch, Mariano. Historia de la ópera en Buenos Aires.
       Buenos Aires: Imprenta del Comercio, 1905. 256 pp.

       Seminal source on the history of opera in Argentina.

73   _____. Historia de los orígenes del teatro nacional
       argentino. Repr. Buenos Aires: Solar/Hachette, 1969.

       First edition 1929. Seminal source for comparison between
       origins of national theater and national opera.

74   _____. Historia del teatro en Buenos Aires. Buenos
       Aires: Establecimiento Tipográfico El Comercio, 1910.

75   Boskaljon, Rudolf F. W. Honderd jaar muziekleven op
       Curaçao. Assen, Netherlands: Van Gorcum, 1958. 188 pp.

       A chronology that records musical activity from 1850 to 1955.
       (M)

76   Braga, Henriqueta Rosa Fernandes. Música sacra evangélica
       no Brasil: Contribuição a sua história. Rio de Janeiro:
       Livraria Kosmos Editora, 1961. 448 pp.

       A historical survey from the 16th to the 20th century with
       an unannotated 22-page bibliography. (M)

77   Calcaño, José Antonio. La ciudad y su música. Crónica
       musical de Caracas. Caracas: Editorial "Conservatorio
       Teresa Carreño," 1958. 518 pp.

       A comprehensive historical survey with 9-page bibliography.
       (M)

78   _____. Contribución al estudio de la música en
       Venezuela. Serie Cuadernos Literarios de la Asociación de
       Escritores Venezolanos. Caracas: Editorial Elite, 1939.
       128 pp.

       Documented historical survey, no bibliography or index.
       (M)

79 _____. Cuatrocientos años de música caraqueña.
Caracas: Círculo Musical, 1967. 98 pp.

General historical survey of Caracas's musical life, 1567–
1967. Biographical information and appendix of historical
documents. (M)

80 Callejo Ferrer, Fernando. Música y músicos puertorriqueños. San Juan, PR: Editorial Coquí, 1971. 283 pp.

First edition, 1915. Historical survey, including a 200–page
biographical dictionary and index.

81 Cánepa Guzmán, Mario. La ópera en Chile (1839–1930).
Santiago de Chile: Editorial del Pacífico, 1976. 305 pp.

82 Carpentier, Alejo. Ese músico que llevo adentro. 3 vols.
La Habana: Editorial Letras Cubanas, 1980. Vol. 1,
479 pp.; vol. 2, 589 pp.; vol. 3, 354 pp.

Extraordinary collection of Carpentier's music criticism.
Review by Stevenson in Inter-American Music Review, 4:2
(Spring-Summer, 1982), 88–90; and by Chase in Latin
American Music Review, 4:2 (Fall-Winter, 1983), 269–271.

83 _____. La música en Cuba. México, DF: Fondo de
Cultura Económica, 1972. 368 pp.

First edition, 1946. Pioneer history of music in Cuba.
Information needs to be updated. However, the insightful
perceptions recorded in this history will not be easily
surpassed.

84 Castellanos, J. Humberto. "Breve historia de la música en
Guatemala." Boletín de Museos y Bibliotecas (Guatemala
City, Biblioteca Nacional), segunda época, 3 (Oct., 1943),
112–121; (April, 1944), 20–28; (July, 1944), 66–74; and
(Oct., 1944), 97––.

85 Chase, Gilbert. Introducción a la música americana contemporánea. Compendios Nova de Iniciación Cultural, 17.
Buenos Aires: Editorial Nova, 1958. 129 pp.

86 Churión, Juan José. El teatro en Caracas. Caracas:
Tipografía Vargas, 1924. 230 pp.

History of opera in Venezuela to 1881, no bibliography or
index. (M)

87   Claro Valdés, Samuel, and Jorge Urrutia Blondel. Historia
      de la música en Chile. Universidad de Chile, Instituto de
      Investigaciones Musicales. Santiago: Editorial ORBE, 1973.
      192 pp.

      Documented historical narrative, pre-Columbian era to 1971.
      Biographical sketches of 98 composers, 74 are 20th century.
      Six-page chronology, appendix with information on music
      periodicals; 189-item unannotated bibliography, no musical
      examples. (M)

88   _____. Oyendo a Chile. Santiago de Chile: Editorial
      Andrés Bello, 1979. 143 pp.

      Important music appreciation text on Chilean music. 42
      illustrations, bibliography, index. Review in Inter-American
      Music Review, 1:2 (Spring-Summer, 1979), 237-238.

89   Coopersmith, Jacob M. Music and Musicians of the Dominican
      Republic. Music Series 15. Washington, DC: Pan American
      Union, 1949. 146 pp.

90   Corrêa de Azevedo, Luiz Heitor. Brief History of Music in
      Brazil. Washington, DC: Division of Music and Visual Arts,
      Department of Cultural Affairs, Pan American Union, 1948.
      92 pp.

91   _____. 150 Anos de Música no Brasil (1800-1950).
      Rio de Janeiro: Livraria José Olympio Editora, 1956.
      423 pp.

      Narrative history of 19th and 20th centuries. Some docu-
      mentation in text. Index of persons and topics, unannotated
      bibliography of 5 pages.

92   _____. Música e Músicos do Brasil; história, crítica,
      comentários. Rio de Janeiro: Livraria Casa do Estudante do
      Brasil, 1950. 410 pp.

      Twenty biographical chapters on Brazilian composers, no
      index or bibliography. (M)

93   Delgadillo, Luis A. "La música indígena y colonial en
      Nicaragua." Revista de Estudios Musicales, 1:3 (April,
      1950), 43-60.

94   Díaz Du-Pond, Carlos. Cincuenta años de ópera en México.
     México, DF: Universidad Nacional Autónoma de México, 1978.
     326 pp.

     Review by Jaime González Quiñones in Latin American Music
     Review, 1:1 (Spring-Summer, 1980), 112-114.

95   Díaz Gainza, José. Historia musical de Bolivia (Epoca
     Precolonial). Potosí: Universidad Tomás Frías, 1962.

     Aboriginal music in precolonial era. Terms, scales, no index
     or bibliography. (M)

96   Diniz, Jaime C. Músicos Pernambucanos do Passado.
     Recife: Universidade Federal de Pernambuco. Vol. 1, 1969,
     222 pp.; Vol. 2, 1971, 219 pp.

     Projected three-volume work on composers of the colonial
     period in the state of Pernambuco. Unannotated bibliog-
     raphy of published and manuscript sources, facsimiles. (M)

97   Dumervé, Constantin. Histoire de la musique en Haiti.
     Port-au-Prince: Imprimerie des Antilles, 1968. 319 pp.

98   Estrada, Julio, ed. La música en México. México, DF:
     Universidad Nacional Autónoma de México, 1984. 5 vols.
     1, Período prehispánico (c.1500 A.C. a 1521 D.C.); 2, Guía
     bibliográfica; 3, Período de la Independencia a la Revolución
     (1810 a 1910); 4, Período nacionalista (1910 a 1958);
     5, Período contemporáneo (1958 a 1980).

99   Fiorda-Kelly, Alfredo. Cronología de las óperas . . .
     cantadas en Buenos Aires. Buenos Aires: Imprenta Riera,
     1934. 83 pp.

     Seminal chronology of opera performances in Buenos Aires,
     particularly important for works produced before the in-
     auguration of the new Teatro Colón of Buenos Aires in 1980.

100 Flores, Bernal. La música en Costa Rica. San José, Costa
     Rica: Editorial Costa Rica, 1978. 142 pp.

     Bibliography, photos, musical examples. Review by Béhague
     in Latin American Music Review, 3:1 (Spring-Summer, 1982),
     128-129. According to Béhague, this is "the most compre-
     hensive historical survey of Costa Rican music to appear, by
     the Eastman trained Professor of Music at the Escuela de
     Artes Musicales of the University of Costa Rica and Director
     of the Department of Music of the Ministry of Culture."

101 Fonseca, Julio. "Apuntes sobre música costarricense." Revista Musical (Costa Rica), 1:3 (Oct., 1940), 35-42; 2:4 (1941), 64-74.

102 _____. "Referencias sobre música costarricense." Revista de estudios musicales (Mendoza, Argentina), 1:2 (April, 1950), 75-97.

103 Franze, Juan Pedro. La participación de la mujer argentina en el campo de la música. Buenos Aires: Centro Nacional de Documentación e Información Educativa, 1972. 16 pp.

104 Friedenthal, Albert. Musik, Tanz und Dichtung bei den Kreolen Amerikas. Berlin: Hans Schnippel, 1913. 328 pp.

105 García, Juan Francisco. Panorama de la música dominicana. Ciudad Trujillo: Publicaciones de la Secretaría de Estado de Educación y Bellas Artes, 1947. 46 pp.

106 Gesualdo, Vicente. Historia de la música en la Argentina, 2d ed. Buenos Aires: Editorial Libros de Hispanoamérica, 1978. 2 vols. I, La época colonial, 1536-1809, 107 pp.; II, La independencia y la época de Rivadavia, 1810-1829, 124 pp.

First edition, Editorial Beta, 1961. Vol. I, 1536-1850; Vol. II, 1851-1900. Superb historical account of colonial and postindependence music in Argentina to 1900. 1851-1900, chronology. Extensive bibliography at end of each volume. Items in this bibliography cannot be incorporated into the present inventory but must be consulted. List of periodicals and index of names.

107 Gómez Rodríguez, José G. Cuadernos biográficos musicales. Vol. I. México, DF: Secretaría de Educación Pública, 1969.

108 González, Jorge Antonio. "La ópera en Cuba." Música, Boletín de la Casa de las Américas, 11 (1972).

Most authoritative source on Cuban opera by the collaborator of Edwin T. Tolón in the pioneer Operas cubanas y sus autores (1943), and author of a definitive study of Cuban opera presently in press.

109 González Sol, Rafael. Datos históricos sobre el arte de la música en El Salvador. San Salvador: Imprenta Mercurio, 1940. 74 pp.

Narrative survey of musical life in El Salvador. (M)

110 Guardia, Ernesto de la, and Roberto Herrera. El arte lírico
     en el Teatro Colón (1908-1933). Buenos Aires: Dirección
     Nacional de Bellas Artes, 1933. 513 pp.

     Pioneer work on the history of this important opera house.

111 Hernández Balaguer, Pablo. Breve historia de la música
     cubana. Santiago de Cuba: Universidad de Oriente, 1964.

112 Kiefer, Bruno. Villa-Lobos e o Modernismo na Música
     Brasileira. Porto Alegre: Movimento, 1981. 179 pp.

     Review in Latin American Music Review, 4:2 (Fall-Winter,
     1982).

113 Lange, Francisco Curt. Boletín Latinoamericano de Música, 6
     (1946), 606 pp. Issue devoted to the music of Brazil.

     Essays by 24 distinguished contributors. Musical supplement
     volume.

114 List, George, and Juan Orrego-Salas. Music in the
     Americas. Inter-American Music Monograph Series 1.
     Bloomington, IN: Indiana University Research Center in
     Anthropology, Folklore and Linguistics. 1967. 257 pp.

     A collection of papers read at the first Inter-American
     Seminar of Composers and the second Inter-American Confer-
     ence on Ethnomusicology. The papers include contributions
     by Luiz Heitor Corrêa de Azevedo, Frank Gillis, Charles
     Haywood, George List, Alan P. Merriam, Bruno Nettl, Carlos
     Vega, and Charles Seeger. Abstracts in RILM, 2:2 (May-
     August, 1968).

115 Macía de Casteleiro, María. La música religiosa en Cuba.
     La Habana: Ucar García, 1956. 137 pp.

     History of Cuban church music in the 19th and 20th
     centuries.

116 Mariz, Vasco. Figuras da Música Brasileira Contemporánea.
     2d ed. São Paulo: Centrais Impresoras Brasileiras, 1970.

     First edition, 1948. Biographical coverage of 17 composers.
     (M)

117 _____. História da Música no Brasil. Rio de Janeiro:
     Instituto Nacional do Livro, Ministerio da Educação e
     Cultura, 1981. 331 pp.

118   Martín, Edgardo. Panorama histórico de la música en Cuba.
      La Habana: Universidad de la Habana, 1971. 257 pp.

      Excellent historical survey of Cuban music. It includes a
      7-page bibliography and 9 analytical indexes, with carefully
      documented statistics. It also lists the names of 63 Cuban
      composers.

119   Maurín Navarro, Emilio. San Juan en la historia de la
      música. San Juan, PR: Editorial Sanjuanina, 1965. 196 pp.

120   Mayer-Serra, Otto. El estado presente de la música en
      México. Washington, DC: Pan American Union, 1946, repr.
      1977.

121   _____ . Panorama de la música hispanoamericana.
      México, DF: Editorial Atlante, 1943. Pp. 379-440. (Separ-
      ata of Vol. II, Enciclopedia de la Música Atlante).

122   _____ . Panorama de la música mexicana, desde la
      independencia hasta la actualidad. México, DF: Fondo de
      Cultura Económica, 1941. 196 pp.

      Includes a 7-page bibliography.

123   Moncada García, Francisco. Pequeñas biografías de grandes
      músicos mexicanos: primera serie. México, DF: Ediciones
      Framong, 1966.

      Not very reliable, but useful for list of composers' names.

124   Morales, Salvador. La música mexicana. México, DF:
      Editorial Universo, c.1981. 204 pp.

125   Moreno Andrade, Segundo Luis. Historia de la música en el
      Ecuador. 3 vols. Quito: Editorial Casa de la Cultura
      Ecuatoriana, 1972.

      Includes coverage of folk and pre-Hispanic music. Vol. II
      deals with the impact of Western music on traditional
      Ecuadorian music; Vol. III lists musical institutions and
      discusses the art musical tradition.

126   _____ . "La música en el Ecuador." In Ecuador en
      cien años de Independencia. Vol. 2. J. Gonzalo Orellana,
      ed. Quito: Imprenta de la Escuela de Artes y Oficios, 1930.
      Pp. 187-276.

      Comprehensive treatment of Ecuador's music.

127   Moyano López, Rafael. La cultura musical cordobesa.
      Córdoba, Argentina: Imprenta de la Universidad, 1941.
      212 pp.

      A narrative survey of musical life in Córdoba since 1860.
      (M)

128   Muñoz Santaella, María Luisa. La música en Puerto Rico:
      panorama histórico-cultural. Sharon, CT: Troutman Press,
      1966. 174 pp.

      A general survey with 5-page bibliography. About this
      source, see Stevenson's annotation in "Caribbean Music
      History: A Selective Annotated Bibliography with Musical
      Supplement," Inter-American Music Review, 4:1 (Fall, 1981),
      54.

129   Muñoz Sanz, Juan Pablo. La música ecuatoriana. Quito:
      Imprenta de la Universidad Central, 1938. 36 pp.

130   Olavarría y Ferrari, Enrique de. Reseña histórica del teatro
      en México, 1538-1911. 3d ed. updated from 1911 to 1961 by
      Salvador Novo. 5 vols. México, DF: Editorial Porrúa, 1961.
      5,380 pp.

      Fundamental, documented chronology of Mexican theater and
      opera. Essential for coverage of history of opera in Mexico.

131   Ordaz, Luis. El teatro argentino. Buenos Aires: Centro
      Editor de América Latina, 1971.

      Basic work for the roots of national opera in popular theater
      on creole subjects.

132   Orrego-Salas, Juan. Involvement with Music: Music in Latin
      America. New York, NY: Harper's College Press, 1976.
      19 pp.

      A general-appreciation survey of music in Latin America by
      the distinguished Chilean composer and musicologist.

133   _____. "Pasado y presente de la música chilena."
      Revista Zig-Zag, 2,892 (1960), 92 ff.

134   Orta Velázquez, Guillermo. Breve historia de la música en
      México. México, DF: Librería de M. Porrúa, 1971. 495 pp.

135   Otero, Higinio. Música y músicos de Mendoza. Desde sus
      orígenes hasta nuestros días. Buenos Aires, 1970.

136 Pardo Tovar, Andrés. La cultura musical en Colombia.
Bogotá: Ediciones Lerner, 1966. 449 pp.

Comprehensive, documented historical survey of Colombian
music from pre-Hispanic era to 1965. 13-page appendix.
Outstanding bibliographic survey of research materials on
Colombia. It includes coverage of popular music,
performance organizations, musical institutions, biographies,
catalogs of composers' works, Colombian music publications,
1851-1964. 62 monographs discussed in chapters on bibliography, with full bibliographic descriptions. (M)

137 Pasarell, Emilio. Orígenes y desarrollo de la afición teatral
en Puerto Rico, 2d ed. San Juan, PR: Departamento de
Instrucción Pública, 1969. 535 pp.

A narrative chronology with 5-page bibliography. First
edition in two volumes, 1951 and 1967. (M)

138 Pérdomo Escobar, José Ignacio. Historia de la música en
Colombia. 5th ed. Bogotá: Editorial ABC, 1980.

First edition, 1945. Standard history of Colombian music.
It includes a 13-page bibliography.

139 _____ . La ópera en Colombia. Bogotá: Litografía
Arco, 1979. 121 pp.

It includes facsimiles, bibliography and plates. Review by
Stevenson, Inter-American Music Review, 3:2 (Spring-
Summer, 1981), 227-228.

140 Pereira Salas, Eugenio. Historia de la música en Chile,
1850-1900. Publicaciones de la Universidad de Chile.
Santiago: Editorial del Pacífico, 1957. 379 pp.

Standard source for 19th century Chilean music by the
distinguished "father" of Chilean musicology.

141 _____ . Los orígenes del arte musical en Chile.
Santiago: Imprenta Universitaria, 1941. 373 pp.

Historical narrative covering pre-Columbian music to 1850.
It includes coverage of folk and popular music and an
11-page bibliography. (M)

142 Pinilla, Enrique. Informe sobre la música en el Perú,
Vol. IX, Historia del Perú. Lima: Editorial Juan Mejía Baca,
1980. 322 pp.

Review by Stevenson, Inter-American Music Review, 4:2
(Spring-Summer, 1982), 108-109.

143   Pinilla Aguilar, José I.   Cultores de la música colombiana.
      Bogotá: Editorial Ariana, 1980.   434 pp.

144   Plaza y Manrique, Ramón de la.   Ensayos sobre el arte en
      Venezuela.   Caracas: Imprenta al Vapor de "La Opinión
      Nacional," 1883.   Reprinted in Colección Clásicos Venezo-
      lanos, Serie Historia 6 (Ediciones de la Presidencia de la
      República), 1977.   xix, x, 262, 56 pp.   Prefaces by Luis
      García Morales, Alfredo Boulton, and José Antonio Calcaño.

      In The New Grove entry on Plaza y Manrique, Stevenson
      indicates it was "published to commemorate Bolívar's birth.
      [Plaza y Manrique's is] the first Latin American music
      history and still one of the best.   It combines extensive
      analysis of aboriginal music with a precise and extremely
      valuable history of European music in Venezuela from the
      founding of Caracas to Plaza's time; it includes a 56-page
      musical appendix."

145   Prieto, Sixto.   "El Perú en la música escénica."   Fénix, 9
      (1953), 278-351.

      A chronological list of Peruvian operas and operas on
      Peruvian subjects, 1658-1927.   Bibliography of 90 items.

146   Raygada, Carlos.   "Panorama musical del Perú."   Boletín
      latinoamericano de música, 2:2 (April, 1936), 169-214.

147   Roberts, John Storm.   The Latin Tinge: The Impact of Latin
      American Music on the United States.   New York, NY:
      Oxford University Press, 1979.

      Review by Stevenson, Inter-American Music Review, 2:2
      (Spring-Summer, 1980), 139.

148   Sáenz Poggio, José.   Historia de la música guatemalteca
      desde la monarquía española hasta fines del año de 1877.
      Guatemala: Imprenta La Aurora, 1878.   80 pp.

149   Salas Viú, Vicente.   La creación musical en Chile, 1900-
      1951.   Santiago: Ediciones de la Universidad de Chile, 1952.
      477 pp.

      General survey of musical life in Chile, 1900-1950, 2-page
      bibliography.   (M)

150   Saldívar, Gabriel.   Historia de la música en México: épocas
      precortesiana y colonial.   México, DF: Secretaría de
      Educación Pública, 1934.   324 pp.

      Historical survey with 9-page bibliography, no index.   (M)

151   Salgado, Susana. Breve historia de la música en el
      Uruguay. Montevideo: AEMUS, 1971. 350 pp.

      Excellent survey of music in Uruguay from 1860 to date of
      publication by the distinguished student of Lauro Ayestarán.

152   Sider, Ronald. "The Art Music of Central America: Its
      Development and Present State." Ph.D. diss., Eastman
      School of Music of the University of Rochester, 1967. Ann
      Arbor, MI: University Microfilms International, 67-11084.
      xiv, 375 pp.

      Excellent survey of Central American music, 5-page
      bibliography.

153   Slonimsky, Nicolas. Music of Latin America. New York,
      NY: Thomas Y. Crowell, 1945. Repr. with new foreword
      and addenda. New York, NY: Da Capo Press, 1972.
      234 pp.

      A pioneer history of music of the entire region, it called
      international attention to Latin American composers in the
      unique style of one of the most original musical minds of any
      period. According to Luiz Heitor Corrêa de Azevedo,
      Slonimsky's achievement remains "the only reference work
      that covered the entire region, country by country, before
      the publication of Béhague's comprehensive 1979 history.
      While much of the information contained in this source has
      been superseded and updated in periodical literature, there
      is good reason why the book remains unique."

154   Stevenson, Robert. "Bogotá." In Ruth Blume, ed., Die
      Musik in Geschichte und Gegenwart, Supplement, A-Dy.
      Kassel und Basel: Bärenreiter Verlag, 1973.

      Definitive documented survey of music in Bogotá from the
      pre-colonial period to 1969, including a one-column
      bibliography. (M)

155   _____. "Cuzco." In MGG, Supplement, cols. 1673-
      1678.

      It surveys music in Cuzco from 1043 to the present,
      1/2-column bibliography. (M)

156   _____. "Guatemala Stadt." In MGG, Supplement,
      Fus-Hy, cols. 551-555.

      Definitive historical survey, 1/3-column bibliography. (M)

157 _____. "Latin America." In Frederick W. Sternfeld, ed., Music in the Modern Age, Vol. 5, Praeger History of Western Music. London: Weidenfeld and Nicolson, 1973. Pp. 407-432.

Classified discographies and bibliographies are additional reference features of this series. (M)

158 _____. "Latin America." In The New Catholic Encyclopedia. Vol. VIII. New York, NY: McGraw Hill, 1967.

Stevenson also contributed numerous individual entries on composers.

159 _____. "Lima." In MGG, Supplement, Hy-Lo, cols. 1138-1139.

Coverage of music in Lima from 1535 to the present, 1/4-column bibliography. (M)

160 _____. Music in Mexico: A Historical Survey. New York, NY: Thomas Y. Crowell, 1952. 300 pp.

Definitive history of music in Mexico, from early aboriginal music to mid-20th century. It includes a 4-page chronology and an 11-page bibliography, index.

161 _____. "Music in Quito: Four Centuries." Hispanic American Historical Review, 43:2 (May, 1963), 247-266.

162 _____. The Music of Peru: Aboriginal and Viceroyal Epochs. Washington, DC: Pan American Union, 1960. xii, 331 pp.

Seminal, documented historical survey with 17-page bibliography and 100-page musical supplement. (M)

163 Subirá, José. Historia de la música española e hispanoamericana. Barcelona: Salvat, 1953.

164 Tolón, Edwin T., and Jorge Antonio González. Historia del teatro en La Habana. Santa Clara, Cuba: Dirección de Publicaciones, Universidad Central de las Villas, 1961. 170 pp.

Seven, out of ten, chapters devoted to opera. Coverage to 1850.

165 _____. Operas cubanas y sus autores. La Habana: Imprenta Ucar, García y Cía, 1943. 472 pp.

Excellent history of Cuban opera, probably superseded only by the history of opera in Cuba by Jorge Antonio González to be published shortly by Editorial Letras Cubanas.

166 Valldepres, Manuel. "La música en la República Dominicana." Inter-American Music Bulletin, 77 (May, 1970), 31-44.

167 Vargas Ugarte, Rubén. "Notas sobre la música en el Perú." Cuadernos de Estudio (Lima), 3:7, 25-35.

168 Vásquez Messmer, Peter. Compositores bolivianos. La Paz: Escuela de Artes Gráficas "Don Bosco," 1975. 96 pp.

169 Vásquez, Rafael. Historia de la música en Guatemala. Guatemala: Tipografía Nacional, 1950. 346 pp.

Comprehensive historical survey covering folk, art, and popular music. No bibliography or index. (M)

170 Vega Miranda, Gilberto. Breviario del recuerdo: antología de músicos nicaragüenses. Managua: Secretaría de Educación Pública, 1945. 212 pp.

Forty-four short biographical entries on Nicaraguan musicians, no bibliography or index. (M)

III. Bibliographies, Music Literature (written and oral traditions) (08)

171 Anuario bibliográfico. Vol. 1--, 1958--. México, DF: Biblioteca Nacional, 1967--. Annual.

Very few music entries to 1962, which appeared in 1974. (M)

172 Anuario bibliográfico colombiano. Vol. 1--, 1951--. Bogotá: Instituto Caro y Cuervo, 1952--. Annual.

173 Anuario bibliográfico costarricense. Vol. 1--, 1956--. San José, Costa Rica: Imprenta Nacional, 1958--. Annual

174 Anuario bibliográfico cubano. Vols. 1-30, 1937-1965. La Habana and Gainesville, FL. Annual.

Title became Bibliografía cubana in 1953. Editor of the Anuario bibliográfico cubano was Fermín Peraza. (M)

175 Anuario bibliográfico mexicano. 1931-1933 and 1940-1942. México, DF: Secretaría de Relaciones Exteriores, 1932-1934, 1942-1944.

After a 25-year interval, publication of an annual biblio- graphic record was resumed as Anuario bibliográfico (item 171). (M)

176 Anuario bibliográfico peruano. Vol. 1--, 1943--. Lima: Biblioteca Nacional, 1945--. Irregular.

177 Anuario bibliográfico uruguayo. 1946-1949. New series, 1968--. Montevideo: Biblioteca Nacional, 1947-1951, 1969--. Annual.

178 Anuario bibliográfico venezolano. 1942-1954. Caracas: Tipografía American, 1944-1960. Irregular.

179 Ardissone, Elena, and Nélida Salvador, compilers. Biblio- grafía de la Revista "Nosotros," 1907-1943. Buenos Aires: Fondo Nacional de las Artes, 1971. 700 pp.

8,557 items indexed from the revista Nosotros, many of which deal with music. It includes an index of authors.

180 Aretz, Isabel. "La etnomusicología en Venezuela: primera bibliografía general." Boletín Interamericano de Música, 55 (Sept., 1966), 3-9; 56 (Nov., 1966), 3-34.

Comprehensive reference work. First part is introduction and bibliographic essay; second part is a classified bibliography of 610 entries that include books, articles, recordings, and printed music. (M)

181 Ayestarán, Flor de María Rodríguez de, and Walter Guido. "Bibliografía de Lauro Ayestarán." Revista Histórica, 39 (Dec., 1968), 525-589.

The Revista Histórica is a publication of the Museo Histórico Nacional of Montevideo, Uruguay. A brief biography accom- panies the extensive, 743-item bibliography of the writings of Lauro Ayestarán (1913-1966), compiled by Walter Guido and by the widow of this noted Uruguayan folklorist and musicologist.

182 Ayestarán, Lauro. "Bibliografía musical uruguaya." Revista de la Biblioteca Nacional, 1 (1966), 13-82.

505 references to books, monographs, music periodicals from Uruguay. The first part is divided into four main sections:

(a) works printed in Uruguay exclusively devoted to music; (b) works printed in Uruguay which contain music scores or important music references; (c) music librettos printed in Uruguay; (d) works printed abroad with detailed information on Uruguayan music and musicians. Of particular importance is the section on Uruguayan music periodicals since this information is not available in any other source. [This annotation is quoted from the Handbook of Latin American Studies, 32 (1970), 481.]

183 _____. Fuentes para el estudio de la música colonial uruguaya. Montevideo: Impresora Uruguaya, 1947. 57 pp.

Bibliography of colonial documents containing references to music dating from 1573 to 1839, a total of 147 items. (M)

184 Baumann, Max Peter. "Bibliographie zur traditionellen Musik Boliviens." Typescript.

A bibliography of over 600 items on Bolivian traditional music, available directly from the compiler. Address: Universität Bamberg, Postfach 1549, D-8600 Bamberg, West Germany.

185 Becco, Horacio Jorge. Contribución para una bibliografía de las ideas latinoamericanas. Series América Latina en su Cultura. Paris: UNESCO, 1981. 230 pp.

Extraordinary contribution to history of ideas. Many items relevant to music.

186 Béhague, Gerard. "Latin American Music: An Annotated Bibliography of Recent Publications." Yearbook for Inter-American Musical Research, 11 (1975), 190-218.

Covers publications from 1970 to 1976. Excellent annotated bibliography of 117 items following the classification in Handbook of Latin American Studies, i.e., general and by countries.

187 Belknap, S. Yancey, comp. "Latin American Performing Arts, An Analytical Index: 1957-1958," Inter-American Music Bulletin, 17 (May, 1960), 109 pp.

An index of articles published in 1957-1958 in eight Latin American music magazines and periodicals, such as Buenos Aires Musical and Pro Arte Musical (La Habana).

188 Bibliografía argentina de artes y letras. Vol. 1--, Jan.-March, 1959. Buenos Aires: Fondo Nacional de las Artes. Quarterly to 1964, semi-annual 1965--.

189   Bibliografía boliviana.   Vol. 1--,   1962--.   Cochabamba,
      Bolivia: Los Amigos del Libro, 1963--. Annual.

      Author and title arrangement, with subject index. Few, but
      some, music items. In his annotation, Marco also remarks
      that Werner Guttentag Tichauer is presently editor.

190   Bibliografía brasileira. Vol. 1--, 1938-1939. Rio de Janeiro:
      Instituto Nacional do Livro, 1941--. Irregular.

      Annotation in Marco reads as follows: "Retrospective cover-
      age for 1938-1955 in irregularly published volumes, 1941-
      1957.   Includes song collections and anthologies but no
      scores. For 1941 there were 17 music entries; 21 for 1955.
      After a nine-year suspension, publication resumed in 1966
      (with coverage of 1963) using a classed Dewey arrangement.
      The 1963 volume contained six music books; that of 1966, 12
      music books."

191   Bibliografía brasileira mensual. Vol. 1--, Nov., 1967. Rio
      de Janeiro: Instituto Nacional do Livro. Monthly.

      Marco indicates about three music books per issue until
      October, 1969, when score coverage began. Issue for
      November, 1969 included 68 music items, that of May, 1971
      contained 84 items.   Includes list of publishers with
      addresses, and list of periodicals.

192   Bibliografía colombiana. Vol. 1--, 1961--. Gainesville, FL.
      Semi-annual.

      Prepared by Cuban bibliographer Fermín Peraza and con-
      tinued by his wife after his death. Books and pamphlets
      published in Colombia and abroad, by Colombians. (M)

193   Bibliografía cubana.   Vol. 1--, 1959-1962--.   La Habana:
      Biblioteca Nacional "José Martí." Annual.

      Marco indicates that this bibliography is edited by Fermín
      Peraza. See also title, Anuario bibliográfico cubana (item
      174).

194   Bibliografía mexicana. Vol. 1--, Jan.-Feb., 1967--. México,
      DF: Biblioteca Nacional. Bimonthly.

195   Bibliografía de la música latinoamericana. La Habana, Cuba:
      Casa de las Américas, 1972. 37 pp.

      Compiled from holdings in Biblioteca Nacional "José Martí";
      Biblioteca Central "Rubén Martínez Villena," University of

Havana; and Biblioteca "José Antonio Echeverría" at the Casa de las Américas.

196 Bibliografía venezolana. Año 1--, Jan.-March, 1970--. Caracas: Centro Bibliográfico Venezolano, 1970 (quarterly); 1971 (semi-annual).

Music under "Bellas Artes." (M)

196a Bibliographic Guide to Latin American Studies. Boston, MA: G. K. Hall, 1978--.

A comprehensive guide to publications about and from all Latin American and Caribbean countries, incorporating the items cataloged during the year for the Benson Latin American Collection and additional titles from the Library of Congress. Provides access in one alphabet by author, title, and subject.

197 Boggs, Ralph Steele. "Bibliografía del folklore mexicano." Boletín de bibliografía antropológica americana, 3:3 (Sept.-Dec., 1939), 1-121.

Appendix, 247 bibliographic entries.

198 _____ . Bibliography of Latin American Folklore. New York, NY: The H. W. Wilson Co., 1940. 109 pp.

199 _____ . "Folklore Bibliography for 1945." Southern Folklore Quarterly, 10:1 (March, 1946), 17-108.

Items listed here by Boggs not cited in Handbook of Latin American Studies.

200 Boletim bibliográfico brasileiro. Nov.-Dec., 1951--. Sept.-Dec., 1967. Rio de Janeiro: Estante Publicações, 1953-1967. Bimonthly, irregular.

201 Boletim bibliográfico da Biblioteca Nacional. Vol. 1--, 1918--. New series, Vol. 1--, 1951--. Rio de Janeiro: Biblioteca Nacional. Quarterly.

Coverage of scores before 1973. Prepared on the basis of materials received by the acquisitions department of the National Library. (M)

202 Bustillos Vallejo, Freddy. Bibliografía boliviana de etnomusicología. La Paz: Instituto Nacional de Antropología, Departamento de Etnomusicología y Folklore, 1982. 21 pp.

202a Catalog of the Latin American Collection of the University of
Texas at Austin. 39 vols.; Supplements, 19 vols. Boston,
MA: G. K. Hall, 1969-1977.

Catalogs materials at the Benson Latin American Collection up
to 1974. The Bibliographic Guide (item 196a) covers
cataloged materials beginning in 1978 (annual). Thus, there
is a gap of four years (1974-1978) between these two complementary sources.

203 Chase, Gilbert. A Guide to the Music of Latin America.
2d ed. rev. and enlarged. Washington, DC: A Joint Publication by the Pan American Union and the Library of
Congress, 1962. Repr., New York, NY: AMS Press, 1972.
393 pp. First edition entitled A Guide to Latin American
Music, Latin American Series 5 (Washington, DC: Library of
Congress, Music Division, 1945). 274 pp.

Fundamental bibliography, items included have to be
evaluated individually. Many of the most important sources
published before 1960 are listed. This Guide stands as a
seminal reference source at the time of publication. Many
items continue to be very valuable, others are superseded
by more recent research. 3,700 items, including books and
articles, listed in the 1962 edition, all briefly annotated.
One of its most useful features is the index of periodicals
and supplement.

204 _____. "Materials for the Study of Latin American
Music." Notes, 13 (March, 1942), 1-12.

205 Chilean Bibliographic News Service. Servicio bibliográfico
chileno. 1940-1971. Santiago: Zamorano y Caperán.
Monthly, later quarterly.

Annual and periodic guides. Book dealers' list for foreign
clientele, the only consistent record of Chilean publications
for three decades. It covers an estimated 90 percent of
Santiago book production. (M)

206 Claro Valdés, Samuel. "Homenajes. Veinticinco años de
labor iberoamericana del doctor Robert Stevenson." Revista
Musical Chilena, 31:139-140 (July-Dec., 1977), 122-134.

Excellent review of Stevenson's monumental contribution to
Latin American musicology to 1977. It annotates and
describes contents of Renaissance and Baroque Musical
Sources in the Americas (1970); Christmas Music from
Baroque Mexico (1974); Latin American Colonial Music
Anthology (1975); A Guide to Caribbean Music History

(1975); Stevenson's critical edition of Tomás Torrejón y Velasco's La púrpura de la rosa (1701), the first New World opera (1976); Autores varios, Vilancicos Portugueses (1976); and three El Dorado recordings.

207 _____. "Inventory of Existing Documentation for the Region of Latin America and the Caribbean, Preliminary Study," in Music in the Life of Man: A World History. Bayreuth meeting, International Music Council of UNESCO, 1981. P. 50.

List of four dissertations on Chilean music, one on Latin American Baroque music completed at the Universidad de Chile.

208 Corrêa de Azevedo, Luiz Heitor, in collaboration with Mercedes Reis Pequeno and Cleofe Person de Matos. Bibliografia Musical Brasileira (1820-1950). Coleção B 1: Bibliografia, 9. Rio de Janeiro: Ministério da Educação e Saúde, Instituto Nacional do Livro, 1952. 252 pp.

1,639 entries. Author index, bibliography organized by subject. Seminal reference work edited by the distinguished Brazilian musicologist and his former students, Mercedes Reis Pequeno and Cleofe Person de Matos, the former presently Head of the Music Divison of Brazil's National Library, the latter an expert on the music of the Brazilian master José Mauricio Nunes Garcia.

209 Cortázar, Augusto Raúl. Guía bibliográfica del folklore argentino, primera contribución. Buenos Aires: Imprenta de la Universidad, 1942. 291 pp. (Instituto de Literatura Argentina, Ricardo Rojas, Director, Facultad de Filosofía y Letras de la Universidad de Buenos Aires--Sección Bibliografía, Tomo I, No. 1).

Invaluable bibliographic tool for Argentine folklore, compiled by this eminent Argentine folklorist and bibliographer, former head of the Folklore Department of the Ethnographic Museum at the Facultad de Filosofía y Letras of the University of Buenos Aires.

210 Cortázar, Augusto Raúl, and Carlos Dellepiane Calcena. Contribución a la bibliografía folklórica argentina (1956-1960). Comisión Internacional Permanente de Folklore, Publicación 3. Buenos Aires: Dirección General de Cultura, 1961. 69 pp.

Extensive, fundamental bibliographic guide to Argentine folklore. This publication is the second issue of which the first is "Contribuciones a la bibliografía folklórica argentina (1950–1955)." Folklore Americano (Lima), 8–9 (1959), 53–70. Folklore Americano was the organ of the Comité Interamericano de Folklore based in Lima, Peru.

211 Current Caribbean Bibliography/Bibliografía actual del Caribe. Vol. 1––, June 1951––. Hato Rey, PR: Caribbean Regional Library. French and Spanish. Annual, irregular; bimonthly for 1971.

Cumulative 1971 volume published in 1973. (M)

212 Dannemann, Manuel. Bibliografía del folklore chileno, 1952–1965. Latin American Folklore Series 2. Austin, TX: University of Texas at Austin, Center for Intercultural Studies in Folklore and Oral History, 1970. 60 pp.

A 425-item fundamental bibliography on Chilean folklore.

213 _____. "Bibliografía folklórica y etnográfica de Carlos Lavín A." Revista Musical Chilena, 21 (Jan.-March, 1967), 85–88.

A bibliography of published and unpublished writings by this eminent Chilean folklorist and composer.

214 Davis, Martha Ellen. Music and Dance in Latin American Urban Contexts: A Selective Bibliography. Urban Anthropology Bibliographies 1). Brockport, NY: State University of New York, Department of Anthropology, 1973. 20 pp.

Forty-two annotated entries covering items published between 1967 and 1977.

215 Deal, Carl, ed. Latin America and the Caribbean: A Dissertation Bibliography. Ann Arbor, MI: University Microfilms International, 1977. Pp. 125–126; Latin America and the Caribbean, II, supplement ed. Marian C. Walters, 1979. P. 62.

7,200 listed titles through 1977, which supersedes University Microfilms International's Latin America: A Catalogue of Dissertations (1974). Marian C. Walters's supplement adds 1,868 dissertations and 100 master theses. Dissertations in music are listed on a total of three pages in both compilations.

216 Espejo Núñez, Julio. "Bibliografía básica de arqueología andina, Vol. V, Música precolombina." Boletín Bibliográfico (Lima), 29:1–4, 70–81.

217 Ethnomusicology, Journal of the Society for Ethnomusicology. Vol. 1--, 1953--. Timothy Rice, present editor.

Since 1953, date of first issue, Ethnomusicology carries a section on "Current Bibliography and Discography." Items on Latin America covered under "The Americas."

218 Ethnomusicology, Journal of the Society for Ethnomusicology. Latin American Issue, 10:1 (Jan., 1966), 1-86.

Contributions by Carlos Vega, Luis Felipe Ramón y Rivera, Gertrud P. Kurath, A. M. Jones, Juan Orrego-Salas, E. Thomas Stanford, George List, and brief contributions by Isabel Aretz, Zdenka Fischmann, Daniel J. Crowley, and George List. Most of these contributions, especially List on Colombia and Aretz on Venezuela, emphasize important bibliographic sources for the study of folk music in those countries.

219 Fern, Leila. Selected References in English on Latin American Music. Music Series 13. Washington, DC: Pan American Union, 1944.

220 Figueroa Thompson, Annie. An Annotated Bibliography of Writings about Music in Puerto Rico. Index and Bibliography Series 12. Ann Arbor, MI: Music Library Association. 34 pp.

Describes books on Puerto Rican music housed at the "José M. Lázaro" Memorial Library at the University of Puerto Rico in Río Piedras. Stevenson annotates this bibliography in the Handbook of Latin American Studies as a "superlative valuable list of 304 annotated titles dating from 1844 to 1972."

221 _____. "Puerto Rican Newspapers and Journals of the Spanish Colonial Period as Source Materials for Musicological Research." Ph.D. diss., Florida State University, School of Library Science (March, 1980). Ann Arbor, MI: University Microfilms International, 80-16679. 501 pp., bibliography.

Impressive achievement summarized in Inter-American Music Review, 4:2 (Spring-Summer, 1982), 91-94.

222 Furt, Jorge M. "Bibliografía de la música folklórica argentina." Boletín de la Asociación Cultural Ameghino, Sección Arte Argentino (1933).

223 García Icazbalceta, Joaquín. Bibliografía mexicana del
     Siglo XVI. México, DF: Librería de Andrade, 1886. Rev.
     and augmented by Agustín Millares Carlo. México, DF:
     Fondo de Cultura Económica, 1954.

224 Inter-American Review of Bibliography. A publication of the
     Department of Cultural Affairs of the Organization of
     American States, 1951--. Index issue, "Catalog of the
     Inter-American Review of Bibliography, 1951-1982," pub-
     lished in 1983. Roberto Etchepareborda, ed.

     Catalog indexes the contents of 32 uninterrupted years of
     publications in the social sciences, humanities, and bibliog-
     raphy on Latin America and the Caribbean. It includes
     articles and reviews of books and articles published from
     1951 to 1982 in 32 volumes comprising 122 issues.

225 Handbook of Latin American Studies. A publication of the
     Hispanic Division, Library of Congress. Dolores Moyano
     Martin, ed. Gainesville, FL: University of Florida Press;
     presently Austin, TX: University of Texas Press, 1936--.
     44 volumes to date. Annual.

     "Music Section," bi-annual, presently edited by Robert
     Stevenson. Fundamental tool for bibliographic control of
     publications on Latin America in the humanities and social
     sciences. Previous editors of the "Music Section" include
     William Berrien (no. 5, 1939); Gilbert Chase (nos. 6-8,
     1940-1942); Charles Seeger (nos. 9-16, 1943-1950); Richard
     A. Waterman (nos. 17-20, 1952-1957); Bruno Nettl (nos. 21-
     25, 1958-1962); Gilbert Chase (nos. 26-30, 1964-1968);
     Gerard Béhague (nos. 32-36, 1970-1974); Robert Stevenson
     (nos. 38--, 1976--).

226 Huerta, Jorge A. A Bibliography of Chicano and Mexican
     Dance, Drama and Music. Oxnard, CA: Colegio Quetzalcoatl,
     1972. 59 pp.

227 Jamaica: A Select Bibliography, 1900-1963. Kingston,
     Jamaica: Jamaica Independence Festival Committee, Jamaica
     Library Service, 1963. 115 pp.

228 Jamaican National Bibliography. Vol. 1--, 1968--. New
     series, Vol. 1, 1975--. Kingston, Jamaica: Institute of
     Jamaica, West Indies Reference Library, 1969--. New series,
     1976--. Annual.

229 Kuss, Malena. "Latin American Music: An Annotated Bibliography of Reference Sources and Research Materials." Denton, TX: Center for Latin American Music Bibliography, 1983. Typescript.

Preliminary draft of a bibliography published in 1984 and enlarged for publication in 1986. (See n. 2, above.)

230 Lapique Becali, Zoila. Música colonial cubana en las publicaciones periódicas (1812-1912). Colección Cubana. Vol. I. La Habana: Editorial Letras Cubanas, 1979. 295 pp.

Narrative history of publications and chronological catalog of publications in which appear references to music. Review by Lester Brothers in Latin American Music Review, 4:1 (Spring-Summer, 1983), 173-176.

231 Latin American Research Review. Journal of the Latin American Studies Association, 1965--. Three issues per year. Gilbert W. Merkx, present editor.

Until 1978, LARR carried a "Current Research Inventory." This section was discontinued after 13:3.

232 Lekis, Lissa. Folk Dances of Latin America. New York, NY: Scarecrow Press, 1958. 309 pp.

Comprehensive bibliographic guide to the literature on Latin American folk music and dance. 611 items, including books and articles, are listed and briefly annotated.

233 List, George. "Ethnomusicology in Colombia." Ethnomusicology, Latin American Issue, 10:1 (Jan., 1966), 70-76.

Includes institutions, researchers, bibliography, and discography.

234 Lotis, Howard, compiler. Latin American Music Materials Available at the University of Pittsburgh and at the Carnegie Library. Pittsburgh, PA: Center for Latin American Studies, University of Pittsburgh, 1981. 145 pp.

235 Mambretti, Mabel. "Aportes para una bibliografía general del folklore, la etnomúsica y afines de Venezuela: años 1968-1970." Revista Venezolana de Folklore, segunda época, 3 (Sept., 1970), 129-148.

A bibliography of 120 items. (M)

236 Marco, Guy A., Ann Garfield, and Sharon P. Ferris. Information on Music: A Handbook of Reference Sources in European Languages. Vol. II. The Americas. Littleton, CO: Libraries Unlimited, Inc., 1977. Pp. 94-210.

An excellent contribution toward bibliographic control of materials on Latin American music. It relies on materials at the Library of Congress and other United States libraries. Review by Stevenson, Inter-American Music Review, 3:1 (Fall, 1980), 113-114.

237 Mattfeld, Julius, compiler. The Folk Music of the Western Hemisphere: A List of References in the New York Public Library. New York, NY: New York Public Library, 1925. 74 pp.

Approximately 230 entries on Latin America, reprinted with additions. (M)

238 Moedana Navarro, Gabriel. "Bibliografía del profesor Vicente T. Mendoza," in 25 Estudios de Folklore. México, DF: Universidad Nacional Autónoma de México, Instituto de Investigaciones Estéticas, 1971. Pp. 9-55.

Homage to Vicente T. Mendoza and Virginia Rodríguez Rivera. Includes reviews and lists 355 entries. (M)

239 "La OEA y la música." Boletín Interamericano de Música, 83 (March-June, 1973), 86-119.

Index issue of the Boletín Interamericano de Música (Inter-American Music Bulletin), a publication of the Music Section, Department of Cultural Affairs, Organization of American States. Indexes articles published to 1972, classified by issue, discipline, subject, and country.

240 O'Leary, Timothy. Ethnographic Bibliography of South America. New Haven, CT: Human Relations Area Files, Behavior Science Bibliographies, 1963. 387 pp.

Seminal bibliographic tool. Arranged alphabetically under tribes within countries or regions. Indispensable for all coverage of South American Indian music.

241 Ortega Ricaurte, Carmen. "Contribución a la bibliografía de la música en Colombia." Revista de la Dirección de Divulgación Cultural, Universidad Nacional de Colombia, 12 (Aug., 1973), 83-255.

Samuel Claro Valdés annotated this entry as "an important contribution to musical bibliography that includes books, articles, and reviews."

242 Pereira Salas, Eugenio. Bio-Bibliografía musical de Chile desde sus orígenes a 1886. Serie de Monografías Anexas a los Anales de la Universidad de Chile. Santiago de Chile: Ediciones de la Universidad de Chile, 1978. 136 pp., musical appendix, 11 pp.

Itemization of his enormous personal library, which Pereira Salas (1904-1979) donated to the Central Library of the University of Chile. Reviews of this fundamental bibliography by Samuel Claro Valdés in Revista Musical Chilena, 33:145, 91-103; and by Stevenson in Inter-American Music Review, 1:2 (Spring-Summer, 1979), 241-242.

243 _____. "Guía bibliográfica para el estudio del folklore chileno." Archivos del folklore chileno, 4 (1952), 1-112. Also issued separately (Santiago, Chile: Universidad de Chile, Instituto de Estudios Musicales, 1952).

An annotated, classified bibliography and discography that includes books, articles, records, music anthologies. 248 music entries. (M)

244 Reis Pequeno, Mercedes de Moura. Música no Rio de Janeiro Imperial, 1822-1870. Exposição comemorativa do primeiro decenio da Seção de Música e Arquivo Sonoro. Rio de Janeiro: Seção de Música e Arquivo Sonoro, Biblioteca Nacional, 1962.

A 100-page illustrated catalog compiled by Mercedes Reis Pequeno, founder and present head of the Music Section of Brazil's National Library.

245 Revista Musical Chilena. Index Issue, 29:129-130 (Jan.-June, 1975), 105 pp.

Retrospective index issue commemorating the 30th anniversary of this distinguished publication (1945-1975), compiled by its director and present editor Luis Merino.

246 Revolutionary Cuba: A Bibliographical Guide, 1966-1968. Coral Gables, FL: University of Miami Press, 1967-1970. Annual.

Materials about and published in Cuba since the Castro régime, edited by Fermín Peraza. (M)

247 Sims, Michael. United States Doctoral Dissertations in Third World Studies, 1869-1978. Waltham, MA: Crossroads Press, 1981. 450 pp.

A listing of 19,000 doctoral dissertations in Third World studies. Arranged by geographic area and indexed by subject, place name, personal name, language, and ethnic group. Includes author's name, year of completion of the dissertation, and degree-granting institution. Areas covered: North Africa, Sub-Saharan Africa, Asia, Latin America and the Caribbean, and the Middle East.

248   Stevenson, Robert. A Guide to Caribbean Music History. Lima: Ediciones "CVLTVRA," 1975. 101 pp. Revised and expanded as "Caribbean Music History: A Selective Annotated Bibliography with Musical Supplement." Inter-American Music Review, 4:1 (Fall, 1981). 112 pp.

Seminal reference source for Caribbean music history, copiously annotated. 1975 edition reviewed by Samuel Claro Valdés in Revista Musical Chilena, 31:139-140 (July-Dec., 1977), 129-130. First edition (1975) includes list of sources (pp. 1-66), index (67-80), musical illustrations (81-101). Review of second edition by Donald Thompson in Latin American Music Review, 4:2 (1983).

249   _____. Inter-American Music Review, Vol. 1:1--, 1978--. Semi-annual.

All articles by Stevenson and his reviews of current literature about Latin American music should be consulted, as the complete contents of issues to date (4:2 [1982]) have not been included in this inventory.

250   _____. "Nuevos recursos para el estudio de la música latinoamericana." Heterofonía, 52:10(1) (Dec., 1976-Jan.-Feb, 1977), 15-24.

Part I, pp. 15-20, lists American theses and dissertations on Latin American topics, with extremely helpful annotations. Coverage of American dissertations continues in 63:11(6) (Nov.-Dec., 1978), 2-7, of the same journal. Part II reviews coverage of Latin America in dictionaries and encyclopedias. It also includes a complete list of biographical entries on Latin Americans in Riemann Musik Lexikon, 1972, 1975.

251   _____. "South American National Library Publications." Notes, 35:1 (Sept., 1978), 31-41.

Annotated list of important literature brought out of South American libraries. Special emphasis on Brazil, Peru, and Venezuela.

252   Súarez Urtubey, Pola.   "Antecedentes de la musicología en la Argentina.   Documentación y exégesis."   Ph.D. diss., Facultad de Artes y Ciencias Musicales de la Universidad Católica Argentina, Buenos Aires, 1971.

Important history of musicology in Argentina, with extensive bibliography of sources.   A scholarly work that should be published.   Available from the author, or from the library of the Catholic University, Buenos Aires, Argentina.

253   _____.   La música en revistas argentinas.   Compilaciones especiales 38.   Buenos Aires: Fondo Nacional de las Artes, Bibliografía Argentina de Artes y Letras, 1969. 70 pp.

Index of articles in four periodicals, 1837 to 1954, 652 entries.   These periodicals are La gaceta musical, La moda, Revista de estudios musicales, and La revista de música.

254   Wagner, Henry R.   Nueva bibliografía mexicana del Siglo XVI.   México, DF: Editorial Polis, 1940.

Wagner's studies in Mexican bibliography are classic.   Important for Mexican incunabula.

255   Welch, Thomas L., and Myriam Figueras.   Travel Accounts and Descriptions of Latin America and the Caribbean, 1800-1920: A Selected Bibliography.   Washington, DC: Publications of the Organization of American States, 1982.   193 pp.

This bibliography lists more than 1,200 titles.

APPENDIX

Répertoire International de Littérature Musicale Classification From RILM Abstracts, 12:2 (1983)

Reference and Research Materials

01   Bibliography and librarianship
02   Libraries, museums, collections
03   Encyclopedias and dictionaries
04   Catalogues and indexes
05   Catalogues, thematic
06   Bibliographies, general
07   Bibliographies, music
08   Bibliographies, music literature
09   Discographies
10   Iconographies
12   Directories and membership lists

Collected Writings

  14 Periodicals and yearbooks
  15 Festschriften
  16 Congress reports, symposium proceedings
  17 Essays, letters, documents, literary texts

History, Western Art Music

  20 The discipline
  21 History, general; collected biography
  22 Antiquity
  23 Middle Ages
  24 Renaissance
  25 Baroque
  26 Classic and pre-Classic
  27 Romantic and post-Romantic
  28 Twentieth century, history
  29 Twentieth century, musical life

Ethnomusicology and Non-Western Art Music

  30 The discipline
  31 General
  32 Africa
  33 Asia
  34 Europe
  35 North America (north of Mexico)
  36 South and Central America
  37 Australia and Oceania
  39 Jazz, pop, and rock

Instruments and Voice

  40 General (including orchestra)
  41 Voice (including choral ensembles)
  42 Keyboard, organ
  43 Keyboard, general
  44 String
  45 Wind
  46 Percussion
  48 Electronic

Performance Practice and Notation

  50 Performance practice, general
  51 Performance practice of music to ca. 1600
  52 Performance practice of music, ca. 1600-1825
  53 Performance practice of music, ca. 1800-1900
  54 Performance practice, twentieth-century music
  55 Notation and paleography
  58 Editing

Theory, Analysis, and Composition

60 General
61 Rhythm, meter, tempo
62 Melody
63 Harmony and counterpoint
64 Form
65 Orchestration, instrumentation, timbre
66 Style and structural analysis
68 Techniques of composition

Pedagogy

70 General
71 Primary and secondary schools
72 Colleges and universities
73 Conservatories

Music and Other Arts

76 Dance
77 Dramatic arts (including film)
78 Poetry and other literature
79 Plastic arts

Music and Related Disciplines

80 General
81 Philosophy, aesthetics, criticism
82 Psychology and hearing
83 Physiology, therapy, medicine
84 Archaeology
85 Engineering and sound recording
86 Physics, mathematics, acoustics, architecture
87 Sociology
89 Printing, engraving, publishing

Music and Liturgy

90 General
91 Jewish
92 Byzantine (and other Eastern)
93 Catholic
94 Protestant
95 Buddhist
96 Hindu
97 Islamic

64. SELECTED BIBLIOGRAPHIC SOURCES IN
LATIN AMERICAN ETHNOMUSICOLOGY

John M. Schechter

Adkins, Cecil, and Alis Dickinson, eds. Doctoral Dissertations in Musicology. 7th North American ed. Philadelphia, PA: American Musicological Society/International Musicological Society, 1984.

American Doctoral Dissertations. University Microfilms International (compiled from Dissertation Abstracts International, for the Association of Research Libraries). Annual.

Aretz, Isabel. "Colecciones de cilindros y trabajos de musicología comparada realizados en Latinoamérica durante los primeros treinta años del siglo XX." Revista Venezolana de Folklore (Caracas), 4, 2ª época (Dec., 1972), 49-65.

Valuable historical overview of early ethnomusicological field research in Latin America.

Béhague, Gerard. "Ecuadorian, Peruvian, and Brazilian Ethnomusicology: A General View." Revista de Música Latinoamericana/Latin American Music Review (LAMR), 3:1 (Spring-Summer, 1982), 17-35.

Bibliographic essay, concluding with a selected bibliography.

_____. "Folk and Traditional Music of Latin America: General Prospect and Research Problems." The World of Music, 25:2 (1982), 3-21.

Surveys present knowledge of traditional and folk musics of Latin America, incorporating some discussion of stylistic features and of ethnomusicological issues.

_____. "Latin American Music: An Annotated Bibliography of Recent Publications." Yearbook for Inter-American Musical Research, 11 (1975), 190-218.

Annotated bibliography, with introductory essay, following the Handbook of Latin American Studies "Music" section format.

Editor's Note. This bibliography was distributed during the panel session on "The Current State of Bibliographic Research in Latin American Ethnomusicology" (see Volume I, pp. 334-345).

_____. Music in Latin America: An Introduction. Engle-
wood Cliffs, NJ: Prentice-Hall, 1979.

"Bibliographic Notes" concludes each chapter.

Chase, Gilbert. A Guide to the Music of Latin America. 2d ed.,
rev. and enlarged. Washington, DC: Pan American Union,
1962. 411 pp. Repr. 1972.

Cordeiro, Daniel Raposo. "Latin America, Spain and Portugal: A
Select Guide to Reference Materials at Syracuse University."
Syracuse, NY: Bird Library of Syracuse University, August,
1983. 16 pp. Typescript.

Dannemann Rothstein, Manuel. Bibliografía del Folklore Chileno:
1952-1965. Latin American Folklore Series 2. Austin, TX:
Center for Intercultural Studies in Folklore and Oral History,
The University of Texas [at Austin], 1970.

Briefly annotated.

Davis, Martha Ellen. Music and Dance in Latin American Urban
Contexts: A Selective Bibliography. Urban Anthropology
Bibliographies 1. Brockport, NY: State University of New
York, Department of Anthropology, 1973. 20 pp.

Spanish- and Portuguese-speaking countries, and publications
within the last decade, only. 42 entries: Brazil (25);
Spanish-speaking South America (10); Mexico, Central America
and Southwest U.S.A. (4); and Hispanic Caribbean (3).

Dissertation Abstracts International. University Microfilms International. Ann Arbor, MI. Annual.

Duckles, Vincent, comp. Music Reference and Research Mater-
ials: An Annotated Bibliography. 3d ed. New York, NY: The
Free Press, 1974; 4th ed., by Michael Keller and Vincent
Duckles, Schirmer Books, 1985.

Under the section "Bibliographies of Music" is the subsection
"Jazz and Popular Music," entries 955-963. Under "Bibliographies of Music Literature" is the subsection "Ethnomusicology," entries 667-697.

Ethnomusicology: Journal of the Society for Ethnomusicology.
"Current Bibliography, Discography, and Filmography":
"Americas." Joseph C. Hickerson, Louise S. Spear, and Carl
Rahkonen, eds. Triannual.

Printed sources, recordings, and films/videotapes.

_____. 10:1 (Jan., 1966). Special Latin American Issue.

Ethnomusicology at UCLA: Newsletter of the Program in Ethnomusicology, UCLA Department of Music. Roger Wright, ed.
Los Angeles, CA, 90024. 1983--.

Figueroa Thompson, Annie. An Annotated Bibliography of
Writings about Music in Puerto Rico. Ann Arbor, MI: Music
Library Association, 1974.

Incorporates references to books, sections and chapters of
books, dissertations, and journal articles; excludes recordings
and printed music. Items date from 1844 to 1972.

Flansburg, Sundra Cee, ed. Music: A Catalog of Selected
Doctoral Dissertation Research. University Microfilms International.

Citations to 1,568 dissertations and master's theses published
1978 to 1983. "Ethnomusicology," pp. 7-8.

Grow, Michael. Scholars' Guide to Washington, D.C. for Latin
American and Caribbean Studies. Washington, DC: Smith-
sonian Institution Press, 1979.

"Collections D. Collections of Music and Other Sound Recordings," pp. 102-106, summarizes music-archival holdings in
embassies, cultural institutes, and, most notably, the Library
of Congress' Music Division, Recorded Sound Section, and
Archive of Folk Song (which became, on October 1, 1981, "The
Archive of Folk Culture").

Handbook of Latin American Studies. Austin, TX: University of
Texas Press.

In Humanities volumes, "Music" section, biennially in even-
numbered years. Current compiler/bibliographer, Robert
Stevenson.

Heintze, James R. American Music Studies: A Classified
Bibliography of Master's Theses. College Music Society
Bibliographies in American Music 8. Detroit, MI: Information
Coordinators, 1984.

Hickerson, Joseph C. [Head, Archive of Folk Culture]. "An
Inventory of the Bibliographies and Other Reference and
Finding Aids Prepared by the Archive of Folk Culture."
Washington, DC: Archive of Folk Culture, Library of
Congress, Aug., 1984. Typescript.

Among the resources mentioned are the following:

1. "Bibliographies in the Field of Ethnomusicology." 1976. 5 pp.

2. "Brazilian Materials in the Archive of Folk Song." 1980. 3 pp.

3. "Folklife and Ethnomusicology Archives and Related Collections in the United States and Canada." (LC Folk Archive Reference Aid [LCFARA] No. 2). 1984. 14 pp.

4. "Folklife and Ethnomusicology Serial Publications in North America." 1982. 16 pp.

5. "Folklife and Ethnomusicology Societies in North America." 1982. 14 pp.

6. "A Guide to the Collection of Recorded Folk Music and Folklore in the Library of Congress." 1983. 6 pp.

7. "Latin American and Caribbean Recordings in the Archive of Folk Song." 1960. 5 pp.

8. "Material Relating to Ethnomusicology." 1967. 5 pp.

9. "Mexican-American Folksong and Music on Field Recordings in the Archive of Folk Song." 1978. 2 pp.

10. "Music of the Incas and Early Peru." 1966. 2 pp.

11. "Peruvian Field Recordings in the Archive of Folk Culture." 1982. 2 pp.

12. "Puerto Rican Folklore and Folk Music." 1968. 2 pp.

13. "Record Companies in North America Specializing in Folk Music, Folklore and Ethnomusicology." 1982. 13 pp.

14. "Theses and Dissertations in the Library of Congress Containing Collections of Folksong and Folk Music." 1981. 6 pp.

15. "Trinidad Field Recordings in the Archive of Folk Culture." 1982. 1 pp.

Hinds, Harold E., Jr. "Latin American Popular Culture. A New Research Frontier: Achievements, Problems and Promise." Journal of Popular Culture, 14:3 (Winter, 1980), 405-412.

_____. "Latin American Popular Culture: Recent Research Trends and a Needs Assessment." Journal of Popular Culture, 18:1 (Summer, 1984), 58-64.

Updates through 1982 publications of the same author's earlier bibliographic essay in the same journal.

Huerta, Jorge A. A Bibliography of Chicano and Mexican Dance, Drama and Music. Oxnard, CA: Colegio Quetzalcoatl, 1972. 59 pp.

References to Mexican books, journals, and phonograph records.

Kunst, Jaap. Ethnomusicology, A Study of Its Nature, Its Problems, Methods and Representative Personalities, to Which Is Added a Bibliography. 3d ed., enl. The Hague: Nijhoff, 1959. 303 pp. (Bibliography is pp. 79–215.) Supplement to the 3d ed., 1960, 45 pp., adds some 500 items to the bibliography and contains new record listings through 1958.

Kuss, Malena. "Charles Seeger and Latin America: Themes and Contributions." Revista Interamericana de Bibliografía/ Inter-American Review of Bibliography, 30:3 (1980), 231–237.

Note 30 cites bibliographic resources useful in the study of Latin American ethnomusicology; several of these sources are incorporated into this bibliography.

_____. "Current State of Bibliographic Research in Latin American Music." Fontes Artis Musicae, 31:4 (Oct.-Dec., 1984), 206–228.

Bibliographic essay confronting the need to integrate bibliographic tools for Latin American music into the international information network; the fact that important lists of materials on Latin American music appear in interdisciplinary bibliographies not well known outside the arena of Latin American studies; the necessity for large-scale, composite tools of bibliographic control for Latin American music materials. Three annotated appendixes elaborate dictionaries, encyclopedias, and literature about lexicographical coverage of Latin America; bibliographies and reference sources for Latin American studies that include music; and bibliographies of music literature.

_____. Latin American Music in Contemporary Reference Sources: A Study Session. Paramount, CA: Academy Printing and Publishing, 1976. 19 pp.

Lotis, Howard. Latin American Music Materials Available at the University of Pittsburgh and at Carnegie Library of Pittsburgh. Pittsburgh, PA: Center for Latin American Studies, University of Pittsburgh, 1981. 146 pp.

Incorporates bibliographies and discographies.

Mead, Rita H. Doctoral Dissertations in American Music: A
Classified Bibliography. I.S.A.M. Monographs 3. Brooklyn,
NY: Brooklyn College Institute for Studies in American Music,
1974.

Dissertations accepted from the 1890s to 1973.

Merriam, Alan P., comp. "An Annotated Bibliography of Theses
and Dissertations in Ethnomusicology and Folk Music Accepted
at American Universities." Ethnomusicology, 4:1 (Jan., 1960),
21-39.

Twenty-three of the 180 theses and dissertations deal prin-
cipally or completely with Latin America.

The Music Index: The Key to Current Music Periodical Literature.
Detroit, MI: Information Services, Inc.

Indexes more than 225 periodicals by subject and author.

Nettl, Bruno. Folk and Traditional Music of the Western Conti-
nents. 2d ed. Englewood Cliffs, NJ: Prentice-Hall, 1973.

Chapter 9, "Latin American Folk Music," with a concluding
"Bibliography and Discography," is by Gerard Béhague;
Chapter 10, "Afro-American Folk Music in North and Latin
America," with a concluding "Bibliography and Discography,"
is by Bruno Nettl and Gerard Béhague.

_____. Reference Materials in Ethnomusicology: A Biblio-
graphic Essay. 2d ed., rev. Detroit Studies in Music
Bibliography 1. Detroit, MI: Information Coordinators, 1967.
40 pp.

Pages 30-40 are a "List of Publications Cited," with full
bibliographic data.

_____. The Study of Ethnomusicology: Twenty-nine Issues
and Concepts. Urbana, IL: University of Illinois Press, 1983.

Chapter 27, "Cultural Grey-Out," discusses processes of
influence of Western music on non-Western societies. A major
bibliography ("Publications Cited") concludes the book.

_____. Theory and Method in Ethnomusicology. New
York, NY: The Free Press, 1964.

Chapter 2, "Bibliographic Resources of Ethnomusicology,"
pp. 27-61, concluding with a "Bibliography" (pp. 58-61), is an
important bibliographic essay, oriented historically; it also
discusses periodicals, bibliographies, and discography.

Nettl, Bruno, ed. <u>Eight Urban Musical Cultures: Tradition and Change</u>. Urbana, IL: University of Illinois Press, 1978.

First sentence of "Introduction" by Bruno Nettl, p. 3: "This volume presents a group of ethnomusicological studies devoted to the fate of traditional music in modern cities of developing or recently developed nations of Asia, Africa, and the Americas." This "Introduction" elaborates the trend of growing scholarly interest in urban musical cultures, and it proposes analytical approaches to the study of urban musics, including urban popular music. One of the essays in the anthology is David K. Stigberg, "<u>Jarocho</u>, <u>Tropical</u>, and 'Pop': Aspects of Musical Life in Veracruz, 1971-72," pp. 260-295.

Olsen, Dale A. "Folk Music of South America: A Musical Mosaic." In Elizabeth May, ed., <u>Musics of Many Cultures: An Introduction</u>. Berkeley, CA: University of California Press, 1980. Pp. 386-425.

Concluding Glossary, Bibliography, Discography, and Films sections.

_____. "Symbol and Function in South American Indian Music." In Elizabeth May, ed., <u>Musics of Many Cultures: An Introduction</u>. Berkeley, CA: University of California Press, 1980. Pp. 363-385.

Concluding Glossary, Bibliography, Discography, and Films sections.

Ortega Ricaurte, Carmen. "Contribución a la bibliografía de la música en Colombia." <u>UN: Revista de la Dirección de Divulgación Cultural, Universidad Nacional de Colombia</u> (Bogotá), 12 (Aug., 1973), 83-252.

Extensive bibliography, with sections on dance, biography, Colombian music history, musical instruments, music pedagogy, art music, Colombian folklore--music and dance, Colombian opera and zarzuela, music criticism, bulletins and journals relevant to the study of Colombian music, and scores published in journals and books (by composer's name).

Rangel, Lúcio. <u>Bibliografía da Música Popular Brasileira</u>. Rio de Janeiro: Livraria São José, Gráfica Olimpica Editora, 1976.

<u>Répertoire International de Littérature Musicale</u> (RILM). International Repertory of Music Literature. RILM Abstracts of Music Literature. New York, NY: International RILM Center, City University of New York. 1 (Jan./April, 1967)--.

An international quarterly devoted to abstracting current literature on music. All abstracts are in English. Current area editor for Latin American Studies: John M. Schechter.

Resound: A Quarterly of the Archives of Traditional Music. Amy E. Novick, ed. Archives of Traditional Music, Maxwell Hall 057, Indiana University, Bloomington, IN 47405.

Sadie, Stanley, ed. The New Grove Dictionary of Music and Musicians. 20 vols. London: Macmillan, 1980.

   A. "Latin America," Vol. 10, pp. 505-534;

      I. "Indian Music," by Isabel Aretz, Bibliography, p. 515.
        1. South America
        2. Central America

     II. "Folk Music," by Gerard Béhague, Bibliography p. 522.
        1. South America
        2. Central America and the Caribbean

    III. "Afro-American Music," by Robert Stevenson and Gerard Béhague, Bibliography, p. 528.
        1. The Colonial Period (Stevenson)
        2. Independence to c. 1900 (Stevenson)
        3. 20th Century (Stevenson)
        4. Folk Music (Béhague)

    IV. "Popular Music," by Gerard Béhague, Bibliography, p. 534.
        1. Mexico and the Caribbean
        2. The Andean Area
        3. Argentina, Uruguay and Brazil

   B. Bibliographies at conclusion of articles on individual countries of Latin America.

_____. The New Grove Dictionary of Musical Instruments. 3 vols. London: Macmillan, 1984.

Articles of varying length on musical instruments worldwide. Many articles contain concluding bibliographic references. Principal author of articles on Latin American musical instruments: John M. Schechter.

Smith, Ronald R. "Latin American Ethnomusicology: A Discussion of Central America and Northern South America." LAMR, 3:1 (Spring/Summer, 1982), 1-16.

Bibliographic essay, incorporating a listing of commercial and field recordings from this region held in the Indiana University Archives of Traditional Music, by: Item--Collector--Accession Number; a concluding bibliography.

Stevenson, Robert. "Nuevos recursos para el estudio de la
música latinoamericana." Heterofonía, 52:10(1) (Dec., 1976/
Jan.-Feb., 1977), 15-24.

Two parts: Part I: Annotated citations to 20 bachelor's,
master's, and doctoral theses pertaining to Latin American
music, including the ethnomusicological dissertations of Olsen,
Robertson-DeCarbo, Kuss, and Girard (see "Doctoral Dissertations in Latin American Ethnomusicology: 1965-1984,"
pp. 673-678, below).   Part II: Discusses treatment of Latin
American music in dictionaries and encyclopedias published
since 1967.

Studies in Latin American Popular Culture.   Harold E. Hinds,
Jr., and Charles Tatum, eds.   Morris, MN; Las Cruces, NM.
English languge. 1982--. Annual.

Addresses all aspects of popular culture in Latin America,
soliciting contributions from all scholarly disciplines.

Temas de Etnomusicología-1.   Buenos Aires: Instituto Nacional de
Musicología "Carlos Vega," Ministerio de Educación y Justicia,
Secretaría de Cultura (Ercilia Moreno Chá, Directora), 1984.
101 pp.

Reports on ethnomusicological field research realized through
the "Carlos Vega" Institute.

Walters, Marian C., ed.   Latin America and the Caribbean,
Part II.   A Dissertation Bibliography.   University Microfilms
International.

1,868 doctoral dissertations and 100 master's theses (updating
Carl W. Deal, ed., Latin America and the Caribbean: A
Dissertation Bibliography, UMI, 1977).   Includes dissertations
abstracted from January, 1960 to June, 1980, and theses
abstracted from December, 1971 to June, 1980.

65. DOCTORAL DISSERTATIONS IN LATIN AMERICAN ETHNOMUSICOLOGY: 1965-1984

John M. Schechter

[Dissertation Abstracts is abbreviated as Dis Abst. University Microfilms is abbreviated as UM.]

Alfaro, Daniel. "Folk Music of the Yucatan Peninsula." Ph.D., Music, University of Colorado at Boulder, 1982. 449 pp. Dis Abst 43:12A, Part 1, p. 3747; UM No. 8309828.

Aretz, Isabel. "Música Tradicional Argentina: La Rioja." Ph.D., Musicology, Catholic University, Argentina, 1967. 600 pp.; as Música Tradicional de La Rioja, Biblioteca INIDEF (Instituto Interamericano de Etnomusicología y Folklore), 2. Caracas: Organización de Estados Americanos and CONAC, 1978. 612 pp.

Asche, Charles Byron. "Cuban Folklore Traditions and Twentieth Century Idioms in the Piano Music of Amadeo Roldán and Alejandro García Caturla." D.M.A., The University of Texas at Austin, 1983. 101 pp. Dis Abst 44:04A, p. 902; UM No. 8319552.

Béhague, Gerard Henri. "Popular Musical Currents in the Art Music of the Early Nationalistic Period in Brazil, circa 1870-1920." Ph.D., Musicology, Tulane University, 1966. 288 pp. Dis Abst 27:05A, p. 1390; UM No. 6610751.

Beyersdorff, Margot Caroline. "Traditional Songs of Quechua of South Andean Peru: From a Diachronic and Synchronic Perspective." [Spanish text] Ph.D., Latin American Literature, University of California, San Diego, 1983. 379 pp. Dis Abst 44:2156A; UM No. 8326116.

Boilès, Charles Lafayette, Jr. "Cognitive Process in Otomi Cult Music." Ph.D., Music, Tulane University, 1969. 187 pp. Dis Abst 30:10B, p. 4470; UM No. 7006380.

Brandt, Max H. "An Ethnomusicological Study of Three Afro-Venezuelan Drum Ensembles of Barlovento." Ph.D., The Queen's University of Belfast, 1979.

Editor's Note. This bibliography was distributed during the panel session on "The Current State of Bibliographic Research in Latin American Ethnomusicology" (see Volume I, pp. 334-345).

Carvalho, José Jorge de. "Ritual and Music of the Sango Cults of Recife, Brazil." Ph.D., Social Anthropology, The Queen's University of Belfast, 1984. 613 pp.

Cashion, Susan Valerie. "Dance Ritual and Cultural Values in a Mexican Village: Festival of Santo Santiago." Ph.D., Education, Stanford University, 1983. 374 pp. Dis Abst 44:05A, p. 1313; UM No. 8320689.

Conway, Frederick James. "Pentecostalism in the Context of Haitian Religion and Health Practice." Ph.D., The American University, 1978. 292 pp. Dis Abst 39:06A, p. 3673; UM No. 7823653.

d'Aquino, Iria. "Capoeira: Strategies for Status, Power and Identity." Ph.D., Anthropology, University of Illinois at Urbana-Champaign, 1983. 229 pp. Dis Abst 44:06A, p. 1850; UM No. 8324532.

Dunstan, Raymond David. "St. Lucian Carnival: A Caribbean Art Form." Ph.D., Anthropology, State University of New York at Stony Brook, 1978. 374 pp. Dis Abst 39:05A, p. 3012; UM No. 7821848.

Euper, Jo Ann. "A Study of the Relationships between Group Musical Experience and Social Integration in Six Honduran Communities." Ph.D., University of Kansas, 1973. Dis Abst 34:12A, Part 1, pp. 7805-7806; UM No. 7412554.

Fogal, Robert Edwin. "Traditional Music and the Middle Class: A Case Study of Mercedes, Province of Buenos Aires, Argentina." Ph.D., Folklore, Indiana University, 1981. 378 pp. Dis Abst 42:07A, p. 3253; UM No. 8128063.

Friedman, Robert Alan. "Making an Abstract World Concrete: Knowledge, Competence and Structural Dimensions of Performance among Batá Drummers in Santería." Ph.D., Folklore, Indiana University, 1982. 335 pp. Dis Abst 43:12A, p. 3999; UM No. 8308858.

Girard, Sharon Elizabeth. "Music of the Requiem in Venezuela: A Study of the Colonial Tradition and Its Background of Folk and Autochthonous Music of the Dead." Ph.D., Musicology, University of California, Los Angeles, 1975. 3 vols., 1142 pp. Dis Abst 36:05A, p. 2478; UM No. 7525203.

Goldberg, Alan Bruce. "Commercial Folklore and Voodoo in Haiti: International Tourism and the Sale of Culture." Ph.D., Folklore, Indiana University, 1981. 318 pp. Dis Abst 42:03A, p. 1228; UM No. 8119054.

Grebe, María Ester. "Generative Models, Symbolic Structures, and Acculturation in the Panpipe Music of the Aimara of Tarapacá, Chile." Ph.D., Social Anthropology, The Queen's University of Belfast, 1980.

Heisley, Robert Michael. "Corridistas de la Huelga: Songmaking and Singing in the Lives of Two Individuals." Ph.D., Folklore, University of California, Los Angeles, 1983. 317 pp. Dis Abst 44:05A, p. 1537; UM No. 8321985.

Hill, Jonathan David. "Wakuenai Society: A Processual-Structural Analysis of Indigenous Cultural Life in the Upper Río Negro Region of Venezuela." Ph.D., Anthropology, Indiana University, 1983. 467 pp. Dis Abst 44:04A, p. 1141; UM No. 8317095.

Hoffnagel, Judith Chambliss. "The Believers: Pentecostalism in a Brazilian City." Ph.D., Anthropology, Indiana University, 1978. 297 pp. Dis Abst 39:02A, p. 962; UM No. 7813206.

Horspool, Glen Arvel. "The Music of the Quiché Maya of Momostenango in Its Cultural Setting." Ph.D., Music, University of California, Los Angeles, 1982. 424 pp. Dis Abst 43:10A, p. 3150; UM No. 8306056.

Kaphan, Iris Selicoff. "Change in Cultural Context and Musical Style: A Connective Process, Formulated and Applied to the Mexican Revolution and Mexican Music." Ph.D., Musicology, University of California, Los Angeles, 1977. 293 pp. Dis Abst 38:09A, p. 5114; UM No. 7801720.

Kauffman, Christopher Paul. "Variation in the Music, Song Texts and Instrumentation of the Papa Aysay Ceremony in Chinchero, an Indigenous Highland Community in Southern Peru." Ph.D., Music, Indiana University, 1977. 418 pp. Dis Abst 38:04A, p. 1728; UM No. 7722600.

Koorn, Dirk. "Folk Music of the Colombian Andes." Ph.D., Ethnomusicology, University of Washington, 1977. 310 pp. Dis Abst 38:09A, p. 5115; UM No. 7800939.

Kuss, María Elena. "Nativistic Strains in Argentine Operas Premiered at the Teatro Colón (1908-1972)." Ph.D., Music, University of California, Los Angeles, 1976. 536 pp. Dis Abst 37:06A, p. 3258; UM No. 7628570.

Lampman, Richard Alan. "The Idea of a Democratic Culture: The Evolution of Popular Music from 1955 to 1975." Ph.D., Purdue University, 1980. 255 pp. Dis Abst 41:06A, p. 2663; UM No. 8027297.

Lashley, Leroy Lennox George. "An Analysis of the Calypso as a Mass Communication Medium: The Social and Political Uses." Ph.D., Howard University, 1982. 245 pp. Dis Abst 44:11A, p. 3195; UM No. 8404060.

Lucas, Theodore Drexel. "The Musical Style of the Shipibo Indians of the Upper Amazon" [with Original Composition: The Revelation of John]. D.M.A, Composition, University of Illinois at Urbana-Champaign, 1970. 430 pp. Dis Abst 31:09A, pp. 4820-4821; UM No. 715168.

Lyon, Patricia Jean. "Singing as Social Interaction among the Wachipaeri of Eastern Peru." Ph.D., Anthropology, University of California, Berkeley, 1967. 154 pp. Dis Abst 28:11B, p. 4393; UM No. 685776.

McCoy, James A. "The Bomba and Aguinaldo of Puerto Rico as They Have Evolved from Indigenous, African and European Cultures." Ph.D., Music, The Florida State University, 1968. 185 pp. Dis Abst 29:07A, p. 2294; UM No. 69590.

Mukuna, Kazadi Wa. "O Contato Musical Transatlântico: Contribuição Banto à Música Popular Brasileira." [Portuguese Text] Ph.D., University of California, Los Angeles, 1978. 291 pp. Dis Abst 39:01A, p. 17; UM No. 7811398.

Nyberg, John Leroy. "An Examination of Vessel Flutes from Pre-Hispanic Cultures of Ecuador." Ph.D., Music, University of Minnesota, 1974. 533 pp. Dis Abst 35:06A, p. 3797; UM No. 7426217.

O'Brien, Linda Lee. "Songs of the Face of the Earth: Ancestor Songs of the Tzutuhil-Maya of Santiago Atitlán, Guatemala." Ph.D., Ethnomusicology, University of California, Los Angeles, 1975. 284 pp. Dis Abst 36:07A, pp. 4098-4099; UM No. 76838.

Olsen, Dale Alan. "Music and Shamanism of the Winikina-Warao Indians: Songs for Curing and Other Theurgy." Ph.D., Ethnomusicology, University of California, Los Angeles, 1973. 2 vol., 566 pp. Dis Abst 34:08A, pp. 5234-5235; UM No. 7328744

Ramírez, Daniel Moriel. "The Peña: A Semiological Analysis of the Latin American Folk Music Movement." Ph.D., University of California, San Diego, 1980. 314 pp. Dis Abst 42:02A, p. 871; No. 8116837.

Reyes Schramm, Adelaida. "The Role of Music in the Interaction of Black Americans and Hispanos in New York City's East Harlem." Ph.D., Ethnomusicology, Columbia University, 1975. 273 pp. Dis Abst 36:03A, p. 1160; UM No. 7518435.

Robertson-DeCarbo, Carol Elizabeth. "Tayil: Musical Communication among the Mapuche of Argentina." Ph.D., Indiana University, 1975. 223 pp. Dis Abst 36:08A, pp. 5385-5386; UM No. 762885.

Schechter, John Mendell. "Music in a Northern Ecuadorian Highland Locus: Diatonic Harp, Genres, Harpists, and Their Ritual Junction in the Quechua Child's Wake" Ph.D., Ethnomusicology, The University of Texas at Austin, 1982. 3 vols., 947 pp. Dis Abst 43:05A, p. 1343; UM No. 8217936.

Seitz, Barbara Joan. "Llaquichina Songs of the Sacha Huarmi (Jungle Woman) and Their Role in Transformational Communication Events in the Ecuadorian Oriente. Ph.D., Music Education, Indiana University, 1982. 431 pp. Dis Abst 44:03A, pp. 698-699; UM No. 8317122.

Sharon, Douglas Gregory. "The Symbol System of a North Peruvian Shaman." Ph.D., Anthropology, University of California, Los Angeles, 1974. Dis Abst 35:05A, p. 2450; UM No. 7424616.

Sheehy, Daniel Edward. "The Son Jarocho: The History, Style, and Repertory of a Changing Mexican Musical Tradition." Ph.D., Ethnomusicology, University of California, Los Angeles, 1979. 401 pp. Dis Abst 40:04A, p. 1744; UM No. 7921454.

Sigmund, Charles Edgar. "Segundo Luis Moreno: His Contributions to Ecuadorian Musicology." Ph.D., Music History and Literature, University of Minnesota, 1971. 2 vols., 520 pp. Dis Abst 32:05A, p. 2733; UM No. 7128287.

Singer, Roberta Louise. "My Music Is Who I Am and What I Do: Latin Popular Music and Identity in New York City." Ph.D., Folklore, Indiana University, 1982. 237 pp. Dis Abst 43:08A, p. 2491; UM No. 8301122.

Smith, Richard Chase. "Deliverance from Chaos for a Song: A Social and a Religious Interpretation of the Ritual Performance of Amuesha Music." Ph.D., Anthropology, Cornell University, 1977. 340 pp. Dis Abst 38:07A, p. 4242; UM No. 7728385.

Smith, Ronald Richard. "The Society of Los Congos of Panama: An Ethnomusicological Study of the Music and Dance-Theater of an Afro-Panamanian Group." Ph.D., Folklore, Indiana University, 1976. 342 pp. Dis Abst 37:04A, p. 2345; UM No. 7621604.

Solís, Theodore. "The Marimba in Mexico City: Contemporary Contexts of a Traditional Regional Ensemble." Ph.D., Musicology, University of Illinois at Urbana-Champaign, 1983. 358 pp. Dis Abst 43:12A, Part 1, p. 3751; UM No. 8310010.

Stigberg, David Kenneth. "Urban Musical Culture in Mexico: Professional Musicianship and Media in the Musical Life of Contemporary Veracruz." Ph.D., Music, University of Illinois at Urbana-Champaign, 1980. 408 pp. Dis Abst 41:06A, p. 2349; UM No. 8026603.

Tompkins, William David. "The Musical Traditions of the Blacks of Coastal Peru." Ph.D., Music, University of California, Los Angeles, 1981. 2 vols., 594 pp. Dis Abst 42:12A, p. 4971; UM No. 8206083.

Vega-Drouet, Hector.   "Historical and Ethnological Survey on Probable African Origins of the Puerto Rican Bomba, Including a Description of Santiago Apostol Festivities at Loiza Aldea." Ph.D., Music, Wesleyan University, 1979.   170 pp.   <u>Dis Abst</u> 40:03A, p. 1148; UM No. 7920645.

Veiga, Manuel Vicente Ribeiro, Jr.   "Toward a Brazilian Ethno-musicology: Amerindian Phases."   Ph.D.,   Ethnomusicology, University   of   California,   Los Angeles,   1981.   357 pp. <u>Dis Abst</u> 42:07A, p. 2930; UM No. 8122872.

Wortman, Mary Alice.   "The Concept of <u>Machismo</u> in the Poetry, Music, and Dance of the Gaucho of the Río de la Plata." Ph.D., Fine Arts, Ohio University, 1972.   214 pp.   <u>Dis Abst</u> 33:08A, p. 4279; UM No. 734252.

66. A SELECTED BIBLIOGRAPHY ON LATIN AMERICAN URBAN POPULAR MUSIC

John M. Schechter

Anonymous. "Music Unites UCLA and Latino Community." Ethnomusicology at UCLA, 2:2 (Winter, 1985), 1.

Béhague, Gerard. "Bossa and Bossas: Recent Changes in Brazilian Urban Popular Music." Ethnomusicology, 17:2 (May, 1973), 209-233.

_____. "Brazilian Musical Values of the 1960s and 1970s: Popular Urban Music from Bossa Nova to Tropicalia." Journal of Popular Culture, 14:3 (Winter, 1980), 437-452.

_____. "Interpenetration of Traditional and Popular Musics in the City of Salvador, Bahia [Brazil]." In Daniel Heartz and Bonnie Wade, eds., Report of the Twelfth Congress [International Musicological Society]: Berkeley 1977. Kassel: Bärenreiter; Philadelphia, PA: American Musicological Society, 1981. Pp. 298-300.

_____. "Notes on Regional and National Trends in Afro-Brazilian Cult Music." In Merlin H. Forster, ed., Tradition and Renewal: Essays on Twentieth-Century Latin American Literature and Culture. Urbana, IL: University of Illinois Press, 1975. Pp. 68-80.

Benmayor, Rina. "La 'Nueva Trova': New Cuban Song." Revista de Música Latinoamericana/Latin American Music Review (LAMR), 2:1 (Spring/Summer, 1981), 11-44.

Blum, Joseph. "Problems of Salsa Research." Ethnomusicology, 22:1 (Jan., 1978), 137-149.

Carrasco Pirard, Eduardo. "The nueva canción in Latin America." International Social Science Journal, 34:4 (1982), 599-623.

Céspedes, Gilka Wara. "New Currents in 'Música Folklórica' in La Paz, Bolivia." LAMR, 5:2 (Fall/Winter, 1984), 217-242.

Crook, Larry. "A Musical Analysis of the Cuban Rumba." LAMR, 3:1 (Spring/Summer, 1982), 92-123.

Editor's Note. This bibliography was distributed during the panel session on "The Current State of Bibliographic Research in Latin American Ethnomusicology" (see Volume I, pp. 334-345).

Duany, Jorge. "Popular Music in Puerto Rico: Toward an Anthropology of Salsa." LAMR, 5:2 (Fall/Winter, 1984), 186-216.

Friedman, Robert. "'If You Don't Play Good They Take the Drum Away': Performance, Communication and Acts in Guaguancó." In C. Card, J. Hasse, R. L. Singer, and R. M. Stone, eds., Discourse in Ethnomusicology: Essays in Honor of George List. Bloomington, IN: Ethnomusicology Publications Group, 1978. Pp. 209-224.

Garrido, Juan S. Historia de la música popular en México: 1896-1973. México, DF: Editorial Extemporáneos, 1974. 189 pp.

Geijerstam, Claes af. Popular Music in Mexico. Albuquerque, NM: University of New Mexico Press, 1976.

Gilmour, D. R. "Rastaman Vibrations: The Influence of Jamaican Musical Style in American Popular Music." (Paper presented at the 1983 NAJE National Convention, Kansas City). Proceedings of NAJE Research, 3 (1983), 40-46.

Gradante, William. "'El Hijo del Pueblo': José Alfredo Jiménez and the Mexican canción ranchera." LAMR, 3:1 (Spring/Summer, 1982), 36-59.

_____. "Mexican Popular Music at Mid-Century: The Role of José Alfredo Jiménez and the canción ranchera." Studies in Latin American Popular Culture, 2 (1983), 99-114.

Kirchheimer, Donna Wilson. "Songs of Revolution by the People's Musicians of Chile." Sing Out!, 22:5 (Sept.-Oct., 1973), 6-13.

Lashley, Leroy Lennox George. "An Analysis of the Calypso as a Mass Communication Medium: The Social and Political Uses." Ph.D. diss., Howard University, 1982. 245 pp. Dis Abst 44:11A, p. 3195; UM No. 8404060.

Limón, José E. "Texas-Mexican Popular Music and Dancing: Some Notes on History and Symbolic Process." LAMR, 4:2 (Fall/Winter, 1983), 229-246.

Marcondes, Marco Antônio, ed. Enciclopédia da Música Brasileira: Erudita, Folclórica e Popular. 2 vols. São Paulo: Art Editora, 1977.

Middleton, R., and D. Horn, eds. Popular Music. Part 1: Folk or Popular? Distinctions, Influences, Continuities. Cambridge: Cambridge University Press, 1981.

_____. Popular Music. Part 2: Theory and Method. Cambridge: Cambridge University Press, 1982.

Moreno, Albrecht. "Bossa nova: Novo Brasil: The Significance of Bossa Nova as a Brazilian Popular Music." Latin American Research Review, 17:2 (1982), 129-141.

Pearse, Andrew. "Music in Caribbean Popular Culture." Revista/Review Interamericana, 8:4 (Winter, 1978-79), 629-639.

Peña, Manuel H. "From Ranchero to Jaitón: Ethnicity and Class in Texas-Mexican Music (Two Styles in the Form of a Pair)." Ethnomusicology, 29:1 (Winter, 1985), 29-55.

_____. "Ritual Structure in a Chicano Dance." LAMR, 1:1 (Spring/Summer, 1980), 47-73.

_____. The Texas-Mexican Conjunto: History of a Working-Class Music. Austin, TX: University of Texas Press, 1985.

Reuter, Jas. "La Música Popular en la Ciudad de México." LAMR, 5:1 (Spring/Summer, 1984), 97-101.

Reyes Schramm, Adelaida. "The Role of Music in the Interaction of Black Americans and Hispanos in New York City's East Harlem." Ph.D. diss., Columbia University, 1975. 273 pp. Dis Abst 36:03A, p. 1160; UM No. 7518435.

_____. "Explorations in Urban Ethnomusicology: Hard Lessons from the Spectacularly Ordinary." 1982 Yearbook for Traditional Music, 14 (1982), 1-14.

Rhodes, Willard. "On the Subject of Ethno-musicology." Ethnomusicology Newsletter, 7 (April, 1956), 1-9.

Roberts, John Storm. The Latin Tinge: The Impact of Latin American Music on the United States. New York, NY: Oxford University Press, 1969.

_____. "¡Salsa!" Stereo Review, 34:3 (March, 1975), 64-68.

Rondón, César Miguel. El Libro de la Salsa: Crónica de la música del Caribe urbano. Caracas: Editorial Arte, 1980.

Roseman, Marina. "The New Rican Village: Taking Control of the Image-Making Machinery." New York Folklore, 6:1-2 (1980), 45-54.

_____. "The New Rican Village: Artists in Control of the Image-Making Machinery." LAMR, 4:1 (Spring/Summer, 1983), 132-167.

Singer, Roberta Louise. "My Music Is Who I Am and What I Do: Latin Popular Music and Identity in New York City." Ph.D. diss., Indiana University, 1982. 237 pp. Dis Abst 43:2491A; UM No. 8301122.

_____. "Tradition and Innovation in Contemporary Latin Popular Music in New York City." LAMR, 4:2 (Fall/Winter, 1983), 183-202.

Solís, Theodore. "Muñecas de Chiapaneco: The Economic Importance of Self-Image in the World of the Mexican Marimba." LAMR, 1:1 (Spring/Summer, 1980), 34-46.

_____. "The Marimba in Mexico City: Contemporary Contexts of a Traditional Regional Ensemble." Ph.D. diss., University of Illinois at Urbana-Champaign, 1983. 358 pp. Dis Abst 43:12A, Part 1, p. 3751; UM No. 8310010.

Stigberg, David K. "Jarocho, Tropical, and 'Pop': Aspects of Musical Life in Veracruz, 1971-72." In Bruno Nettl, ed., Eight Urban Musical Cultures: Tradition and Change. Urbana, IL: University of Illinois Press, 1978. Pp. 260-295.

_____. "Mexican Popular Musical Culture and the Tradition of música tropical in the City of Veracruz." Studies in Latin American Popular Culture, 1 (1982), 151-163.

_____. "Urban Musical Culture in Mexico: Professional Musicianship and Media in the Musical Life of Contemporary Veracruz." Ph.D. diss., University of Illinois at Urbana-Champaign, 1980. 408 pp. Dis Abst 41:06A, p. 2349; UM No. 8026603.

Theil, Gordon. "Popular Music Sound Recordings: Recommendations on Selection, Arrangement and Cataloging." Phonographic Bulletin, 38 (March, 1984), 29-33.

Turino, Thomas. "The Urban-Mestizo Charango Tradition in Southern Peru: A Statement of Shifting Identity." Ethnomusicology, 28:2 (May, 1984), 253-270.

Vasconcellos, Gilberto. Música Popular: De Olho na Fresta. Rio de Janeiro: Graal, 1977.

Vega, Carlos. "Mesomusic: An Essay on the Music of the Masses." Ethnomusicology, 10:1 (Jan., 1966), 1-17.

Waddey, Ralph C. "Viola de Samba and Samba de Viola in the Recôncavo of Bahia (Brazil)." In two parts: [Part I: Viola de Samba], in LAMR, 1:2 (Fall/Winter, 1980), 196-212; Part II: Samba de Viola, in LAMR, 2:2 (Fall/Winter, 1981), 252-279.

White, Garth. "Traditional Musical Practice in Jamaica and Its Influence on the Birth of Modern Jamaican Popular Music." African-Caribbean Institute of Jamaica Newsletter, 7 (March, 1982), 41-68.

Winders, J. A. "Reggae, Rastafarians and Revolution: Rock Music in the Third World." Journal of Popular Culture, 17:1 (1983), 61-73.

67. BIBLIOGRAPHY OF BRAZILIAN CHAPBOOK LITERATURE

Laurence Hallewell and Cavan McCarthy

CHAPBOOKS OF OTHER COUNTRIES

General

*1. Weiss, Harry B. A Book about Chapbooks. The People's Literature of By-Gone Times. Trenton, NJ: The author. 149 pp.

England, Scotland, Ireland, France, Italy, Germany, Holland, United States.

English-Speaking Countries
General

2. Neuberg, Victor E. Chapbooks: A Guide to Reference Material on English, Scottish and American Chapbook Literature of the 18th and 19th Centuries. London: Vine Press, 1964 (88 pp. Mimeo); 2d ed., London: Woburn Press, 1972 (81 pp.)

Librarianship

*3. Endelman, Judith E., and Diane K. Bauerle. "Computerized Access to a Chapbook Collection." College and Research Libraries News, 46:7 (July/August, 1985), 340–342.

England

4. Ashton, John. Chapbooks of the 18th Century. London: Chatto & Windus, 1882; repr. New York, NY: Blom, 1967.

5. Halliwell-Philips, James Orchard. A Catalogue of Chapbooks, Garlands and Popular Histories. London, 1849; repr. Detroit, MI: Singing Tree Press, 1968.

The first (?) serious treatment of the subject in English.

Editor's Note. This bibliography was originally prepared as an appendix to the authors' "Brazilian Chapbook Literature" (Volume I, pp. 361–379). The entries marked with an asterisk were personally examined by the authors.

*6.   Hindley, Charles. The History of the Catnach Press. . . . London, 1887; repr. Detroit, MI: Singing Tree Press, 1968.

7.   _____. The Life and Times of James Catnach, Late of Seven Dials, Ballad Monger. London: Reeves and Turner, 1878. 432 pp.

Catnach was the best-known early nineteenth-century London chapbook publisher. Seven Dials, Charing Cross, was then a notorious slum district.

*8.   Rogers, Pat. Literature and Popular Culture. Brighton, Sussex: Harvester Press, 1985. Esp. chapts. 7 and 8.

9.   Rollins, Hyder Edward. An Annotated Index to the Ballad Entries, 1555-1709 in the Registers of the Company of Stationers of London. Chapel Hill, NC: University of North Carolina Press, 1924. 324 pp.

10.   Shepard, Leslie. The History of Street Literature: The Story of Broadside Ballads, Chapbooks, Proclamations, News-sheets, Election Bills, Tracts, Pamphlets, Cocks, Catchpennies and Other Ephemera. London: David and Charles, 1973.

*11.   _____. John Pitts, Ballad Printer of Seven Dials, London, 1765-1844. . . . London: Private Libraries Association, 1969. 160 pp.

Pitts was Catnach's chief rival.

*12.   Spufford, Margaret. Small Books and Pleasant Histories: Popular Fiction and Its Readership in 17th Century England. London: Methuen, 1981. 275 pp.

Time span covered is somewhat greater than her title suggests.

13   Thomson, Frances M. Newcastle Chapbooks in Newcastle upon Tyne University Library. Newcastle: Oriel Press, 1969. 109 pp.

Newcastle-on-Tyne was probably the most important English provincial center of chapbook publishing.

Scotland

14.   Harvey, William. Scottish Chapbook Literature. Paisley: A. Gardner, 1903.

United States

*15. Weiss, Harry B. American Chapbooks. Trenton, NJ: The author, 1938. 32 pp.

Reprinted as a chapter in his A Book about Chapbooks [item 1].

16. Winslow, O. Elizabeth. American Broadside Verse. New Haven, CT: Yale University Press, 1930.

Nigeria

17. Dodson, Don. "Onitsha Pamphlets: Culture in the Marketplace." Ph.D diss., Stanford University, Stanford, CA, 1974.

*18. McCarthy, Caval Michael. "Printing in Onitsha: Some Personal Observations on the Production of Nigerian Market Literature." African Research and Documentation, 35 (Aug., 1983), 22-25.

19. Obiechira, Emmanuel N. Onitsha Market Literature. New York, NY: Africana, 1972.

Western Europe

Germany

20. Coupe, William. The German Illustrated Broadsheet in the 17th Century: Historical and Iconographical Studies. 2 vols. Baden-Baden, 1966-1967.

21. Kopp, Arthur. "Niederdeutsche Liederdrucke aus dem 16. Jahrhundert." Centralblatt für Bibliothekswesen (Leipzig), 19 (1902), 509-529.

Netherlands

22. Boekenoogen, G. J. "De nederlandsche volksboeken." Tijdschrift voor boek- en bibliothekwezen (The Hague), 3 (1905), 107-142.

France

23. Assier, Alexandre. La Bibliothèque Bleue depuis Jean Oudet Ier jusqu'à M. Baudot, 1600-1863. Paris: Champion, 1874.

24. Bollème, Geneviève. La Bibliothèque Bleue: littérature populaire en France du 17e au 19e siècle. Paris: Julliard, 1971.

25. Bonnefoy, Claude. La littérature de colportage. Paris: Flammes et Fumées, 1971.

*26. Mandrou, Robert. De la culture populaire au 17e et 18e siècles: la Bibliothèque Bleue de Troyes. Paris: Stock, 1964. 222 pp.

27. Nisard, Charles. Histoire des livres populaires ou de la littérature de colportage depuis l'origine de l'imprimerie jusqu'à l'établissement de la commission d'examen des livres de colportage. Paris: Aymot, 1854.

   Basic work, resulting from Napoleon III's investigation of the chapbook industry (motivated by his desire to suppress political criticism).

Italy

28. Axon, William Edward Armytage. "Some 20th-century Italian Chapbooks." The Library (London), n.s., 5 (1904), 239-255.

The Far East
China

29. Maclagan, P. J. "Notes on Some Chinese Chap-books." The China Review (Hong Kong), 98:22 (1897), 782-786; 98:23 (1898), 163-167.

Japan

30. Zolbrod, Leon M. "Kusazochi: Chapbooks of Japan." Transactions of the Asiatic Society of Japan, ser. 3, 10 (1968), 116-147.

Hispanic Countries
Spain

31. Caballero Bonald, José Manuel. Pliegos de cordel. Barcelona: Seix y Barral, 1963.

32. Caro Baroja, Julio. Ensayo sobre la literatura de cordel. Madrid: Edición de la Revista de Occidente, 1969.

33. García de Enterría, María Cruz. Sociedad y poesía de cordel en el barroco. Madrid: Taurus, 1973.

34. Marco, Joaquín. Literatura popular en España en los siglos 18 y 19: una aproximación a los pliegos de cordel. 2 vols. Madrid: Taurus, 1977.

35. Sánchez Borbón, Azalea. "Pedro Malasartes en las letras hispánicas." Ph.D. diss., Tulane University, New Orleans, 1970.

36. Soons, Alan. "Spanish Ballad and News-Relation in Chapbook Form: The Index of a Mentality." Kentucky Romance Quarterly, 20 (1973), 3-17.

37. Wilson, Edward M. "Tradition and Change in Some Late Spanish Chapbooks." Hispanic Review, 25 (1957), 194-216.

Mexico

38. McDowell, John H. "The Mexican Corrido: Form and Theme in a Ballad Tradition." Journal of American Folklore, 85 (1976), 205-220.

39. María y Campos, Armando de. La Revolución Mexicana a través de los corridos populares. 2 vols. México, DF: Biblioteca del Instituto Nacional de Estudios Históricos de la Revolución Mexicana, 1962.

40. Mendoza, Vicente T. El corrido de la Revolución Mexicana. México, DF: Biblioteca del Instituto Nacional de Estudios Históricos, 1956.

41. _____. El romance español y el corrido mexicano. 2d ed. México, DF: Fondo de Cultura Económica, 1959.

42. Paredes, Américo. "The Ancestry of Mexico's Corridos." Journal of American Folklore, 76 (1963), 1-15.

43. Sorrano Martínez, Caledonio. El Coyote: corrido de la Revolución. México, DF: [The author?], 1951.

Nicaragua

44. Mejía Sánchez, Ernesto. "Romances y corridos nicaragüenses." Anuario de la Sociedad Folklórica de México, 5 (1944/45), 78.

Argentina

45. Fernández Latour de Botas, Olga. "Poesía popular impresa de la Colección Lehmann-Nitsche." Cuadernos del Instituto Nacional de Antropología (Buenos Aires), 5 (1964/65).

Chile

*46. Lenz, Rodolfo. "Sobre la poesía popular chilena: contribu-
ción al folklore chileno." Anales de la Universidad de Chile,
78:143(2) (Jan./Feb., 1919), 511-622.

Article actually written in 1894, and reporting that chapbooks had already almost died out in Chile.

Portugal

47. Arouca, Walter. "Literatura de cordel portuguesa." A tarde
(Salvador, Bahia), July 1, 1975.

48. Bell, Aubrey FitzGerald. A literatura portuguesa. Coimbra:
Imprensa da Universidade, 1931. Pp. 457-470. "Literatura
popular."

Translation of item 49.

*49. _____. Portuguese Literature. Oxford: Clarendon
Press, 1922. Pp. 338-347. Appendix 1, "Literature of the
People."

Most chapbooks cited in Oporto editions of c. 1912.

50. Braga, Theóphilo. O povo portuguez nos seus costumes,
crenças e tradições. 2 vols. Lisbon: Ferreira, 1885.

51. Coelho, Francisco Adolpho. Cantos populares portuguezes.
Lisbon: Plantier, 1879.

52. Hardung, Victor Eugênio. Histórias jocosas a cavalo num
barbante. Oporto: Nova Crítica, 1980.

Presumably a reprint of a nineteenth-century edition.

53. _____. Romanceiro português. Leipzig: Brockhaus,
1877.

54. Hulet, Claude. "Two folheto versions of João de Calais,"
Second Symposium for Portuguese Traditions, University of
California, Los Angeles, May 8, 1978.

*55. Sharrer, Harvey L. "Eighteenth Century Chapbook Adapta-
tions of the Historia de Flores y Blancaflor by Antônio da
Silva, mestre de gramática." Hispanic Review, 52 (Winter,
1984), 59-74.

*56.   Slater, Candace.   "Why One Evil King Could Not Be a
       Brazilian: A Comparison of Portuguese and Brazilian Litera-
       tura de Cordel." Luso-Brazilian Review, 18:2 (Winter,
       1981), 279-295.

       Detailed comparison of the two national traditions.

BRAZILIAN CHAPBOOK LITERATURE

Bibliographies

Separately Published

57.   Biderman, Sol. Catálogo da Coleção de literatura de cordel
       coligida sob os auspícios da Fundação Ford por Sol e Madial
       Tereza Biderman. Marília, SP: Faculdade de Filosofia,
       Ciências e Letras, 1970. 79 pp.

58.   Literatura popular em verso. Vol. 1, Catálogo.   Rio de
       Janeiro: Casa de Rui Barbosa, 1961. 394 pp.

*59.   Luyten, Joseph M. Bibliografia especializada sobre literatura
       popular em verso. São Paulo: ECA/USP, [1981?]. 104 pp.

       Bibliography of 1,213 unannotated entries by author (sub-
       arranged under each letter of the alphabet by format).

In Periodicals

60.   Menezes, Eduardo Diatay Bezerra de. "Bibliografia comple-
       mentar (literatura de cordel e cultura popular)." Revista de
       ciências sociais (Fortaleza), 8:1/2 (1977), 241-263.

61.   Tavares Júnior, Luiz, and Maria Tereza de Morais. "Levan-
       tamento bibliográfico de literatura de cordel." Revista de
       ciências sociais (Fortaleza), 8:1/2 (1977), 233-240.

Exhibition Catalog

*62.   A xilografia popular e a literatura de cordel: [Catálogo
       duma exposição na Casa de Rui Barbosa, aberta no dia 2 de
       julho de 1985. Projeto e coordinação geral de Origenes
       Lessa]. Rio de Janeiro: Fundação Casa Rui Barbosa, 1985.
       38 pp.

Biobibliography

*63.   Almeida, Atila Augusto F. de, and "José Alves Sobrinho"
       (José Clementino de Souto). Dicionário bio-bibliográfico de

repentistas e poetas de bancada. 2 vols. João Pessoa, PB: Editora Universitária, 1978.

General Works

Periodicals

*64. A Ordem, afterward, O Brasil Poético: orgão oficial da Ordem Brasileira dos Poetas da Literatura de Cordel 1(1)--. Rua Alvarenga Peixoto 158, Liberdade, CP 916, Salvador, Bahia: Prof. Marinha Mora, February, 1977--.

Standard Works

*65. Slater, Candace. Stories on a String: The Brazilian Literatura de Cordel. Berkeley, CA: University of California Press, 1982. 313 pp.

Researched in the North-East, Rio and São Paulo, 1977-1979. Appendix B, pp. 244-261: "[73] Popular poets interviewed" with brief biographical data. Bibliography divided into 190 English-language and 293 Portuguese- language items. Some entries represent general background, e.g., Freyre's Mansions and the Shanties. Reviewed by Malcolm Silverman, Interamerican Review of Bibliography, 32(3/4) (1982), 381-382.

*66. _____. A vida no barbante: a literatura de cordel no Brasil. Rio de Janeiro: Civilização Brasileira, 1984.

Translation by Otávio Alves Velho of Stories on a String [item 65]. Reviewed by Wilson Martins, "Literatura? Popular?," Jornal do Brasil (Rio de Janeiro), July 20, 1985.

Monographs

67. Batista, Francisco das Chagas. Cantadores e poetas populares. Parahyba do Norte: Batista Irmãos, 1929.

Author was leading cordel publisher of the first quarter of the present century.

68. Cascudo, Luís da Câmara. Vaqueiros e cantadores: folclore poético do sertão de Pernambuco, Paraíba, Rio Grande do Norte e Ceará. Porto Alegre, RS: Globo, 1939; repr. Rio de Janeiro: Edições de Ouro, 1970. 274 pp.

The great Rio Grande do Norte folklorist's first book on cordel.

69. Curran, Mark J. Literatura de cordel. Recife: Editora
     Universitária, 1973.

     Author is professor at Arizona State University.

70. Diêgues Júnior, Manuel. Literatura de cordel. Rio de
     Janeiro: Campanha de Defesa do Folclore Brasileiro do MEC,
     1975. 38 pp.

     Portuguese origins and traditional themes.

*71. Londres, Maria José Fialho. Cordel: do encantamento às
     histórias de luta. São Paulo: Duas Cidades, 1983. 318 pp.

     Portuguese-language version of her doctoral dissertation
     [item 72].

72. _____. "Littérature du peuple au Brésil, du conte
     merveilleux aux histoires de lutte." Ph.D. diss., École des
     Hautes Études en Sciences Sociales, Université de Paris III,
     Paris, 1978.

*73. Machado, Franklin ("Franklin Maxado Nordestino"). O que é
     literatura de cordel. Rio de Janeiro: Codecri, 1980.

     Introduction by most influential middle-class devotee and
     practitioner.

*74. Noblat, Ricardo. A literatura de cordel nordestina. Rio de
     Janeiro: Bloch, 1976. Issued as a free supplement with
     Fatos e fotos/Gente, 786 (Oct. 3, 1976).

*75. Romero, Sylvio [Vasconcelos da Silveira Ramos]. Estudos
     sobre a poesia popular do Brasil. 2 vols. Rio de Janeiro,
     1879-1880; repr. Petrópolis, RJ: Vozes, 1977.

     Earliest important account. Author, the leading literary
     historian and critic of his day, a northeasterner (from
     Sergipe) and a professor at the Colégio Pedro II, considered
     cordel already in decline and likely to survive--if at
     all--only in the sertão.

76. Santos, Luiz Cristovão dos. Brasil dé-chapeu-de couro.
     Rio de Janeiro: Civilização Brasileira, 1958.

Collected Articles

*77. Caderno de Letras, 3(2) número especial de literatura
     popular. João Pessoa: Universidade Federal de Paraíba,
     July, 1978.

78. Proença, Manoel Cavalcanti, ed.   Literatura de cordel.
     São Paulo: ECA/USP, 1971.

Articles

79. Barroso, Gustavo. "Literatura de cordel." A manhã (Rio de
     Janeiro), Feb. 10, 17, 24, 1950.

80. Coutinho, Edilberto. "O grito popular de cordel." Cultura
     (Brasília, MEC), 8:2 (April/June, 1978), 102-107.

81. Curran, Mark J. "Literatura de Cordel: Its Distribution and
     Adaptation to the Brazilian Mass Market." Studies in Latin
     American Popular Culture, 1 (1982), 164-178.

82. Diegues Júnior, Manuel. "Literatura de cordel." Revista do
     livro (Rio de Janeiro, INL), 12:38 (1969), 51-57.

*83. Hallewell, Laurence. Books in Brazil: A History of the Pub-
     lishing Trade. Metuchen, NJ: Scarecrow, 1982. Pp. 383-
     396 et seq., "Chapbooks."

*84. _____ . O livro no Brasil: sua história. São Paulo:
     T. A. Queiroz, 1985. Pp. 534-552, "Folhetos populares," "O
     conteudo . . . ," "O futuro . . . ," "Ilustradores . . . ,"
     "E o cordel entra no mercado de massa."

     Revised and updated translation of item 83.

85. Lessa, Origenes. "Literatura popular em versos." Anhembi,
     21 (1955), 60-87.

86. Pinto, Alexina de Magalhães. "Poesias populares." Alma-
     naque brasileiro Garnier, 8 (1910), 217-222.

*87. Slater, Candace. "Cordel and canção in Today's Brazil."
     Latin American Research Review, 17:3 (1982), 29-53.

*88. Venâncio, J. Carlos, and Luís Alves Júnior, eds. Literatura
     de cordel, antologia. Vol. 1. São Paulo: Global, 1976.
     "Literatura popular em verso, literatura popular nordestina,
     literatura de cordel: uma introdução," by Mário Souto Maior.

Scholarship

*89. Castelo Branco, Heloisa. "Cordel, a literatura mais rica do
     mundo para um especialista da Sorbonne." Jornal do Brasil,
     Dec. 16, 1977.

*90. Ciccacio, Ana Maria. "Na Paraíba, uma universidade aberta à cultura popular." Estado de São Paulo, Aug. 27, 1978.

*91. "Cordel brasileiro levado à Sorbonne." Tribuna da Bahia, Nov. 3, 1972.

92. Fundação Casa de Rui Barbosa. Centro de pesquisa. "Literatura de cordel na Casa de Rui Barbosa." Cultura (Brasília, MEC), 10:36 (April/June, 1981), 11-12.

93. MacGregor Villarroel, Mary. "Brazilian Folk Narrative Scholarship: A Critical Survey and Selective Annotated Bibliography." Ph.D. diss., University of California, Los Angeles, 1981.

*94. Noblat, Ricardo. "Ganhando status: um simpósio universitário estuda o cordel." Veja, 529 (Oct. 25, 1978), 151-152.

Origins

*95. Augusto, João. "As origens do cordel no Brasil." Jornal do Brasil, April 14, 1973.

96. Benjamin, Roberto E. Câmara. Breve noticia de antecedentes franceses e ingleses da literatura de cordel nordestino." Revista tempo universitário (Natal, UFRN), 6 (1980), 171-188.

97. Melo, Veríssimo de. "Origens da literatura de cordel." Revista tempo universitário (Natal, UFRN), 1 (1976), 51-56.

[See also items 56, 70].

Background and Relationships
Cordel and Society

98. Arantes Neto, Antônio Augusto. "Some Sociological Aspects of the Literatura de Cordel." Ph.D. diss., Cambridge University, Cambridge, UK, 1977.

99. Cortez, Marcius Frederico. "Relações de classes na literatura de cordel." Revista de Civilização Brasileira, 5/6, 293-294.

*100. Proença, Ivan Cavalcanti. A ideologia do cordel. Rio de Janeiro: Imago, 1976. 111 pp.

Cordel and Literature

*101. Balden, Nancy T. "Popular Poetry in the Novels of Jorge Amado." Journal of Latin American Lore, 2:1 (1976), 3-22.

*102. Coutinho, Edilberto. "Aproximação com a literatura de cordel e o cordel na literatura." Cadernos brasileiros, 12:58 (1970), 45-52.

103. Perrone, Charles. "O cancioneiro popular no romance brasileiro da trinta." Cultura (Brasília, MEC), 9:33 (Oct./Dec., 1979), 40-47.

Cordel and the Alternative Press

104. "Cordel sem folclore: entrevista com Franklin Maxado." Pasquim, 592 (Oct. 31, 1980).

*105. Machado, Franklin ("Franklin Maxado Nordestino"). O cordel televivo: futuro, presente e passado da literatura de cordel. Rio de Janeiro: Codecri, 1984. 107 pp.

       Includes radio, LP, and other nonprint media for publishing cordel.

106. Pereira, Carlos Alberto Messederi. Retrato de época: poesia marginal, anos '70. Rio de Janeiro: Funarte, 1981. 363 pp.

Geography of Cordel

Northeast

107. Aires, Félix. O Maranhão na poesia popular. São Luís: Sioge, 1977.

108. _____. O Piauí na poesia popular. Rio de Janeiro: Artenova, 1975.

109. Campos, Renato Carneiro. "Folhetos populares na zona dos engenhos de Pernambuco." Boletim do Instituto Joaquim Nabuco de Pesquisas Sociais (Recife), 4 (1955).

110. Suassuna, Ariano. "Nota sobre a poesia popular nordestina." DECA: Revista do Departamento de Extensão Cultural e Artística (Recife), 4:5 (1962).

Rio de Janeiro

111. Frade, Cáscia. Literatura de cordel no Grande Rio. Rio de Janeiro: Instituto Estadual do Patrimônio Cultural, Divisão de Folclore, 1978.

*112. Machado, Franklin ("Franklin Maxado Nordestino"). "Um poeta bahiano denuncia: 'O Rio agora é o centro de comercialização do cordel.'" Diário de Pernambuco, May 27, 1981. [Continuation of item 114].

113. Pinto, Milton José. O cordel do Grande Rio. Rio de Janeiro: Departamento de Cultura, 1978. 23 pp.

*114. Rivas, Lêda. "Um poeta bahiano denuncia: 'O Rio agora é o centro de comercialização do cordel.'" Diário de Pernambuco, May 17, 1981. [Continued by item 112].

115. Slater, Candace. "Joe Bumpkin in the Wilds of Rio de Janeiro." Journal of Latin American Lore, 6:1 (1980), 5-53.

São Paulo

*116. Luyten, Joseph Maria. A literatura de cordel em São Paulo: saudosismo e agressividade. São Paulo: Loyola, 1981. 206 pp.

Production, Publication, Distribution

117. Arantes Neto, Antônio Augusto. Pelo estudo dos folhetos no contexto de sua produção. Campinas: UNICAMP, 1978. Repr. in Arte em revista, 2:3 (March, 1980), 45-51.

118. Benjamin, Robert E. Câmara. "Literatura de cordel: produção e distribuição." 2º Ciclo da INTERCOM, São Paulo, Setembro 1979. 20 pp. Repr. in José Marques de Melo, ed., Comunicações e classes subalternas. São Paulo: Cortez, 1980. Pp. 105-119, "Literatura de cordel: produção e distribuição no nordeste brasileiro." pp. 105-119.

119. Cadengue, Rogério Bastos. Os problemas de produção da literatura de cordel. São Bernardo de Campo: Instituto Metropolitano de Ensino Superior, 1980.

120. Curran, Mark J. "Literatura de Cordel Today: The Poets and the Publishers." Journal of Latin American Lore, 6:1 (1980), 55-75.

See also his "Literatura de Cordel: Its Distribution . . ." [item 81].

121. Pereira, Thelmo de Jesus. "A expressão gráfica da literatura de cordel nordestina." REMAG: Revista métodos de artes gráficas, 15 (1965), 18-63.

122. Souza, Liêdo Maranhão de. "Cordel: agentes e folheteiros."
      Equipe (Recife), 71:1 (1974), 3-6.

123. _____. O mercado, sua praça e a cultura popular do
      nordeste. Recife: Secretaria de Educação e Cultura do
      Município, 1977.

Illustrations and Covers

General

*124. Costella, Antônio. Introdução à gravura e história da xilo-
       grafia. Campos do Jordão: Mantiqueira, 1984. Pp. 93-97,
       "Xilogravura popular do Nordeste."

125. Luyten, Joseph Maria.   "A ilustração na literatura de
      cordel." Revista Comunicações e Artes (São Paulo), 8
      (1979), 15-16.

*126. Machado, Franklin ("Franklin Maxado Nordestino"). Cordel,
       xilogravura e ilustrações. Rio de Janeiro: Codecri, 1982.
       90 pp.

       Includes a bibliography of 50 items.

127. Maior, Mário Souto. "A xilogravura popular na literatura de
      cordel." Brasil açucareiro, 71:1 (Aug., 1968), 85-87; 75
      (1970), 45-53.

128. Passos, Claribalte.   "A arte de xilogravura na terra do
      açúcar." Brasil açucareiro, 82 (1973), 39-42.

129. Pontual, Roberto.   "Notas sobre a xilogravura popular
      brasileira." Revista de cultura Vozes 64(8) (Sept., 1970),
      53-59; repr. Folkcomunicação (São Paulo), 1971.

130. Senna, Homero, ed.   Xilografos nordestinos.   Rio de
      Janeiro: Casa de Rui Barbosa, 1977. 218 pp.

*131. Souza, Liêdo Maranhão de. O folheto popular: sua capa e
       seus ilustradores. Recife: Massangara, 1981. 94 pp.

       Historical account.

132. Suassuna, Ariano. Xilogravura do nordeste. Recife: Museu
      de Arte Popular, 1968.

133. Valadares, Clarival do Prado. "Arte popular (xilogravuras
      de cordel)." Revista de cultura Vozes, 64(9) (Nov., 1970),
      71-74.

Individual Artists

José Francisco Borges

*134. "Abrindo caminho." Veja, 479 (Nov. 9, 1977), 108.

José Soares da Silva

*135. "Dila é escolhido entre duzentos gravadores." Estado de São Paulo, July 16, 1972, p. 22.

*136. Fonseca, Homero. "A vocação irresistível e pessoal de Dila, o multiplicado de Lampião." Jornal do Brasil, April 7, 1979, B1.

Jerônimo Soares

137. Cavalcante, Carlos. "Jerônimo Soares: a xilogravura sobre temas nordestinos." Diário de Pernambuco, Jan. 25, 1978.

138. Luyten, Joseph Maria. Cinco xilogravuras populares. São Paulo: The author, 1980. "Jerônimo Soares, um grande gravador."

The Text

Language

139. Mota, Leonardo. Violeiros do norte: poesia e linguagem do sertão nordestino. 3d ed. [Fortaleza]: Imprensa Universitária do Ceará, 1962. 329 pp.

140. Rector, Mônica. "Ambuiguité(s) dans la littérature de cordel." Cahiers du monde hispanique et luso-brésilien, 5 (1980), 107-121.

Poetry

141. Correia, Marlene de Castro. "O saber poético da literatura de cordel." Cultura, 1:3 (July/Sept., 1971), 48-53.

142. Estudos e ensaios folclóricos em homenagem a Benato Almeida. Rio de Janeiro: Seção de publicações do MRE, 1960. "A poesia dos cantadores do Nordeste" by Manuel Diégues Júnior, pp. 621-637.

*143. Queiroz, Paulo. "Os generos de cantoria segundo Braulio Tavares." O norte. Suplemento Domingo (João Pessoa), Aug. 21, 1977.

Versions

144. Nascimento, Braulio de. "Arquetipo e versão na literatura
      de cordel." Revista de cultura sergipana (Aracaju), 1
      (1977), 41–46.

Individual Authors and Publishers

João Martins de Ataíde

*145. Carvalho, Socrates Torres de. "Aos 75 anos João Martins de
       Athayde vive das glórias: deixou de fazer poemas o mais
       famoso versejedor do nordeste." Última hora, May 28, 1953.

146. Cavalcanti, José Lins do Rego. Poesia e vida. Rio de
      Janeiro: Universal, 1945. "O poeta João Martins de Ataíde,"
      pp. 161–162.

Leandro Gomes de Barros

*147. Batista, Sebastião Nunes. Bibliografia prévia de Leandro
       Gomes de Barros. Rio de Janeiro: Biblioteca Nacional, 1971.
       "Nota preliminar" by Wilson Losada.

*148. Literatura popular em verso: antologia. Vol. 2. Campina
       Grande, PB: MEC/Fundação Universitária Regional do
       Nordeste, 1976. "Introdução à obra de Leandro Gomes de
       Barros" by Horário de Almeida.

149. Silva, Telma Camargo de. Leandro Gomes de Barros: du
      merveilleux au politique. Paris: École des Hautes Études en
      Sciences Sociales, 1977. 154 pp.

Francisco das Chagas Batista

*150. Batista, Francisco das Chagas. Antologia. Rio de Janeiro:
       Casa de Rui Barbosa, 1977. "Notícia biobibliográfica" by
       Sebastião Nunes Batista, pp. 1–33.

Sebastião Nunes Batista

*151. Lamentação dos poetas na morte de Sebastião Nunes Batista:
       [antologia]. Rio de Janeiro: Fundação Casa de Rui Barbosa,
       1982. 16 pp.

Rodolfo Coelho Cavalcante

*152. Curran, Mark L. "Politics in the Brazilian Literatura de
       Cordel . . ." Studies in Latin American Popular Culture, 3
       (1984), 115–126.

153. _____. "Rodolfo Coelho Cavalcante: Brazil's Popular Poet and Propagandist of the Literatura de Cordel." The Politics of Culture, 5 (1976), 11-24.

*154. José, Emiliano. "Sessenta anos de poesia de Cavalcante, trovador da Bahia." Afinal, 1:13 (Nov. 27, 1984), 40.

José Gomes

155. "Ele, o tal Cuíca de Santo Amaro." Viver Bahia (Salvador), 3 (July/Sept., 1977).

Luzeiro Editora

*156. Cavalcante, Rodolfo Coelho. "Luzeiro Editora Ltda. e os trovadores da literatura de cordel." Brasil poético, 3:7 (Aug., 1977), 1.

[See also the section on Luzeiro Editora in item 116].

Raimundo Santa Helena

*157. Alencar, Edigar de. "Conflagração no cordel." O dia (Rio de Janeiro), April 21, 1985.

*158. Broxado. "Cidadania fluminense para Santa Helena, rei do cordel." O dia (Rio de Janeiro), Oct. 26, 1984.

*159. Caballero, Mara. "O cordelista Santa Helena sai de casa." Jornal do Brasil, Oct. 8, 1984.

*160. "Política faz poeta abandonar o cordel." Última hora, Oct. 8, 1984.

This and item 159 recount machinations of PDS presidential candidate Paulo Maluf seeking to commit writers of cordel to supporting his campaign.

Manuel Camilo dos Santos

*161. Lessa, Origenes. "Final menor para São Sarué." O norte (João Pessoa), March 21, 1979, 2:1.

José Francisco Soares

162. Baptista, Maria Edileuza. "A história do poeta-repórter que não foi agricultor, não deu para pedreiro e vive feliz escrevendo cordel." Jornal do commercio (Recife), Feb. 1, 1978), C8.

[See also item 245].

Cantadores

163.	Barroso, Gustavo. <u>Ao som da viola</u>. Rio de Janeiro: Leite Ribeiro, 1921.

164.	Mota, Leandro. <u>Cantadores</u>. 3d ed. Fortaleza: Imprensa Universitária do Ceará, 1961.

165.	Rolim, Maria Luisa. "Cantadores são perseguidos nas feiras do nordeste." <u>Diário de Pernambuco</u>, May 20, 1979.

	[See also items 67 and 68].

Classification

*166.	Beirao, Nirlando. "Sabe que existe um cordel de rico?" <u>Istoé</u>, 2:43 (Oct. 19, 1977), 35.

167.	Camargo, Nara Pereira de. "Usos da forma da literatura de cordel." <u>Uma questão editorial</u> (São Paulo, ECA/USP), 1:1 (June 23, 1978), 21-36.

168.	Diégues Júnior, Manuel. "Tentativa de classificação de literatura de cordel." <u>Cultura</u> (Brasília), 8:30 (July/ Dec., 1978), 34-41; 9:33 (Oct./Dec., 1979), 40-49.

169.	Moran, Emílio F. "Some Semantic Categories in Brazilian Caboclo Folk Narratives." <u>Luso-Brazilian Review</u>, 11:2 (Winter, 1974), 212-230.

*170.	Souza, Liêdo Maranhão de. <u>Classificação popular da literatura de cordel</u>. Petrópolis: Vozes, 1976. 104 pp.

Subjects and Themes
Communication, News, Journalism

171.	Araujo, Alceu Maynard de, ed. <u>Cordel e comunicação</u>. São Paulo: ECA/USP, 1971.

*172.	Batista, Sebastião Nunes. "A comunicação e a síntese na literatura de cordel." <u>Caderno de letras</u> (João Pessoa, Universidade Federal da Paraíba), 2:3 (July, 1978), 39-53.

173.	Baur, Mariza. "Literatura de cordel, o jornal do sertão." <u>Gazeta de Pinheiros</u> (Pinheiros, SP), Jan. 18, 1974.

174.	Beltrão, Luiz. <u>Comunicação e folclore</u>. São Paulo: Melhoramentos, 1971.

175. Cantel, Raymond. Temas da atualidade na literatura de cordel. Trans. Adelia Lúcia Borges. São Paulo: ECA/USP, 1972.

176. Husseini, Maria Marta Guerra. "Literatura de cordel enquanto meio de comunicação no nordeste brasileiro." Revista do Arquivo Municipal (São Paulo), 188 (1976), 117-295.

177. Lima, José Ossian. "Cordel e jornalismo." Revista de comunicação social (Fortaleza, Universidade Federal do Ceará), 5 (1975), 22-40.

178. Santa Cruz, Luiz. "A poesia como veículo de comunicação social." Cadernos de jornalismo e comunicação (Rio de Janeiro), 19 (Feb. 1969), 66-74; repr. in A. M. de Araujo, ed., Cordel e comunicação [item 171].

Carolingian Cycle and Traditional Stories

179. Batista, Sebastião Nunes. "Carlos Magno na poesia popular nordestina." Revista brasileira de folclore, 11:30 (May/Aug., 1971), 143-170.

180. Cantel, Raymond M. "La persistencia de los temas medievales de Europa en la literatura popular del nordeste brasileño." Actas del Tercer Congreso Internacional de Hispanistas, Mexico City, 1970. Pp. 176-185.

*181. Cascudo, Luís da Câmara. Cinco livros do povo. Rio de Janeiro: Olympio, 1953; 2d ed., João Pessoa: Editora Universitária da UFPb, [1979?]. 499 pp.

182. _____. "Roland no Brasil." Revista de Ocidente (Lisbon), 62:286 (Feb. 1962); also published as offprint, Natal, RN, 1962.

*183. Ferreira, Jerusa Pires. Cavalaria em cordel: os passos das águas mortas. São Paulo: HUCITEC, 1979. 140 pp.

Based on M.A. thesis, Salvador, Universidade Federal da Bahia, 1977.

184. Leão, Pepita de. Carlos Magno e seus cavaleiros. Porto Alegre: Globo, 1967. 282 pp.

History and Historical Subjects

185. Calheiros, Walmir. "A conquista da lua na literatura de cordel." Gazeta de Alagoas (Maceió), Aug. 17, 1969.

186. Calmon, Pedro. A história do Brasil na poesia do povo. Rio de Janeiro: Editora "A Noite," [194_?]; repr. Bloch, 1973.

Thieves, Rogues, Outlaws

187. Daus, Ronald. Der epische Zyklus der Cangaceiros in der Volkspoesie Nordostbrasiliens. Bibliotheca Ibero-Americanas, Band 12. Berlin: Berlins Coloquium Verlag, 1969.

Based on Ph.D. diss., University of Kiel, 1966.

188. Lewin, Linda. "Oral Tradition and Elite Myth: The Legend of the 'Good' Thief Antônio Silvino in Brazilian Popular Culture." Journal of Latin American Lore, 5 (1980), 157-204.

189. Melo, Veríssimo de. O ataque de Lampião a Mossoró através do romanceiro popular. Natal, RN: Departamento de Imprensa, 1953.

190. Andrade, Mário de. O baile das quatro artes. Vol. 14. Obras completas de Mário de Andrade. São Paulo: Martins, 1963. "O romanceiro de Lampião," p. 118.

191. Maior, Mário Souto. "Antônio Silvino no romanceiro de cordel." Revista brasileira de folclore, 10 (1970), 45-53.

192. Soares, Teixeira. "Andanças de Pedro Malasartes." Revista brasileira de cultura (Rio de Janeiro), 19 (Jan./March, 1974), 71-80.

[See also item 35].

Fantasy and Myth

193. Azevedo, Carlos Alberto. Fantástico na literatura de cordel. Recife: MEC & Instituto Joaquim Nabuco de Pesquisas Sociais, 1978.

194. _____. "O heróico e o messânico na literatura de cordel." Revista de cultura Vozes, 67:9 (1973), 51-54; 68:1 (1974), 73-76.

Continuation of item 193.

195. Macedo, Nertan. "Mitos nordestinos na poesia popular." Brasil açucareiro, 70 (Aug., 1968), 64-66.

196. Tavares Júnior, Luís. "O discurso fantástico na narrativa do cordel." Revista Aspectos (Fortaleza), 8 (1975).

Religion

197. Araujo, João Dias de. "Imagem de Jesus Cristo na literatura de cordel." Revista de cultura Vozes, 68:7 (1974), 41-48.

198. Barreto, Luiz Antônio. "A Bíblia na literatura de cordel: primeira versão do 'Gênesis.'" Revista brasileira de cultura, 7 (1971), 137-155.

199. Benjamin, Roberto E. Câmara. "A religião nos folhetos populares." Revista de cultura Vozes, 62:2 (1970), 21-24.

200. Calasans, José. Ciclo folclórico do Bom Jesus Conselheiro. Bahia: Tipografia Beneditina, 1950.

201. Koshiyana, Alice Mitika. Análise de conteudo da literatura de cordel: presença de valores religiosos. São Paulo: ECA/USP, 1972.

Religion: The Devil

202. Borges, Francisca Neuma Fechine, et al. "Deus e o diabo na literatura popular em verso: modelo hipotético de narrativa." Primeira Jornada de Estudos Linguísticos GELNE, João Pessoa (UFPb).

*203. _____. "Encarnação do diabo em folhetos e obras eruditas nordestinas." Caderno de letras (João Pessoa), 2:3 (July, 1978), 77-93.

204. _____. "Les incarnations du diable dans les feuillets de littérature orale et dans les oeuvres érudites du Nord-Est brésilien." Cahiers de littérature orale (Paris), 5 (1980), 64-87.

Translation of item 203.

*205. Mello, Linalda de Arruda. "O pacto com o diabo." Caderno de letras, 2:3 (July, 1978), 65-76.

206. Pimentel, Altimar de Alencar. O diabo e outras entidades míticas no conto popular. Brasília: Coordenada, 1969. 101 pp.

*207. _____. "O herói demoníaco." Caderno de letras, 2:3 (July, 1978), 59-64.

208. Pontes, Mário. "O diabo na literatura de cordel." Revista de cultura Vozes, 64 (1970), 29-35.

209. _____. "A presença demoníaco no poesia popular do nordeste." Revista brasileira de folclore, 12:34 (Sept./Dec., 1972), 261-284.

*210. Santa Cruz, Luís. "O diabo na literatura de cordel." Cadernos brasileiros, 5:5 (1963), 3-14.

Religion: The Pope

211. Candelária, Inocêncio. "O papa na poesia." Diário de Mogi (Mogi das Cruzes, SP), Sept. 18, 1980.

212. Melo, Veríssimo de. "Atentado ao papa na poesia de cordel." A república (Natal, RN), May 21, 1981.

Religion: Mysticism, Eschatology, Messianism, Popular Religion

213. Biderman, Sol. "Literatura de cordel escatológica." Estado de São Paulo, Suplemento literário, Feb. 18, 1967.

214. _____. "Messianismo e escatologia na literatura de cordel." Ph.D. diss., Universidade de São Paulo, São Paulo, 1970.

215. Calasans, José. Os ABC de Canudos. Bahia: Comissão Baiana de Folclore, 1965.

216. Cantel, Raymond M. "Les prophètes dans la littérature populaire du Brésil." Cahiers du monde hispanique et luso-brésilien, 15 (1970), 57-72.

217. Lodoy, Raul G. da Motta. "Padre Cícero na literatura de cordel." O Fluminense (Niteroi, RJ), Oct. 12, 1975.

*218. Souza, Magna Celi Meira de. "Misticismo e fanatismo nos folhetos de feira e nas obras eruditas brasileiras." Caderno de letras (João Pessoa), 2:3 (July, 1978), 94-104.

[See also item 196].

Literature and Literary Figures

219. Candelária, Inocêncio. "Camões no cordel." Diário de Mogi (Mogi das Cruzes, SP), April 8, 1980.

220. Gomes, Deny. "Presença de Camões na literatura de cordel." Diário de Pernambuco, Jan. 9, 1981.

221. Matos, Edilene. Castro Alves no folheto de cordel. Salvador, BA: Núcleo de Pesquisa e Cultura de Literatura de Cordel, 1981.

Women, Sex, Erotica

*222. Japiassu, Moacir. "Cultura popular: o nordeste vai atacar de 'pornocordel.'" Istoé, 79 (June 28, 1978), 44-47.

223. Melo, Veríssimo de. "Topless em cordel." A república (Natal, RN), May 22, 1980.

224. Ramos, Léo Borges. "O erotismo na literatura de cordel." Ele e ela, 9:101 (Sept., 1977), 48-52.

225. Maior, Mário Souto. "O sexo na literatura de cordel." Ele e ela, 6:69 (Jan., 1975), 59-62.

226. Tahan, Ana Maria B. "A mulher na literatura de cordel." Folha de São Paulo, Nov. 20, 1974.

Social Questions

227. Diégues Júnior, Manuel. "Cidade e vida urbana em folhetos populares." Cultura (Brasília, MEC), 3 (1973), 59-67.

228. Farias, João. "A cachaça na literatura de cordel." Boletim da Comissão Fluminense de Folclore (Niteroi, RJ), 1:2 (April, 1970), 23-25.

229. Franklin, Jeová. "O preconceito racial na literatura de cordel." Revista de cultura Vozes, 64:8 (Oct., 1970), 35-39.

230. Melo, Veríssimo de. "Migrações em cordel." A república (Natal, RN), July 26, 1980.

231. Menezes, Eduardo Diatay Bezerra de. "Estrutura agrária: protesto e alternativas na poesia popular do nordeste." Revista de ciências sociais, 11:1/2 (1980), 29-61.

232. Moura, Clóvis. O preconceito de cor na literatura de cordel. São Paulo: Editora Resenha Universitária, 1976. 87 pp.

*233. Slater, Candace. "Setting Out for São Paulo: Internal Migration as a Theme in Brazilian Popular Literature." New Scholar, 8:1/2 (1982), 245-256.

Politics and Obituaries

234. Brandão, Théo. "As eleições e a literatura de cordel." Diário de Notícias. Suplemento literário (Rio de Janeiro), Nov. 13, 1960, p. 2.

235. Cantel, Raymond M. "Les poètes populaires du Nordeste brésilien et les morts célèbres." Cahiers du monde hispanique et luso-brésilien, (19__), 20-39.

236. Carrazoni, Adão. "A morte do estadista na literatura de cordel." Jornal de Brasília, Aug. 24, 1977.

237. "Criativo, o M.D.B. de Pernambuco usa até o cordel." Estado de São Paulo, Sept. 17, 1978.

238. Curran, Mark J. Introduction and Selected Bibliography of History and Politics in Brazilian Popular Poetry. Tempe, AZ: Center for Latin American Studies of Arizona State University, 1971.

*239. _____. "Politics in the Brazilian Literatura de Cordel: The View of Rodolfo Coelho Cavalcante." Studies in Latin American Popular Culture, 3 (1984), 115-126.

240. "Está sendo vendida em versos a famosa carta de Vargas." Diário da noite (Rio de Janeiro), Sept. 6, 1954.

241. Faria Filho, Luiz de. "A literatura (política) de cordel." O globo, May 12, 13, 14, 1975.

242. "JK e Vargas em folhetos de cordel." Folha de São Paulo, Sept. 20, 1976.

243. Lessa, Origenes. Getúlio Vargas na literatura de cordel. Rio de Janeiro: Documentário, 1973. 150 pp.

Governmental and Propaganda Uses

244. "Cordel diz a operário como evitar acidentes." Diário do Grande ABC (São Bernardo, SP), Aug. 12, 1977.

*245. "Cordel para tudo." Veja, 453 (May 11, 1977), 100.

Cordel to order by José Soares, for advertising and propaganda by government and business. [See also item 237].

The Future of Cordel

*246. Cavalcanti, Pedro. "Cordel ameaçado." Veja, 396 (April 7, 1976), 96.

An interview with Raymond Cantel: dangers of cordel catering to tourists, of the consequences of the spread of transistor radios, and of technical improvements in the manner of cordel publishing leading to homogeneity of orthography and grammar.

*247. Falcão, Luiz Augusto. "A crise do cordel." Afinal, 1:13 (Nov. 27, 1984), 38-40.

Sales falling, costs rising, output decreasing.

*248. "Literatura de cordel: SOS." Jornal de letras, Sept., 1971, 1.

The government, or somebody, must do something.

Anthologies

*249. Barros, Leandro Gomes de. Antologia: literatura popular em versos. João Pessoa: Editora Universitária da UFPb, [1978?].

250. Batista, Sebastião Nunes. Antologia da literatura de cordel. Natal, RN: Fundação José Augusto, 1977.

*251. Casa de Rui Barbosa, Rio de Janeiro. Literatura popular em verso. Antologia. 4 vols. Rio de Janeiro: MEC, 1964-1978.

ACRONYMS

AACR2	Anglo-American Cataloging Rules, 2d edition
AEMUS	Asociación de Estudiantes de Música (Uruguay)
AGPR	Archivo General de Puerto Rico
ALA	American Library Association
AP	Acción Popular (Peru)
APELCU	Asociación de Poetas y Escritores Libres de Cuba
APRA	Alianza Popular Revolucionario Americana (Peru)
ARL	Association of Research Libraries (U.S.A.)
ATLA	American Theological Library Association
BCC	Bronx Community College (U.S.A.)
BRS	Bibliographic Retrieval System
CADEC	Christian Action for Development in the Eastern Caribbean
CASA	Centro de Acción Social Autónomo (U.S.A.)
CBS	Columbia Broadcasting System (U.S.A.)
CC	Cataloging category
CCC	Consejo Central Conspirativo (Colombia)
CEAS	Centro de Estudos e Ação Social (Brazil)
CEDLA	Centro de Estudios y Documentación Latinoamericanos (Netherlands)
CEESTEM	Centro de Estudios Económicos y Sociales del Tercer Mundo (Canada)
CEFNOMEX	Centro de Estudios Fronterizos del Norte de México
CELADE	Centro Latinoamericano de Demografía (Chile)
CELADEC	Comisión Evangélica Latino Americana de Educación Cristiana (Peru)
CELAM	Consejo Episcopal Latino-Americano
CEP	Centro de Estudios y Publicaciones (Peru)
CEPAL	Comisión Económica para América Latina y el Caribe

CUNY   City University of New York (U.S.A.)

DESCO   Centro de Estudios y Promoción del Desarrollo (Peru)

DINACOS   (Dirección Nacional de Comunicación Social (Chile)

EDUCA   Editorial Universitaria Centroamericana (Costa Rica)

EMBRAPA   Empresa Brasileira de Pesquisa Agropecuária

ERIC   Educational Resources Information Center (U.S.A.)

E.U.   Estados Unidos / United States

FAPES   Fundación Argentina para la Promoción del Desarrollo
            Económico y Social

FIP   Frente de Izquierda Popular (Argentina)

FREJULI   Frente Justicialista de Liberación (Argentina)

GGB   Grupo Gay da Bahia (Brazil)

GRECMU   Grupo de Estudios sobre la Condición de la Mujer en
            Uruguay

HAHR   Hispanic American Historical Review

HAPI   Hispanic American Periodicals Review

ICAIC   Instituto Cubano del Arte e Industria Cinematográficos

IDOC   International Documentation and Communication Centre
            (Italy)

IDRC   International Development Research Centre (Canada)

IECLB   Igreja Evangélica de Confissão Luterana no Brasil

ILADES   Instituto Latinoamericano de Doctrina y Estudios Sociales
            (Chile)

ILL   Inter-Library Loan

INIDEF   Instituto Interamericano de Etnomusicología y Folklore
            (Venezuela)

ISAM   Institute for Studies in American Music (U.S.A.)

IU   Izquierda Unida (Peru)

JUNAPLA   Junta Nacional de Planificación y Coordinación Económica
            (Ecuador)

LACAP   Latin American Cooperative Acquisitions Program

LAJSA   Latin American Jewish Studies Association (U.S.A.)

LAMP   Latin American Microform Project (U.S.A.)

CEPAM	Centro Ecuatoriano para la Promoción y Acción de la Mujer
CEREP	Centro de Estudios de la Realidad Puertorriqueña
CETEC	Universidad Centro de Estudios Técnicos (Dominican Republic)
CEUR	Centro de Estudios Urbanos y Regionales (Argentina)
CFP	Concentración de Fuerzas Populares (Ecuador)
CIA	Central Intelligence Agency (U.S.A.)
CIDHAL	Comunicación, Intercambio y Desarrollo Humano en América Latina
CIDOC	Centro Intercultural de Documentación (Mexico)
CIEDUR	Centro Interdisciplinario de Estudios sobre el Desarrollo (Uruguay)
CIELO	Comité de Intelectuales y Escritores Libres de Oposición (U.S.A.)
CIEP	Centro de Investigación y Experimentación Pedagógica (Uruguay)
CIESE	Centro de Investigaciones y Estudios Socio-Económicos (Ecuador)
CIESU	Centro de Informaciones y Estudios del Uruguay
CINVE	Centro de Investigaciones Económicas (Uruguay)
CIP	Cataloging-in-Publication
CIS	Centro de Investigaciones Sociales (Puerto Rico)
CISR	Conference Internationale de Sociologie Réligieuse (Italy)
CLAEH	Centro Latinoamericano de Economía Humana
CLAR	Confederación Latinoamericana de Religiosos (Colombia)
CLAT	Central Latinoamericana de Trabajadores
CODE	Convergencia Democrática (Peru)
COELI	Centre Oecuménique de Liaisons Internationales (Belgium)
COHA	Council on Hemispheric Affairs (U.S.A.)
CONAC	Consejo Nacional de la Cultura (Venezuela)
CRL	The Center for Research Libraries (U.S.A.)
CUNA	Consejo Unitario Nacional Agrario (Peru)

CUNY	City University of New York (U.S.A.)
DESCO	Centro de Estudios y Promoción del Desarrollo (Peru)
DINACOS	(Dirección Nacional de Comunicación Social (Chile)
EDUCA	Editorial Universitaria Centroamericana (Costa Rica)
EMBRAPA	Empresa Brasileira de Pesquisa Agropecuária
ERIC	Educational Resources Information Center (U.S.A.)
E.U.	Estados Unidos / United States
FAPES	Fundación Argentina para la Promoción del Desarrollo Económico y Social
FIP	Frente de Izquierda Popular (Argentina)
FREJULI	Frente Justicialista de Liberación (Argentina)
GGB	Grupo Gay da Bahia (Brazil)
GRECMU	Grupo de Estudios sobre la Condición de la Mujer en Uruguay
HAHR	<u>Hispanic American Historical Review</u>
HAPI	<u>Hispanic American Periodicals Review</u>
ICAIC	Instituto Cubano del Arte e Industria Cinematográficos
IDOC	International Documentation and Communication Centre (Italy)
IDRC	International Development Research Centre (Canada)
IECLB	Igreja Evangélica de Confissão Luterana no Brasil
ILADES	Instituto Latinoamericano de Doctrina y Estudios Sociales (Chile)
ILL	Inter-Library Loan
INIDEF	Instituto Interamericano de Etnomusicología y Folklore (Venezuela)
ISAM	Institute for Studies in American Music (U.S.A.)
IU	Izquierda Unida (Peru)
JUNAPLA	Junta Nacional de Planificación y Coordinación Económica (Ecuador)
LACAP	Latin American Cooperative Acquisitions Program
LAJSA	Latin American Jewish Studies Association (U.S.A.)
LAMP	Latin American Microform Project (U.S.A.)

LAMR   Latin American Music Review

LARR   Latin American Research Review

LARU   Latin American Research Unit (Canada)

LAWG   Latin American Working Group (Canada)

LC   Library of Congress (U.S.A.)

LCFARA   LC Folk Archive Reference Aid

MALDEF   Mexican American Legal Defense and Educational Fund

MAPA   Mexican American Political Association

MARC   Machine-Readable Cataloging

MAS   Movimiento al Socialismo (Argentina)

MBH   Movimiento de Bases Hayistas (Peru)

MECHA   Movimiento Estudiantil Chicano de Aztlán (U.S.A.)

MGG   Musik in Geschichte und Gegenwart

MID   Movimiento de Integración y Desarrollo (Argentina)

MLC   Minimal Level Cataloging

NACLA   North American Congress on Latin America (U.S.A.)

NAJE   National Association of Jazz Educators (U.S.A.)

NCIP   North American Collections Inventory Project

NEH   National Endowment for the Humanities (U.S.A.)

NLBR   National Level Bibliographic Record

NOTIS   Northwestern On-Line Total Integrated System
            (U.S.A.)

NUC   National Union Catalog

NUCMC   National Union Catalog of Manuscript Collections

OAS   Organization of American States

OCLC   Online Computer Library Center (U.S.A.)

ODEPLAN   Oficina de Planificación Nacional (Chile)

ONDEPJOV   Oficina Nacional de Pueblos Jóvenes (Peru)

PAP   Partido Aprista Peruano

PC   Partido Comunista

PDC	Partido Demócrata Cristiano (Chile)
PI	Partido Intransigente (Argentina)
PIN	Partido de la Izquierda Nacional (Argentina)
PMLA	Publications of the Modern Language Association of America
PO	Partido Obrero (Argentina)
PPC	Partido Popular Cristiano (Peru)
PRI	Partido Revolucionario Institucional (Mexico)
PSR	Partido Socialista Revolucionario (Colombia)
REB	Revista Eclesiástica Brasileira
RILM	Répertoire International de Littérature Musicale
RISM	Répertoire International des Sources Musicales
RLB	Research Libraries Group, Inc. (U.S.A.)
RLIN	Research Libraries Information Network (U.S.A.)
SADAIC	Sociedad de Artistas y Compositores (Argentina)
SCCR	Stanford Center for Chicano Research (U.S.A.)
SE	Sin editorial
SEAM	Southeast Asian Microform Project (U.S.A.)
SERPAC	Servicio Pastoral de Comunicaciones, Diócesis de Neuquén (Argentina)
SINAMOS	Sistema Nacional de Apoyo a la Movilización Social (Peru)
SLAGH	Secretariado Latino-Americano de Grupos Homosexuales (Brazil)
SLAPC	Studies in Latin American Popular Culture
SMO	Servicio Militar Obligatorio
SMSA	Standard Metropolitan Statistical Area
SODRE	Servicio Oficial de Difusión Radio Eléctrica (Uruguay)
SPLAJS	Serial Publications in Latin American Jewish Studies
SUNY	State University of New York (U.S.A.)
TFP	Sociedad Uruguaya de la Tradición, Familia y Propiedad

TSF   Theological Students Fellowship (U.S.A.)

UCR   Unión Cívica Radical (Argentina)

UJC   Unión de Jóvenes Comunistas (Cuba)

UKCIP   United Kingdom Cataloging-in-Publication

UMAP   Unidades Militares de Ayuda a la Producción (Cuba)

UMI   University Microfilms International (U.S.A.)

UNEAC   Unión de Escritores y Artistas de Cuba

UNESCO   United Nations Educational, Scientific, and Cultural
           Organization

UNIMARC   Universal Machine-Readable Cataloging

USBE   Universal Serials and Book Exchange (U.S.A.)

USIA   United States Information Agency

WID   Women in Development (U.S.A.)

WOLA   Washington Office on Latin America

YIVO   Institute for Jewish Research (Yidisher Visnshaft-
           lekher Institut)

ABOUT THE AUTHORS

JUAN ABREU is a Mariel Generation artist and writer living in Miami. His most recent book is Libro de las exhortaciones al amor, and he continues to exhibit his paintings in galleries in the United States.

MARGARITA ANDERSON IMBERT is former Selection Officer for Hispanic materials, Harvard College Library. She resides in Belmont, Massachusetts.

REINALDO ARENAS published in his native Cuba until he became a prohibited writer. Since 1980 he has resided in New York City. He has received fellowships from the Guggenheim and Cintas Foundations, and he has taught at Cornell University and Florida International University. His many works include Celestino antes del alba (1967); El mundo alucinante (1969); El Central (1981); Termina el desfile (1981); Cantando en el pozo (1982); and Arturo, la estrella más brillante (1984).

PATRICIA AUFDERHEIDE is a visiting professor at the Center for International Studies, Duke University.

JOHN BLAZO is a member of the Maryknoll Order, and has worked extensively in Central America.

MARIA CRISTINA CAPEL owns and operates the Librería del Plata, based in Buenos Aires, Argentina.

DONALD S. CASTRO is Professor of History and Dean of Instruction, California State Polytechnic University, Pomona, California. He is pursuing research in Argentine demographic history.

MARIA DE LOS ANGELES CASTRO is Professor of History and also Director of the Centro de Investigaciones Históricas, Universidad de Puerto Rico (Río Piedras). She has published works on nineteenth-century architecture in San Juan as well as a bibliographic guide to Puerto Rican history entitled Los primeros pasos (1984).

MARTHA DAVIDSON is a free-lance picture researcher living in Cambridge, Massachusetts. She is currently preparing A Guide to Mexican Picture Collections, scheduled for publication early in 1987.

CARL DEAL is Director of Library Collections, University of Illinois at Urbana-Champaign, having formerly served there as the Latin American Bibliographer. He was Executive Director of the Latin American Studies Association from 1978 to 1981.

RONALD H. DOLKART, Professor of History, California State University, Bakersfield, is conducting research on modern Argentina. He co-edited Prologue to Perón: Argentina in Depression and War, 1930–1943 (1975).

ENID F. D'OYLEY is a Bibliographer in the Robarts Library, University of Toronto. She has written imaginative works including Animal Fables and Other Tales Retold and The Bridge of Dreams, as well as bibliographic and scholarly compilations.

JUDITH LAIKIN ELKIN is Professor of History, Ohio State University. Her many publications have reflected her research interests in Latin American Jews and in Jewish women in Latin cultures.

ROSA M. FERIA is the librarian for the Librería Linardi y Risso, Montevideo, Uruguay.

RENATA LELLEP FERNANDEZ holds a Ph.D. in Anthropology from Rutgers University. Her research addresses topics relating public policy, cultural practice, and symbolic relationships.

DANILO H. FIGUEREDO is Latin American Specialist, New York Public Library.

GERVASIO LUIS GARCIA is Professor of History, Universidad de Puerto Rico (Río Piedras). His publications include the monographs Desafío y solidaridad (1982); Primeros fermentos de organización obrera en Puerto Rico, 1873–1898 (1983); and Historia crítica, historia sin coartadas (1985).

REINALDO GARCIA RAMOS is a member of the Mariel Generation writers. He currently works as a journalist for New York City's Spanish-language press.

MAURICIO GERSON was educated in his native Mexico and in the United States. He works as a producer and director at New Jersey Network, and has received an Emmy Award.

MINA JANE GROTHEY is Ibero-American Reference Librarian, Zimmerman Library, University of New Mexico. She served as SALALM's President during 1986/87.

MARK L. GROVER is Latin American Studies Bibliographer, Brigham Young University. He contributed to the 1981 bibliography The Catholic Left in Latin America, and is pursuing research on the Mormon Church in Latin America.

LAURA GUTIERREZ-WITT is Head Librarian, Benson Latin American Collection, The University of Texas at Austin.

LAURENCE HALLEWELL is Latin American Bibliographer, Ohio State University. He has written the study Books in Brazil (1982), among many other works.

DAN C. HAZEN is Librarian for Hispanic Collections, University of California, Berkeley. He served as President for SALALM XXX.

JOHN R. HEBERT is Assistant Chief of the Hispanic Division, The Library of Congress.

PEDRO HERNAN HENRIQUEZ is currently affiliated with Harvard University.

ROBERT HOWES works in the Official Publications Library, Humanities and Social Sciences Division, The British Library.

AUSTIN HOYT, television producer and journalist, is best known for his PBS documentaries on Vietnam and for the series "Crisis in Central America."

MICHAEL F. JIMENEZ is Assistant Professor, Department of History, Princeton University.

MARGARET H. JOHNSON heads the Hispanic Section, Department of Printed Books, The British Library.

MALENA KUSS directs the Center for Latin American Music Bibliography, School of Music, North Texas State University. She has published Latin American Music: An Annotated Bibliography of Reference Sources and Research Materials (1984), and has several expanded bibliographies in preparation.

ASUNCION LAVRIN is Professor of History, Howard University. She edited Latin American Women: Historical Perspectives (1978, published in Spanish in 1985), and has written The Ideology of Feminism in the Southern Cone, 1900-1940 (1986).

DANIEL H. LEVINE is Professor of Political Science, University of Michigan, Ann Arbor. He has published widely on religion and politics in Latin America, and recently edited the volume Religion and Political Conflict in Latin America (1986).

KAREN J. LINDVALL is Latin American Bibliographer, University of California, San Diego.

CAVAN McCARTHY is Professor of Library Science, Universidade Federal de Pernambuco, Brazil. His 1982 doctoral dissertation was entitled "The Automation of Libraries and Bibliographic Information Systems in Brazil."

ROBERT A. McNEIL is Head of the Hispanic Section, Bodleian Library, Oxford University.

MARCO ANTONIO MASON is a sociologist and president of OMNI Resources Corporation, a consulting firm dedicated to research, training, and marketing development. His principal research interests include adjustment patterns of the Caribbean population in the United States, cross-cultural health issues in the urban setting, and the impact of U.S. immigration policy on ethnic communities.

SONIA MERUBIA is Serials Records and Acquisition Librarian, Benson Latin American Collection, The University of Texas, at Austin.

CARMEN MI COSTA DE RAMOS is Head Librarian, Puerto Rican Collection, Universidad de Puerto Rico (Río Piedras).

RICHARD J. MOORE has written widely on the urban poor in Latin America. He is currently a Senior Research Associate, National Association of Schools of Public Affairs and Adminis-tration, where he pursues research on policy reform in Latin America.

LUIZ MOTT is Professor of Anthropology, Universidade da Bahia, Brazil. He also founded the Grupo Gay da Bahia.

SHARON A. MOYNAHAN is Latin American Cataloging Team Leader, General Library, University of New Mexico.

LUISA PEREZ heads the Reference Department, West Dade Regional Library, Miami-Dade Public Library System, Miami, Florida.

FERNANDO PICO is Professor of History, Universidad de Puerto Rico (Río Piedras). He has published widely on Puerto Rican history including, most recently, his Historia general de Puerto Rico (1986).

ALVARO RISSO is co-owner of the Librería Linardi y Risso, Montevideo, Uruguay.

NICOLAS ROSSI owns and operates Libros Argentinos para Todo el Mundo, headquartered in Buenos Aires, Argentina.

JOHN M. SCHECHTER is Assistant Professor, Department of Music, University of California, Santa Cruz. His 1982 disserta-tion was entitled "Music in a Northern Ecuadorian Highland Locus: Diatonic Harp, Genres, Harpists, and Their Ritual Junction in the Quechua Child's Wake."

JUDITH SELAKOFF is the Librarian for the Research Institute for the Study of Man, located in New York City.

CECELIA L. SHORES heads the Acquisitions Department, The Center for Research Libraries, Chicago. She also administers the Latin American Microform Project, and the other Special Microform Projects affiliated with CRL.

CHARLES L. STANSIFER directs the Center of Latin American Studies, University of Kansas. His publications include several essays on contemporary Nicaragua.

ROBERTO G. TRUJILLO is Chief of the Foreign Language and Area Collections Department, Stanford University Libraries, as well as Curator for Stanford's Chicano Collections. He has compiled a number of bibliographies of Chicano publications.

ROBERT VALERO is Professor of Spanish, Georgetown University. His writings include the volume of poetry entitled Desde un oscuro ángulo (1983).

BARBARA G. VALK is Coordinator for Bibliographic Development, Latin American Center, University of California, Los Angeles. She also edits the Hispanic American Periodicals Index.

NANCY E. VAN DEUSEN recently received her M.L.S. from the University of Texas at Austin. She currently resides in Lima, Peru.

LESBIA ORTA VARONA is Microforms and Reserve Librarian, University of Miami.

DAVID ZUBATSKY is Research Library Relations Officer for the Online Computer Library Center (OCLC). He served as Washington University's Latin American bibliographer during much of the 1970s, and has published in a variety of fields. His Latin American Literary Authors: An Annotated Guide to Bibliographies is scheduled for publication in 1986.

CONFERENCE PROGRAM

Seminar on the Acquisition of
Latin American Library Materials XXX
19 - 23 June 1985

Latin American Masses and Minorities:
Their Images and Realities

Princeton University Library
Program in Latin American Studies
Woodrow Wilson School of Public and International Affairs
Princeton, New Jersey

1985

8:00 a.m.-6:00 p.m.   Lower Lobby
REGISTRATION

8:00-9:30 a.m.

Subcommittee on Non-Print Media	Coffee Shop
Membership Committee	Coffee Shop
Subcommittee on Cuban Bibliography	Library
Subcommittee of OCLC Users	Coffee Shop
Subcommittee of RLG Members	Private Dining Room
Subcommittee on Library Education	Lower Lobby Room

9:45-11:15 a.m.

Editorial Board	Library
Committee on Policy, Research, and Investigation	Dining Room
Library/Bookdealer/Publisher Relations	Private Dining Room
Subcommittee on Gifts & Exchanges	Dining Room
Joint Committee on Official Publications	Coffee Shop
Constitution and Bylaws Committee	Lower Lobby Room

11:30-1:00 p.m.

Finance Committee	Library
Nominating Committee (Ballot Counting)	Lower Lobby Room
Subcommittee on Reference Services	Coffee Shop
Subcommittee on National-Level Cooperation	Dining Room
Subcommittee on Bibliographic Instruction	Dining Room
Subcommittee on Cataloging and Bibliographic Technology	Private Dining Room

1:00-2:15 p.m.
Lunch

2:15-4:15 p.m.

Committee on Library Operations and Services	Library
Committee on Interlibrary Cooperation	Private Dining Room
Committee on Acquisitions	Coffee Shop
Committee on Bibliography	Dining Room

2:30-3:30 p.m. Firestone Library, Second Floor, Data Base Management
An introduction to the RLIN system
Ellen Greenblatt, Princeton University

3:00-4:00 p.m. Firestone Library, Second Floor, Frelinghuysen Room
An introduction to technical processing (a slide-tape program)
Luisa Paster, Princeton University

4:15-5:15 p.m. Private Dining Room
HAPI

Barbara Valk, Chair, University of California-Los Angeles

5:30-7:30 p.m.
LAMP Executive Committee Dinner

Laura Gutiérrez-Witt, Chair, University of Texas-Austin

5:30-7:45
Dinner

7:45-10:00 p.m. Private Dining Room
Executive Board

8:00-10:30 p.m. Television Room
"History and Development of Latinos on the Screen"
Mauricio Gerson, Producer/Director (New Jersey Network)

Schmidtmeyer, Peter. *Travels into Chile, over the Andes, in the years 1820 and 1821, with some sketches of the productions and agriculture; mines and metallurgy; inhabitants, history, and other features of America, particularly of Chile, and Arauco.* (London: Longman, Hurst, Rees, Orme, Brown, and Green, 1824.)

9:00 a.m.-7:00 p.m.   Lobby
REGISTRATION

9:00-11:00 a.m.   Forbes College Television Room
"Crisis in Central America" Frontline documentary film

9:00-11:30 a.m.   Room 8
LAMP

Laura Gutiérrez-Witt, Chair, University of Texas-Austin

11:30-1:00 p.m.   Room 3
Guide to Resources

Paula H. Covington, Chair, Vanderbilt University

12:30-1:15 p.m.   Room 8
New Member Orientation
Donald Wisdom, Library of Congress

1:00 p.m.   State Dining Room
Book Exhibition Opening

1:30-2:50
Lunch

1:30-2:50
Serials Acquisition Interest Group No-Host Lunch
Jacqueline A. Rice

1:30-2:30 p.m.   Firestone Library, Second Floor, Data Base Management
An introduction to the RLIN system
Ellen Greenblatt, Princeton University

3:00-3:45 p.m.   Dodds Auditorium
OPENING SESSION

Dan C. Hazen, President, SALALM XXX, Visiting Scholar, Stanford
University

Donald E. Stokes, Dean, Woodrow Wilson School of Public and
International Affairs and Professor of Politics and Public Affairs

Paul E. Sigmund, Director, Program in Latin American Studies and
Professor of Politics

Donald W. Koepp, University Librarian

Peter T. Johnson, Bibliographer for Latin America, Spain and Portugal

Ann Hartness-Kane, University of Texas-Austin

Rapporteur General: Charles S. Fineman, Northwestern University

3:45-4:30 p.m.   State Dining Room
El té (sin leche) con los libreros

4:30-7:00 p.m.   Dodds Auditorium
RESEARCH PANEL I: "Media and the Creation of Image"

Danilo H. Figueredo, Chair, New York Public Library

Focus: On how information is gathered, processed and presented; emphasizes
the differences in the interpretation of Latin American current events as
recorded by newspapers, magazines, radio, TV and motion pictures.

New York Times coverage of Latin America
  Warren Hoge, *New York Times*

Latin American events and the Hispanic press: policy guidelines
  Heberto Padilla, *El Diario-La Prensa*, New York City

Hispanic news coverage
  Gustavo Godoy, S.I.N. Television Network

"Crisis in Central America"
  Hoyt Austin, Public Television - Frontline

The world interpreted by the international press
  Mauricio Gerson, New Jersey Network

Bernardo Avalos, *Información Sistemática*, Mexico City (discussant)

Rapporteur: Karen J. Lindvall, University of California-San Diego

7:30-9:00 p.m.   Forbes College Terrace
BOOKDEALERS' RECEPTION

Zumárraga, Juan de, 1468-1548. [Doctrina breve] *Doctrina breve muy
provechosa de las cosas que pertenecen a la fe catholica y a nuestra
cristianidad en estilo llano para cumun inteligencia.* (Tenuchtitlan,
Mexico: Juan Cromberger, 1544.)
The Scheide Library

21 June
Friday
Woodrow Wilson School

8:45-11:00 a.m. Dodds Auditorium

RESEARCH PANEL II: "Masses and Minorities through Time"

Peter T. Johnson, Chair, Princeton University

Focus: On specific groups of people in the past; problems of reconstructing their individual and collective experiences; significance of difficulties encountered in research with documentation.

Political movements
  Michael Jiménez, Princeton University

Las comunidades rurales en Puerto Rico
  Fernando Picó, S.J., Universidad de Puerto Rico-Río Piedras

Labor organization
  Gervasio Luis García, Universidad de Puerto Rico-Río Piedras

Women
  Asunción Lavrin, Howard University

Jews
  Judith Elkin, University of Michigan-Ann Arbor

Rapporteur: David Block, Cornell University

11:00-11:30 a.m. State Dining Room

Bookdealers' coffeebreak

11:30 a.m.-1:30 p.m. Dodds Auditorium

RESEARCH PANEL III: "Popular Culture"

Mary Henry, Chair, New York University

Focus: On literature, fotonovelas, comics, cinema, photographs as popular art; origins of expression; relationships to prevailing social and cultural conditions; problems encountered in research.

Photographs and pictorial research
  Martha Davidson, Picture Collections: Latin America and The Caribbean

The movies and the masses
  Patricia Aufderheide, *In These Times*

Popular art forms
  James A. Findlay, Rhode Island School of Design

Fotonovelas and comics
  Renata Lellep Fernández, Rutgers University

Rapporteur: Elba G. Barzelatto, Princeton Public Library

11:30-1:30 p.m. Bowl 1

RESEARCH PANEL IV: "Religion: Liberation Theology and the Evangelical and Pentecostal Churches"

Mark Grover, Chair, Brigham Young University

Focus: On religion and society; activities of churches in a political and social context; membership and gender and leadership considerations.

Religion, church and state
  Deborah Huntington, North American Congress on Latin America

Folk and popular religion
  Daniel Levine, University of Michigan-Ann Arbor

Liberation theology
  Brother John Blazo, Maryknoll Order

Religion and rebellion
  Phillip Berryman, American Friends Service Committee

Rapporteur: Jane R. Orttung, Rutgers University

1:30-2:45 p.m.

Lunch
Catalogers' No-Host Lunch with Ben Tucker, Library of Congress

1:30-2:30 p.m.   Firestone Library, Second Floor, Data Base Management

Introduction to the RLIN system (in Spanish)
  Luisa Paster, Princeton University
  Waldina Zullo, Princeton University

2:45-4:45 p.m. Dodds Auditorium

RESEARCH PANEL V: "Migration and Immigration"

Nélida Pérez, Chair, Centro de Estudios Puertorriqueños, Hunter College, City University of New York

Focus: On movement and settlement of non-elite groups over time; causes for migration and immigration; adjustment in the new area; physical and psychological considerations; economic and political considerations.

Problems in contemporary research on inter-American migration
  Christopher Mitchell, New York University

Squatter settlements
  Richard J. T. Moore, Princeton University

The other migrations: Caribbean migration to Western Europe
  Mark M. Miller, University of Delaware and the *International Migration Review*

Migration
  Saskia Sassen-Koob, Queens College, City University of New York

Rapporteur: David Block, Cornell University

RESEARCH/LIBRARY PANEL I: "Overseas Communities and Library Collections"

Diana Lachatenere, Chair, Schomburg Center for Research in Black Culture, New York Public Library

Focus: On constitution and evolution of these communities; their national survivals vs. integrative measures.

Anglophonic West Indies
  Marcos Mason, Omni Enterprises
  Judith Selakoff, Research Institute for the Study of Man

Cubans
  Lesbia Varona, University of Miami

Dominicans
  Sonia Bú-Larancuent, Asociación Comunal de Dominicanos Progresistas (New York City)

Haitians
  Lionel Legros, Haitian Information Center (Brooklyn)

Rapporteur: Ana María Cobos, University of California-Los Angeles

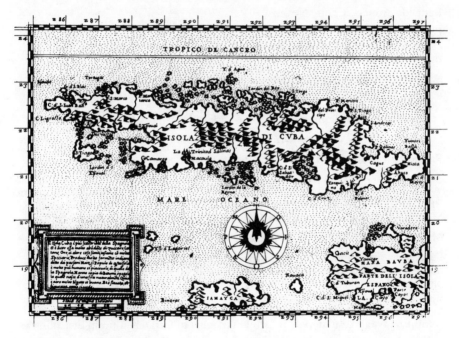

Cuba   Venice [1564?]
Richard Halliburton Map Collection

2:45-4:45 p.m. Bowl 2

RESEARCH/LIBRARY PANEL II: "Documenting Black Culture in the Americas"

Howard Dodson, Chair, Schomburg Center for Research in Black Culture, New York Public Library

Focus: On selected aspects of black culture, past and present; the creation of the literature or documentation; its collection by libraries.

Haiti
L. François Hoffmann, Princeton University

The Caribbean
Franklin Knight, The Johns Hopkins University

Brazil
Mary Karasch, Oakland University

Rapporteur: Sheila A. Milam, Harvard University

4:45-5:00 p.m.
Break

5:00-6:30 p.m. Bowl 1

RESEARCH/LIBRARY PANEL III: "Mariel: Antecedentes y Consecuencias"

Reinaldo Arenas, Chair, Novelist

Focus: Describes and analyzes the intellectual environment in Cuba for writers and artists during the 1970s and discusses the activities of those members of the Mariel Generation (1980) now writing in the United States.

René Cifuentes, co-editor, *Mariel*

Miguel Correa, Novelist

Reinaldo García Ramos, *El Diario-La Prensa* (New York City)

Roberto Valero, Georgetown University (respondent)

Rapporteur: Rafael Coutín, University of North Carolina-Chapel Hill

5:00-6:30 p.m. Dodds Auditorium

RESEARCH/LIBRARY PANEL IV: "The Music of Latin American Masses and Minorities: Access, Relevance and Availability of Bibliographic Resources"

Malena Kuss, Chair, North Texas State University

Focus: On the relevance of existing bibliographic tools to specialists in fields other than music, with emphasis on: (1) the need to integrate existing bibliographic tools into the international information network; (2) criteria for the preparation of tools addressed specifically to the non-specialist; and (3) the need for composite tools of bibliographic control that would consolidate and centralize available materials in single volumes to facilitate a multi-disciplinary approach.

Ronald H. Dolkart, California State University at Bakersfield

Donald S. Castro, California State Polytechnic University-Pomona

John Schechter, University of Washington

8

Lettera di Amerigo vespucci delle isole nuouamente trouate in quattro suoi viaggi.

Vespucci, Amerigo, 1451-1512.   *Lettera di Amerigo Vespucci delle isole nuovamente trouate in quattro suoi viaggi.* (Florence: Pietro Pacini da Pescia, 1505-1506.)
The Scheide Library

7:00-9:00 p.m.
No-host dinner meeting of bibliographers responsible for Iberian Peninsula imprints
Ellen Brow, Harvard University

9:15-10:30 p.m.   Dodds Auditorium
Motion picture: *Manos a la Obra: The Story of Operation Bootstrap.* Gervasio Luis García, Commentator, Universidad de Puerto Rico-Río Piedras

9:00-11:00 a.m.   Bowl 2

LIBRARY PANEL I: "Historical Dimensions of Collections"

Lionel V. Loroña, Chair, New York Public Library

Focus: On how and when significant collections of materials on revolutionary movements, ethnic groups, or topics were formed; role of individual and institutional initiative.

Robert McNeil, Oxford University

Margaret Johnson, British Library

Lee H. Williams, Yale University

Georgette Magassy Dorn, Library of Congress

Margarita Anderson-Imbert, Harvard University

Ann Hartness-Kane, University of Texas-Austin

Howard Dodson, Schomburg Center for Research in Black Culture, New York Public Library

Roberto Trujillo, Stanford University

Rapporteur: David Block, Cornell University

9:00-11:00 a.m.   Bowl 1

LIBRARY PANEL II: "The Literature of Outsiders I"

G. Rodney Phillips, Chair, New York Public Library

Focus: On literature of mass appeal; its creation and significance in society; collecting and organizing it; research users.

Literary women and their works
Enid D'Oyley, University of Toronto

Chicano literature
Barbara J. Robinson, University of California-Riverside

Puerto Rican literature of the migration
Juan Flores, City University of New York

Cordel
Laurence Hallewell, Ohio State University

Rapporteur: Jackie M. Dooley, University of California-San Diego

9:00-11:00 a.m.   Dodds Auditorium
LIBRARY PANEL III: "Political Movements: Nicaragua as a Case Study"

Ruth Kaplan, Chair, North American Congress on Latin America

Focus: On literature produced by participants; identifying and collecting it.

Charles L. Stansifer, University of Kansas

Helen Cunningham, *Business Latin America*

George Black, North American Congress on Latin America

Alfonso Vijil, Libros Latinos

David Atlee Phillips, Writer and formerly of the CIA

Rapporteur: Daniel A. Foley, Tulane University

9:00-11:00 a.m.   Bowl 5
LIBRARY PANEL IV: "The Literature of Outsiders II"

Paula H. Covington, Chair, Vanderbilt University

Focus: On literature created by special interest groups; research potentials.

Political prisoners
Luisa Pérez, Miami Public Library

Women and revolution
Ellen Calmus, Journalist

Gay literature in the humanities and social sciences
Robert W. Howes, British Library

Rapporteur: Lesbia O. Varona, University of Miami

11:00-11:30 a.m.   State Dining Room
Bookdealers' coffeebreak

11:30-1:30 p.m.   Bowl 1
WORKSHOP I: "Women"

Karen Lindvall, Chair, University of California-San Diego

Biography of Latin American women
Sara de Mundo Lo, University of Illinois-Champaign-Urbana

Latin American women in the literature of the social sciences and the humanities
Dolores Moyano Martin, Library of Congress

Argentine women's organizations
Gabriela Sonntag-Grigera, American Community Schools (Buenos Aires)

The Archives of the International Women's Tribune Center
Martita Midence, International Women's Tribune Center

Women in the *maquiladoras*
Karen Lindvall, University of California-San Diego

Latin American women and liberation theology
Mina Jane Grothey, University of New Mexico

11

WORKSHOP II: "Puerto Rico"

Nélida Pérez, Chair, Centro de Estudios Puertorriqueños, Hunter College, City University of New York

Focus: On non-elite groups; publishers and publications, from the Island and the U.S.; government documents; research centers; oral history; on diverse aspects of publishing and collecting.

María de los Angeles Castro, Universidad de Puerto Rico-Río Piedras

Carmen Mí Costa de Ramos, Universidad de Puerto Rico-Río Piedras

José Olmo, Rutgers University

Amilcar Tirado, Centro de Estudios Puertorriqueños, Hunter College, City University of New York

Mawe, John, 1764-1829. *Travels in the interior of Brazil, particularly in the gold and diamond districts of that country, by authority of the Prince Regent of Portugal: including a voyage to the Rio de la Plata and an historical sketch of the revolution of Buenos Aires.* (London: Longman, Hurst, Reese, Orme, and Brown, 1812.)

11:30-1:30 p.m. Room 8

WORKSHOP III: "Base Level Cataloging"

Sharon Moynahan, Chair, University of New Mexico

Focus: The access and research implications of cataloging description and classification which does not meet full USMARC standards. How does a library balance the loss of certain access points, such as subject headings, against the likelihood of an ever increasing and inaccessible backlog? Viewpoints from various sectors of the library community should illustrate the complexity of the problem and the importance of a well-constructed solution.

Cecilia Sercan, Cornell University

David Zubatsky, OCLC

Mark Grover, Brigham Young University

Rick Ricard, Library of Congress

1:30-3:30 p.m.

Lunch

3:30-5:30 p.m. Dodds Auditorium

WORKSHOP IV: "The Creation of Literature of Political Transition: Sources and Acquisitions"

Basil Malish, Chair, Library of Congress

Focus: On political parties and interest groups involved with campaign literature; how to identify and obtain diverse materials.

Argentina
  Nicolás Rossi, Libros Argentinos
  María Cristina Capel, Librería del Plata

Uruguay
  Juan Risso, Librería Linardi y Risso

Bolivia
  Alfredo Montalvo, Editorial Inca

Nicaragua
  Alfonso Vijil, Libros Latinos

Chile
  P. H. Henríquez, Institute for International Development, Harvard University

3:30-5:30 p.m.   Room 8

WORKSHOP V: "Solving Reference Questions: Small and Medium Sized Libraries"

Joseph P. Consoli, Chair, Princeton University

Focus: Discussion of selected reference questions received from university students and scholars during the past year which bear upon sources produced by non-trade publishers and emphasize topics involving masses and minorities; how questions were interpreted; sources used; solutions.

   Carmen Mí Costa de Ramos, Universidad de Puerto Rico-Río Piedras

   Mercedes Benítez-Sharpless, Lafayette College

   Mary George, Princeton University

   Sue Norman, Dickinson College

   Marian Goslinga, Florida International University

3:30-5:30 p.m.   Bowl 5

WORKSHOP VI: "Solving Reference Questions: Large Research Libraries"

Georgette Magassy Dorn, Chair, Library of Congress

Focus: Discussion of selected reference questions received from university students and scholars during the past year which bear upon sources produced by non-trade publishers and emphasize topics involving masses and minorities; how questions were interpreted; sources used; solutions.

   Rosa Abella, University of Miami

   Danilo H. Figueredo, New York Public Library

   Iliana Sonntag, San Diego State University

   Ann Hartness-Kane, University of Texas-Austin

   Mina Jane Grothey, University of New Mexico

   Margaret Johnson, British Library

3:30-5:30 p.m.   Room 3

   Interest Group in Spanish and Portuguese Paleography
   Patricia Marks, Princeton University
   David Block, Cornell University

9:00-10:30 p.m.   Dodds Auditorium

   Motion picture: *Improper Conduct* (Néstor Almendros and Orlando
   Jiménez-Leal, Directors) Reinaldo Arenas, commentator

14

23 June
Sunday
Woodrow Wilson School

9:00-11:30 a.m.   Dodds Auditorium
LIBRARY PANEL V: "Can Research Libraries Support the Study of Latin America's Masses and Minorities through the Age of Information Technology? An Agenda for the Future"

Dan C. Hazen, Chair, Stanford University

Focus: On the organizational, conceptual, structural, and technological constraints, local and national, that limit libraries as they address the types of needs highlighted during this conference; explorations of strategies for the future.

Complexities of cooperation
  John Hébert, Library of Congress
  Carl Deal, University of Illinois-Champaign-Urbana (respondent)

National context
  Laura Gutiérrez-Witt, University of Texas-Austin
  Cecelia Shores, Center for Research Libraries, LAMP (respondent)
  Juanita Doares, New York Public Library (respondent)

New technology
  David Zubatsky, OCLC
  Barbara Valk, University of California-Los Angeles
  Roberto Trujillo, Stanford University (respondent)

Rapporteur: Rachel B. Miller, University of Kansas

11:30-12:30 p.m.
Subcommittee and committee meetings   Rooms 5, 7, 10, 11,
(as necessary)   and Bowl 5

12:30-1:30 p.m.
Committee on Library Operations and Services   Room 3

Committee on Interlibrary Cooperation   Room 9

Committee on Acquisitions   Room 8

Committee on Bibliography   Room 12

1:30-3:30 p.m.
Lunch

2:15-3:30 p.m.   Room 8
Executive Board

3:30-5:00 p.m.   Dodds Auditorium
CLOSING SESSION
  Dan C. Hazen, Stanford University
  Suzanne Hodgman, University of Wisconsin-Madison

Rapporteur General: Charles S. Fineman, Northwestern University

6:30-8:00 p.m.   Forbes College Terrace
  CLOSING RECEPTION by the Program in Latin American Studies and the
  Woodrow Wilson School of Public and International Affairs

INSTRVCION CON

TRA LAS CERIMONIAS,
y Ritos que vſan los Indios confor-
me al tiempo de ſu infi-
delidad.

CAPITVLO PRIMERO
Delas idolatrias.

 O M V N es caſi a todos los Indios adorar Guacas,
Idolos, Quebradas, Peñas, o Piedras grandes, Cer-
ros, Cumbres de montes, Manantiales, Fuentes, y
finalmente qualquier coſa de naturaleza que pa-
rezca notable y differenciada de las demas.
2. Item es comun adorar el Sol, la luna, Eſtrellas, el Lu
zero dela mañana, y el dela tarde, las Cabrillas, y
otras eſtrellas.

3. Itê los defunctos, o ſus ſepulturas, aſsi delos antepaſſados, como delos
Indios ya Chriſtianos.

4. Los Serranos particularmente adoran el relampago, el Trueno, el Rayo
llamandolo Sanctiago. Item el arco del Cielo (el qual tambien es reue-
renciado delos indios delos Llanos.) Item las tempeſtades, los toruelli
nos, o remolinos de viento, las lluuias, el granizo. Item los Serranos
adoran los montones de piedras que hazen ellos meſmos enlas llanadas
o encruzijadas, o en cumbreras de montes, que enel Cuzco y enlos Co-
llas ſe llaman Apachitas, y en otras partes las llaman Cotorayac run, i o
por otros vocablos. Finalmente adoran qualeſquiera otros mochade-
ros de piedras donde hallan auerle echado piedras, coca, mayz, ſugas,
trapos y otras coſas differentes. Y en algunas partes de los Llanos aun
ay deſto no poco.

5. Los Yungas eſpecialmente delos Andes, o otros Indios que viuen en
                                                            A   tierras